Benedict Arnold

THE TRAITOR WITHIN

Benedict Arnold

THE TRAITOR WITHIN

David C. King

New Lights Press
P.O. Box 326
Hillsdale, NY 12529

Book and cover design by Jessika Hazelton

Printed in the United States of America

The Troy Book Makers • Troy, New York • thetroybookmakers.com

To order additional copies of this title,
contact your favorite local bookstore
or visit www.tbmbooks.com

ISBN: 978-1-61468-1182

To Sharon
For being the perfect partner

Acknowledgments

My thanks to Susan Novotny (Market Block Books, Troy, NY and The Book House, Albany, NY) and Eric Wilska (The Bookloft, Great Barrington, MA) for creating The Troy Book Makers and making so much possible for so many. At The Troy Book Makers, the advice and editorial work of Jessika Hazelton has been outstanding. And thanks to Jennifer Spanier for superb indexing.

I also want to acknowledge the help of the following in making this book happen: Sandy Flitterman-Lewis, Rutgers University, for ideas, assistance, and support; Lauren Losaw for assistance in locating resources; Karen Ball for research help; Nehoma Horwitt for encouragement, questions, and curiosity. And a very special thanks to my wife Sharon, *sine qua non*.

Contents

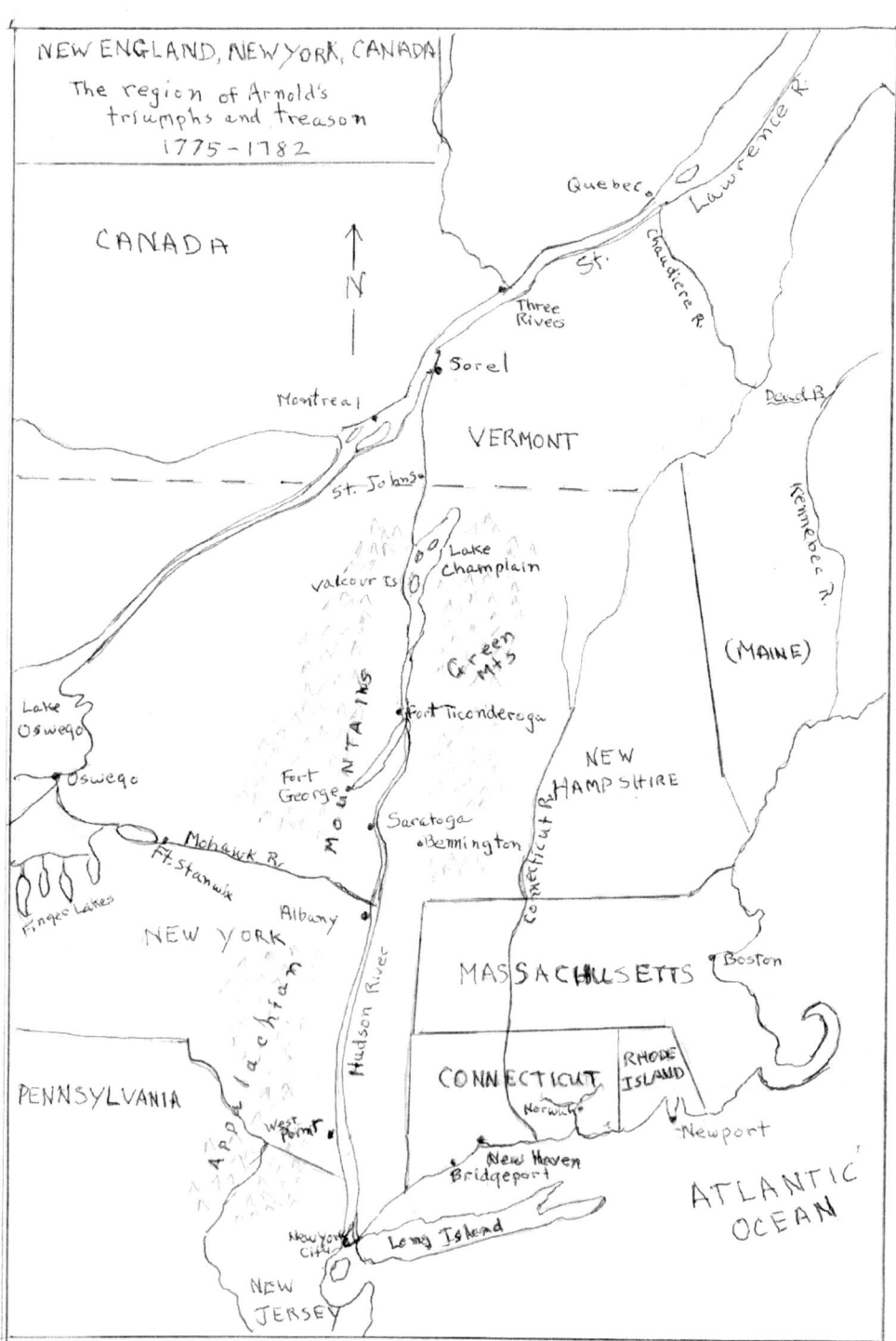

NEW ENGLAND, NEW YORK, CANADA
The region of Arnold's triumphs and treason
1775-1782

Preface

> Analysis cannot do justice to Arnold's story. It must be narrated through its zigzag course during the four years before it took its dark turn underground to treachery and catastrophe.
>
> Carl Van Doren, *Secret History of the American Revolution*. New York, NY, Viking Press, 1941, p. 145.

From 1780, the year of Benedict Arnold's treason, to today, Arnold has been viewed as the archetypal Dark Angel. Many of our wars have produced traitors, but none has ever had such a powerful impact on his time or been so vilified by history. Arnold, after all, nearly scuttled the American Revolution. Only because of luck and poor timing did he fail in his attempt to turn over to the British the complex of forts centered at West Point.

For four years, Benedict Arnold was America's most heroic and successful battlefield leader, hailed as Commander-in-Chief George Washington's "fighting general." But as soon as his treasonous scheme was discovered, and he managed to escape to British lines, Americans did all they could to diminish or forget his contributions to independence and to emphasize his guilt for "treason black as Hell."

Over the next two hundred years, histories and biographies painted Arnold as a tortured soul, whose need for money, along with a desire for revenge against those who opposed him, drove him to treachery. Recent biographers have offered kinder interpretations. The most prominent of revisionists has been James Kirby Martin; his 1997 biography was titled *Benedict Arnold, Revolutionary Hero: An American Warrior Reconsidered* (New York University Press, 1997).

Martin's major thesis is that Arnold had become convinced that the American Revolution was failing, largely because of bankrupt leadership; this failure left the way open for America's new ally, France, to move in and take over if the British withdrew. He believed it would be better to restore relations with Great Britain rather than be ruled by the French. (The British had already offered home rule—and much of the Americans' demands short of independence.) Arnold even seemed to view himself as a sort of Pied Piper of turncoats who would draw thousands of discouraged rebels back to the fold. If this interpretation is valid, he emerges as a misguided Patriot, convinced he was acting for the good of the country.

Through the several interpretations of Arnold's life, there is still an air of mystery about the man. Even after reading all the explanations of his motives, one is left with the feeling that something is missing; the many different accounts are not satisfying.

My purpose in writing *Benedict Arnold: The Traitor Within* is to examine the mystery again, to find out what's been missing. This effort involves an examination of his life and military career to find what there was inside this proud, dedicated patriot that led to his apparently sudden decision to offer himself to the enemy he had fought against so valiantly for nearly five years.

The major discoveries I've made fall into three categories:

First, in reviewing the major events of his life, I've been struck by the patterns that emerge. Time after time, a great success was followed by devastating loss or defeat. Over time, he may have been so beaten down by defeats and by his enemies that he finally reacted with a wild desire to strike back.

Second, there were critical matters of timing. In terms of his desperate need for money, for example, this need is given as a major reason for his decision to sell out his country. The timing seems strange, however, because only a few weeks before his first contact with British headquarters, the government of New York State offered him, as a reward for his heroic services, a gift of two fine estates near Lake Champlain, plus 40,000 acres of land. With the likelihood of such a gift, did he really have to sell his services to the enemy for money?

Third, and most important, what was the actual role of his wife, Margaret "Peggy" Shippen? Most biographers (but not all) are certain that she was involved, but all agree that hers was only a supportive role. I'm convinced that she was deeply involved in the plot from the beginning; in fact, there is considerable evidence that she may have been the instigator or a co-conspirator. Much of my evidence is circumstantial, but the weight of that evidence makes the case.

Although I'm trying to add new clarity to Benedict Arnold's story, this in no way is designed to diminish his guilt in committing such a horrifying betrayal of all that American patriots were striving to achieve. In addition, I have only admiration for the contributions of modern historians and biographers who have combed through the vast historical record, a record that is maddeningly silent on several key questions. We have no documents to prove what was in his mind, or in Peggy's, as they wove their complex web of deceit and betrayal. But we do have enough evidence to peel away more layers of the mystery and to come closer to the truth.

CHAPTER ONE

Early Patterns

FEW PEOPLE IN COLONIAL AMERICA BEGAN LIFE with more advantages than did Benedict Arnold. By his mid-teens, however, young Benedict learned that advantages were not guarantees; fate could intervene in totally unexpected ways.

Born in 1741, Benedict must have learned early that his family held a special place in the society of Norwich, Connecticut. When the family entered church on Sundays, for example, he followed his parents walking with quiet dignity to the front row of pews, which was always reserved for them. For his father, the fourth Benedict Arnold, this recognition of status was gratifying because he had spent years striving to restore the family to a position of wealth and prestige following a period of declining fortunes.

In addition to belonging to one of the leading families in Norwich, one of the advantages in young Benedict Arnold's life was the promise of taking over his father's successful business. Another advantage was that the Arnold name was one of the most illustrious in the brief history of colonial New England. The first Arnold—William—had arrived in the 1630s, during the great Puritan migration to Massachusetts Bay Colony. Troubled by the strict rules of the Puritans, William soon joined the dissenter Roger Williams in his break-away move to Rhode Island. With his son, the first Benedict Arnold, William purchased huge tracts of land, then resold smaller parcels to the steady flow of new settlers. In addition to the family's growing wealth, Benedict I was chosen to succeed Roger Williams as governor of Rhode Island and served several terms until his death in 1678.

The Arnold fortune declined over the next forty years, largely because each head of the family (Benedict I, II, and III) divided their once-extensive land holdings equally among all the heirs. As a result, the death of Benedict III in

1719 left the prospects for the fourth Benedict limited to an apprenticeship as a cooper. The idea of spending his career making barrels did not appeal to Benedict IV, so he moved from Rhode Island to Norwich Town, Connecticut with his brother Oliver.

Norwich had become a booming port town, located upstream from the coast at the point where the Thames River divided into two. The town's location enabled it to compete with New London, on the coast. Norwich had better access to the inland farms and, by the 1700s, growing agricultural prosperity gave farm families the ability to trade for household furnishings and a few luxury items.

Benedict IV took advantage of the opportunities. He built a fortune as a merchant, purchasing ships to trade between the islands of the West Indies and ports in the American colonies. He also married a wealthy widow named Hannah Waterman King, and was enabled to take over management of the King mercantile holdings for his wife.

Hannah and Benedict IV seemed to have a warm and loving relationship. They had six children, the first, named Benedict, died within his first year, probably from diphtheria, also called "throat distemper." When another son was born on January 14, 1741, the parents followed a common practice by naming him the fifth Benedict, skipping over the deceased infant in the numbering. Of the six children, only Benedict V and a younger daughter, Hannah, lived to adulthood.

Benedict grew up in a close-knit and supportive family, which established patterns for a promising future. He received the best possible formal education, with the likelihood of going on to one of colonial America's few colleges, probably Yale, located in nearby New Haven. To prepare him for college, Benedict was sent away to boarding schools. In addition, his father's trade ventures—he was now known as Captain Arnold—offered a ready-made career for the boy.

Mythical Boyhood

Practically all biographies of Benedict Arnold have repeated the many stories of Benedict's troublesome boyhood. One story, for example, related a favorite prank of stealing a baby bird from its nest, then torturing it in front of the adult birds. Another tale described Benedict tipping over a cannon on the village green, filling the barrel with gunpowder and lighting it. The resulting explosion nearly killed him and made the earth tremble. In another incident, he led a gang of boys in stealing barrels of tar, planning a great bonfire. When a constable stopped them, Benedict tore off his coat and challenged the man to fight him.

The many stories like these were designed to show that Arnold's boyhood revealed characteristics that would eventually lead to treason. It was not until the 1990s that the research of historian James Kirby Martin [James Kirby Martin. *Benedict Arnold: Revolutionary Hero*. (New York University Press, 1997)] showed that these tales first appeared in print or were mentioned soon after Arnold's treason was discovered, not before. There were no contemporary accounts of his antisocial behavior. Martin hypothesized that Revolutionary War veterans invented these stories to diminish Arnold's reputation as perhaps the greatest battlefield hero of the Revolution, and also to demonstrate that, even as a boy Benedict was aggressive, often violent, determined to have his way, and reckless.

An earlier biographer, Willard Wallace [*Traitorous Hero*, Harper & Brothers, 1954] suggests that some of the stories may have been true, "but were given undue importance by contemporaries eager to testify, after Arnold's treachery, to the blackness of his youth. He was in all probability neither better nor worse than other children, though perhaps more energetic, proud, and willful than most." 1.

Upheaval

Although Benedict Arnold's boyhood may not have been as colorful as it is usually pictured, the pattern of privilege and promise is accurate. However, the youth's life did not remain smooth and predictable. A series of dramatic events led to upheaval in his personal life, destroying much of the hope for his future.

In the 1740s, much of New England was rocked by the religious upheaval that became known as The Great Awakening. Itinerant preachers touched off a period of highly emotional conversions to a search for God's grace. Benedict's parents became devoted to this strict observance of Calvinistic doctrine—avoiding God's punishment for sins. Hannah became particularly concerned with her son's moral state, constantly admonishing him to look after his soul.

Benedict did not accept much of Hannah's more Calvinistic new faith, but this did not lead to the kind of bickering and dissension that tore apart other families. Hannah made sure that Benedict went to good boarding schools; the second one was operated by her relative, the Reverend Cogswell. While she encouraged the schoolmaster not to 'spare the rod,' she was gentle in her religious instructions and reminder to her son. While he was away at the Reverend Cogswell's school, about twenty miles from Norwich, for example, she made sure he had plenty of spending money. In a letter in which she sent him thirty shillings (and the Captain added ten more, for a total translated into nearly 300 modern dollars), she admonished him that God would be watching to see how wisely he used it.

While the religious controversies of The Great Awakening helped shape Benedict's views on the role of religion in his life, far more shattering was the painful lesson that a family's social status did not protect them from the many epidemics that lowered life expectancy throughout Colonial America. Diseases such as smallpox, measles, scarlet fever, and diphtheria swept through entire regions, decimated populations, and left grieving families in their wake. The first of the Arnolds' children—Benedict—had died in his first year, probably of diphtheria, a disease that literally choked the victim to death. Hannah gave birth to five other children. There were two more boys: the Benedict who survived and Absalom King Arnold who died in 1750. Of the three girls, only Hannah survived to adulthood. The girls—Elizabeth, 3 and Mary, 8—died within months of each other during epidemics of the mid-1750s.

Hannah and Captain Arnold were devastated by the loss of four of their six children. They could take some comfort from the fact that Hannah pulled through the epidemic that took her sisters, and that Benedict was away at school. Hannah's letters to him gave the broad outlines of the events, but she told him not to come home, for fear that he too would become a victim.

The deaths of the two girls was particularly hard on Benedict's father. All four children had died before reaching age ten, and the tragedies had struck when his business was in serious trouble. The repeated warfare between the British and

French reached a new level of crisis with the Seven Years War (1756-1763). The family's business went into a steep decline from which it never recovered.

Benedict's father responded by starting to drink—not just in the manner of mid-18th century merchants, but to drink heavily, so heavily that within two years he was lost in a fog of alcoholism. Young Benedict, away at school, knew the situation was bad, but it was still a shock when he received a letter from his mother saying they no longer had money to pay for his school. The fifteen-year-old came home to his family and to the realization that his formal education had ended; there would be no advancement to Yale or any other college. The family's finances were in shambles, and it was soon clear that there would be no family business for him to take over.

Far worse for Benedict and his sister Hannah was the humiliation of seeing their father staggering through the streets of Norwich, the object of derision and jokes. On occasion he was arrested for public drunkenness and Benedict had to bring him home. The leaders of their church held meetings at which they chastised him and threatened him with excommunication. His wife Hannah, who had always held the family together, died in 1759 at age 52. That was the final blow. When Arnold's father died two years later, his passing was probably something of a blessing to his two remaining offspring.

The scars from those years remained with Arnold for the rest of his life. He hated the way people had behaved toward his father; and he developed a deep distrust of men in positions of privilege or power. Determined to restore the prestige of the family name, he became furious when anyone challenged his honor or his actions, sometimes "demanding satisfaction" through a duel. This wounded pride transformed him into a man driven by ambition.

Apprentice Years

As soon as the family business began to fail, Benedict Arnold's mother Hannah had searched for other ways to give him a good start in a career. She persuaded two relatives—Joshua and Daniel Lathrop—to sign him on as an apprentice in their apothecary business. They were soon delighted with their young employee, providing him with steadily-increasing responsibilities and opportunities.

Apothecaries were more than pharmacists in the eighteenth century. The Lathrops, for example, sold surgical equipment and medicines to the British Navy and Army, but they also traded in an array of merchandise from fruits and fabrics to furniture and coffins.

Benedict's apprenticeship years have been the occasion for more tales about him in biographies of his life. According to the stories, he ran away from the Lathrops' apothecary shop on two occasions to join the New York Militia in order to fight alongside the British against the French in Canada. (New York paid higher enlistment bounties than did the New England colonies.) Although the fifteen-year-old boy never got into a battle, the biographers wrote, the episodes reflected several pre-treason traits: a desire to fight and to achieve military glory; a willingness to break the rules in order to achieve his goals; greed—enlisting in New York for a higher bounty.

Several recent biographers have stated that these stories are not supported by the historical evidence; in fact, they seem to be based on errors in interpreting the documents. The name B. Arnold appears several times in the enlistment rolls of the New York Militia, but there are different spellings of what could be thought as misspellings of Benedict, such as "Benedick" and "Bowdik." Physical descriptions don't match, none mentions the town of Norwich, and the occupation is listed as laborer and weaver. Benedict Arnold often said, "I was a coward until I was fifteen years of age." Biographer Jim Murphy has argued that "It's hardly likely that such a boy would dash headlong into a bloody fight."2.

More convincing arguments against his having been a runaway involve his relationship with his employers. Joshua and Daniel Lathrop were graduates of Yale and became highly successful in their business. They quickly saw that Benedict was intelligent, hard working and eager to learn. At first, he worked in the apothecary shop, where he learned the details of selling and dealing with customers. From the beginning, he lived in the elegant home of Daniel and Jerusha Lathrop. Mrs. Lathrop took to Benedict and was soon treating him like a son. She continued some of his schooling and instructed him in adult behavior, such as how to act toward people of inferior or superior position.

In terms of running away to join the militia, it does not seem likely that the Lathrops would tolerate having a runaway in their tightly run business or their embracing household. Also, they clearly had plans for Benedict. By the time he was eighteen, they were sending him on their trading ships to the West Indies and then to England. These experiences helped him to develop a knowledge of, and fondness for, ships and sailing. The Lathrops had such confidence in their apprentice that, when he was twenty, they helped set him up in his own apothecary business in New Haven, providing him with merchandise on credit valued at about $20,000 in early 21st century money.

There was one exception to the questionable reliability of the militia stories. In 1757 there was a general call to arms for all able-bodied men throughout Connecticut. The crisis, during the Seven Years War, occurred when a French army invaded from Canada; after capturing Fort William Henry, the French began pushing south toward Albany.

If young Arnold did get into a militia uniform and began marching, he did not get far. The French became concerned about their supply lines, withdrew to Canada, and the militia was disbanded.

A Successful Young Man

In 1760, when Benedict moved to New Haven, he opened his small shop on the Lathrop model. He hung out a sign which announced:

B. Arnold Druggist

Book Seller, Etc.

From London

Sibi Totique ("For himself and for all.")

With the help of the Lathrops, he stocked his shelves with a wide array of merchandise—books, jewelry, cosmetics, and, as one broadside mentioned, "a very elegant assortment of mezzotint pictures, prints, maps, stationery and paper hangings for rooms."3. He also had an array of medicines and herbs, including "Spirits of Scurvy Grass," "James's Fever Powder," and "Francis's Female Elixer."

He had picked up some knowledge of healing practices from Daniel Lathrop and, by applying what he knew, he soon was being referred to as "Doctor" Arnold.

The business was successful from the start, and twice he had to move to larger shop spaces. His sister Hannah moved to New Haven, sharing his home and helping in the business. In spite of tales about Benedict chasing away suitors, Hannah remained dedicated to her older brother for life.

In his third year in business, Benedict formed a partnership with another rising young merchant named Adam Babcock. They purchased three good-sized ships and opened trade with the West Indies, Canada, London, and ports on the North American coast. With Hannah and a hired clerk to manage the shop, Benedict was free to spend much of his time at sea. A large portion of his profits came from buying horses, grain, lumber, and pork in Canada, products that brought high prices from the plantation owners in the West Indies. Molasses for making rum was one of the major products traded from the islands to New England.

The steady growth of Arnold's business was aided by the booming economy of New Haven. Between 1750 and 1765, the population quadrupled from 2,000 to 8,000.

Arnold loved the rough and sometimes dangerous life at sea. He was often away from New Haven for long periods of six months or more, and he relied on his sister Hannah to manage the business. The occasionally rough manners and language that "Captain" Arnold acquired led the established society of New Haven to consider him an "upstart" and "crude." Some, however, accepted him, including the Mansfield family; he married twenty-two-year-old Margaret "Peggy" Mansfield in 1767, and became close friends with her father. Margaret bore him three sons: Benedict VI, born February 14, 1768; Richard, August 22, 1769; and Henry, September 10, 1772.

The Arnolds seemed to have a loving relationship, although there were questions and some signs of trouble. While he was away on his long trading voyages he wrote romantic letters to her and agonized over why Peggy didn't write to him more often. He sometimes wrote impassioned exclamations, such as, "Oh, when shall we be so happy to meet and part no more."4. There are few remaining letters written by her and none indicating her reactions to the many stories of his mistresses or bouts of venereal disease, or tavern fights and occasional duels.

Over a period of thirteen years, from 1762 to early 1775, Arnold encountered countless obstacles to success. British taxes and customs collections nearly drove him out of business. He also had trouble collecting money owed him, and this led him to try to dodge creditors; these dodges almost cost him time in debtors prison.

Much of his trouble with British customs resulted from policies developed in the wake of Great Britain's stunning victory in the Seven Years' War (1756-1763). King George III and his ministers, in order to raise revenue to pay for the War and their expanded empire, launched a series of new acts, including the Currency Act, the Sugar Act, the Proclamation of 1763 (to prevent land-hungry settlers from moving beyond the crest of the Appalachians), and in 1765, a Quartering Act and the Stamp Act. For enforcement, the Royal Navy assigned ships and men to stop smuggling. In late 1765, Benedict joined other merchants in ignoring the Stamp Act and engaging in increasingly creative smuggling.

Arnold's business, as well as his marriage, suffered in the 1770s, when the story spread that the Captain was seriously ill with venereal disease. Although none of Peggy's letters on the subject survive, she must have been shocked by the lurid stories. Benedict not only denied the tales in his most ferocious manner, but he also persuaded several well-known business associates to sign statements supporting his protestations of innocence. The gossip soon faded.

Through it all, the business grew steadily and, by the time he was thirty years old, he was one of the wealthiest men in New Haven. He ordered the building of a handsome mansion and he was particularly proud of the structure's pillars which, he felt, symbolized his position as a leading citizen.

He also bought the Norwich house he had grown up in, which the family had been forced to sell during his father's business failure. Benedict had no use for the house, but it must have seemed a good way to demonstrate his growing economic power to the Norwichites who had been so unkind to his father. He then turned around and sold the house a year later for a substantial profit—a move that might have been his way of showing his disdain for the town and its people.

Arnold had made great strides in restoring the family's wealth, but he still had far to go in the matter of prestige or honor. He might have made gains by building political alliances with government figures who could provide support. His friendship with his father-in-law could have been a useful first step since Samuel Mansfield was high sheriff of New Haven County and could have provided introductions, but Arnold was not interested. This go-it-alone attitude turned out to be a serious mistake. His military career was to suffer frequently because he had no well known men in government to speak for him.

He did display a sort of political awareness in developing opposition to British Customs policy—an opposition joined by practically all colonial merchants. For these men, smuggling became a necessity in order for them to make a living. They did not consider smuggling to be a crime, but rather an act of patriotism; since they had no voice or vote in the creation of those taxes, the customs duties were not legal, so smuggling was not illegal.

The first sign of deep political conviction was in his response to the Boston Massacre in 1770. He was horrified by the shooting of five unarmed Bostonians by British soldiers, then further outraged when the soldiers were found not guilty. "Good God!" he wrote, "are the Americans all asleep and tamely giving up their liberties, or are they all turned philosophers that they don't take immediate vengeance on such miscreants."5.

Over the next five years, the dispute between Great Britain and her thirteen American colonies grew steadily worse. In December 1773, a band of Patriots took part in a widespread protest against British East India Company tea by dumping a shipment of it into Boston Harbor. The British responded swiftly. The port of Boston was ordered closed until the tea should be paid for. Thomas Gage arrived with 3,500 redcoats to enforce this and several other new laws, known as the Coercive Acts (or, in America, the Intolerable Acts).

Arnold became determined to be a major figure in any military action that developed. Perhaps gaining military prominence was a way to restore the honor of the family name. The first step was to form a militia unit in New Haven. His offer was approved and his men were delighted with their dashing new uniforms, designed by their commanding officer—Captain Arnold.

The early years of Benedict Arnold's story displayed a pattern that would be repeated throughout his life. Until his mid-teens, he seemed to be on a path that guaranteed success in life, including a formal education, which was rare in the 18th century, and a successful business that would be his. Then everything collapsed and quite suddenly the bright promise vanished, and he had to face the humiliation of sudden poverty, selling the family home, and witnessing his father becoming a shameful public spectacle.

As he would do throughout his future career, Arnold worked hard to overcome the obstacles. Within ten years of starting out, he had become one of the wealthiest men in New Haven, had built a magnificent house, and was happily married with three sons. Once again, his life was in a good place, with a promising future.

CHAPTER TWO

Ticonderoga and Crown Point

BENEDICT ARNOLD FORMED HIS NEW HAVEN MILITIA unit in 1774, calling it the Governor's Foot Guards. He outfitted them in striking uniforms of his own design, featuring scarlet jackets with silver buttons, white ruffled shirts, and black boots. Although the Guards were short of weapons and ammunition, Arnold hired a professional to train them in military routine. The idea of leading men into battle would be appealing to Arnold, and he thought that military glory would be a perfect way to restore the family's reputation.

In April, 1775, the people of New Haven were electrified by news of the fighting at Lexington and Concord—the opening battles of the American Revolution. Arnold's Foot Guards voted to join the militia units gathering outside Boston, but New Haven officials did not want to be involved until they knew more. Consequently, when Captain Arnold asked for keys to the town's magazine of military supplies, they refused. Arnold exploded. "None but Almighty God shall prevent my marching!" he shouted. 1. Within minutes he had the key and the Governor's Foot Guards were soon on the road to Cambridge, outside Boston.

The men were excited and confident. As Arnold proudly led his Guards through farm villages, and people emerged from their homes to cheer them on, he had a brief encounter with a Connecticut militia officer—Colonel Samuel Parsons—who was on his way home from Cambridge. It was a meeting that was destined to have a powerful influence on Arnold's dreams of military glory. Parsons told him about the many militia companies camped outside Boston with headquarters at Cambridge. But, he said, the patriots had little hope of forcing the British to evacuate Boston unless they could acquire artillery.

That need for artillery set off sparks in Arnold's mind. He excitedly told

Parsons about Fort Ticonderoga, a huge, star-shaped British fortress on the Hudson River that controlled the southern approach to Lake Champlain. The Hudson-Champlain corridor separated New England from New York and the West; it also formed the natural invasion route for any British force moving south from Canada. On trading trips to Montreal, Canadian merchants had told him that the fort had been badly damaged during the French and Indian War (1756-1763) and the British had done little in the way of repairs. There were now only a few dozen British soldiers guarding the crumbling battlements. Most important, Arnold told Parsons, the fort held nearly one hundred cannons, many of them made of brass. The story was much the same at Crown Point, a small fort built on a peninsula a few miles north on the lake.

When the two men parted, Arnold hurried on to Cambridge, his mind now filled with visions of military adventure. He was sure he could capture both Ticonderoga and Crown Point with only two- or three hundred men. Taking those forts would protect the colonies from British invasion and some of the cannons could be transported overland to the patriots outside Boston.

After finding housing for his Foot Guards, Arnold met with the Massachusetts Committee of Public Safety, the acting government of the colony. He described his plan for capturing Ticonderoga and Crown Point, and the committee immediately approved it. Arnold was made a colonel in the colony's militia and given written authority and money for raising up to 400 militiamen in western Massachusetts.

Arnold immediately set off on the 150-mile ride to western Massachusetts and eastern New York, with only a friend to accompany him. Other of his officers followed, planning to recruit troops as they went. "Colonel" Arnold was in high spirits, thrilled by the idea of leading his men into battle.

His buoyant mood did not last long. As he neared his destination, he was shocked to discover that another volunteer outfit was going to reach Ticonderoga ahead of him. Arnold himself had unwittingly set his rival force in motion: Connecticut's Colonel Parsons had reported his Cambridge-Road meeting with Arnold to members of the Connecticut Assembly. Without any real authority, these men appointed Captain Edward Mott to lead about sixty men to Ticonderoga; they also asked for a larger force to be raised by Ethan Allen, a big, tough frontier leader from the "Hampshire Grants" (soon to be renamed Vermont).

Riding like a man possessed—and nearly killing his horse—Arnold caught up with Allen and his men on May 8. Ethan Allen's followers were known as the "Green Mountain Boys"—a rowdy, often unruly bunch, but willing to follow Allen anywhere. Allen was one of the most colorful figures of the Revolution. He stood well over six feet tall, had immense strength, and possessed a great capacity for alcohol, especially his favorite drink, called a "Stonewall" (rum mixed with hard cider). He was not a smart man, but he was clever, especially at advancing his own reputation.

When the two leaders finally met, Arnold expressed his fury and claimed to have the only legitimate authority to lead. But Allen had nearly 200 men around him, while Benedict Arnold was still waiting for his first recruits to arrive. After hours of heated argument, Allen shrewdly offered co-leadership to his rival, because he recognized that Arnold's written orders from Massachusetts were the only legitimate authority. Arnold was far from pleased, but he knew he had no choice but to agree. Allen's Green Mountain Boys, who had little regard for Colonel Arnold, were ready to mutiny until Allen persuaded them to accept the compromise.

The attack on Fort Ticonderoga turned into something of a comedy. On the night of May 9-10, 1775, the co-leaders managed to get about eighty men across Lake Champlain in rowboat relays by the time dawn approached. Imagine the shock of the lone British sentry when he confronted Arnold in his bright scarlet coat and big Ethan Allen decked out in yellow breeches and a striking green coat with over-sized gold epaulets.

The sentry quickly retreated and Green Mountain Boys poured through the gate. Allen and Arnold encountered the sleepy second-in-command as he struggled to pull on his pants. When he asked by what authority the two men demanded surrender of the fort, Allen bellowed, "In the name of the great Jehovah and the Continental Congress!" When they found the fort commander, he quickly saw that his position was hopeless and surrendered the fort.

at Ticonderoga and Crown Point, as well as an invasion of Canada. In London, British leaders said that the attacks succeeded only because British defenders were totally unprepared since they had no reason to expect attacks that were really acts of war. They denounced Benedict Arnold as a "horse jockey"—a man who did nothing more than buy and sell horses. They also had little respect for a man of low social standing; and they were certain that Arnold and his followers would break and run when they confronted British troops.

The attacks also upset many Americans, including members of the new Continental Congress, which began meeting in Philadelphia on the very day that Allen and Arnold captured Fort Ticonderoga. Many of the delegates had felt justified in taking up arms to defend their rights, as they had done at Lexington and Concord. They were planning on resolving their differences with King George III and Parliament. The brash action of Arnold, Allen and the others would make a peaceful settlement more difficult, if not impossible.

If Arnold was stunned by these reactions to his military achievements, they were nothing compared to the abuse he encountered in the weeks that followed. Although he was skilled as a soldier and as a ship's captain, as well as a very successful merchant, he was a political novice. He had no political allies in Connecticut or Massachusetts; no one in government or the military was ready to speak up for him. On the contrary, there were several men who were determined to destroy him politically. He turned out to be an easy target.

Ethan Allen displayed his shrewdness in his reports about the capture of Ticonderoga. His written account to New York's government stated, "I took the fortress of Ticonderoga," but to give the event legitimacy, he added, "Colonel Arnold entered the fortress with me." 3. But in his report to the Massachusetts Provincial Congress, he did not mention Arnold at all, although he did find ways to praise his allies. James Easton, for example, "behaved with great zeal and fortitude . . . in the assault"; John Brown " .

. . was an able counselor, and was personally in the attack"; and the Green Mountain Boys "behaved with resistless fury." 4.

Allen was also clever in having these reports delivered by hand, with Easton going to the Massachusetts Congress. (Easton had asked Arnold to promote him to colonel, but Arnold thought him a coward and so turned him down.) From Ethan Allen's perspective, Easton was the perfect person to talk about Benedict Arnold. While Arnold was preparing to attack St. Johns, Easton was appearing before the Massachusetts Provincial Congress elaborating on his written report about Ticonderoga and completing his character assassination of Arnold.

Allen had been careful not to criticize Arnold. That task was taken care of by Edward Mott, who had led the Connecticut militiamen to Ticonderoga. In his report, Mott said that Arnold's attempts to assume command of the attacking force had nearly caused a mutiny among the men. Only the leadership of Allen and Easton had saved the mission from the near-disaster caused by Benedict Arnold.

Weeks of debate and confusion followed—in Congress and also in the governments of Massachusetts and Connecticut. Some members of government wanted reconciliation with England, which would probably involve returning Forts Ticonderoga and Crown Point to the British. Other delegates believed that the British would soon launch a major invasion from Canada south down the Champlain-Hudson River corridor; they believed it was best to attack first.

Through these weeks from May to July, Benedict Arnold's reputation continued to take a beating from the attacks by Allen, Easton, Mott, and Brown. In late June, the beleaguered and disgusted Arnold resigned his commission. Easton was promoted to colonel and given command of Arnold's regiment, John Brown was made a major in the same regiment, and Ethan Allen was hailed as the "Hero of Ticonderoga." Their victory over Arnold could not have been more complete.

The bloodless victory at Ticonderoga and Crown Point was a momentous one, but it revealed one of the patterns of Benedict Arnold's life. He hoped to emerge as the leader of the victory, but after the hatchet job on his character by Allen, Easton, and others, it was Ethan Allen who became known as the hero.

Out of the political chaos of that spring, surprising new thinking emerged: Congress decided to launch an invasion of Canada. The hope was that the new Continental Army, commanded by General George Washington, could conquer Canada, perhaps making it the fourteenth colony, before large numbers of British troops arrived. Leaders of Congress did not mention Benedict Arnold as possible leader of the invasion force. Instead, they selected Major General Philip Schuyler of New York, who had served in Congress and in the French and Indian War.

Arnold was deeply disappointed at being passed over, but he decided to meet with Schuyler in the hope that the aristocratic New Yorker might offer him something. Schuyler already had a good opinion of him, having learned about his daring raid on St. Johns. The two men met at Schuyler's sprawling estate near Albany and the major general was pleased by Arnold's detailed knowledge of the Champlain region. Arnold, in turn, could hope that Schuyler might help him obtain a new commission.

Just as Schuyler's friendship seemed to offer Arnold a bit of hope, he was hit with a devastating personal tragedy: news reached him at Schuyler's estate that his wife Peggy had died suddenly on June 19—two weeks earlier. Three days later, her father, "Papa" Mansfield, who had become Arnold's close friend, also died. Peggy, who was only thirty, probably succumbed to one of the epidemic fevers that frequently swept through the colonies.

Arnold was overwhelmed with grief. He had always looked forward to being with her in their magnificent New Haven home, "where mutual love and friendship doubled our joys . . ." 5. He left Albany for the lonely ride home, eager to see his sister Hannah and his three young sons (the oldest was just seven). He was relieved to find that Hannah had taken care of the funeral arrangements and had kept his business affairs in good order.

For the next few weeks, Arnold was in despair. His life had reached its lowest point. His courageous efforts in the patriot cause had ended in defeat and humiliation, and the loss of his beloved wife left an aching hole in his life. But

Hannah refused to let him give up. She told him that she would do her best to be a "good mother" to the boys and would maintain his home as well as his various business interests.

Arnold's natural resilience took over, and by late July he was ready for action. Once again, he headed for Cambridge, with a new plan already taking shape in his mind: The planned invasion of Canada, to be led by General Schuyler, would use the Hudson-Champlain corridor; Arnold planned to meet with General Washington and propose leading a second invasion of Canada, this one through the forests of Maine. It was a bold scheme—and that made it typical of Benedict Arnold.

CHAPTER THREE

The Wilderness March

AT CAMBRIDGE, GENERAL WASHINGTON READILY APPROVED Arnold's plan to lead a second invasion of Canada. They agreed on a force of 1,100 men that would march through the Maine wilderness, following the Kennebec River and other waterways to the Chaudiere River, which would lead straight to Quebec, the capital of British Canada.

The main American army, under General Schuyler, would advance from the west, through St. Johns and Montreal, then meet up with Arnold's force outside Quebec.

While Benedict had been excited about the Ticonderoga campaign, at least until events and men turned against him, he considered this invasion of Quebec "the opportunity of a lifetime." He would plan it and lead it, responsible only to General Washington, not to political figures.

This "march" through the Maine wilderness was destined to become one of the great survival stories in America's history. It would also make Benedict Arnold a national hero.

As soon as Washington and Schuyler approved the plan, Arnold worked with ferocious speed to prepare for the journey. Timing was important. The Schuyler-led troops were already in Canadian territory. It was necessary for both armies to reach Quebec at nearly the same time in order to have a coordinated attack.

While waiting for Schuyler's approval, Arnold had carefully selected regiments and individuals from the thousands of men camped around Cambridge, keeping the British hemmed in around Boston. The heat of late summer, the boredom of the siege, and the promise of action, brought far more volunteers than were needed.

Arnold selected three companies of riflemen and ten companies of muskets. While most troops in the American Revolution used muskets, the riflemen formed a distinctive breed and soon acquired a romantic image as well as a reputation as expert marksmen. Their long rifles had gun barrels with interior grooves—or "rifles"—which caused the bullet to spin and to leave the gun in a straight line. Muskets had smooth barrels which allowed the bullet to rattle from side to side, causing the shell to leave the barrel in an erratic flight.

The difference in the weapons was important. At long range, the rifles were remarkably accurate. British troops soon called them "the world's deadliest widow-makers." Rifles, however, were less effective in close combat, partly because they took more time to load. Muskets, on the other hand, were useful at short range where the lack of accuracy was less noticeable; muskets could also be fitted with bayonets, while rifles could not.

Arnold's three companies of riflemen, two from Pennsylvania and one from Virginia, were rough outdoorsmen. They wore fringed hunting shirts, Indian leggings, broad-brimmed hats, and moccasins, with scalping knives and tomahawks strapped to their belts. As snipers, and for launching an attack, riflemen had no equals. The riflemen were met with some derision because of their clothing when they had first arrived at Cambridge, but they quickly earned respect. Arnold placed Captain Daniel Morgan in command of all the rifle companies. Morgan was a big, barrel-chested frontiersman, with a booming voice and a commanding presence. He was to become one of the outstanding generals of the Continental Army.

By mid-September, Arnold had his army ready to go. He had worked tirelessly to overcome countless difficulties in getting to this point, including arranging money for many of the men who were worried because they would have no pay due them until they were in Canada. He had all the men, except the rifle companies, supplied with new coats, linen frocks, blankets, shoes, guns, and tents.

On the crisp, sun-filled morning of September 19, 1775, there was a sense of excitement in the air as crowds gathered to watch 1,050 troops board the eleven fishing boats that would carry them up the coast to the Kennebec River. A surprising number of men kept journals, including Private Abner Stocking, who described the departure: "We got underway with a pleasant breeze, our drums beating, fifes playing, and colours flying. Many pretty girls stood upon the shore, I suppose weeping for the departure of their sweethearts. At eleven o' clock . . . we left the entrance of the harbor and bore away for the Kennebec River." 1.

The sea journey was hampered by thunderstorms, dense fogs, a difficult entry to the Kennebec, plus seasickness. After three days, the boats anchored at Reuben Colburn's shipyard. Early in September, Arnold had met with Colburn in Cambridge and ordered the building of 200 *bateaux*. These were simple boats that could be propelled by oars, paddles, or poles. Each bateau was large enough to carry six or seven men, plus supplies.

All 200 boats were completed, but when Arnold saw how poorly they were made, he flew into a rage. In the rush to finish their task, the builders had used green lumber that quickly warped, the boards pulled apart, and leaks developed. Although Colburn's men, with help from carpenters in Arnold's force, made what repairs they could, and added twelve new boats, it was clear that the bateaux were going to be a constant problem. That was only the first of countless disasters that were soon to threaten the lives of the entire expedition.

After transferring the supplies from the fishing boats to the bateaux, they were ready for what Arnold called "our plunge into the wilderness." He had divided the army into four companies. Two advance companies set out on September 28th, the rest following a day later. Arnold traveled by canoe so he could move back and forth along the long line of march.

When they reached one of the last clusters of settlers' cabins, the inhabitants helped him understand the second devastating problem: In mapping out the expedition, Benedict had relied on the only known charts, which had been made in 1761 by a British engineer, Lieutenant John Montresor. His calculation of the distances turned out to be far off. He had estimated the total distance to Quebec to be 180 miles; the actual distance would turn out to be 385 miles—more than double the estimate.

Benedict did not seem troubled by the new estimate of the distance. He had tremendous confidence in his ability to overcome obstacles. In physical terms, he was very strong and athletic. (Although many accounts describe him as short and stocky, about 5'4" in height, that height was at least average, and some descriptions place him at 5'7" or even 5'9"—well above average. His broad shoulders may have made him appear stocky.) From boyhood, he had always astounded people with his abilities in running, swimming, jumping, climbing, or riding.

Arnold also was completely fearless. He seemed to have a deep-seated faith in his destiny or fortune. Particularly in his military life, he felt that as long as he could act decisively, he would succeed. In terms of the journey ahead, he boldly told his men: "I believe, by the best information I can procure, we shall be able to complete the march in twenty days." 2.

The men, however, soon began to encounter the first of the incredible obstacles that were to threaten the march. Daily travel, without special problems, was grueling. Caleb Haskell, another diarist, wrote early in the march: "We begin to see that we shall have a scene of trouble to go through in this river, the water is so swift and the shoal full of rocks, ripples and falls, which oblige us to wade a great part of the way." 3.

The very first of the many waterfalls they were to encounter—Ticonic Falls—revealed more severe hardships: the portages. The bateaux were hauled out of the river, and nearly 65 tons of supplies were taken out. Handspikes were passed beneath each 400-pound boat, fore and aft, and four men struggled to carry the clumsy craft to a point above the falls.

At the next portage, on October 1st, the men were up to their waists in the frigid, swirling water. Their hands, constantly wet, became blistered and raw from hauling the bateaux. When they finally lay down to sleep that night, they were still soaked through; they awoke to find their clothes frozen, one wrote, "as thick as a pane of glass."

After more difficult portages, Benedict realized the men were exhausted by how hard he was pushing them. He constantly had in mind the solemn warning from Washington as Arnold prepared to leave: "The safety and welfare of the whole continent might depend upon the success of the Kennebec expedition." 4.

The men were relieved when Arnold called for a halt of a few days to repair the bateaux and examine the food supplies. The boats had been badly battered by rocks and rough water, often causing the seams to split. Dr. Isaac Senter, a 22-year-old surgeon from New Hampshire, another diarist, described the results:

> ... By this time, many of our bateaux were nothing but wrecks, some stove to pieces, etc. The carpenters were employed repairing them, while the rest of the army were busy in carrying over the provisions, etc.... The [dried] fish lying loose in the bateaux ... were spoiled by being continually washed with fresh water running into the bateaux. The bread casks not being waterproof, admitted the water in plenty, swelled the bread, bursts the casks, as well as soured the whole bread. 5.

Dr. Senter and Arnold also discovered that the salt beef had been poorly prepared by the packers and nearly all of it had to be thrown away.

After repacking the remaining provisions, the army pushed on. They were soon battered by weather and the wilderness more severely than ever. On October 11th, the three lead divisions began struggling through the Great Carrying Place, where they left the Kennebec River. Heavy rains turned the land into a quagmire. The men had to push west across three ponds separated by long, hard portages. The men carried bateaux and supplies on their backs over flinty rock ledges and into lowland marshes where they were often hip deep in mud and water. Many men were becoming ill with nausea and diarrhea, some from drinking brackish marsh water, others from spoiled provisions.

The tireless Benedict Arnold seemed to be everywhere as the men struggled over the rugged terrain, helping a group laboring uphill with a bateau, lifting a trooper who slipped into a deep swamp, aiding another with a twisted knee who could no longer walk. Wherever he went, he encouraged the men with kind and cheerful words, exhibiting his extraordinary strength and determination.

After the Great Carrying Place, they reached the Dead River, which brought more and different hardships. The river was constantly winding and, following three days of torrential rain, flooded its banks more than a mile on either side. The men who were marching by land had to make

to reach Quebec before Montgomery. In a strange twist of fate, the Americans took Montreal so quickly in part because of the leadership of Colonel John Brown—Arnold's enemy from Ticonderoga days.

Arnold's Heroism

At some point in the incredible march through the Maine wilderness, almost any other commander would have decided that the hardships were too great and turned back. But Arnold continued to push on with the gritty determination that saved the lives of his men. In the months that followed, Arnold was hailed for his heroic achievement. General Schuyler, in a letter to Congress, wrote that "Colonel Arnold's march does him great honor; some future historian will make it the subject of admiration to his readers." 12. James Warren called Arnold "a genius, who led a march under such circumstances, and attended with such difficulties that no modern story can equal." 13. He compared it to the famous historic march in the third century B.C. during Rome's war with Carthage, when the Carthaginian General Hannibal led his army (with some men riding elephants) through the snow-clogged Alps in order to attack Rome. Others picked up on the Hannibal image and began referring to Arnold as "America's Hannibal."

In a letter to Arnold, General Washington wrote, "My thanks are due, and sincerely offered to you, for your enterprising and persevering spirit." 14. He also offered him command of a regiment as a new army was formed for 1776. And, in a letter to Schuyler, Washington said, "The merit of this gentleman is certainly great, and I heartily wish that Fortune may distinguish him as one of her favourites. I am convinced that he will do every thing that prudence and valour shall suggest." 15.

While his new status as a hero was gratifying, Arnold was keenly aware that the praise was far from unanimous. As 1775 drew to a close, Congress showed no sign of promoting him to the rank of major general. In addition, his old enemies from the capture of Ticonderoga, including James Easton and John Brown, were still at work in their efforts to tear down his reputation.

The outcome of the battle for Quebec was soon to provide his detractors with more ammunition.

CHAPTER FOUR

Quebec—"The Forlorn Hope"

BENEDICT ARNOLD AND HIS RAGGED ARMY LEARNED that crossing the mile-wide St. Lawrence could be a daunting task. The weather remained bitterly cold, with frequent squalls of blinding snow. Two British warships were riding at anchor in the middle of the river, ready to blast any American boats—and their occupants—into small pieces. In addition, several patrol boats zigzagged up and down the river.

The Americans quietly began the crossing relays in about thirty birch-bark canoes and small boats on the moonless night of November 12, 1775. Arnold used experienced seamen to operate the canoes and boats. They guided their craft beneath the very gunwales of the warships and landed the troops in the shadow of the walled city.

After landing, the troops made their way part-way up the cliff, close to the lower city gates. As morning approached, 500 men had made the crossing. But an exchange of gunfire with a patrol boat persuaded Arnold to send a message to the 200 men still on the south bank to stay there and wait for another chance to make the crossing.

Morgan and other officers urged Arnold to launch a quick strike, taking advantage of surprise to capture the city before the defenders could organize. Arnold was sorely tempted to give the order, and several historians have said it might have worked; the British were badly disorganized, they were undermanned, and they lacked firm leadership. But Benedict did not dare risk it. If the surprise attack failed, it could ruin Washington's grand design for a two-army attack on the capital of British Canada. Reluctantly, he gave the order to climb to the top and set up a camp on the far side of the city.

While they waited for Montgomery's army to join them, Arnold's men found many of the French-Canadian residents to be friendly and helpful, especially while the money carried by Arnold held. A number of men acquired comfortable housing, and many were able to purchase clothing, shoes, and food, although there was little in the way of muskets or ammunition.

The Quebec defenders had seen Arnold's men soon after they arrived, and a sporadic exchange of gunfire began. The only artillery the Patriots had were a few small cannons they had managed to drag through the Maine wilderness, and these were useless against Quebec's thick stone walls. The most effective weapons the Americans did have were Dan Morgan's riflemen. With their long guns, they managed to pick off several wall-top sentries, enough to make the defenders a little uneasy.

Arnold realized that his army was far too weak to attack Quebec or even to start a siege. He figured that a force of at least 2,000 men and heavy artillery would be needed. Since his army consisted of only 500 men on the north side of the St. Lawrence, he could only hope that Montgomery could supply enough men and artillery to give the Americans a chance.

In the west, Montgomery's men moved easily into Montreal. Two days earlier, Governor Carleton had loaded his men and supplies on a flotilla of small boats for a race to Quebec. (Montgomery negotiated the surrender of Montreal, promising to pay fair prices for any supplies they took and to respect the people's religion.) Farther upriver at Sorel, American troops attacked Carleton's flotilla, forcing three boats to surrender and capturing the troops that had been defending Montreal. Guy Carleton managed to escape in a small boat and made his way to Quebec, where he assumed command of the city's defenses. He was confident the city could hold until the spring thaw when British ships could get through, bringing thousands of fresh troops.

Just before Carleton's return to Quebec, Arnold tried to lure the city's defenders into an open battle outside the walls, much as British general Wolfe had done to defeat Montcalm in the decisive battle of the Seven Years War (1756-1763). But the British simply scoffed at the challenge. In fact, when they saw the shabbily-dressed rebels, many without shoes, they laughed and jeered from the safety of their stone walls.

Benedict quickly realized his mistake and now feared that the enemy would attack the Americans. To avoid disaster, he ordered a night march on November 19, traveling twenty miles west where they set up camp at Pointe-aux-Trembles to wait for Montgomery. The march had been hard on the shivering soldiers, leading one of the shoeless Patriots to write, "We might have been tracked all the way by the blood from our shattered hoofs." 1.

By late November, the Americans learned that Montgomery's force was just thirty miles west of Pointe-aux-Trembles, bringing artillery and munitions, as well as plentiful supplies of clothing and guns. This was a happy interlude for Arnold's men, and they were able to bring the south bank detachment across the river.

Montgomery and Arnold finally met on December 1st, and from the beginning they got along well. Both were in their thirties, confident in their abilities, and neither was jealous of the other. Benedict seemed to get along well with officers who respected him such as Schuyler, Washington, and now Montgomery. Montgomery admired Arnold and, in a letter to Schuyler, noted that "he , , , is active, intelligent, and enterprising." And, of Arnold's wilderness marchers, he said, "There is a style of discipline among them, much superior to what I have been used to see in this campaign." 2.

The two generals were eager to capture Quebec, but they were keenly aware of what they were up against. Their combined forces numbered well under 1,500, about half the number defending Quebec. Several hundred Americans were suffering with smallpox, an often fatal disease, which many thought had been brought into the garrison by infected women sent by the Quebec defenders. In addition, some of the men whose enlistments were expiring had already started for home. Most of the militiamen were farmers or fishermen, many with families, and they were eager to be home to plant crops or prepare nets and boats for the spring. The men in both Arnold's and Montgomery's forces had already experienced the difficult enlistments and the winter weather in Canada did not promise improvement.

Arnold and Montgomery decided to test the possibilities of an assault on the city. They had their men build cannon emplacements out of ice and snow, hoping that an artillery bombardment would soften up Quebec's defenses. The attempt was a rather pathetic failure. Carleton had about 150 cannons available and he used the heaviest artillery to destroy the Americans' batteries, knocking them all out of action.

Montgomery and Arnold had one hope left: an assault on the city under cover of a nighttime blizzard. This decision caused some dissension among Arnold's men, especially in the company led by Captain Oliver Hanchet. Hanchet had already refused his commander's order to move supplies closer to Quebec's walls, insisting it was too dangerous. Normally, Arnold would have arrested Hanchet for such insubordination, but the army was so desperate for manpower that he had to tread lightly.

When Hanchet, supported by Brown and others, said he wanted to form an independent corps, separate from Arnold, Benedict was furious and humiliated, but knew he had to turn the matter over to Montgomery as commander of the combined armies. Montgomery used all the calm reasoning and persuasive skills that Arnold lacked to convince the officers and their men to stay with the assault and to continue to serve under Arnold.

Finally, on the night of December 30, the kind of fierce blizzard that Montgomery and Arnold had been waiting for moved in. With the wind picking up, the men quickly moved into position, now eager for action.

The American plan was for a two-pronged attack on the Lower Town near river level. Montgomery would lead his troops on the right flank, along the St. Lawrence, and Arnold on the left flank, along the Charles River. The two armies would then unite inside the walls and drive up into the Upper Town.

Arnold planned to spearhead the assault with a small force of hand-picked volunteers. He called this band the "Forlorn Hope." He was excited and bursting with energy. Once again, this was his dream—leading his men in a heroic attack on an enemy stronghold, pinning everything on a single throw of the dice. Victory would be momentous. Not just Quebec, but all of Canada could be in American hands. There would no longer be a danger of a British invasion from the north.

The bold American plan seems quixotic, and yet it might have succeeded. The fact that it seemed doomed from the start was due largely to bad luck.

Shortly after midnight on December 31st, two regiments of Canadian volunteers launched diversionary attacks, followed by the attacks of Montgomery's and Arnold's men. There was an immediate crash of cannons, mortars, rockets, and muskets, mixed with the steady beat of drums and the constant clang of church bells, the city's alarm system.

While Arnold led his men through deep snow past a row of brick warehouses, Montgomery made his way up a twisting path. He paused to wait for about 200 men to assemble, then led the way through a break in a barricade. At a distance of about forty paces, the British defenders managed to set off a single cannon loaded with grapeshot. The blast smashed into Montgomery and those closest to him, killing about ten instantly, the loss of their general and his two captains devastated the troops. With no one giving firm orders to continue, the assault turned into a disorganized retreat.

At the same time, Arnold led his men into a dark alleyway in the Lower Town, seeing little but the flash of muskets. They came to a barricade with two mounted guns. One gun fired, missing everything, but the other gun slammed a shell into Arnold's leg, knocking him to the ground. As he struggled to his feet, he shouted for his men to keep coming. But he could feel his boot filling with blood, he wrote later, and "the loss of blood rendered me very weak. . . . As the main body of troops came up, with some assistance I made my way to the hospital, near a mile on foot, being obliged to draw one leg after me, and a great part of the way under the continual fire of the enemy from the walls, at no greater distance than fifty yards. I providentially escaped, though several were shot down at my side." 3.

As Arnold painfully struggled to the rear, big Daniel Morgan assumed command. He ordered the men to use ladders to scale the barricades, and, to help them overcome their fear, he was the first to scramble over and leap into the town. For a few minutes Morgan and the men following him had remarkable success. They forced their way through street after street, taking scores of prisoners.

During a pause in the shooting, Morgan called a quick council of war. Many of his officers were missing, having lost their way in the storm and failing to find their way into the town. Morgan's men were on the edge of the Upper

Town and Morgan suggested that they press on. But his men disagreed, arguing that it was best to wait. They had more prisoners than men and, more important, Morgan later wrote, "General Montgomery was certainly coming down the river St. Lawrence and would join us in a few minutes, so that we were sure of conquest if we acted with caution. To these arguments," he concluded ruefully, "I sacrificed my own opinion and we lost the town." 4.

Morgan's assessment was right. Montgomery had already been killed and his troops, instead of battling toward Morgan, were in retreat. The British quickly recovered and battled back. They took control of houses around the Americans. Private George Morison described the beginning of the end:

> Our main body now appears, having taken a wrong route through narrow and crooked streets. . . . A furious discharge of musketry is let loose upon us from behind houses. In an instant we are assailed . . . by thrice our number. . . .
>
> [Ahead of us] the awful voice of Morgan is heard, whose gigantic stature and terrible appearance carries dismay among the foe wherever he comes. . . . They call on us to surrender, but we surrender them our bullets and retreat to the first battery. Here we maintain ourselves until ten o'clock [in the morning], when surrounded . . . many of our officers and men slain, and no hope of escape. We are reluctantly compelled to surrender . . . having fought manfully for three hours. 5.

Moments later, Morgan found himself surrounded and forced to surrender. With tears of frustration streaming down his face, he surrendered his sword to a priest rather than to a British officer. The battle for Quebec was over. Roughly one hundred Americans had been killed or wounded and four hundred taken prisoner.

In the hospital, Arnold learned of the battle's progress from the wounded men as they were brought in. He fully expected that Governor Carleton would soon attack but he refused requests to retreat. Instead, he remained in his bed armed with two pistols determined to kill as many as he could.

But Carleton did not attack. Instead, he was content to remain in the safety of the walled city and wait for the spring and the arrival of fresh British troops.

Retreat, And . . .

From January to May, 1776, the situation in Canada remained uncertain. From the British perspective, Carleton held the remnants of the American army as prisoners, planning to take them aboard prison ships in the spring. Arnold and the Americans saw the matter quite differently. From their point of view, they were maintaining a siege of Quebec and would renew their assault as soon as they could. Arnold wrote frequently to Congress and General Washington, asking for reinforcements and for a healthy officer to take his place. In a letter to his sister, Arnold wrote, "I have no thought of leaving this proud town, until I first enter it in triumph. 6.

He continued to hope he could renew the assault on Quebec in the spring and occupy the city before the British reinforcements arrived. He was encouraged by the news that Congress had finally recognized the importance of Canada and new regiments were already on their way, traveling north on the Hudson-Champlain route.

The winter was slow to retreat, however, slowing the American relief regiments and making life miserable for Arnold and his men outside Quebec. Fierce blizzards were common and the temperature often stayed below -25 degrees F for days at a time. The Americans attempted to harass the defenders when work groups tried to collect firewood; a number of houses were burned down in the process.

On April 2, Major General David Wooster arrived from Montreal to replace Arnold who was still suffering from his leg wound, aggravated by a fall from his horse just as he was starting to ride again. Wooster, who was old and reportedly alcoholic, showed no interest in discussing his plans with Arnold, so Benedict headed for Montreal to complete his recovery.

Wooster failed badly in a matter of a few weeks, first in attempts to bombard the city from the Heights of Abraham. Governor Carleton's defenders simply returned the fire with more powerful artillery. When Wooster's plan to burn the British ships in the harbor also failed, he was replaced by General John Thomas.

Thomas quickly saw that the American siege was useless without more men and more artillery. He found that his command consisted of only 1,900 men, with less than half that number fit for duty. In the first days of May, Thomas learned that at least fifteen British ships were making their way through the breaking ice on the St. Lawrence River, carrying about 8,000 British regulars and German mercenaries. The new British force was led by two of England's most famous generals: John Burgoyne and Simon Fraser. The approach of these reinforcements effectively ended the American efforts to capture Quebec.

Governor Carleton, who had not once moved outside Quebec to attack Arnold's force, learned that the Americans were preparing to retreat and decided it was time to attack. With a band of 900, including the first 200 troops off the ships, the British and Canadians advanced against the American lines, where only 250 men were in condition to oppose them. When the Americans saw the size of the force attacking them, they panicked and fled, leaving 200 sick or wounded comrades. Carleton chose not to pursue the 250, but returned to the city to help organize the rest of the reinforcements.

By mid-May, there were more than 13,000 British at Quebec. Small brigades, numbering 400 to 700, set off to attack the few remaining Patriot strongholds in Canada.

At the same time, in Philadelphia, the delegates to Congress were beginning to consider the bold move of declaring independence. In May, all of the colonies were beginning to organize state governments as suggested by Congress. Over the next weeks of discussion about a declaration, there was a general feeling in Congress and among the Patriot population that the American forces in Canada were likely to succeed. In fact, in early June, while Congress was debating the first resolution for independence, General John Sullivan arrived at St. Johns, Canada, with a brigade of 3,300, and was joined by four regiments sent by Washington. The troops plus ample supplies of food, ammunition, and weapons seemed to indicate a new assault on Quebec. No one could have anticipated the disaster that was already destroying the American dream of conquering Canada.

... Disaster

The beginning of the American defeat began in mid-May when a force of 400 was ordered to defend a stronghold called The Cedars, about 30 miles east of Montreal. But when a British force of 650 advanced toward them, the American major surrendered his entire garrison without a fight, even though a relief column was on the way from Montreal. In what was becoming a regular pattern for the Americans, the relief column of 100 under Major Henry Sherburne was surrounded only four miles from The Cedars and was forced to surrender.

Benedict Arnold had reached St. Johns when he learned of the American defeats. He immediately turned back to help, picking up fleeing soldiers on the way. The advancing British, which now included 500 Indians, heard of Arnold's approach; they sent a messenger to warn him that, if he attacked, the American prisoners would be turned over to the Indians. Arnold negotiated, agreed to take the American prisoners for later exchange, and returned to Montreal.

In early June, when General John Sullivan arrived at St. Johns with the large body of reinforcements, it looked as if the Americans could reverse the trend of disorganized flight and defeats. Sullivan was confident that he was just the man to lead the resurgence. His first move was to send 2,000 men in bateaux to attack a British stronghold at Trois Rivieres, about halfway between Montreal and Quebec.

The attack on Trois Rivieres turned into one more bungled defeat. Planning on a predawn surprise attack, the main force became lost and wandered into a swamp. These troops, under Anthony Wayne, managed to locate the fort and attacked, but fell back under heavy fire. The Americans scattered into the forest, hounded by Indians and Canadian volunteers. The battle cost at least 230 who surrendered and more than 400 dead or missing. British losses were fewer than twenty. Many of Sullivan's survivors made it to Sorel.

In Montreal, Benedict Arnold, who had learned that he had been promoted to brigadier general, recognized that their cause was hopeless. He led his 300 defenders out of the town and headed for St. Johns with the British pursuers closing in. At Sorel, General Sullivan reached a similar conclusion and ordered a retreat to Lake Champlain. He loaded his 2,500 men onto bateaux and fled ahead of the British fleet. As they retreated up the Richelieu River, they were pursued by more than 4,000 British regulars led by Generals Burgoyne and Fraser. The redcoats, one reported, were delighted to see "the rebels flying before us in the greatest Terror."

Arnold had sent the wounded and sick ahead to Ile aux Noix, but only two men could be spared to row each boat. This enabled the able-bodied to continue fighting a rearguard action. Arnold paused at Ile aux Noix, where Sullivan's force joined them. The Americans now numbered 8,000, but more than half were suffering from smallpox, malaria, or dysentery, as well as hunger, exhaustion, and the demoralization of defeat. Historian Richard Ketchum wrote, "The hand of death lay on this army, and everywhere men were crying out piteously for help." 7. A surgeon traveling with them said, "It broke my heart, and I wept till I had no more power to weep." 8.

Somehow, with Arnold's leadership, the battered Patriot army staggered south to Crown Point, and some to Ticonderoga. Men were dying of smallpox at the rate of ten to fifteen a day. A visiting chaplain wrote, "I did not look into a tent or hut [at Crown Point] in which I did not find either a dead or dying man." 9.

By the end of June, the question was: How long would Carleton and Burgoyne wait before assembling a fleet on Lake Champlain to launch an invasion of the American colonies? Such an invasion could end America's Revolution.

Arnold: Pro and Con

The campaign for Canada had lasted only about nine months, beginning with Arnold's heroic march through the Maine wilderness and the Schuyler-Montgomery invasion on the Hudson-Champlain corridor. By the time the battered American army reached Crown Point and Ticonderoga, many Americans now saw the campaign as a humiliating disaster. When John Adams, a key leader in Congress, heard of the army's arrival at Crown Point, he wrote:

> Our army . . . is an object of wretchedness enough to fill a human mind with horror: disgraced, defeated, discontented, dispirited, diseased, naked, undisciplined, eaten up with vermin, no clothes, beds, blankets; no medicines, no victuals but salt pork and flour. . . . 10.

Of the roughly 5,200 who reached Crown Point, 2,800 required hospitalization; the rest, an observer wrote, were "emaciated and entirely broken down in strength, spirits, and discipline." 11.

What was Benedict Arnold's role in the mission's failure? A few weeks earlier, Congress had sent a committee of three highly respected men to try to find out why the campaign was failing. The three, headed by 70-year-old Benjamin Franklin, included Samuel Chase and Charles Carroll. After meeting with Arnold and others, Carroll offered this assessment of Arnold:

> Believe me, if this war continues, and Arnold should not be
> taken off pretty early, he will turn out to be a great man. He
> has great vivacity, perseverance, resources, intrepidity, and a
> cool judgment . . . 12.

Others had praise for Arnold, including the British. In a letter to General Burgoyne, for example, the British Secretary for American Affairs, wrote: "I am sorry Arnold escaped [from Canada] . . . I think he has shown himself the most enterprising man among the rebels." 13.

General Washington also recognized Arnold's achievements in Canada. He wrote to Congress, "The merit of this gentleman is certainly great; I heartily wish that fortune may distinguish him as one of her favorites." And in a note to Arnold the commander in chief wrote, "My thanks are due, and sincerely offered to you, for your enterprising and persevering spirit." 14. Congress rewarded him by promoting him to the rank of major general.

There were also critics of Arnold's role in Canada. His old enemies—John Brown, James Easton, and Moses Hazen—again went on the attack. All three had felt the sting of Arnold's criticism, especially regarding the mishandling of private property in Canada. Immediately after the retreat to Crown Point and Ticonderoga, the trio went to Philadelphia to present their charges against Arnold to Congress and to counter his charges against them. Arnold was 250 miles away at Ticonderoga and could not defend himself.

With so many charges against Arnold bombarding Congress, the delegates began to think there must be some truth to them. Brown's arguments seemed to be particularly persuasive. As Arnold's recent biographer James Kirby Martin has written: "Since Brown could say whatever he pleased [with Arnold unable to respond], he spewed out a scurrilous tale about Arnold operating as a notorious pillager in Canada, all of which, he promised, would soon be demonstrated. . . ." 15.

Angered by what was taking place, Samuel Chase wrote to Arnold, "I cannot but request all persons to suspend their opinion and to give you an opportunity of being heard," then added a warning, "Your best friends are not your countrymen."

Arnold was outraged when the decisions of the judges were announced in August, 1776. Nearly all of the charges against Brown, Easton, and Hazen were dropped. Brown and Easton received promotions as well as back pay to 1775. Hazen's case continued for several months, and the charges against Arnold also lingered until they were eventually dropped.

In Ticonderoga, Arnold received some solace from the announcement by General Horatio Gates, the new commander in the North, that Arnold would be in command of the defense of Lake Champlain. But he still felt that Congress had betrayed his patriotism and his service to his country, damaging his sense of honor. He confided his feelings to Horatio Gates: "I cannot but think it extremely cruel, when I have sacrificed my ease, health, and a great part of my private property, in the cause of my country, to be [vilified] as a robber and thief—at a time, too, when I have it not in my power to be heard in my own defense." 16.

From his first trip to Fort Ticonderoga in the spring of 1775 (with Ethan Allen) to his return with the battered American army little more than a year later, Benedict Arnold had been on a remarkable, thrill-packed journey. The cannons taken at Ticonderoga had been vital in enabling Washington's forces to drive the British out of Boston.

Then, in the extraordinary march through the uncharted wilderness of Maine, Arnold had displayed amazing courage, compassion, and leadership. His men knew they owed their lives to him and they became devoted to him for life. The attack on Quebec had failed, in large part because of Montgomery's death and his crippling wound at the very start of the fighting, but again he displayed extraordinary leadership and courage in getting the remnants of the army to the relative safety of Crown Point and Fort Ticonderoga.

In spite of his heroism, Arnold stirred up a hornet's nest of controversy and criticism. This hostility was partly caused by his own impatience with those who got in his way, especially officers who were not his superiors. In times of danger, when quick action or decisions were needed, Arnold had no equal. But when people like Brown or Easton crossed him, he became aggressive and arrogant, confident that he was right and anyone who didn't agree with him was an idiot or an enemy.

Those who opposed him often charged that he frequently stole property from merchants or enemy officers. There may have been some truth to these charges, although nothing was ever proved against him. Historians feel that Arnold's problem stemmed from his rush to act, leaving details about finances to be settled later. His viewpoint seemed to be that Congress—and other government agencies—should provide whatever the army needed; what amounts were to be repaid could be dealt with when the fighting was over. The question about Arnold's honesty and integrity continued until he committed his amazing act of treason.

In the autumn of 1776, Arnold was about to embark on one of his most incredible adventures. In fact, some historians feel this was Arnold's most heroic moment. All of his previous exploits had been as an army leader; his newest action was to be as a naval commander.

Chapter Five

Meantime...

In the early months of 1776, Benedict Arnold lay in a hospital outside Quebec, frustrated by his slow recovery from his leg wound, but still determined to maintain a siege of the city. At the same time, his influence on the war was being felt 200 miles away outside Boston. There, General George Washington, Commander-in-Chief of the Continental Army, was preparing for a showdown with the British occupying Boston.

The showdown turned out not to be necessary, in large part because of Benedict Arnold. Over the winter, General Seymour Knox arrived with fifty-seven cannons that had been hauled by ox-drawn sleds, struggling over snow-covered hills and icy streams from Fort Ticonderoga to Washington's headquarters at Cambridge. Working quietly and swiftly, Continental troops overnight positioned the cannons on the heights overlooking the city.

In the morning, the British in Boston were shocked to see dozens of cannons aimed at them. Rather than risk a bombardment, the British boarded ships and evacuated the city in March, 1776, sailing north to Canada. Washington, who was hailed as a hero for building up the army that helped force the evacuation, knew the British would be back. He began moving the army to New York City, figuring (rightly, as it turned out) that the British would strike there.

After the heady victory in liberating Boston in March, the rest of 1776 was a strange mixture of highs and lows, victories and defeats. In the spring, for example, the British hoped to achieve a quick victory in the South, planning to capture Charleston, South Carolina, where, they believed, Loyalists would rush to help the British. Instead, Patriots organized a powerful defense on Sullivan Island. Led by Colonel William Moultrie, the Southern militia crushed the attacking British and forced them to retreat in late June, 1776. Two British warships lost about two hundred men, killed and wounded; American casualties were only twelve killed and twenty-four wounded. It would be more than two years before the British tried the South again.

At almost the same time, however, on June 29, a Patriot soldier looked out a second story window on New York's Staten Island and was stunned to see that "the whole bay was full of ships. I declare I thought all London was afloat." 1. By August, the British had landed 32,000 soldiers, supported by thirty warships, carrying 1,200 guns and 15,000 sailors.

To oppose this huge invasion force, Washington had only about 20,000 men, mostly half-trained militia; there was no naval support, and very little artillery. From late June on, the British redcoats advanced steadily across Long Island, Brooklyn, and Manhattan.

While the Patriots were winning in South Carolina and losing badly in New York City in the summer of 1776, Congress was meeting in Philadelphia to consider Thomas Jefferson's draft of the Declaration of Independence. On July 2, the declaration was approved, and the thirteen colonies became the Thirteen United States. Throughout July and August, the Declaration was read aloud and cheered in one community after another.

The Declaration of Independence gave Patriots a morale boost, but the army could not stop the British from crushing all opposition. Their warships were able to sail the rivers surrounding Manhattan, raking the streets with shells and bullets, and forcing the Patriots to retreat again and again. After New York City was abandoned, the British captured the forts and outposts along the Hudson River.

From September on, Washington spent four agonizing months trying to hold together his army while retreating across New Jersey with the British in pursuit. Finally, they crossed the Delaware River into Pennsylvania. By now, Washington's army had melted to fewer than 4,000 men. There had been many casualties, and others had gone home when their enlistments were up. Washington's strategy was simple: make sure there was always an army in the field; avoid a pitched battle at all costs because that could destroy his army.

In December, Washington was on the edge of despair. "I think the game is pretty near up," he wrote. 2.

But the game was not up. Both Washington and Arnold were about to display their respective genius in strategy and leadership.

As the British made their turns, Arnold would send his best ships into the open water to start the battle, then retreat into Valcour harbor to join the rest of the flotilla in battle formation.

In the hope of improving his fleet's chances, Arnold decided to put on an act of bravado. He began boasting often and publicly that he intended to take the fight to the British, even attacking St. Johns inside Canada. He knew that spies would pick up these claims and report to Carleton. There was evidence that Arnold's ploy worked well enough to make Carleton more cautious. In late August, Arnold began sending squadrons of several ships to explore the lake, even in the north. Instead of challenging these incursions, Carleton moved his fleet closer into Canadian waters. He did not order the ships to start their advance south until October 6.

The extra time enabled Arnold to give his crews valuable sailing experience, as well as some gunnery practice, although lack of ammunition limited actual shooting. These weeks also gave Arnold ample time to display his leadership skills, and the men responded with steadily increasing confidence. They also had glimpses of his extraordinary courage. On August 26, for example, the ships were sailing easily southward when a furious storm, hidden by the hills, suddenly burst onto the fleet. Arnold ordered the captains to sail due south. One of the gundalows did not respond quickly enough and began drifting toward land and certain disaster.

Arnold saw the danger and responded instantly. He leaped into a small boat and ordered the oarsmen to row toward the troubled gundalow. The frightened men obeyed, rowing furiously through the towering waves until they were close enough for Arnold to stand up and shout through a speaking horn, directing the gundalow's captain how to lower the sail. It worked and the gundalow was saved. The men of the fleet had heard stories of their commander's fearlessness in the face of danger. Now they had seen it first-hand and they were beginning to see him as a leader they would follow anywhere.

The battle began much as Arnold had outlined it, and as it turned out, he also had luck on his side. On the morning of October 11, about 10 am, the Americans watched as the British fleet sailed past the island. Arnold had hoped that overconfidence in their power would convince the British that there was no need to send a scouting patrol. That's exactly what happened and the enemy fleet was two miles below Valcour Island before they spotted the Americans and began their turn into the wind.

From the raised quarterdeck of the *Congress* row galley, Commodore Arnold led the three row galleys out of their Valcour Island harbor and opened fire. The battle began in late morning and raged throughout the day. The air was filled with the almost constant roar of cannons, along with the crack of muskets and rattle of swivel guns. The din was mixed with shouted oaths and commands, the cries of the wounded, and the war whoops of Indians. Arnold rushed from cannon to cannon, often aiming the gun himself. Like other officers, his face, hands and uniform were black with gun powder. His shouts of directions and encouragement seemed to boost all the men's spirits.

After the initial exchange, Arnold ordered his row galleys back into Valcour's harbor to form a solid defensive line. One of the galleys maneuvered poorly and was badly shot up, eventually running aground. The Americans fought valiantly against the greater number and firepower of the enemy, suffering about fifty casualties and the loss of some ships. British losses were similar but they were better able to afford them.

The battle had been pretty much of a draw. However, as darkness approached and the shooting stopped, Carleton's fleet formed a solid barrier across the mouth of Valcour Bay. The British also had troops and Indian warriors swarming over the hills, including on Valcour Island. Although Arnold's men had done well, it was clear that they were now trapped. They could not possibly fight their way out in the morning. The British leaders were confident that they would force the rebels to surrender or destroy them.

Arnold and his officers decided it was better to risk a breakout and then try to race to the safety of Crown Point and Ticonderoga. Under cover of darkness and fog the Patriot ships moved out single file, with oars muffled, hugging the rocky New York coast. Arnold even had the wounded moved below decks so their moans or cries would not be heard by the British.

After several tense hours, the American flotilla was clear of the bay and began the race to Crown Point. In the morning, as the fog lifted, the stunned

British discovered that Valcour Bay was empty. Furious, Carleton ordered his fleet commanders to give chase. Crown Point was more than forty miles to the south, so he was confident they could catch up to the rebels.

The damaged American ships had trouble staying ahead. Three of the gundalows were so badly damaged that they had to be sunk. Arnold ordered one of the row galleys to lead the remaining nine vessels toward Crown Point, while the other two row galleys would try to delay the British. It was vital, Arnold told his captains, that at least a few ships got through; they would be proof that Carleton had not gained complete control of Lake Champlain.

After one row galley surrendered, the other, the *Congress*, commanded by Arnold, faced the British. He knew that the longer he and his men delayed the enemy, the better chance the remaining ships would have to reach Crown Point. For more than two hours, Arnold and his crew put up a brave fight against a total of seven enemy ships. Rather than surrender, Arnold made a sudden dash between two British ships, ran the *Congress* on shore and set it ablaze, rather than let the British capture it. That was a point of honor to him, and one that was widely praised.

Arnold and his crewmen raced on foot toward Crown Point. They caught up with five of his ships that had made it through. They boarded the row galley and sailed to Crown Point and then, on to Ticonderoga. It was a great triumph for Arnold and his men. But he and Gates were still fearful that Carleton was about to launch an attack on Crown Point and Ticonderoga.

Carleton, however, did not dare risk it. He had been surprised by the fighting ability of the rebels. Consequently, on November 2nd, he began withdrawing his ships to Canada, planning to launch a new invasion in the spring of 1777. In England, the king's ministers were not pleased. To them, it seemed impossible that a handful of rebel ships, led by the "horse jockey" Arnold, could battle a British fleet to a standstill. For the 1777 invasion, they wanted a man who was more willing to fight. They chose General John Burgoyne.

Heroism Questioned . . .

When Arnold returned to Ticonderoga, he was treated as a hero. Gates, in his general orders for October 14, expressed thanks to "General Arnold, and the officers, seamen, and marines of the fleet for the gallant defense they made against the great superiority of the enemy's force. Such magnanimous behavior will establish the fame of American arms throughout the globe." 6.

In a letter to General Schuyler, Gates expressed his thanks that "it has pleased Providence to preserve General Arnold. Few men ever met with so many hairbreadth escapes in so short a space of time." The praise was echoed by members of Congress. Benjamin Rush wrote that "General Arnold . . . has conducted himself like a hero." Virginia's Richard Henry Lee praised all of Arnold's men: " . . . our people bravely maintained the unequal contest, conducting themselves with a valor that has extorted applause even from their enemies, and which certainly deserved a better fortune." 7.

The British added to the praise. A British officer who served in the Lake Champlain battle, wrote that the rebels' retreat "did great honor to General Arnold." And a popular British publication stated that "Arnold's desperate resistance [had greatly added to] that renown which he had acquired on land in the Canada expedition. He had not only acted the part of a brave soldier, but . . . also amply filled that of an able naval commander. . . . [Not even] the most experienced seamen could have found a greater variety of resources . . . to compensate for the want of force, than he did." The publication concluded that Arnold had "raised his character still higher than it was before with his countrymen." 8.

As always seemed to be the case, critics of Arnold emerged quickly. The main attack came from Brigadier General William Maxwell, who called Arnold "our evil genius to the north." He charged that Arnold must have used "a good deal of industry [to lose] our fine fleet [which] by all impartial accounts, was by far the strongest." 9.

At first, few people paid much attention to Maxwell's charges. But over the next several weeks, doubts emerged about Arnold's conduct. Some wondered if he had been serious when he boasted that he would carry the fight to the enemy, even invading Canadian territory. Was it possible, as James Wilkinson later charged, that the lake battle had taken place because of an "excess of rashness and folly [in order] to exalt his character for animal courage, on the blood of men equally brave." 10. James Wilkinson, who was to become one of the most notorious figures in American history, showed his tendency to advance his career by switching loyalties. As Arnold's aide during the retreat from Canada, he had nothing but praise for his general. Six months later, he had become Gates's aide and joined the chorus of Benedict Arnold's critics.

Although not many saw evil in Arnold's actions, a growing number wondered about his decision to fight at Valcour Bay; maybe, they thought, it would have been a better strategy to retreat to Crown Point or Ticonderoga and save the fleet. By November, then, Arnold's brilliant defense of Lake Champlain seemed much less heroic. Instead of acknowledging that his actions had convinced Carleton to withdraw to Canada, many in Congress now seemed to feel that his drive for personal glory led him to sacrifice men and ships. There was no one in the Congress willing to defend his honor. Even Richard Henry Lee, who had earlier praised him, now accused him of acting in a "fiery, hot, and impetuous" manner, instead of withdrawing in the face of a fleet "so much superior to his force." 11.

In later years, historians were more willing to recognize that Arnold's actions with his banged-together ships, were actually crucial to the future success of the Patriots' cause. The famous naval historian Alfred Thayer Mahan wrote in the late 19th century that the Americans were strong enough to force the British to surrender at the Battle of Saratoga because of " . . . the invaluable delay secured to them by their little navy on Lake Champlain created by the indomitable energy, and handled with the indomitable courage of the traitor Benedict Arnold." He added, "Never had any force, big or small, lived to better purpose or died more gloriously . . ." 12.

In the following months, Arnold had new chances to prove his courage and leadership.

CHAPTER SEVEN

Heroics And Politics

By EARLY 1777, LESS THAN TWO YEARS AFTER the start of America's Revolution, Benedict Arnold had become one of the Patriots' most heroic figures. People praised his many exploits, which included: acquiring the vital artillery from Ticonderoga and St. Johns; risking starvation and death in the almost mythical march through the Maine wilderness; exercising gritty leadership in the battle for Quebec; and performing extraordinary feats on Lake Champlain.

At the same time, however, some Americans—including leading members of Congress—saw him as dangerous and untrustworthy. His critics, including Easton, Brown, and Hazen, attacked him relentlessly in newspapers and in Congress. Several of the charges, including shady financial dealings, tended to stick, even though proofs were lacking or questionable. Several members of Congress developed an abiding distrust of Arnold. Some felt that the repeated accusations were likely to have some validity.

General Washington was keenly aware of Congressional uneasiness regarding Arnold. He also knew that nearly all members of Congress were determined to maintain firm civilian control over the military. They didn't want Arnold—or Washington for that matter—to become too popular. A military dictatorship would quickly end the Patriot cause.

After the Battle of Lake Champlain, Arnold saw little action for the next six months. He rested at Ticonderoga for a few days and prepared to go to New Haven to see his three sons and his sister Hannah for the first time in nearly a year and a half. The plan changed suddenly when Gates received an urgent plea for help from General Washington in Pennsylvania. General Gates organized eight regiments of Continental Army troops and headed south. Arnold joined them, then raced ahead to reach Washington's headquarters on the Delaware River in mid-December.

Washington told Arnold about his plan to recross the Delaware and attack Britain's hired allies—the Hessians—stationed at Trenton, New Jersey. Arnold, of course, was eager to be part of the surprise attack, especially after the months of losses and retreats that Washington's army had experienced. Washington, however, had other plans for his fighting general. He asked Arnold to hurry to New England where a British force of about 7,000 had landed at Newport, Rhode Island. The commander-in-chief wanted him to rally Patriot militia to prevent British forces from moving inland.

Enthusiasm for the Patriot cause had dipped badly during the months of military disasters. The one bright spot had been Arnold's heroism on Lake Champlain. Washington hoped that Benedict's presence in New England would encourage more militiamen to sign up. Arnold immediately headed north.

He stopped in New Haven for a few days, basking in the affection of his three sons and his sister Hannah. The oldest boy, Benedict, was about to turn nine, Richard was seven and Henry was four. Benedict was also pleased by the warm reception he received from the people of New Haven, who were thrilled by his courageous defense on Lake Champlain. When he left for Providence, he was accompanied by the same warm response of people for the entire journey.

In Rhode Island, he found that the British were in firm control of Newport and the surrounding area. American General John Spencer had fewer than 5,000 half-trained militia to try to hold them at bay. While Arnold was eager to develop a plan for dislodging the British, he knew he needed more men to have a chance.

From his arrival at Providence on January 12, until the end of the month, he had little success recruiting militia. He wrote to Washington with a description of his battle plan, and added that, because of the lack of troops, "I believe your Excellency will not think it prudent for us to make a general attack." 1. Washington quickly responded, saying that no attack should be attempted unless there was "certainty of success."

Arnold was deeply disappointed to learn that his role in Rhode Island was to be defensive, with little chance for combat. Even the defensive posture seemed less demanding when the Americans learned that Sir Henry Clinton, the British commander, did not intend to attack Providence. Instead, he had decided to go into winter quarters at Newport. In fact, Clinton had received permission to spend the winter in England.

Spencer and Arnold agreed that Benedict should go to Boston to try to raise three or four regiments of Continental troops, rather than militia. On his journey, he learned about three of his old friends—Daniel Morgan, Eleazer Oswald, and John Lamb—who had been captured at Quebec. In November, Arnold had asked General Washington to see if he could speed their release in a prisoner exchange. The exchange was completed and all three were already rebuilding their military careers. Oswald, who rode with Arnold on the way to Boston, told him that Morgan was organizing a new regiment of Virginia riflemen; John Lamb, who had survived a disfiguring face wound, had been promoted and given orders to organize the Continental Army's 2nd Artillery Regiment. Congress, however, had provided no funds for cannons, horses, and other materials. Lamb used his own money and borrowed more, but he was still well short. Arnold sent word through Oswald, who was to be an officer in the new regiment, for Lamb to go to Hannah Arnold to receive a note for 1,000 pounds.

That act of generosity was typical of Benedict's attitude about money. He knew he might not be repaid by John Lamb, but as long as he had the money, that was how he wanted to use it.

Arnold's Romantic Interlude

In Boston, Benedict wanted to make a good impression, so he contacted an old acquaintance, Paul Revere, for help in selecting the best uniform accoutrements. One reason for the sartorial splendor was that he had met a pretty young Bostonian named Elizabeth "Betsy" De Blois. Benedict enlisted the aid of Lucy Knox, wife of General Henry Knox, Washington's over-sized artillery officer. Arnold, in a letter to Lucy, asked her to arrange the delivery of a trunk of gowns to the "heavenly Miss De Blois."

Benedict's gift showed a remarkable lack of taste. The dresses had been confiscated from an enemy shipment, but even if delivered in person, they would not have constituted a sophisticated offering. Perhaps not surprisingly, Miss De Blois refused the gift and did not encourage further overtures by the impetuous general. Arnold left Boston a loser in love and with few new recruits.

Arnold had little time to fret over his failure to win the hand of Miss De Blois. In early March, 1777, he received a letter from Washington with crushing news: Congress had voted to promote five men to the rank of major general. All five had less experience than Arnold and none had shown anything approaching his ability. But all five were now his superiors and he became the oldest remaining brigadier general. This news was a blow to Benedict's pride that some biographers feel he never recovered from.

Washington had not been consulted by Congress in the choices made, and he was stunned to see no mention of Benedict Arnold. In his letter to Arnold, he cautioned him not to "take any hasty steps" until the matter could be looked into. Washington also wrote privately to his friend in Congress Richard Henry Lee, saying he was

> anxious to know whether General Arnold's non-promotion was owing to accident or design, and the cause of it. Surely a more active, a more spirited, and sensible officer, fills no department of your army. Not seeing him then in the list of major generals, and no mention made of him, has given me uneasiness, as it is not to be presumed (being the oldest brigadier) that he will continue in service under such a slight. 2.

Arnold was both shocked and hurt by the news of his non-promotion. On March 14 he wrote to Washington that he thought the action by Congress was "a very civil way of requesting my resignation, as unqualified for the office I hold. . . . When I entered the service of my country my character was unimpeached. I have sacrificed my interest, ease and happiness in her cause. . . ." He added that he wanted a court of inquiry into his conduct, but in deference to Washington's request, "I shall certainly avoid any hasty step . . . that may tend to the injury of my country." 3.

Washington continued to be troubled by what was happening to Arnold.

But he was keenly aware that Congress had become very touchy in their dealings with the military's officers, especially generals, convinced that civilian government had to keep tight control over its officers, including Benedict Arnold and even George Washington. Knowing this, Washington still turned again to his friend Lee. "I could wish to see Arnold promoted to the rank of major general," he wrote, and that he should be given seniority over the others. It is by men of [Arnold's] activity and spirit the cause is to be supported." 4.

What neither Washington nor Arnold knew was that the enemies of both men were becoming more bold. The winter of 1776-1777 provided severe tests for both men.

Enemies Old and New

About the time that Arnold learned of his non-promotion, he also learned that one of his old enemies—John Brown—had submitted a petition to Congress. Brown listed thirteen "crimes" Arnold had committed and urged Congress to arrest and court-martial him. Brown also attacked Arnold for his "unjustifiable, false, wicked, and malicious accusation" that Brown had stolen property at Ticonderoga. 5. "Money is this man's god," the petition concluded, "and to get enough of it he would sacrifice his country." 6.

One of several facts that Arnold was not yet aware of was that the petition had been delivered to Congress by General Gates—the man who had worked closely with Arnold through the Lake Champlain crisis and praised him for his heroic actions, and who had then rushed south to aid Washington.

Instead of rushing to meet Washington, however, Gates suddenly slowed down. Washington was upset, particularly because another general he had counted on—General Charles Lee—was also inexplicably slow.

What had gone wrong, especially with Gates? Why did he so suddenly seem to turn against both Arnold and Washington?

The answer was that both Gates and Lee had come to think of Washington as an inept bungler. They believed that his mismanagement had enabled the British to take control of New York City and then sweep across New Jersey, nearly destroying the remnants of Washington's army. When the commander-in-chief ordered the two generals to move with speed, they simply refused. Both Gates and Lee were now so intent on advancing their own careers, they didn't care about endangering the Revolution.

Lee was so slow that a British force caught up with him and captured him. Major General John Sullivan took command of his 2,000 troops and quickly had them across the Delaware with Washington.

When Gates finally arrived in camp, he immediately argued with Washington about the commander's plan for a secret attack on Trenton. Gates insisted the Patriots should move deeper into Pennsylvania. Washington would not listen, so Gates, claiming illness, left and went to Baltimore where Congress had relocated. There he met with friends in Congress, seeking their support to have him replace Schuyler in the Northern District. His eventual goal was to replace Washington as commander-in-chief.

It was in Baltimore that Gates delivered Brown's anti-Arnold petition to Congress. Gates had apparently been troubled by the public acclaim Arnold had received after Lake Champlain. He now viewed the naval hero as a rival for power, not an ally. By early 1777, Gates seemed determined to destroy Arnold's career.

Battlefield Heroics . . . Again

Since the British showed no sign of moving inland, Arnold felt it was safe for him to return to New Haven, spend some time with his family, and prepare to go to Philadelphia to try to clear his name with Congress. The day before he was to leave, a courier arrived with the news that a British force had landed at Norwalk, Connecticut and was marching toward Danbury where the Patriots had a major supply depot. Arnold immediately headed for Danbury.

Benedict rode swiftly but stopped long enough at every town for militiamen to join him to defend Connecticut from British invaders. He hoped for an outpouring of citizen soldiers, something like the thousands who had answered the call at Lexington and Concord, and then at Bunker Hill. But only about 100 followed him, including Brigadier General David Wooster, a New Haven neighbor, and briefly the commander outside Quebec.

At the town of Redding he met militia general Gold S. Silliman in command of about 500 men. Silliman told him that earlier in the day, a force of 2,000 British had taken Danbury without opposition. The redcoats had destroyed tons of supplies and weapons, then torched the town, leveling nearly every house. The British, under the command of William Tryon, the former Loyalist governor of Connecticut, headed for the coast, planning to board their ships before the Patriots could organize any opposition.

Arnold was well aware that his militia force, which numbered less than 600 and with little training, were no match for the invaders, but he was determined to show that Americans would defend their lands. He divided his little army, having Wooster harass them from the rear, while he and Silliman raced cross-country to Ridgefield, where they planned to block the road to the coast.

When Wooster caught up to the British and opened fire, Tryon stopped instantly and ordered a full-scale counter-attack, supported by the fire from six field cannons. The Patriot militia panicked and fled. Wooster was seriously wounded; his son rushed to help him. When a redcoat ordered the younger Wooster to surrender, he refused and the redcoat ran him through with a a bayonet, killing him instantly. David Wooster died a few days later.

Wooster's attack did gain valuable time, allowing Arnold and Silliman to lead their men cross-country to Ridgefield, where they set up a barricade of logs, rocks, and overturned wagons. Quietly urging his men to remain calm, Arnold rode back and forth behind the defense.

The British appeared in mid-afternoon and Tryon immediately ordered an attack. The frightened Americans, outnumbered about 20 to 3, held their line. Surprised by the Patriots' stubborn defense, Tryon ordered a flanking attack. Being attacked from two sides was too much for the American militiamen. They faltered, then started to run.

Arnold ordered a retreat. In his diary, he described the action that followed:

> [I] turned my horse to retreat just as General Agnew's infantry, running down the hill from the rocks, fired a complete round at my humble person. The Lord knows why I was not killed, nine bullets went through my poor horse, which fell

dead at once, and my feet were entangled in the stirrups, but I was not wounded.

'Surrender, you are my prisoner,' cried a grenadier, as he rushed forward with a fixed bayonet to run me through. 'Not yet,' I remarked; and this little interchange of conversation had given me time to draw a pistol from its holster with which I shot the soldier dead. 7.

The day's fighting was over. The British had suffered heavy losses, so Tryon decided to pause for the night, rather than risk marching fifteen miles to the coast in the dark. Arnold spent the night riding the countryside, urging militia to join him in fighting the invading British.

Once again, few militia joined him by morning. Both Arnold and Washington were increasingly disturbed by the unwillingness of the American people to defend their homes and the Patriot cause. Washington called it a "langor [sic] that prevails everywhere." 8. Arnold, a delegate for Congress said, could not understand how the people of Connecticut could put up with "such an insult without resistance or proper revenge." And Arnold himself said of the citizen-soldiers, "I wish never to see another of them in action." 9.

In spite of the problems, Arnold was still ready to fight. As the British neared the coast, he had his men use hit-and-run tactics, since they were too badly outnumbered for a direct attack. Arnold was again in the thick of the fighting, riding along the line, urging the militia to stay steady. A surprised witness wrote that he "exhibited the greatest marks of bravery, coolness, and fortitude . . . ignoring the enemy's fire of musketry and grape shot." 10.

In a climax that echoed the Ridgefield encounter, Arnold's horse was hit and crumbled to the ground, but this time Arnold was thrown clear, although a musket ball tore through the collar of his coat. Seeing their commander down was too much for the Connecticut militiamen. They broke and ran, giving the British a clear path to their ships waiting off the coast.

Once again, even the British praised Arnold, calling him "a devilish fighting fellow." 11. The members of Congress did an about-face and immediately promoted him to the rank of major general on May 2. While that move was welcome, the delegates did not address the matter of seniority, so the other five major generals still outranked him.

John Adams, who would become the nation's second president, had an unusual idea for honoring Arnold's heroic stand. He wanted to have a medal created, much as Congress had done to honor Washington for the liberation of Boston. Adams thought that such a medal would encourage men to enlist in the Continental Army. He described the medal:

> ... I wish we could make a beginning, by striking a medal with a platoon firing at General Arnold, on horseback, his horse falling dead under him and he deliberately disentangling his feet from the stirrups and taking his pistols out of his holsters before his retreat.

On the reverse, the medal would show Arnold "mounted on a fresh horse, receiving another discharge of musketry, with a wound in the neck of his horse. . . ." 12.Adams was convinced that people had not seen such examples of outstanding bravery on the battlefield.

Matters of Honor

Congress never acted on Adams's idea of a medal honoring Benedict Arnold, largely because there were so many doubts about his character. (In addition to the medal struck for Washington in 1776, seven others were created during the Revolution.)

Arnold knew nothing about the idea of a medal, but he was still deeply troubled by the failure of Congress to establish his seniority over the other five major generals. He was also troubled by the notion that neither General Gates nor Washington seemed to be granting him whole-hearted support.

Eager to find out where he stood, Arnold left New Haven and rode to Washington's new headquarters in Morristown. He didn't realize how much Washington admired him. The commander-in-chief warned friends in Congress that no general was likely to remain in service after losing his seniority to less qualified men. He always advised his young general to be patient and bide his time. But when Arnold arrived unexpectedly and showed him the petition

Brown had sent to Congress, Washington changed his mind and encouraged him to go to Congress. He realized that Congress was not behaving honorably in their treatment of Arnold.

The members of Congress greeted him warmly and presented him with a fine horse to replace the two he had lost. While they put off discussing the problem of seniority, they did appoint a committee—the Board of War—to consider his claim for expenses in the Quebec campaign. The board's statement declared "entire satisfaction . . . concerning the general's character and conduct, so cruelly and groundlessly [attacked in John Brown's] publication." 13.

Arnold was still seething over the matter of seniority. He wondered if Congress was trying to quiet him with the gift of a horse. But he was reluctant to resign and leave the army. He loved the excitement of battle. He knew that he had no equal in assessing a military situation, making a quick strategic decision, and inspiring his men to do whatever he asked. He was also convinced that his military career offered the best hope of restoring his family's honor and wealth.

Over the next few weeks, however, he observed that his friend and mentor, General Philip Schuyler, was struggling with enemies in Congress to hold onto his position as head of the Northern Military District. And he watched General Horatio Gates, his former friend and ally, turn against Schuyler, against Arnold himself, and even against Washington.

If so much depended on the whims of Congress, what chance did Arnold have, especially since he lacked political allies? Consequently, on July 10, 1777, Arnold reluctantly wrote a letter of resignation to Congress. He explained that he did not resign his commission out of "a spirit of resentment (though my feelings are deeply wounded), but because of a real conviction that it is not in my power to serve my country in the present rank I hold." Not advancing him above the other major generals was, he wrote, an "implied impeachment of my character and declaration of Congress that they thought me unqualified for the post that fell to me in the common line of promotions." 14

Arnold handed in the resignation and prepared to leave Philadelphia. He assumed his military career had ended but once again, fate intervened and changed his plans.

While Arnold was still in Philadelphia, Washington received two stunning reports: First, General Howe had loaded 15,000 troops on 260 transport ships. Was he planning to move south to attack Washington's 7,500-man army? Or, would he move north, up the Hudson to connect with the British moving south from Canada? Either move could be disastrous for the Patriot cause.

The other report was that the British in Canada, now under General Burgoyne, had launched their invasion down the Champlain-Hudson corridor. With more than 10,000 men, including German mercenaries and Indians, Burgoyne's force could easily overwhelm the Patriot army under Schuyler, based at Albany. General Arthur St. Clair who was supposed to defend Ticonderoga, took one look at the approaching British and abandoned the fort on July 5 without firing a shot. Burgoyne had now paused at Skenesboro to wait for supplies before making his final push for Albany.

On July 10, Washington asked Congress for 6,000 new troops and Congress, finally realizing that the Revolution was in danger, readily agreed. Congress also agreed when Washington requested that Benedict Arnold be sent north to train these recruits. In making the request, Washington revealed how highly he regarded the hero of Champlain and Danbury. He pointed out that Arnold ". . . is active, judicious, and brave, and an officer in whom the militia will repose great confidence." 15.

Congress managed the matter of Arnold's resignation by simply ignoring it. Arnold was understandably delighted that he was still in uniform and was being sent to the likely locale of the next important fighting. The approaching battles, in fact, would turn out to be the turning point of the American Revolution. And once again, Benedict Arnold was to play a pivotal role.

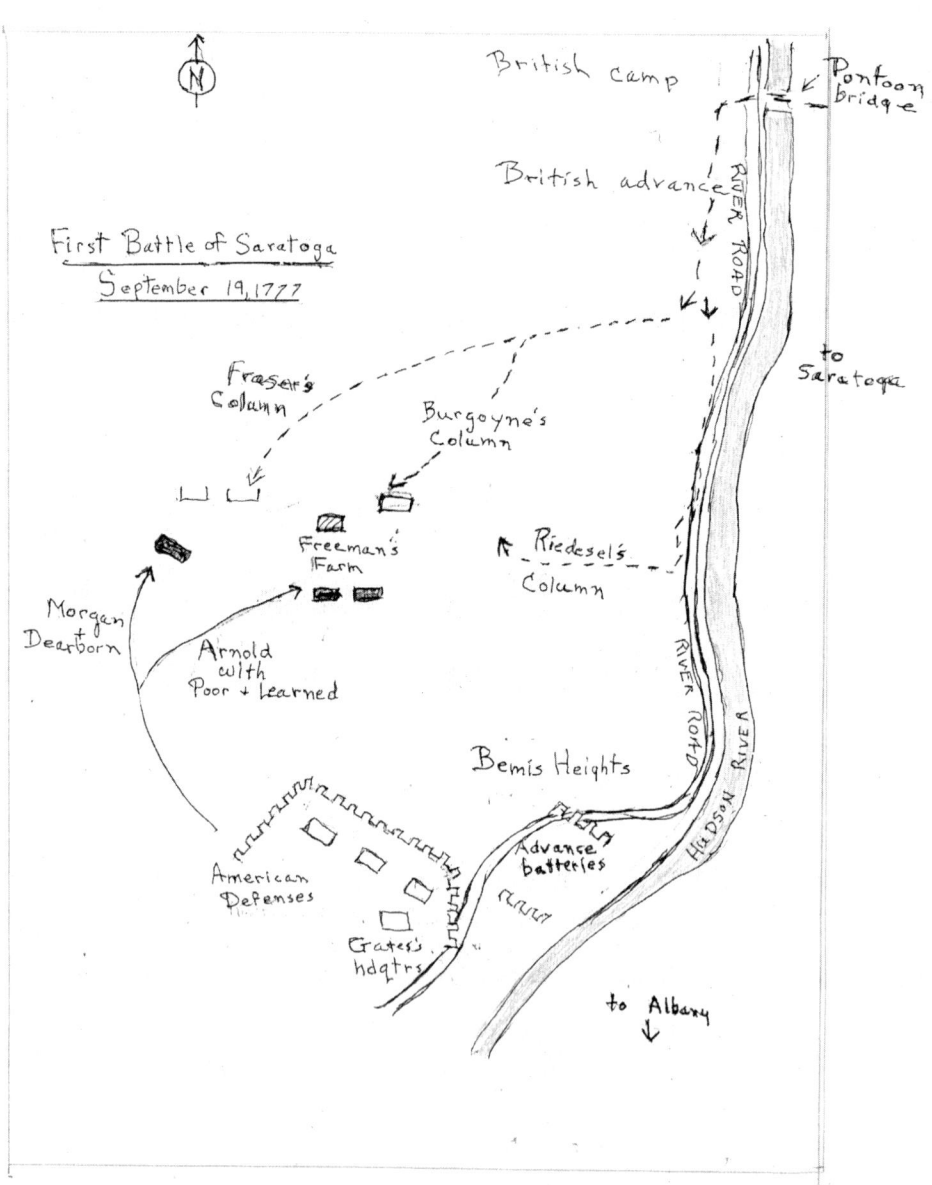

First Battle of Saratoga
September 19, 1777

British camp

Pontoon bridge

British advance

RIVER ROAD

to Saratoga

Fraser's Column

Burgoyne's Column

Freeman's Farm

Riedesel's Column

Morgan Dearborn

Arnold with Poor & Learned

Bemis Heights

RIVER ROAD

HUDSON RIVER

American Defenses

Advance batteries

Gates's hdqtrs

to Albany

CHAPTER EIGHT

The Battle of Saratoga, Part I

In June, 1777, British General John Burgoyne led his 10,000-man invasion force south from Canada on the Lake Champlain-Hudson River corridor. His army looked invincible, and "Gentleman Johnny" was brimming with confidence. He was a dashing figure, an actor, a playwright and a hero of the Seven Years' War (1756-1763), immensely popular with his troops and with the government leaders in London.

As the long procession of soldiers, horses, oxen, wagons, and field artillery rumbled south, along with scores of supply boats following on the lake and river, the commanding officers were sure they would easily smash through the American defenses to Albany. There they would meet General Howe's army coming north from New York City and a third, smaller army under Colonel Barry St. Leger coming east along the Mohawk River.

In the beginning, the British and their Hessian allies moved swiftly. On July 5, they took Fort Ticonderoga, one of the keys to American defenses. The fort's defenders, commanded by Major General Arthur St. Clair, fled without firing a shot. With the enemy close behind, St. Clair's men made a torturous retreat through rugged, wooded hills, losing nearly 400 men (killed, wounded, or captured) in a running battle to Fort Edward. Although the Patriots managed to strike back several times, inflicting fairly heavy casualties, the loss of the fort and the scattering of St. Clair's men, constituted a devastating defeat for the American cause.

Burgoyne now paused at Skenesboro to wait for supplies from Canada. The delay stretched out to three weeks. No one could see it yet, but the long wait revealed several weaknesses in the British invasion. One serious problem was the time needed to move a huge army through the dense wilderness of the Hudson River Valley. Burgoyne had allowed many of his officers to bring their wives, and some also brought their children. This slowed down the army's movements and added to the logistical problems of transporting food, as well as weapons, 138 pieces of field artillery, and ammunition.

Another weakness emerged from Burgoyne's personality. He was enjoying himself and felt no need to rush. Baroness von Riedesel, wife of the general who commanded the Hessians, wrote in her diary that Burgoyne was "... having a jolly time, spending half the night singing and drinking and amusing himself with the wife of a commissary, who was his mistress and, like him, loved champagne." 1.

During the three-week lull, Arnold received his orders from General Washington, headed north, and reached Fort Edward on July 22. He met with Schuyler and helped him plan defense strategies. Their greatest worry was being short of troops. Few volunteers had answered Schuyler's repeated appeals for militia that he sent throughout New England and New York. He was also troubled by the news that another British force was moving east across New York state. With too few men, he wrote, "I am to face a powerful enemy from the north, flushed with success, and pressed at the same time from the west." 2.

When the British and Hessians neared Fort Edward in late July, Schuyler had no choice but to retreat closer to Albany. Burgoyne now felt that finishing off the rebels would be quick and easy. He sent glowing reports to London, where he was hailed as a conquering hero. He issued a proclamation, calling on the rebels to surrender, or else . . . Major General Friedrich von Riedesel, commander of the Hessians, echoed that confidence, saying that Burgoyne's campaign would be a "march of annihilation."

Schuyler did what he could with the time gained by Burgoyne's delay. He sent several hundred woodsmen into the thick forests, where they cut down trees to block pathways, destroyed bridges, and rolled boulders into streams to make passage difficult. When the British resumed their march, they could not advance more than a mile a day. As the work crews struggled forward, the Americans could hear the thud of their axes in their effort to rebuild more than thirty bridges. Arnold was sent ahead with a squad of soldiers to harass the enemy column so they could attack it at weak points.

The planning and energy poured into these efforts began to pay off. In fact, the work of Schuyler and Arnold made it possible for the Patriots to put up a strong defense. Their efforts were helped by other developments. General Washington, for example, could not spare much man power, but he did send Colonel Daniel Morgan and his regiment of riflemen, knowing how well Morgan and Arnold had worked together in the Quebec campaign. He also sent General John Glover's Marblehead seamen who had ferried Washington across the Delaware the previous December.

Two other developments involved Burgoyne's flanks—first on the left flank, then on his right.

Burgoyne: Storm Clouds On His Left

While Burgoyne waited for supply wagons to arrive from Canada, he also was in desperate need of horses, cattle, and oxen. Scouts told him there were large numbers of animals in the Hampshire Grants (Vermont) and that many of the people were loyalists who would be eager to welcome the British and Hessians. This sounded like easy pickings to Burgoyne, so in mid-August, he sent a force of about 600 Hessians, British, and Indians, all under the command of German Lieutenant Colonel Friedrick Baum, toward Bennington (Vermont) to round up as many animals as possible.

Neither Burgoyne nor Riedesel worried about the militia under Seth Warner, since they had retreated into northern Vermont. But they did not count on the extraordinary abilities of John Stark. Like Benedict Arnold, Stark had been passed over for promotion by Congress. He went home to Vermont, and became a general of militia. When he learned that Baum's force was coming, he managed to raise 1,500 militiamen in less than a week. And Seth Warner, with about 300 men, promised to meet Stark at Bennington.

When Baum saw some of Stark's men approaching, he paused on a hill and prepared to greet the men he assumed were loyalists, coming to join them. Too late, he realized the truth as Stark's men burst from the woods and attacked from all sides. Baum's force was saved from total disaster only by their hilltop location and the approach of 550 additional men sent by a worried Riedesel. The enemy force was soon overwhelmed, however, especially after a shell hit an ammunition wagon causing a tremendous explosion. Stark's men rushed up the hill and used sabers, bayonets, and butts of their muskets to destroy Baum's force. The Indians fled, but hundreds of Hessians and British were cut down or forced to surrender. The arrival of Seth Warner's militia helped crush most of the 550 Hessian reinforcements.

The Battle of Bennington was a stunning victory for the Patriots. The American casualties were light, while the British and Hessians lost roughly 800 men, killed, wounded, or taken prisoner. That number amounted to nearly ten percent of Burgoyne's invasion force. In a report to London, Burgoyne wrote that the population of Vermont was "the most active and most rebellious race on the continent, and hangs like a gathering storm on my left." 3.

Burgoyne consoled himself with the knowledge that Colonel St. Leger was at Oswego in New York State and would soon be arriving on the Hudson. He did not yet know that St. Leger had also run into trouble. In his case, the trouble was Benedict Arnold.

... And On His Right

British Lieutenant Barry St. Leger led an expedition of nearly 1,000 British, Hessian, and Loyalist troops from Montreal to Oswego, New York, There, on July 25, they were joined by about 1,000 Iroquois warriors led by a remarkable man named Thayendanegea, or Joseph Brant. Brant had lived among whites for many years and had served as secretary to Guy Johnson, the British Superintendent of Indian Affiars. (Johnson had helped persuade most of the Iroquois nations to side with the British throughout the American Revolution.)

Confident of success, St. Leger led his army of 2,000 men toward Albany. The only obstacle in his path was Fort Stanwix on the Mohawk River. The fort was held by about 750 men commanded by Colonel Peter Ganesvoort. They were restoring the fort and planning to rename it Fort Schuyler. When Ganesvoort refused to surrender the fort, St. Leger had his men surround it.

Arnold's Rescue of Fort Stanwix

East of Fort Stanwix, Militia General Nicholas Herkimer organized a force of about 800 militiamen to march to the relief of the fort. Scouts reported the march to St. Leger, and he sent Brant's Indians to set up an ambush. Herkimer's men marched into the ambush near Oriskany, suffering heavy losses, including a wound to Herkimer that was to prove fatal. Bleeding heavily, Herkimer had himself propped up under a tree, sitting on his saddle, puffing his pipe, and directing a counter attack. He had lost more than 150 men, plus another 50 taken prisoner, most of whom would be tortured and scalped. He ordered the survivors back to Fort Dayton, where he died a few days later.

When General Schuyler, at Saratoga, learned about the battle of Oriskany, he realized that if Fort Stanwix now surrendered, St. Leger would have an open path to Albany. That would force Schuyler's outnumbered men to fight both Burgoyne from the north and St. Leger, from the west.

Against the advice of his officers, Schuyler sent a force of 900 Continentals to aid the fort and Arnold agreed to lead them. Outnumbered two to one by St. Leger's army, Arnold was reluctant to try a direct attack, so he decided to try a ruse. He had a prisoner, a Loyalist named Hon Yost Schuyler, who had been sentenced to die for anti-patriotic activities. When his family appealed for his life, Arnold offered him his freedom if he would give false information to the Indians serving under St. Leger.

The plan sounded quixotic, but there were several reasons it could work. Hon Yost was considered "simple-minded," but he was clever enough to understand what Arnold wanted. The Indians knew him and were familiar with spells in which he "spoke in tongues"—a kind of gibberish that convinced them that he could communicate with the Great Spirit and therefore could not lie.

Hon Yost became enthusiastic about the scheme. He practiced saying in the Iroquois language that the greatly feared General Arnold was coming at the head of a huge army. He even shot holes in his coat to make it appear that he had barely escaped Arnold's guards. He also took several Oneidas with him to support his story. In addition, as extra insurance, Arnold kept Hon Yost's brother as a hostage in case of a betrayal.

Arnold's ruse was wildly successful. The Indians quickly packed up. They had been disappointed in St. Leger and in the heavy losses they had suffered in the ambush at Oriskany. When St. Leger tried to persuade them not to leave, "they grew furious," he wrote, "seized upon the officers' liquor and clothes, and became more formidable than the enemy. . . ." 4. Abandoned by the Indians, who made up half his army, St. Leger had no choice but to raise the siege and head back to Lake Oswego and the boats that would take him back to Canada.

Arnold left two militia regiments to support the fort and headed back to the Hudson. Once again, Arnold had displayed his extraordinary talents. By saving Fort Stanwix, his actions enabled the Americans to avoid fighting on two fronts.

The Murder of Jane McCrea

During July and August, Burgoyne's Indian allies caused him increasing grief and trouble by launching a campaign of murder, scalping, and plunder. The climax came when two warriors came into camp waving a fresh scalp of long blond hair. The scalp was quickly recognized as that of Jane McCrea, the fiancé of a Loyalist officer, Lieutenant David Jones.

The incident turned into one of the most famous murders in early American history. Over the years, the case became clouded in romance, legend, and myth, and also interpreted in countless stories and paintings. The most popular story—and probably the most factual—was that Lieutenant Jones had paid two warriors to bring her safely from her home to the British camp. A British officer wrote that

> . . . They at first treated her with every mark of civility . . . and were conducting her into camp, when within a mile of it, a dispute arose between the two [over] whose prisoner she was; and words growing very high, one of them . . . fearful of losing the reward . . . most inhumanely struck his tomahawk into her skull and she instantly expired. 5.

Although Burgoyne had tried to hold the Indians in check, the murder fed a rumor that Burgoyne was paying a bounty for rebel scalps. Stories of the murder spread like wildfire throughout New York and New England. Hundreds of men grabbed their muskets and headed for the Patriot camp.

The Eve of Battle

On his way back from Fort Stanwix (renamed Fort Schuyler), Arnold received the jolting news that his friend Schuyler was being replaced by General

Horatio Gates, now a favorite of Congress. Schuyler was humiliated and so disappointed he could not manage to talk to anyone for several days. He wrote of "the Indignity of being relieved of the command of the army at a time when an Engagement must soon take place." 6.

Benedict Arnold was also furious with Congress when he learned that his request to have his seniority restored was turned down. He was also displeased that Gates was now his commanding officer. In their first meeting, Gates offered no word of thanks for his role in defeating St. Leger. Later, in his diary, Arnold wrote: "Gates only grunted when I returned victorious. Congress decreed to Herkimer a monument; to Ganesvoort a vote of thanks and a command; to Willet [second in command at Stanwix] public praise and an elegant sword; to me nothing." 7.

Although both Arnold and Schuyler were deeply disappointed, the mood in the American camp had changed completely from the previous doubts and fears. The victories at Bennington and then Fort Stanwix had caused dramatic changes in both armies. Burgoyne had suffered the loss of St. Leger's army as well as heavy casualties at Bennington. He was now cut off from Canada, and in desperate need of supplies. American General John Glover wrote in a letter:

> I think matters look fair on our side and I have not the least doubt of beating or compelling Mr. Burgoyne to turn back at least to Ticonderoga, if not to Canada. His situation is dangerous, which he must see and know if he is not blind, and if he is not strong enough to move down to fight us, he cannot remain where he is without giving us a great advantage. 8.

Even the arrival of Gates added to the growing Patriot confidence, although he had no battle experience and had done little to earn his promotion. However, he was popular in Congress and with the soldiers from New England, men who had not cared much for Schuyler and his aristocratic manner. Finally, the arrival of Morgan and his 330 riflemen was cheered. In addition to their sharp-shooting skills, the Patriots believed the woodsmen would keep the Indians under control.

Everyone knew that a battle was coming, and many expected it to be huge—a do-or-die struggle for both sides. Colonel Alexander Scammell wrote to his brother that Burgoyne's army "is driven to desperation and a most bloody Battle must ensue." 9.

The two-part battle of Saratoga turned out to be the turning point of the American Revolution and is considered one of the most important battles in history. Not surprisingly, Benedict Arnold played a vital part in the conflict.

The First Battle of Freeman's Farm

The Hudson Valley in the region of Saratoga was a picturesque area of steep, forested bluffs rising 300 feet above the river. The bluffs were separated by ravines with narrow streams winding down to the river.

On one of the bluffs, called Bemis Heights, the Patriots found an ideal place for defense. An engineer named Thaddeus Kosciuozko, a volunteer from Poland who had joined the Patriot cause, planned a strong defensive network of three-sided breastworks, nearly a mile long, bristling with cannons. This solid fortification was completed by mid-September. The strong defense of Lake Champlain had given the Patriots nearly twelve months to establish the outstanding defense. General Gates was pleased with the defense. He did not believe in going out to meet the enemy and felt comfortable in staying in the fortress-like defenses and waiting for the British to come to him.

At about the time the American defenses were being completed, Burgoyne had a bridge of boats built across the river and his army moved to the west bank of the Hudson. The river below the crossing had rough rapids, making it impossible for supplies to reach Burgoyne by boat. It was now necessary for Burgoyne to rely on much slower wagons.

When Gates's scouts spotted Burgoyne's army crossing the Hudson, the general ordered his commanders to prepare for battle. He had divided his army into two wings. Gates commanded the right wing and he wisely placed Arnold in command on the left. He did not trust Arnold's tendency to rush into battle, so this arrangement allowed him to direct Arnold's actions. New militia troops were coming in every day, encouraged by the victories at Bennington and Fort Stanwix, and in response to the murder of Jane McCrea. By mid-September, the Americans numbered nearly 10,000, while Burgoyne was now limited to less than 7,000.

The morning of September 19 dawned cold and damp, a sharp change from days of blistering heat. A thick fog blanketed the ravines until mid-morning. When Gates informed his officers that they would fight from behind the breastworks, General Arnold was horrified. He knew that, from the river, Burgoyne's artillery could smash holes in the Americans' right wing and follow with a bayonet attack. He argued that allowing the British to gain the initiative would be suicide.

The land in front of the American line was called Freeman's Farm. The farm included a large cleared field, with dense woods beyond. Arnold wanted to move into the woods and, from there, attack Burgoyne's right, forcing them into that clearing. Gates resisted. Other officers supported Arnold's aggressive plan and Gates finally gave in, at least partly. He would allow Arnold to send Morgan's riflemen, backed by Dearborn's light infantry, to move into the woods flanking Freeman's Farm.

Burgoyne ordered his army forward in three columns. Riedesel, commanding most of the Germans, advanced on the left flank along the river. General Simon Fraser was on the right, and Burgoyne commanded the center. Fraser's men found the rugged terrain difficult and by the time they were far enough west to attack, they were more than two miles from the center column. Finally, around two o'clock, all three columns were in position, and cannons were fired to signal the assault on the American lines.

Burgoyne's plan was to catch the Americans by surprise, and it probably would have worked, with Fraser's troops charging down on the American defenses. But Arnold's idea of moving out to meet the enemy meant that it was the British who were surprised. Morgan's riflemen, some climbing high in trees, hit the advancing British hard, picking off the officers with deadly accuracy. As Fraser's men reeled back into the clearing, Morgan's and Dearborn's men charged after them, but were suddenly stopped cold by the center of Burgoyne's line.

The fighting then became general, with the two sides blasting at each other for four hours. The clearing was frequently filled with smoke, as well as the boom of cannons and the rattle of musket fire. By late afternoon, the clearing was littered with the dead and wounded of both sides. No one dared go to the aid of the wounded because the enemy was so close.

Men on both sides were astounded by the sheer magnitude of noise and violence. British Lieutenant William Digby wrote that he had never imagined such an "explosion of fire . . ."

> . . . the heavy artillery, joining in concert like great peals of thunder, assisted by the echoes of the woods, almost deafened us with the noise. . . . The crash of cannon and musketry never ceased till darkness parted us, when they retired to their camp, leaving us masters of the field; but it was a dear bought victory if I can give it that name, as we lost many brave men. 10.

Burgoyne could—and did—claim victory, simply because his troops were still on part of the battlefield, while the Americans went back to their camp. Although the British had lost 600 men (160 dead, 364 wounded, and 42 missing), twice the total of American losses, Burgoyne confidently wrote to his commander of the garrison at Ticonderoga: "We have had a smart and very honorable action, and are now encamped in front of the field, which must demonstrate our victory beyond the power of even an American newspaper to explain away." 11.

There was some dispute over Benedict Arnold's role in the battle. His insistence on carrying the fighting to the British, rather than waiting behind the Bemis Heights defensive works, was certainly crucial in enabling the Americans to fight Burgoyne's army to a standstill. For example, the redcoats' 62nd regiment, which took the brunt of the first attack by Morgan's and Dearborn's regiments, suffered a casualty rate of more than 80 percent.

Did General Arnold lead his men into the battle, or did he remain at headquarters with Gates? The uncertainty about his precise role was created by Colonel James Wilkinson, Gates's adjutant, who insisted, "General Arnold was not out of camp during the whole action." 12.

James Wilkinson was an ambitious young man. In fact, he was so ambitious that he would let nothing stand in the way of his own advancement. He became notorious for changing his loyalties. Wilkinson was with Arnold on his march to Quebec. He became Arnold's aide and stood by him in several difficult situations. Sensing that Arnold was on his way out, he suddenly changed sides and became General Gates's aide, helping to make Gates the "Hero of Saratoga." A few years later, he joined with Aaron Burr in a scheme to create an empire in what is now the American Southwest, but then turned on Burr, who was tried for treason.

A number of men contradicted Wilkinson and provided testimony of Arnold's pivotal role in the action. General Enoch Poor, for example, wrote that "Arnold rushed into the thickest of the fight with his usual recklessness, and at times acted like a madman." 13. Captain Ebenezer Wakefield later wrote that Arnold "inspired by the fury of a demon, led a charge by riding in front of the line, his eyes flashing, pointing with his sword . . . with a voice that rang as clear as a trumpet, called upon the men to follow him, . . . and . . . he hurled them like a tornado on the British line." According to Wakefield, "nothing could exceed the bravery of Arnold on this day. . . . There seemed to shoot out from him a magnetic flame that electrified his men and made heroes of all within his influence. He seemed the very genius of war." 14. Henry Brockholst Livingstone, Arnold's aide, said, "Arnold alone is due the honor of our late victory. [He had become] the life and soul of the troops [enjoying] the confidence and affection of his officers and soldiers. They would, to a person, follow him to conquest or death." 15.

Even General Burgoyne, in explaining the conflict to Parliament, wrote that he had expected "Gates would receive the attack in his [defensive] lines." But, "when Arnold chose to give rather than receive the attack," he disrupted Burgoyne's entire battle plan. 16. However, the failure of Gates to emerge from his defenses enabled Burgoyne's forces to stay on the Freeman's Farm land when darkness ended the fighting. The most serious blunder Gates made was refusing Arnold when he pleaded for reinforcements at a point when Benedict was certain that one final push would rout the British right and center. Instead he ordered Arnold back to headquarters then sent out Learned's brigade with no senior officer to lead them. They lost their way and did not help in the final push.

The fighting spirit and ability of the Americans surprised the British. As one officer wrote: "The courage and obstinacy with which the Americans fought were the astonishment of everyone. [They had shown] they were not the contemptible enemy we had . . . imagined them, incapable of standing a regular engagement." 17.

Thomas Anburey, a British volunteer, wrote that "[Although] the glory of the day remained on our side, I am fearful the real advantages resulting from this hard-fought battle will rest on that of the Americans, our army being so much weakened by this engagement as not to be of sufficient strength to venture forth and improve the victory, which may, in the end, put a stop to our intended expedition; the only apparent benefit gained is that we keep possession of the ground where the engagement began." 18.

Baroness von Riedesel added her thoughts on why the Americans fought so well: "Every man [in the region] is a born soldier and a good marksman. . . .The thought of fighting for their country and for freedom made them braver than ever." 19.`

Both sides knew that the fighting at Freeman's Farm had not ended the battle. Burgoyne knew his best hope, probably the only hope, was to push through to Albany and hope that Clinton would move north to meet him, squeezing Gates's army between them. Until the battle could be resumed, Burgoyne decided to stay where he was, and ordered his field commanders to build a series of redoubts (barricades) and entrenchments a little to the north of Bemis Heights. He also wrote to Clinton urging him to speed his march north.

Heroism Denied

As the Freeman's Farm battle drew to a close, Gates sent a messenger to order Arnold back to headquarters. The timing could not have been worse. Arnold had just taken control of several brigades—groups who had become separated from their regiments, and was about to launch a final attack when the order came. By the time he was back in camp, Arnold was furious. And that was just the beginning.

Gates had no intention of letting Benedict Arnold receive credit for the outstanding Patriot success in the Freeman's Farm battle. He was keenly aware of the praise Arnold was receiving from the officers and men of the army and militia. Captain Ebenezer Wakefield, for example, wrote that "Arnold was not only the hero of the field . . . but he had won the admiration of the whole army." 20. To make sure that such praise did not reach beyond the camp, Gates wrote his official report of the battle to Congress without mentioning Benedict Arnold.

By this time, Arnold had had enough. He asked to be discharged from Gates's command. Gates issued a pass for Arnold to go to Washington's headquarters. A number of officers urged him not to leave, so he remained in camp, a general with no troops, ignored at strategy meetings, but not wanting to leave on the eve of what promised to be the decisive battle.

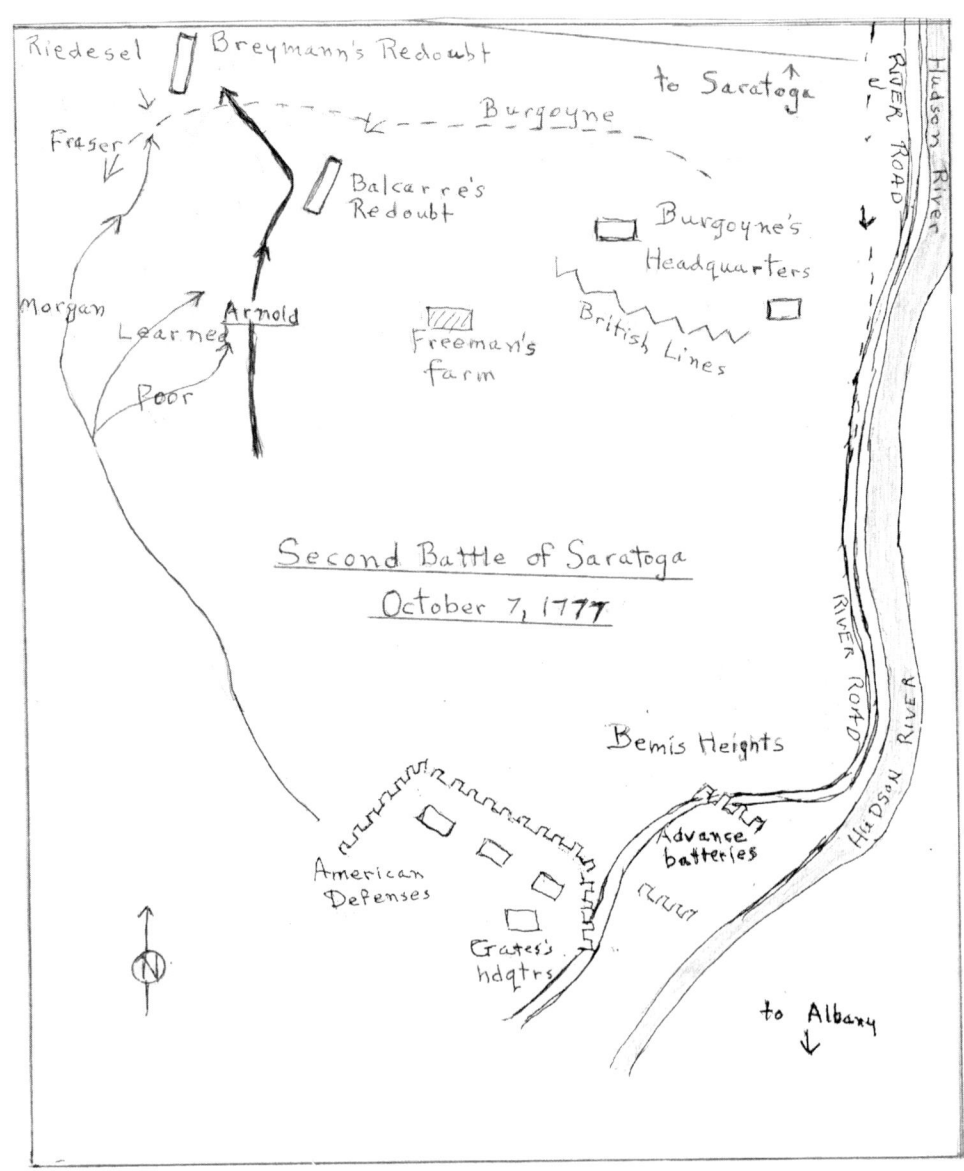

Second Battle of Saratoga
October 7, 1777

Riedesel · Breymann's Redoubt · to Saratoga

Burgoyne

Fraser

Balcarre's Redoubt

Burgoyne's Headquarters

Morgan · Learned · Arnold · Poor

Freeman's farm

British Lines

Bemis Heights

American Defenses

Advance batteries

Gates's hdqtrs

RIVER ROAD · Hudson River · RIVER ROAD · Hudson River

to Albany

N

Chapter Nine

The Turning Point, Part II

As thick fog settled over the Saratoga battlefield on the morning of September 20, most of the troops on both sides expected the fighting to resume in a day or two. Instead, an uneasy lull settled over the battle region—a lull that lasted nearly three weeks.

This gap between the two parts of the Battle of Saratoga was hardly a time of rest or inactivity. There were skirmishes every day and night. These were more wearing on the British, since they had no reserves, while new recruits came into the American camp in ever-increasing numbers. In fact, over the course of the eighteen-day lull, Burgoyne's army was becoming steadily weaker, with barely 6,000 men available, while Gates's growing force reached almost 13,000 by the end of September.

The continuing strain on the British was described by Lieutenant Thomas Anburey in his journal:

> . . . The armies are so near that not a night passes but there is firing and continual attacks on the advanced picquets. . . . We are now become so habituated to fire that the soldiers seem to be indifferent to it, and eat and sleep when it is very near them. The officers rest in their cloaths, and the field officers are up frequently in the night.

Anbury also noted a special cause of stress:

> We have, within these few evenings—exclusive of other alarms --been under arms most of the night, as there has been a great noise, like the howling of dogs. . . . The [fourth] night the noise was much greater. [Soldiers were sent to investigate; they discovered the noise] to have arisen from large droves of

wolves that came after the [partially buried] dead bodies. They were similar to a pack of hounds; for one, setting up a cry, they all joined; and when they approached a corpse their noise was hideous till they had scratched it up. 1.

Burgoyne's Delays and Attrition

Immediately after the battle at Freeman's Farm, General Burgoyne had seemed as confident as ever. He felt certain that General Henry Clinton, now in command in New York City, would approach with the second major part of the invasion plan. The two British armies would then squeeze Gates's army between them, ensuring Burgoyne's greatest triumph.

However, day after day passed with no word from Clinton. Burgoyne sent messages, but never knew that the messengers never got through. They had been caught by Patriots, forced to cough up the bullet-size message capsules, and were then executed as spies.

Finally, late in September, he heard from Clinton. Sir Henry wrote that he would make a push to the north about September 25, "if you think 2,000 men can assist you …" 2. Burgoyne was delighted. For some reason he seemed to think the additional 2,000 men, especially if coming from the south, would save the campaign. He decided to stay where he was, strengthen his defenses, and wait for Clinton. His weak right flank, which Arnold and Morgan had attacked on September 19, was now strengthened by the building of two fortifications, called *redoubts*. The largest, the Balcarres Redoubt, was a mound of logs and earth, twelve to fourteen feet high, which stretched for 500 yards. The smaller Breymann Redoubt ran for half that length, with two crude cabins filling the space in between.

Days continued to pass with no more word from Clinton. By October 1st, the mild days gave way to freezing nights. The trees on the hillsides of the Berkshires and Taconics were turning brilliant shades of red, orange, yellow, and green—a grim kind of beauty for the invaders because it meant the onset of a very uncertain winter. Mornings brought frost and touches of snow to the hills, while thick fog filled the river valleys.

In the British and German camps, hungry soldiers now shivered through the nights with empty stomachs. Even with strict rationing, food staples—mostly salt pork and flour—were running dangerously low. The soldiers, along with wives and children, relied on foraging wheat and corn from fields the owners dared not approach because of the fighting. The need for 200 men or more to guard each foraging party added to the soldiers' weariness.

In addition to illness and deaths, the British-Hessian ranks were diminished by desertions and captures. Burgoyne had also lost most of his Indian warriors, originally numbering about 1,000. He had trusted that the rugged, wooded landscape would be ideal for Iroquois-style warfare. Instead, he lamented, "not a man of them was to be brought within the sound of a rifle shot." 3. Barely 100 remained by late September.

Finally, on October 4, Burgoyne knew he dared wait no longer for Clinton. Apparently, as *Saratoga* historian Richard M. Ketchum has pointed out, Burgoyne was not aware that Clinton planned only to make a limited thrust north, because he was unwilling to endanger the major base at New York City. Also, Sir William Howe, the British supreme commander, who was now pressuring Washington near Philadelphia, would not have approved a major campaign. (On October 7, Clinton did make his move: after capturing two Patriot Hudson River forts, he withdrew to New York.)

On the night of October 4th, Burgoyne called his general for a war council. He later wrote of the meeting:

> No intelligence having been received of the expected coop-
> eration . . . it was judged advisable to make a movement to
> the enemy's left, not only to discover whether there were any
> possible means of forcing a passage, should it be necessary to
> advance, or of dislodging him for the convenience of a retreat,
> but also to cover a forage [mission] of the army, which was in
> the greatest distress on account of the scarcity. 4.

Burgoyne's generals felt that his plan of sending all but 800 men on the attack was too risky, so he scaled it down to a "reconnaissance in force" of about

2,200. Riedesel, commander of the hired Germans, felt he had to go along with the plan, although he argued it would have been wiser to recross the Hudson, establish themselves closer to Ticonderoga, and there wait for Clinton. Burgoyne, of course, was not at all ready to retreat.

The attack was planned for the morning of October 6th or 7th.

Showdown at Freeman's Farm

Throughout the long delay between battles, Benedict Arnold remained in the Patriot camp, miserable, humiliated, and alone. His feud with Horatio Gates grew steadily worse, with frequent shouting matches. The arguments were so fierce that one of Arnold's aides worried in a letter to Schuyler, "General Arnold is so much offended at the treatment Gates has given him that I have not the least doubt the latter will be called on [for a duel]." Schuyler answered: "Perhaps [Gates] is so very sure of success that he does not wish Arnold to come in for a share of it." 5.

On the morning of October 7th, scouts reported the beginning of the British advance. Burgoyne again sent General Fraser's force to try to circle the American left, sending even more men than in September, hoping to place artillery to hit the American fortification from one side, while Riedesel's artillery opened up from the Hudson.

For three hours, General Gates did almost nothing, until he finally sent Morgan and Dearborn "to begin the game." The firing did not begin until the afternoon, when a British force opened fire on a group of the Americans, then launched a bayonet attack. The Americans held their ground and fired volleys that forced the redcoats to retreat.

The sound of the gunfire was almost too much for Arnold. He paced back and forth, futilely trying to see the action through binoculars. The gunfire sounds increased as Morgan's riflemen circled the enemy right and forced them to retreat into the woods, while Dearborn's men caught them in a withering crossfire. The advance was finally stopped when Hessian colonel, the Earl of Balcarres, rallied his men behind their redoubt.

Gates had briefly allowed Arnold, accompanied by General Lincoln, to survey the battlefield. When they returned, Arnold insisted that Gates commit a strong force on the left to support Morgan and Dearborn. Gates snapped, "General Arnold, I have nothing for you to do. You have no business here." 6.

Minutes after that rebuke, Arnold leaped on a borrowed horse and galloped to the battlefield. At this point, Benedict Arnold took over the battle. Military historian W. J. Wood wrote of Arnold's critical role: "Gates was not there, nor did he ever show himself outside his headquarters. Benedict Arnold *was* there, and that fact turned the next phase of Bemis Heights into a decisive battle." 7.

Arnold came up to Learned's brigade, being held in reserve along with several regiments of Connecticut militia. When told where the militia were from, he shouted: "My old Norwich and New London friends! God bless you!" The men cheered as he spurred his horse forward. "Now come on, boys, if the day is long enough, we'll have them in hell before night." 8.

Learned willingly let Arnold take command, and he led a charge against the Balcarres Redoubt. Under heavy fire, the Americans had almost pushed their way through the tangled logs and sharpened sticks, but the British and Hessian resistance was so fierce that Arnold ordered a withdrawal.

He made a quick survey of the battlefield and realized he had attacked the strongest of the redoubts. He wheeled his horse to the left and made a wild gallop between the two armies, with bullets flying in both directions. A Connecticut militiaman wrote: "He behaved, as I then thought, more like a madman than a cool and discreet officer." 9. But British historian Sir John Fortescue saw it differently: "With true military instinct," he wrote, "Arnold seized the opportunity to order a general attack upon the British entrenchments." 10. Meantime, Gates, learning that Arnold had left the camp, sent Major John Armstrong to bring him back, but Armstrong wisely stayed out of the way.

There was no stopping Benedict Arnold now. Sweeping up parts of different regiments, the attack gained strength, with Arnold out in front on horseback, waving his sword, and shouting encouragement to the men. The British and Germans were soon in a chaotic, every-man-for-himself retreat. Either Arnold or Morgan noticed that British General Simon Fraser, mounted on a big gray horse was rallying large numbers to make a stand, and one of them ordered a marksman to bring him down from a great distance, which he did with his third shot. Hit in the stomach, Fraser slumped over his saddle as two aides led him away. (He died the next day.) Burgoyne, seeing his friend and most important general hit, seemed to lose heart; he may also have realized that he was not going to win this critical struggle, and he ordered his men to withdraw into their battlements.

General Arnold could have been satisfied with driving the enemy from the field, but as long as the two redoubts remained and Burgoyne could come back again, he had no intention of stopping. In a hastily created plan with Morgan, Arnold would circle around the rear of Breymann's Redoubt, while Morgan and Dearborn attacked from the front. The double assault took the defenders by surprise. Colonel Breymann tried to rally his men, shouting and threatening to kill anyone who fled, but he was shot, possibly by one of his own men, and the defense began to crumble.

As Arnold led one charge through gunfire and clouds of smoke into the redoubt, Morgan's men attacked from the front. The Hessians, plus some British and Canadians, were now in full, frantic flight. A few of the Hessians stopped to fire one last volley. One of the musket balls slammed into Arnold's leg— the same leg that had been seriously wounded in Quebec. Several bullets hit his horse, and the animal crashed to the ground, landing heavily on Arnold's stricken leg, causing several compound fractures.

Arnold continued to shout encouragement to "my brave boys," as Morgan's men poured into the redoubt, forcing the few remaining British and Hessians to surrender. Morgan's and Dearborn's men rushed to pull Arnold from under his horse. One of the men was about to bayonet the Hessian youth whose shot had felled Arnold. The stricken general shouted not to kill him; he was only doing his duty.

Patriot soldiers made a makeshift litter out of blankets and carried Arnold to Gates's headquarters. With no doctor on the battlefield, Benedict must have been in unbelievable pain, but he remained conscious long enough to accept the praise and congratulations of many of the officers and men. Horatio Gates said nothing to him, and apparently never wrote to ask about his recovery. Arnold was placed on a cart for a bouncing, 30-mile ride to the Continental Army Hospital in Albany. Although his survival was uncertain, he adamantly refused to let doctors amputate the bloody leg with half a dozen bones jutting through the skin.

Darkness was settling over the battlefield as Arnold was carted off. Over the next twenty-four hours, the impact of his leadership on the battle was suggested by the losses on both sides. The British lost 184 killed, 264 wounded, and 183 captured—a total of 631, including 31 officers. And the Germans had 94 killed, 67 wounded, and 102 taken prisoner. Burgoyne's total losses, then, were 894, nearly half of his attacking force. The American losses were remarkably light: an estimated 30 killed and 100 wounded.

Retreat and Surrender

The next morning, Burgoyne's battered army remained behind strong defensive works, facing an ever-growing army of militia as well as the Continentals who had borne the brunt of the fighting. By mid-October, General Gates had more than 16,000 troops at his command. Burgoyne's retreat and the final decision to surrender involved delays and indecision. He seemed to cling to the hope that Clinton might still come to his rescue.

Finally, on the night of the 8th, the army began its slow, painful retreat north. Through the night and the next day, they had advanced only eight miles. A wind-driven rain made the march even more miserable. Gates, nearly as slow to move as Burgoyne, managed to send several militia units to race up the east side of the Hudson to take positions north of the British, cutting off their retreat beyond the village of Saratoga. Morgan's riflemen and other units advanced to the west of the British, completing the net that encircled Burgoyne.

After several days more, the British reached Saratoga, where they torched General Schuyler's estate, and tried to set up a defensive perimeter. Baron von Riedesel describes their condition:

> . . . the ground was covered with dead horses that had either
> been killed by the enemy's bullets or by exhaustion, as there

had been no forage for several days. . . . Even for the wounded, no spot could be found which could afford them a safe shelter—not even . . . long [enough] for a surgeon to bind up their ghastly wounds. The whole camp was now a scene of constant fighting. . . . The sick and wounded would drag themselves along into a quiet corner of the woods and lie down to die on the damp ground. . . . 11.

Even in the midst of the suffering and bloodshed, there were incidents of remarkable kindness extended to an enemy. The case of British Major John Dyke Acland and Lady Acland provides a good example. The major, wounded in both legs, was captured and taken to the army hospital in Albany. His distraught young wife traveled with Baroness von Riedesel on the retreat, until the baroness finally persuaded her to seek a pass to American lines in the hope of joining her husband. Burgoyne wrote the pass and Lady Acland, accompanied by a minister and two others, that night boarded an open boat for a rain-drenched journey down the Hudson to American lines.

With a drum beating a parley, the boat was allowed to land its passengers. Major Dearborn, who was in command of the American line, invited the very wet and quite pregnant ladyship to his house for a cup of tea and a night's rest before a blazing fire. In the morning, General Gates had her escorted to her husband in Albany. Gates, in a letter to his wife, called her ladyship "the most amiable, delicate piece of Quality you ever beheld." 12. (After the major's eleven-week recovery, the couple traveled to British headquarters in New York City.)

On October 13, Burgoyne held a "solemn council of war," at which his generals agreed that surrender was now their only option. After three days of negotiations, surrender ceremonies were held on October 17th at Saratoga between Burgoyne, resplendent in his carefully-preserved scarlet uniform and the bespectacled Gates in a plain blue coat, managing to look much like his nickname of "Granny Gates."

The immediate results of Saratoga were staggering. General John Burgoyne's once glittering invasion force of 10,000 trained troops had been knocked out of the war. The ragged remnants of that army, now stacking their weapons at Saratoga, included nine generals, nearly 400 other officers, and more than 5,000 troops of lesser rank.

The long-term results made the battle even more significant as *the* turning point of the American Revolution. The victory finally persuaded France to enter the war as a full-fledged ally of the United States. This meant a vital infusion of weapons, ammunition, and other war material, as well as troops and the powerful French navy. In addition, England now faced the likelihood of a land war in Europe against France and its allies.

The timing of the victory was also crucial. The main Continental Army, led by Washington, had just lost two major battles to the British under Howe at Germantown and Brandywine Creek in Pennsylvania, forcing Congress to flee to the town of York. The two defeats had caused a serious decline in Patriot morale. Within Congress and the army, an underground movement—later known as the Conway cabal—developed with the apparent aim of removing Washington and replacing him with General Gates. Saratoga changed everything.

Still another positive outcome of the battle was that thousands of militiamen learned the value of discipline. They had beaten a professional European army—an enemy that assumed Americans would run away when confronted by trained British redcoats. Instead the militia volunteers learned to listen to their officers and to observe the Continentals, with the result that they stood fast, even in the face of a bayonet charge.

As the British and Germans marched between rows of Americans to stack their weapons, they were relieved and gratified to find that "not a single man gave any evidence or the slightest impression of feeling hatred, mockery, or malicious pleasure or pride for our miserable fate; [instead] it seemed rather as though they desired to do us honor." Lord Francis Napier added: "They behaved with the greatest decency and propriety, not even a smile appearing in any of their countenances. . . ." 13.

Benedict Arnold, of course, was not present for the British retreat or the surrender ceremonies. He received frequent reports from visitors and asked countless questions. What troubled him most, in addition to his shattered leg and uncertain future, was that Gates was there to accept Burgoyne's sword and receive credit for the victory. Several years later Arnold wrote in his diary:

> ... I effaced myself and saved America. For Saratoga will be placed by future historians among the fifteen decisive battles of the world. It was the Blenheim of the Revolution; and the future historian shall say, 'One General won it; and that was not the General in command.' 14.

At the time of the surrender, Arnold was not yet aware of how much harm Horatio Gates could do him, aided by his equally ambitious assistant, James Wilkinson.

The Rise and Fall of Horatio Gates

Following the surrender at Saratoga, members of Congress could not find enough ways to pile praise and honors on General Gates. They voted to have a special gold medal struck to honor his leadership, the first such medal since the gold piece commemorating General Washington for forcing the British to evacuate Boston in 1776.

No one in Congress seemed troubled by Gates's failure to make more than the briefest mention of Benedict Arnold, or that he sent no report to Washington, the commander-in-chief. Instead, Gates heaped praise on Wilkinson, calling him a "military genius." He urged Congress to reward his aide. This was done and Wilkinson emerged as a brevet brigadier; his elevation to general status shocked and dismayed the army's generals. Some wondered if serving in the Continental Army was worth the personal sacrifices, when men like Wilkinson could be promoted without any sacrifices.

Wilkinson did his best to promote his own cause. He pigeon-holed members of Congress, especially those who supported Gates. In letters to friends, he insisted that "Benedict Arnold neither rendered service nor deserved credit" for Saratoga. 15.

The Congressional approval of General Gates became less certain when terms of the surrender were studied. Gates had granted Burgoyne almost everything he asked for. He even agreed to call the treaty a "convention" rather than a "capitulation." The British and Germans were to be marched to Boston, where they would board transport ships to England, where they agreed not to return to the war.

A majority in Congress, as well as Washington, agreed that the terms were far too lenient. Early in 1778, Congress used technicalities to change those conditions. While Burgoyne and his aides were allowed to return to England, the rest of the defeated army was marched to the interior of Virginia for the remainder of the war. Gates was not criticized for his negotiations. As Henry Laurens said in announcing the gold medal: "Your name, Sir, will be written in the breasts of the grateful Americans of the present age and sent down to posterity in characters which will remain indelible when the gold [of the medal] shall have changed in appearance." 16.

In spite of his few mistakes and his lack of real involvement in the battle, Horatio Gates was to go down in history as "The Hero of Saratoga."

General Gates enjoyed his status as hero until the summer of 1780. With the American forces in the South in some disarray, Congress decided to send Gates to create stability. Washington was not consulted, probably because he would not have approved.

Against the advice of his officers, Gates launched his half-trained militia against a British force at Camden, South Carolina in the pre-dawn hours of August 16, 1780. The Battle of Camden quickly became a bloody defeat for the Americans. Gates fled the battlefield and by nightfall was in North Carolina, more than sixty miles north of Camden.

An embarrassed Congress immediately recalled Gates, and this time asked Washington to name a successor. The commander-in-chief named General Nathanael Greene to command the Southern Department; Greene proceeded to conduct a brilliant duel with the British under Cornwallis that led to the final battle at Yorktown. Although Gates remained the second-ranking general, the luster was off his status as hero. Disenchanted Congressmen ignored Gates's request for a court of inquiry to clear his name.

Gates's critics had a grand time with the Camden fiasco, especially when Gates rode another 120 miles north in just two days. Alexander Hamilton wrote: "Was there ever such an instance of a general running away . . . from his whole army? And was there ever so precipitous a flight? . . . It does admirable credit to the activity of a man at his time of life." 17. And a Loyalist newspaper in New York ran a long advertisement by "Horatio Gates" seeking information about a lost or missing army.

The Gates embarrassment came too late to help Benedict Arnold. A month after the Battle of Camden, Arnold's reputation was destroyed by the exposure of his far greater betrayal.

Benedict Arnold's Turning Point?

When Arnold was carried off the battlefield at the conclusion of his heroism at Freeman's Farm, Major Dearborn bent down to him and asked where he had been hit. According to Dearborn, Arnold answered that it was the same leg and wished "the ball had passed his heart." 18.

Had the shot killed him, he might have died as the martyred hero of Saratoga. It would have made it much harder for Gates and Wilkinson to eclipse his role. And he would have gained the fame he craved as one of the great battlefield leaders in America's history.

Instead, Benedict faced a bleak future in the army's hospital in Albany. Day after day he lay in agonizing pain, while doctors insisted that the leg had to come off to avoid gangrene. He repeatedly resisted their "damned nonsense," even though pieces of bone were jutting through his mangled flesh. In an effort to straighten the leg and stabilize it, the doctors constructed a "fracture box"— a sort of wooden cast that forced Arnold to lie on his back, virtually motionless, a maddening confinement, especially for a man of action.

Arnold's condition remained unchanged through October, November, and December. Finally, in January, 1778, he felt well enough to sit up, but the movement burst open the wound, and he fell back on the bed as searing pain shot through his leg and body. Several more weeks passed before he succeeded in sitting up. From that point through the spring the leg healed quickly, although he would remain disabled for life. The long confinement had caused the muscles to atrophy, and the injured leg emerged two inches shorter.

During these weeks of agony, Arnold had little to do but to think, and to reflect on how Gates and Wilkinson had stolen from him the fruits of victory. Throughout his military career, he had hurled himself into one military crisis after another. He had been the ideal field commander—absolutely fearless and determined, with a unique ability to see the pitfalls and possibilities in every situation; he was a constant source of inspiration to his men, while also showing a deep concern for their well-being. Henry Brockholst Livingstone, who served as Arnold's aide during the Saratoga campaign, wrote that "Arnold alone is due the honor of our late victory; [he had become] the life and soul of his troops, [enjoying] the confidence and affection of his officers and soldiers. They would, to a person, follow him to conquest or death." 19.

Arnold had been certain that these heroic efforts would help to restore his family name, honor, and fortune. Instead, he spent the discouraging months of convalescence wondering how everything could have gone so wrong.

The authors of two recent studies offered the following assessments of Benedict Arnold at this stage:

> Richard M. Ketchum, *Saratoga, Turning Point of the American Revolution* (1997): "Benedict Arnold was now thirty-six years old, a major general, and the kind of field commander generals dream about—fearless and daring, a natural leader, with stamina and determination that allowed nothing to stand in his way. . . .
>
> On the strength of his record there was no question about Arnold's remarkable ability as a battlefield leader, but behind the record and beneath the surface was a man driven by terrible self-doubts and a hunger for fame, social acceptance, money, and rank that had thus far, been denied him. He was a man whose pride was easily wounded, one who could accept neither opposition to his ideas nor criticism while at the same time being totally insensitive to the feelings of others." 20.
>
> James Kirby Martin, *Benedict Arnold* (1997): "As the New

Year dawned, deep and bitter resentment was infusing Arnold's troubled soul. As he grappled with the prospect of life as a virtual cripple, he kept asking himself what it had all been for, why the personal sacrifice when his only reward was defamed personal honor. With time passing so slowly, Arnold kept searching for reasonable answers to his question, but he could not find them." 21.

But was there more? Was the disappointment and resentment enough to explain his decision to betray the cause he had fought and bled for? He wanted fame for his military leadership; he also wanted to restore his family name and his fortune. Could turning traitor bring him closer to any of those goals?

Early 1778 may be too soon to draw conclusions about why Arnold became America's most notorious traitor. For more conclusive evidence we need to explore further the twisted, tortured path of the next three years.

The co-conspirators—John Andre., Peggy Shippen Arnold, and Benedict Arnold

Arnold's men struggling against the flooded Dead River.

American and British ships exchange fire at Valcour Island, Oct. 11, 1776.

Arnold receiving a life-threatening wound at the second Battle of Saratoga.

CHAPTER TEN

Twists And Turns

THE FIRST SIX MONTHS OF 1778 WERE times of great uncertainty for Arnold, with many unexpected twists and turns. The year began with his slow-and-only-partial recovery from his wound. In mid-January, about the time of his abortive attempt to sit up, he received a letter from Washington.

Mis-Communication With Washington

The commander apologized for not contacting him sooner (but did not take the time to explain how he had been struggling against the internal enemies who were trying to replace him with Horatio Gates). Washington asked "whether you are upon your legs again, and if you are not, may I flatter myself that you will be soon? . . . No one wishes more sincerely for this event than I do." He ended the letter by stating "the earnest wish to have your services [in] the ensuing campaign; [Washington promised] . . . a command which I trust will be agreeable to yourself and of great advantage to the public." 1.

Arnold was slow to respond to his commander's warm words. Washington had no way of knowing that his fighting general was battling pain and depression from the re-opening of his wound. He was also furious about the ways he had been humiliated by General Gates and by Congress, and also by the outlandish praise Congress had heaped on Gates.

Six weeks passed before Arnold finally answered Washington, on March 12, from Middletown, Connecticut, where he had been staying with friends. He also apologized for taking so much time to reply, blaming his wounds for the delay. The wounds, he explained, had been "closed" but had recently "broke out again, occasioned by some loose splinters of bone remaining in the leg, which will not be serviceable until they are extracted. . . . It will take time, perhaps two, and possibly five or six months." 2. He could not say when he would be able to travel to headquarters "and take the command your Excellency has been so good as to reserve for me."

Washington wrote again in early May to describe a gift he wished to give Arnold. The gift had come from France—three sets of epaulets and sword knots. The commander was to keep one set and to use the other two to honor special individuals. He wrote that he wished to present one set to Arnold, "as a testimony of my sincere regard and approbation of your conduct." 3.

General Washington was not a demonstrative person and had difficulty expressing his feelings, especially to men, so this gift of decorative epaulets and sword knots probably represented as much warmth as he could manage. To Arnold, however, with his feelings of betrayal by the cause for which he had given so much, the gift may have seemed a hollow gesture. Arnold barely mentioned it in his memoirs. The gift and the reaction show how little the two men understood each other. Washington clearly had little idea of the bitterness and disappointment that was poisoning Arnold's soul.

Two weeks later, with no advance notice, a carriage pulled up at Washington's headquarters at Valley Forge, and Benedict Arnold painfully stepped out, leaning heavily on a crutch. From Washington's point of view, Arnold probably appeared to be a dedicated Patriot, determined to be ready for the next campaign. Although the commander must have been startled by the severity of Arnold's disability, he could still hope that Benedict would again be his fighting general.

Military Governor of Philadelphia

Convinced that General Arnold was not yet able to take a field command, Washington offered him another post: The British were about to evacuate Philadelphia and General Howe was returning to New York. As soon as the British left in June, 1778, Benedict Arnold would become military governor of the city. Washington's appointment was understandable. Since his favorite general could hardly stand, much less sit a horse or give orders in the field, a few months at a governor's desk seemed like a good solution until he was more fully recovered.

The commander had rarely made a more ill-advised appointment; it thrust

Arnold into a maelstrom of political conflict and intrigue that he was not equipped to handle. Congress was moving back to Philadelphia from York, so old conflicts would inevitably be renewed, and delegates could watch him closely for any mistakes. In addition, a new state government had been formed and its leader, Joseph Reed, was determined to protect the state's independent powers in the face of any encroachments by Congress, or interference by Military Governor Benedict Arnold.

In addition, the situation would reveal some of Benedict's most serious flaws. Knowing that he was famous only as a battlefield leader, he became determined to show that he came from a famous family and was the equal of the very best in Philadelphia society. He also had decided that he would now look after his own interests, since his many sacrifices for the Revolution had gained him little. He seemed to want all that had been denied him—wealth, honors, and respect. In the months ahead, his desires were seen by many as signs of greed, aggressiveness, and arrogance.

In spite of his weaknesses, which his enemies attacked frequently, the better side of his nature sometimes emerged. He could be gracious in society and, more important, he displayed kindness and compassion toward those in need.

Here are some of the highlights of his career as military governor:

As soon as the British evacuated Philadelphia in June, 1778, Military Governor Benedict Arnold quickly established his new lifestyle. He leased one of the finest mansions in the city—the one that the British commander General Howe had occupied. He dressed in splendid new uniforms and purchased the finest furnishings for the house. He employed a housekeeper, a cook, a coachman, and a groom, as well as seven lesser servants. His sister Hannah and his three sons moved to Philadelphia, and the family rode about the city in a handsome carriage, served by a team of four and liveried attendants. Governor Arnold also became known for elegant dinners, to which he invited leading citizens, including many who had remained neutral or cooperated with the British during the occupation.

Arnold used his own money for most of these expenses. When Hannah detailed how high the bills were running, he blamed Congress for much of the financial tangle, in part because he had received no pay for more than three years of military service, nor had he been reimbursed for the many expenses and losses he had encountered. In one of his many criticisms of Congress, he wrote: "It is a matter much to be lamented that our army is permitted to starve in a land of plenty; [those responsible] should be capitally punished." 4.

In the summer of 1778, he found a way to help the orphaned children of Dr. Joseph Warren, one of the first heroes of the Revolution, who had been killed at Bunker Hill. Warren had been instrumental in sending Arnold to Ticonderoga in 1775. He wrote to Miss Mercy Scollay, who had been engaged to be the doctor's second wife and was now caring for his son and daughter. Since Massachusetts had done nothing to assist them, Arnold wrote that he was sending five hundred dollars to help. This was not simply a matter of sending money. He added, "I wish to have Richard clothed handsomely, and sent to the best school in Boston. [For] any expense you are at, please call on me . . . and it will be paid with thanks." 5.

Two months later, he sent Mercy another five hundred dollars and promised to keep after Congress to help. He kept his promise and repeatedly agitated for Congress to step in. The delegates finally did act and provided funds for the families of deceased officers. Mercy Scollay received this pronouncement a few weeks after Arnold's treason was exposed.

Joseph Reed of the Council of Pennsylvania was to prove the most dangerous of all of Arnold's enemies. Reed had taken a dislike to Arnold as soon as they met in 1778, and he was determined to oppose the military governor whenever he could. The ardent Patriots in the state's government were eager to punish Philadelphia's Loyalists for aiding the British or cooperating with them, during the British occupation.

Reed had a long list of Loyalists, including many Quakers, whom he wanted tried and, if found guilty, executed. The execution of two Quakers had already taken place before Arnold took office. The new military governor first collided with the state leader when Arnold decreed an end to all executions. He had the vigorous support of Washington, who wanted him to pursue a policy of reconciliation.

The state's Patriot leaders wanted not only to get rid of Loyalists, but also to seize their property as well. When Reed acquired the house of Joseph Galloway, a well-known Loyalist, he again crossed swords with Arnold. Reed had the state militia evict Galloway's wife Grace. When she refused to leave, they carried her out in a chair. Benedict was outraged. He could not stop the eviction, but he sent his housekeeper to assist her and gave her the use of his carriage.

Arnold also antagonized the Pennsylvania Patriots by pursuing private business interests. He purchased a schooner and outfitted it as a privateer. He also learned of a warehouse in New Jersey that was filled with merchandise, including wine, medical supplies, and civilian clothing. Arnold used government wagons to haul the merchandise to Philadelphia, where it was sold and the profits split between Arnold and two partners.

Arnold felt justified in pursuing these ventures because he was responsible for entertaining important visitors from foreign countries, from Congress, and from the army, and these responsibilities created the need for a well-staffed household. The practice of using one's position for personal gain was not illegal, and many others had engaged in it, including leading Patriots. But many people considered the practice tawdry and unsavory. Washington had referred to a "dirty, mercenary spirit" creeping into the Revolution. Nevertheless when Joseph Reed reported Benedict Arnold's dealings to the commander-in-chief, Washington did nothing.

Reed and his Pennsylvania Council stepped up their criticism of Benedict Arnold, often in newspaper articles. One letter to a pro-Reed newspaper declared, "When I meet your carriage in the streets, and think of the splendor in which you live and revel . . . it is impossible to avoid the question, 'From whence have these riches flowed if you did not plunder Montreal.'" 6.

Anti-Arnold forces brought up all the old, unproven charges against him. Arnold responded to many of the charges, but that seemed only to encourage more attacks. He was fortunate that 1778, after a slow beginning, also brought signs of a better life for the troubled general.

Lonely Months

During his long convalescence at the army hospital in Albany, Benedict was confined to bed and the fracture box for four painful and lonely months. Spending day after day in this situation must have made him desperate for human companionship, especially the warmth and physical closeness of a woman. He had been devastated by the death of his wife, and had had no meaningful relationship since. This loneliness might not have mattered much on the battlefield or during the worst weeks of pain and fogginess induced by laudanum or small amounts of opium mixed with alcohol—a common painkilling dependency.

By late January 1778, however, he became well enough to feel the loneliness of his life. During the early spring, Benedict made a spirited bid to re-open his courtship with Elizabeth De Blois. He wrote long, passionate letters to her in Boston, and again enlisted the aid of Lucy Knox. Miss De Blois was somewhat kinder to him this time, even congratulating him on his military achievements, but insisted that they stop the correspondence. He wrote one more time, and receiving no response, had to admit that the matter was closed.

He soon received his appointment as military governor, and became so busy that he had no time to be crushed by the rejection. In fact, only days after his arrival in Philadelphia, he met Margaret "Peggy" Shippen, and a new courtship began.

Love and Marriage

One of the Loyalist families Benedict met on his arrival in Philadelphia was the Shippens—a wealthy merchant family with three lovely, lively, and intelligent daughters. The youngest—Peggy—was just turning eighteen that month of June. She was widely regarded as the most beautiful and accomplished belle of Philadelphia. She could use her prettiness to have young men constantly fawning over her; as one British naval officer wrote, "We were all in love with her." 7. Peggy quickly captured Benedict's attention. In fact, in very little time, he was hopelessly in love.

By all accounts, Peggy Shippen was a remarkable young woman. After examining contemporary accounts of her, historian Willard Sterne Randall described her as " . . . tiny, blond, dainty of face and figure, with steady, wide-set blue-gray eyes. . . . Appearing to be shy, she was bright and quick and capable of conversing at length about politics and business to anyone." 8.

During the previous year, when the British occupied Philadelphia, Peggy, her two sisters and their friends were invited to concerts, plays, and parties by young British officers almost every evening. Peggy was often in the company of Captain John Andre, a good-looking actor, playwright and poet, as well as the aide-de-camp to General Henry Clinton, who was soon to replace Howe as supreme commander of British forces in America.

Benedict began an intense but controlled courtship (no trunks full of gowns). His efforts must have seemed awkward at first. He was twenty years older and still could not walk, or even stand, without difficulty and pain. The British were gone, but a swarm of agile young men, including Continental soldiers, was now buzzing around her.

Although Arnold's courtship looked like an uphill struggle, he had several things in his favor. First, he was a great military hero, who cut a dashing figure in his major general's uniform. Even his war wound was regarded as a badge of his heroism. He had rather swarthy good looks, with strangely powerful gray eyes. Historian John Richard Allen compiled a composite description based on contemporary accounts: "He was well formed, muscular, capable of great endurance, active, graceful in his movements and exceptionally adept at athletic exercise." 9.

People often spoke of Benedict as arrogant and crude, but he also possessed remarkable charm and eloquence. The best description of this aspect of his personality was a statement by Charles Carroll of Maryland, one of three commissioners sent by Congress to Canada in 1776 (with Benjamin Franklin and Samuel Chase) to find out what was going wrong with the invasion of Quebec. Carroll was greatly impressed by Arnold. He wrote: "An officer bred up at Versailles could not have behaved with more delicate ease and good breeding. . . . If this war continues and Arnold should not be taken off pretty early, he will turn out a great man. He has great vivacity, perseverance, resources, integrity and a cool judgment." 10.

During the summer of 1778, Benedict became a regular at the Shippen home for afternoon tea or dinner. He often escorted Peggy and her sisters to social functions. The Shippens were polite to Arnold, but they were also very uneasy about the idea of having their youngest daughter courted by the most notorious rebel leader. But the couple was also aware that the general was doing more than anyone to protect their freedom and their property. While Peggy's father, Edward Shippen, was not opposed to the courtship, he had not given his approval because he hoped the marriage could be put off until the spring of 1779. He was uneasy about the state of Arnold's finances. He quite likely advised his daughter to be cautious.

The courtship proceeded in a slow and stately manner through the summer, autumn, and winter. He was with Peggy almost daily, and even though the couple was chaperoned by her parents in the Shippen home, they seemed to have ample time alone together.

On September 25, Benedict wrote his proposal letter to Peggy. The letter was romantic and passionate, but also remarkably unusual—unusual because large portions of it were copied word for word from his proposal to Betsy De Blois. Perhaps he felt that his letter to Betsy had achieved an eloquence he could not hope to duplicate. Whatever the case, here are key parts of the letter:

> Twenty times have I taken up my pen to write to you, and as often has my trembling hand refused to obey the dictates of my heart—a heart which, though calm and serene amidst the clashing of arms and all the din and horrors of war, trembles with diffidence and fear of giving offence when it attempts to address you on a subject so important to its happiness. Dear madam, your charms have lighted up a flame in my bosom which can never be extinguished, your heavenly image is too deeply impressed ever to be effaced. . . . On you alone my happiness depends.

As he had done with Betsy, he urged Peggy to suffer

> your heavenly bosom . . . to expand with a sensation more soft, more tender than friendship. . . . Whatever my fate may be, my most ardent wish is for your happiness, and my latest breath will be to implore the blessing of heaven on the idol and only wish of my heart. 11.

Benedict's ardor failed to persuade Peggy to give her consent, and this must have been very difficult for him. After months of enforced celibacy, he had to suppress his desires and behave as an eighteenth century courtier. Toward the close of 1778, family members and friends began to wonder about the long delay. One relative wrote: "Pray tell me, will Cousin Peggy follow your example? Everyone tells me so with such confidence that I am laughed at for my unbelief. Does she know her own mind yet?" Another cousin expressed her surprise in a late January 1779 letter: "... When is he likely to convert our little Peggy? They say she intends to surrender soon. I thought the fort would not hold out so long. Well after all there is nothing like perseverance, and a regular attack." 12.

Peggy finally gave in, and the wedding took place in the Shippen mansion on April 8, 1779. During the marriage ceremony, Arnold had to be supported by a soldier. His pride was probably hurt further during the reception by having his leg propped on a camp stool. But he had also achieved his greatest victory—he had finally won Peggy Shippen's hand.

This happiest of occasions, however, could not spare him from the determined antagonism of his adversaries.

Intrigue and the First Steps to Treason

In February 1779, Arnold left Philadelphia to meet with Schuyler and others in Albany to finalize New York's property gift—a gift of property and land as a reward for his heroic services. But before he had gone many miles, Joseph Reed stepped in. As soon as he heard about New York's planned gift to Arnold, Reed and his Pennsylvania Council filed formal charges against Arnold, accusing him of eight crimes involving misuse of his office, the charges to be tried in state court. Reed later added that, as long as Arnold remained in office, the state would no longer call out the militia to fight the British, nor would they pay to support the Continental Army.

The timing of Reed's rash action could not have been worse. Arnold was already on his way north when an aide caught up with him and delivered the news. Arnold was crushed. He didn't know what to do—to continue on to New York, or go back to Philadelphia to face the charges.

He did neither. Instead, he went to Washington's headquarters in Morristown and met with the general. Washington, too, was furious and convinced Arnold to ask for a Congressional hearing. Congress referred the charges to a committee, which quickly cleared him of the first six charges for lack of evidence. The two remaining charges involved the use of military wagons, so they would be heard by a military court.

Arnold's problems with Reed and his committee had now expanded into a conflict between Congress and a state. The threat of withholding militia from the Patriot forces could endanger the hope of defeating the British. Members of Congress and the Pennsylvania Council, after an all-night debate, reached a compromise. A new committee was formed, which ordered a new trial for Arnold—on the same eight charges.

Benedict could not believe what was happening to him. Another trial meant more long hours spent gathering all his evidence again. Matters were made worse when he wrote Washington, asking that the trial take place quickly. Washington had originally scheduled a hearing on the two military questions to take place on May 1, but Reed now asked for an indefinite delay, most likely because he still had no evidence.

Once again, Arnold was shocked when Washington agreed to the postponement. It seemed that not only had Congress turned its back on him, but so had Washington, the one man on whom he had always depended. Desperate for support, Arnold wrote an anguished letter to the commander:

> If your Excellency thinks me criminal, for Heaven's sake, let
> me be immediately tried and, if found guilty, executed. I want
> no favor; I ask only justice. . . . Having made every sacrifice of
> fortune and blood, and become a cripple in the service of my
> country, I little expected to meet the ungrateful returns I have
> received from my countrymen. But as Congress have stamped
> ingratitude as the current coin. I must take it. . . .
> I have nothing left but the little reputation I had gained in the
> army. Delay in the present case is worse than death. 14.

Arnold had also expressed his despair in a letter to Peggy shortly before they were married. "I am heartily tired with my journey," he wrote, "and almost so with human nature. I daily discover so much baseness and ingratitude among mankind that I almost blush at being of the same species." 15.

Even the Loyalist *Royal Gazette* commented on the shabby treatment Arnold was receiving: The newspaper first praised him as "more distinguished for valour and perseverance [than any other American commander]. General Arnold heretofore has been styled another Hannibal, but losing a leg in the service of Congress, the latter considering him unfit for any further exercise of his military talents, permit him thus to fall into the unmerciful fangs of the executive council of Pennsylvania." 16.

Arnold's fight to clear his name was to continue through 1779 and into 1780. He never made the trip to New York State to try to finalize the property gift. Why didn't he take advantage of that time to travel north for meetings with Schuyler and others to try to finalize the reward? If successful, the gift would have helped to ease his troubled finances.

Instead, early in May—less than a month after his marriage to Peggy—Benedict made his first contact with the British, the initial step on his zig-zag road to treason. He contacted a Loyalist shopkeeper in Philadelphia named Joseph Stansbury. Arnold probably learned about Stansbury's availability as a courier from his bride; Peggy, in turn, would have known about the man through her relationship with Captain John Andre.

Stansbury accepted Arnold's statement and left for New York the next morning. Arnold's message was simple: he would "help to defeat the American rebels" and restore America to the British Empire. With help from a Loyalist minister named Jonathan Odell, Stansbury went to British Headquarters, where he met with General Clinton's adjutant, John Andre, now a major, who had just become head of Clinton's secret service.

Andre must have been stunned by Stansbury's message, and not surprisingly, he proceeded with considerable caution. In fact, over the next five months the Andre-Arnold correspondence involved the two men trying to find ways to trust one another while also gaining their respective goals. One of the first steps was to arrange a system of secret communication. Both men would have the two books on which a code was based: primarily Blackstone's *Commentaries* and also Bailey's *Dictionary*. The code was made of three digits, indicating 1) the page number, 2) the line number, and 3) the word number. An alternative involved using invisible ink, with "A" designating acid for decoding, or "F" for fire (heat).

However, Andre apparently wanted to have greater assurance of secrecy, so he involved Peggy in the correspondence. He suggested that "The lady might write to me at the same time with one of her intimates. She will guess who I mean, the latter remaining ignorant of interlining and sending the letter. I will write myself to the friend to give occasion for a reply." 17. The friend chosen was Peggy Chew, who was Peggy Arnold's closest friend and had also acted in an extravaganza designed by Andre (part of a huge farewell celebration at the time of the British departure from Philadelphia). [Peggy Shippen was forbidden from participating by her father who said the costume designed by Andre was too revealing.]

From May 1779 to October the communication between Andre and Arnold became a slow dance of disappointment and frustration for both sides. First, the exchange of messages was extremely dangerous. Stansbury and Odell could not always deliver messages in person, so trustworthy men or women had to be found. The letters between Peggy Chew and Andre were exchanged under a flag of truce, as was done for normally innocent letters. These, and other matters, often meant a delay of up to six weeks between the sending of a letter and a response.

Most troubling was the failure of either side to obtain satisfaction from the other. Arnold wanted some assurance that he would receive at least a minimum sum for his betrayal; he asked Clinton for assurance of 10,000 pounds. Clinton, however, was reluctant to make a commitment until he was certain that Arnold was serious and could offer something substantial. One suggestion from Andre was that Arnold rejoin Washington's army, obtain a field command, and then manage to surrender five or six thousand men. Andre also suggested that a field command could make possible a meeting between Arnold and himself which, he felt certain, would satisfy both sides.

By October, Arnold was fed up. He had frequently sent information to Andre about troop movements, the location of the French fleet and army, plus other matters, but nothing led Clinton to make a commitment of money. Benedict broke off all communication with the British. It was not until May of the following year (1780) that he was willing to try again. Peggy continued to correspond with Andre, mostly on matters of fabrics and accessories that he could obtain for her.

By the autumn of 1779, then, little had been accomplished, except that Arnold had crossed his Rubicon into a land of betrayal. How could he turn back? If he ever took a field command against the British, they would simply expose his communication with Andre and the game would be up. He had maneuvered himself into a most uncomfortable situation.

Unanswered Questions

One of the most difficult questions about Arnold's decision to become a traitor is why he chose May of 1779 to commit himself. He had just married Peggy Shippen and had recently purchased the beautiful estate of Mount Pleasant. While it's true that his trial had been postponed until January, he did not have to rush. Why not take advantage of the long delay? They could have settled into married life, enjoyed their new home, and Benedict could have taken time to go to New York to try to work out the state's generous offer.

At nearly the same time, Arnold wrote his frenzied letter to Washington when the commander agreed to delay Benedict's trial. How could delay of the trial be "worse than death"? And the trial itself was not going to involve anything so serious as to require Benedict Arnold's execution.

Somehow in that month of May events seemed to speed up in Arnold's mind to a frantic pace—the marriage, the new trial, Washington's postponement of it, and Benedict's anguished letter. One wonders why these events led to treason within three weeks of the wedding.

Is it possible that Benedict's marriage to Peggy was an important factor? Most historians and biographers have not thought so. Some have not even mentioned her possible influence on his decision. However, the simple matter of timing makes it worth exploring. She certainly would have felt deeply for her new husband's anguish so expressed in his letter to Washington. She had close friends among the British, and she probably was aware that shopkeeper Stansbury would make a perfect go-between. It would seem only natural for her to urge him to ease his suffering by at least talking with someone in the British camp. Is there proof? The full discussion of her involvement, and the evidence, is in Chapter Thirteen.

CHAPTER ELEVEN

The Tortured Road To Betrayal

AFTER HE BROKE OFF COMMUNICATION WITH Major John Andre in October, 1779, Benedict lived through more than six months of turmoil, frustration, and isolation. He became more desperate than ever to restore his reputation and to gain financial stability. He may have been motivated by the quixotic notion that, if successful in these efforts, he could simply drop the plan to join the British. Apparently he was not concerned about the British exposing his steps toward treason, since he had spent much of his life fighting off accusations.

From October to the following May, however, nothing went Arnold's way. Reed and his Council of Pennsylvania attacked him relentlessly. Congress continued to treat him shabbily, and his finances became more, not less, tangled.

"Fort Wilson" and Isolation

An incident in the autumn of 1779 made Benedict feel both alone and in danger. By October, a steady decline in the value of Continental currency, combined with the French army's purchases of local farm produce, led to severe food shortages in Philadelphia. Bands of disgruntled men began roaming the streets, seeking those they thought were profiting from the skyrocketing prices. When a number of those suspected were harried by a large armed mob, they fled to the home of James Wilson.

There were soon about thirty men barricaded in what they called "Fort Wilson." Most of the men were staunch Patriots, and three of them, including Wilson, were signers of the Declaration of Independence. Benedict Arnold came to help and took command of defense on the second floor; General Thomas Mifflin directed on the first floor.

The defenders turned back the first attack after a brisk exchange of musket fire. The mob suffered about twenty casualties, including four killed; a few defenders suffered minor injuries. The mob regrouped and attacked again, battering down the front door, and bayoneting one defender before retreating. The attackers were preparing for their third assault when Continental troops arrived and the emergency was over.

Arnold, however, remained a target of anger. People in the street yelled at him and threw stones at his carriage. When a crowd gathered around the Arnold home, he dashed off a note to Congress asking for Continentals to protect him and his family. In a curt message, Congress refused to help and advised him that he should have turned to "the executive authority of the state of Pennsylvania" (Joseph Reed and Co.), adding that Congress had full confidence in the state's ability "to protect every honest citizen ... and highly disapprove the insulations of every individual to the contrary." 1. Arnold had asked for help for an "honest citizen" which the state government could not seem to provide.

Although Arnold apologized for the "misunderstanding," and local authorities managed to disperse the crowd, he was deeply shaken. First, he had been disappointed in his dangerous negotiations with the British. Next, he found himself still battling with Joseph Reed and his Council who were clearly determined to destroy him. Now he found that, even with his life threatened, he had no friends in Congress. Feeling isolated and humiliated was bad enough, but that was just the beginning. Joseph Reed and his council, as well as Congress, were about to make matters worse.

The Long Court Battle

As early as February, 1779, the Pennsylvania Council had brought eight charges against Benedict Arnold when he was on his way to meet with General Schuyler in New York. Reed wanted the trial held in a state court, and for maximum exposure he had copies of the charges sent to Congress, General Washington, and authorities in every state, as well as every major newspaper. Since the charges, including several hearings before Congress and two trials, were not settled for a year, the public had time to consider the Council's statement that

Arnold was " . . . oppressive to the faithful subjects of this state, unworthy of his rank and station, highly discouraging to those who have manifested their attachment to the liberties and interests of America, and disrespectful to the supreme executive authority." 2.

Joseph Reed made matters worse by charging that Arnold "fled" the state *after* the charges were made, not before, making it clear that he was trying to elude the trial. Reed and his Council were determined to bring Arnold down, and there were plenty of shady dealings that he was guilty of. The Council's problem was that their eight charges were simply too flimsy. Some charges were merely statements of their intense dislike of the man; for example, that he had made "an indecent and disrespectful refusal" to explain the use of public wagons; and that he showed favoritism to Loyalists. Regarding the few charges that might have hurt Arnold, they could find no evidence.

Although the case against Arnold seemed so weak, the matter dragged on for a year. He continually defended himself with righteous indignation; or, as Van Doren stated it: "Arnold, who was more guilty than the council could know, denied any guilt with his usual bold vigor." 3.

The Council was fortunate that Congress did not dare clamp down on the case because they could not afford to antagonize Pennsylvania. Nevertheless, the congressional committee to which the charges were submitted repeatedly asked for evidence, and when there was none, were forced to dismiss most of the charges for lack of evidence. Two charges regarding the use of public wagons were to be turned over to Washington for a court-martial.

At first, Arnold was pleased and wrote to Congress his hope for a speedy trial. Washington set a date of May 1, 1779, but Reed's objections led to delays so that he could contact witnesses and gather evidence. The delays led Benedict to write his frenzied letter ("Delay . . . is worse than death") to Washington. Finally, in June, advances by the British forced a postponement until the campaigning season was over. Not until late December, 1779, did the court-martial finally hold hearings in Morristown, New Jersey.

The main charges against him involved using public wagons to move private goods and allowing a trading vessel (the *Charming Nancy*) to clear port when others were denied. Benedict's defense was eloquent and persuasive, especially his opening statement:

> When the present necessary war against Great Britain commenced, I was in easy circumstances and enjoyed a fair prospect of improving them. I was happy in domestic connections and blessed with a rising family who claimed my care and attention. The liberties of my country were in danger. The voice of my country called upon all her faithful sons to join in her defense. With cheerfulness, I obeyed the call. I sacrificed domestic ease and happiness to the service of my country, and in her service have I sacrificed a great part of a handsome fortune. I was one of the first who appeared in the field and, from that time to the present hour, have not abandoned her service.

Arnold then responded to all of the original eight charges against him, saying that he considered the attacks against him by Reed and his Council to be "a vile prostitution of power." Referring to the charge that he had closed the city's shops but arranged to make large purchases for his own uses, he claimed that, if guilty, he would be "the vilest of men." He concluded, "The blood I have spent in defence of my country will be insufficient to obliterate the stain." 4.

In typical Benedict Arnold fashion, he did not mention that he had, in fact, profited from closing the shops. He was fortunate that Reed and his Council could not find his secret correspondence with the two men who shared the sales and profits with him.

The court-martial delivered its verdict on January 26, 1780. The officers found only that his use of public wagons was "imprudent and improper" and sentenced him "to receive a reprimand from his Excellency the commander-in-chief." 5.

Through the months of feeling betrayed and isolated, Benedict had held out the hope that Washington would always stand by him. Now, with the court's decision so humiliating, he thought that the commander-in-chief might ignore the verdict, or merely say a few words in private. Even the men of the Pennsylvania Council seemed to feel that Arnold had already suffered more than a man could bear. In an unusual letter to Congress, the Council wrote,

"We find his sufferings for, and services to, his country so deeply impressed upon our minds as to obliterate every opposing sentiment, and therefore beg leave to request that Congress will be pleased to dispense with the part of the sentence which imposes a public censure, and may most affect the feelings of a brave and gallant officer." 6.

Arnold endured more delays by Congress; the court-martial verdict was delivered in January, but it was April before Congress sent its report to Washington. And the commander-in-chief took seriously the court's verdict which required him to issue a reprimand and he decided it must be a public statement. In fact, the reprimand became famous for its statement of ethics in the military:

> Our profession is the chastest of all. Even the shadow of a fault tarnishes the luster of our finest achievements. The least inadvertence may rob us of the public favor so hard to be acquired. I reprimand you for having forgotten that, in proportion as you have made yourself formidable to your enemies, you should have been guarded and temperate in your deportment toward your fellow citizens. Exhibit anew those qualities which have placed you on the list of our most valued commanders. 7.

The Tangled Web of Finances

While Benedict suffered through a year of confusion and humiliation leading to the court-martial verdict, he also struggled with Congress over his finances during the same year, from April 1779 to April 1780. The seemingly endless hearings, reports, and rumors led General Charles Lee to comment that Arnold "was served up as a constant dish of scandal to the breakfast of every table on the continent . . . in this general rage for abuse." 8.

Beginning in April 1779, the attempt to straighten out Arnold's finances was bounced between Congress and the Board of the Treasury. No one seemed willing or able to deal with the complexities. After months of wrangling, the Treasury Board did allow Arnold a credit of $51,993, but refused to grant an additional $3,300. In the final analysis of all the accounts, the Board concluded that Arnold owed the United States a balance of $2,328 for the Canadian Campaign.

The Board's report, issued on April 27, 1780 infuriated Arnold, and he demanded an appeal, arguing that members of the Treasury Board had engaged in a vendetta against him. His anger, and his insistence on the additional $3,300 owed him above the $51,9993 already granted has led some writers to conclude that he was in desperate need of money.

Recent biographers have disputed the conclusion that the need for money was a major motive for his decision to turn to the British. For example, Jim Murphy argues that Benedict's finances were not desperate. He points out that Congress still owed him pay for nearly four years of military service; he was also owed money for various business dealings. The total owed him came to 12,000 pounds, which he could never collect if he turned traitor. Also, his homes, property, warehouses, carriages, and horses would all be confiscated by state and national governments. In other words, Murphy concludes, Arnold stood to lose large sums by turning traitor.

Congress did act on Arnold's appeal in May 1780, appointing a three-man committee to consider his appeal and the report of the Board. There was no final resolution of the financial tangle.

What Led to Full-Fledged Treason?

In May 1780, Benedict renewed contact with the British through Stansbury, and in early June wrote that he expected to be placed in command of West Point. The Hudson River complex of forts, it turned out, had become central to Arnold's planning. He was now dedicating himself to helping America's enemy, by giving them the key to the nation's defenses.

Why did he suddenly recommit himself to treachery? If money was not the motive, what other factors were involved? The following are major elements described by biographers and historians:

First, throughout his long struggle with Congress, the Board of the Treasury, and the Executive Council of Pennsylvania, he achieved few victories to counter-balance the endless assaults on his pride. One of the rare moments of happiness was the birth of his son, Edward, on March 19, 1780.

When Washington issued his reprimand, which he regarded as extremely mild, Arnold was crushed. This has been seen by several writers as the last straw for Benedict; the one person he had always counted on appeared to have turned against him, accepting the accusations of Joseph Reed over Arnold's often-emotional defenses. His feelings of isolation and humiliation were so deep it could have created a powerful desire for revenge.

Second, in the critical years of 1779 and 1780, the American Revolution seemed to be on the brink of failure. The patriotic enthusiasm that had brought out tens of thousands of militia volunteers to fight for independence in 1775 had been dissipated by years of warfare, shortages, and failure of leadership. The army, which had numbered more than 27,000 in 1775 was reduced to less than 3,500 by 1780.

The plight of the army in the winter of 1779-1780 was even worse than at Valley Forge. A committee of Congress, headed by General Schuyler, reported on May 10 that the soldiers were losing patience and that "their starving condition, their want of pay, and the variety of hardship they have been driven to sustain, has soured their tempers, and produced a spirit of discontent which begins to display itself under a complexion of the most alarming hue." 9.

One of the soldiers—Joseph Plumb Martin—described conditions in less flowery terms; by 1780:

> We . . . still kept upon the parade in groups, venting our spleen
> at our country and government, then at our officers, and then
> at our imbecility in staying there and starving in detail for an
> ungrateful people who did not care what became of us, so they
> could enjoy themselves while we were keeping a cruel enemy
> from them. 10.

Many Patriot leaders were convinced that the failures of Congress were bringing the country close to collapse. General Washington, in a letter to a Congressman, wrote that he was "certain . . . that unless Congress speaks in a more decisive tone; unless they are vested with powers by the several states . . . or assume them as a matter of right; and they, and the states respectively, act with more energy . . . that our Cause is lost." 11. James Madison added that Congress had become so weak that "They can neither enlist, pay nor feed a single soldier, nor execute any other purpose but as the means are first put in their hands." 12.

Since this was the Congress that had treated Benedict badly on so many occasions, he may have come to feel that the well-mannered British would treat him with greater respect. In addition, the royal treasury had real money, not the rapidly-depleting Continental currency. Another temptation for Arnold could have been the act of Parliament, passed in January 1779, offering to grant all the Americans' demands short of independence. This would enable Benedict to picture himself as the great peace maker.

Many others had also become disillusioned with the Patriot cause and large numbers turned to the British. Deserters, called "scuffs," often left to help their families or to avoid starvation. By 1780, growing numbers joined Loyalist militia. Major General Nathanael Greene wrote to Virginia Governor Thomas Jefferson to report that much of the state had sided with the British. "The enemy," he said, "have raised seven independent companies in a single day and we have the mortification to find that most of the prisoners we take are inhabitants of America." 13.

Several writers have suggested that Arnold's distrust of France was a contributing factor in his decision. Many Americans were also suspicious of what the French would do when and if the British were defeated. The Loyalist *Royal Gazette* in New York printed an article that was circulated throughout New England, warning that, as soon as French troops landed, revolutionary governments would quickly give way to "the establishment of the French government, laws and customs. . . ." 14.

However, as Carl Van Doren commented in his *Secret History of the American Revolution*: "In spite of Arnold's later claim that he had been opposed to independence and the French alliance, he seems never to have put a syllable of dissatisfaction on record anywhere before May 1779." 15.

There are, then, a number of factors that could have influenced Benedict's ultimate decision: the signs that the Revolution was failing; the weakness of Congress and the Pennsylvania Council, including their unfair treatment of Arnold; the feeling that Washington had betrayed him; distrust of the French, contrasted with the British willingness to grant Americans everything they demanded, except independence. In addition, his need, or desire, for money cannot be entirely ruled out, in spite of the evidence that he was owed an even greater sum than he was demanding from the British. He had lost an important source of income when he stepped down as military governor during his long court battle. At the same time, his courtship and marriage had increased his expenses considerably. And, throughout his life, most of the conflicts he was engaged in involved money in some way.

In trying to sort through all of the factors operating in Arnold's tortured mind, one is struck by the feeling that no combination of these elements offers a satisfactory explanation for the greatest betrayal in America's history. But, when combined with the weaknesses in Benedict's character, the picture becomes clearer.

Benedict's Character Flaws

Benedict Arnold is regarded as one of the great battlefield leaders in our history—brave to the point of recklessness, an inspiration to his men, and possessing a unique ability to respond quickly in any military emergency. But he was not a great man. Other leading figures, including Washington, Jefferson, and Franklin, had suffered frequently at the hands of political enemies, but they all held on to their larger vision of winning independence.

Many contemporary observers as well as modern writers, have felt that Arnold's self-confidence often spilled over into arrogance. This frequently led him to react to any charges as nothing but personal attacks. He had a remarkable ability to deny—apparently even to himself—that he was at fault in any way.

This confidence could also lead to an inflated sense of his own value or importance. When he first opened negotiations with Major Andre, for example, he chose the code name "Monk," a reference to George Monk, a 17th century English general who switched sides after the death of Oliver Cromwell and restored the monarchy (Charles II), becoming a great patriotic hero in the process. Arnold could picture himself as a new patriot, changing sides to restore America to its proper place within the British Empire. He was certain that thousands would follow his lead.

Benedict was also convinced that his services and sacrifices for his country warranted special consideration. Throughout the almost endless hearings and trials, he made frequent reference to his having become a cripple in his service to the cause of independence. He used his disability to gain his goals, most significantly when he told Washington he could not accept a field command but could manage the command of West Point.

At one point in his court battles, he came up with the idea of forming a naval expedition to the West Indies. In order to obtain Washington's permission for three or four hundred troops, he managed to give the impression that the initiative had come from the Board of Admiralty. The plan flopped quickly when Washington decided he could not spare the men and the Admiralty Board also dropped it. However, the episode revealed Arnold's tendency to bend the truth to suit his purposes.

Finally, as biographer Willard Wallace noted, "He was a pathetic case of insecurity." He desperately wanted to be accepted as an equal by the "first families." But, "one of his obsessions was that riches ensured respectability and that the means by which those riches were gained was immaterial." 16.

There is no way to measure how each of these potential motivations worked on Benedict's flawed character. One other element involves the possible role of his wife Peggy. Modern writers have been convinced that she was involved in the treason but could not have influenced the decision of someone as strong willed as Arnold. Analyzing her actions in the next two chapters will clarify the picture.

Chapter Twelve

"Treason of the Blackest Dye"

In May 1780, Benedict made his decision to re-open negotiations with Major Andre and General Clinton. The coded messages bounced back and forth through the summer until Arnold and Andre arranged for a secret meeting in September.

For this round of negotiations, Benedict decided to offer a prize Clinton would have to find exciting: he would have himself appointed the commandant of West Point and then turn it over to the British for a sum of at least 20,000 pounds. West Point quickly became the centerpiece of the exchanges.

The West Point Fixation

West Point was a string of four major forts, plus a blockhouse, and several hilltop fortifications stretching for fifteen miles along the lower Hudson River, guarding the river and the 1,097-foot-long chain designed to prevent British warships from sailing upriver. General Washington often referred to West Point as "the Key to America." With the French now establishing their base at Rhode Island and Washington's army in New Jersey, West Point provided a connecting link for communication and troop movements. In British hands, however, America would be cut in two.

In May or June, Arnold notified Andre and Clinton that he expected to be appointed to the command of West Point. At the same time, he wrote to his friend Schuyler, hinting that he was interested in the post. Schuyler's reply is lost, but in early June, after a meeting with Washington, he reported to Benedict:

> He [Washington] expressed a desire to do whatever was agreeable to you, dwelt on your abilities, your merits, your sufferings and on the well-earned claims you have on your

country, and intimated that as soon as his arrangements for the campaign should take place that he would properly consider you. I believe you will have an alternative proposal, either to take charge of an important post, with an honourable command, or your station in the field. Your reputation, my dear sir, so established, your honourable scars, put it decidedly in your power to take either. A state [NY] . . . will wish to see its banners entrusted to you. If the command at West Point is offered, it will be honourable; if a division in the field, you must judge whether you can support the fatigues, circumstanced as you are. 1.

In typical Benedict Arnold fashion, he interpreted Schuyler's conjecture to mean that Washington was promising that West Point was his. On June 12, Arnold met with Washington in Morristown, but there is no record of what was said; on the same day, however, he wrote to the British that "Mr. Moore [his new code name] expects to have the command of West Point" 2. offered to him by early July. Washington was intending to launch a full campaign against New York, with French help, and he had wanted to give Arnold command of the entire left wing of the army. After both Schuyler and New York Congressman Robert Livingston wrote to Washington urging him to give West Point to Benedict, Washington finally agreed.

By mid-July, Benedict was on his way to West Point, after asking Congress for money in advance of the four years' pay he was owed. Congress advanced him $25,000, and as he left Philadelphia for the last time, he was hoping to acquire an even larger sum from Clinton.

The Greatest Treachery

Arnold had a huge scare on August 1, when he met with Washington while part of the army was crossing the Hudson at King's Ferry. The commander-in-chief was so eager to close in on New York that he again offered his fighting general command of the army's left wing. Arnold was shocked when Washington's General Orders announced from Peekskill that the army's left wing was to be commanded by Major General Benedict Arnold.

The matter was finally straightened out and Arnold was soon safely settled in the house of Beverley Robinson, Benedict's new headquarters, across the river from West Point. It would be interesting to know what was going on in his mind as he wiggled out of what should have been the promotion of a lifetime. The man who was devoted to action and longed to restore his family's honor would have been in command of one-third of the army in what could have been the decisive campaign of the war. All that was now being swept away by his betrayal. Did he consider accepting the promotion, then plan to deny any accusations the British might make? Probably not, considering what the next incident reveals about how far he had fallen into heinous treachery.

On September 15, 1780, Benedict received a letter from Washington with a confidential postscript:

> I shall be at Peekskill on Sunday evening, on my way to Hartford to meet the French Admiral [Ternay] and General [Rochambeau]. You will be pleased to send down a guard of a captain and 50 at that time, and direct the quartermaster to have a night's forage for about 40 horses. You will keep this to yourself, as I want to keep my journey a secret. 3.

Arnold immediately replied to the commander that the guard and forage would be provided. At the same time, he wrote a cipher letter to Clinton: "General Washington will be at King's Ferry Sunday evening next on his way to Hartford to meet the French Admiral and General. And will lodge at Peekskill." 4.

That was an astounding betrayal, even for Benedict Arnold. He was willing to give up the country's most important leader, and a man who had been his mentor and who had admired and trusted him through years of turmoil. The British already had a sloop of war, the *Vulture*, in the Hudson not far from Peekskill, with others available, making a river attack quite possible. No attempt to capture Washington took place—either because the timing was off or Clinton did not have complete confidence in Arnold yet. In either case, no one ever knew of this black spot in Benedict's heart until Clinton's papers were made available after 1900.

Finalizing Plans

By August, Benedict had assured Major Andre and General Clinton that he planned to be in command at West Point and would then turn it over to the British for 20,000 pounds. Sir Henry was thrilled by the idea. If Washington attacked New York, the British could move up the Hudson, take control of the West Point complex and then push south, driving the Americans into Virginia. Like Arnold, Clinton was confident that thousands of rebels would follow Arnold's lead and restore their loyalty to the Crown.

Two problems stood in the way of completing the deal: Communications between New York and West Point became increasingly difficult, and Clinton was cautious about trusting Arnold. He continually refused to agree to the sum Benedict asked for and wanted some proof of his intentions, such as arranging the capture of 5,000-6,000 American troops, or gaining the release of Burgoyne's Saratoga forces still being kept prisoner. For Benedict's part, the American turncoat insisted on knowing exactly how much he would receive.

By mid-August, Clinton was ready to take a chance, but first he wanted a meeting between Arnold and Andre to finalize the details. Problems with communication and logistics forced delays until late September.

Just before the scheduled meeting, Arnold was thrilled by the arrival of Peggy and their infant son. He had planned for her journey with great care, sending his aide, Major David Franks, to Philadelphia to bring her north. Arnold had carefully listed each of the six overnight stops they would make and even suggested that a feather bed in a wagon would be more comfortable for Peggy and their son than a closed carriage. Benedict Arnold biographer Willard Wallace observed: "Arnold was overjoyed to have Peggy with him again and not simply as a co-conspirator. After weeks of separation, their reunion had the element of a honeymoon but one spiced with knowledge of the dangerous game they were playing." 5.

In the effort to bring Andre to Arnold, there were several missteps in the early weeks of September. At one point, as Arnold was being rowed south to meet Andre at Dobbs Ferry, his barge was fired on by the British; Arnold was nearly killed but managed to get away. The often-delayed meeting was rescheduled for the night of September 21.

The Andre-Arnold Meeting

In the long cast of characters in the saga of Benedict Arnold, John Andre is one of the most fascinating and compelling figures. In a 1902 introduction to Andre's journal, Henry Cabot Lodge offered this description of the man:

> There is a pleasant tinge of romance about the man himself, for he was young, handsome, and possessed of many accomplishments, clever, agreeable, popular. . . . The favorite of his commanders, a trusted staff-officer, advancing easily along the road to promotion, beloved among his fellows, popular in Society, he passes suddenly out of the sunshine of a young prosperity into the darkness of a desperate enterprise, becomes the paymaster of treason, a disguised fugitive, a prisoner, a convicted spy, and dies at last by the hangman's hand. 6.

On the night of September 21, the conspirators planned to meet at the home of Joshua Smith on the banks of the Hudson, about 15 miles south of West Point. Smith, who knew nothing of the conspiracy, was rowed to the *Vulture* by two of his tenant farmers and picked up a "businessman" named John Anderson, the code name Andre had used from the beginning. Andre wore his British uniform, but it was completely hidden by a cape. (Clinton had warned him to stay in uniform, or he could be executed as a spy if caught behind American lines.)

Andre and Arnold finally met around midnight at Smith's home. Few details of the meeting are known, but Arnold did give him his written analysis of the fort along with details about where the defenses were weakest. He probably also mentioned that Washington would be stopping at the fort on Monday. Since the meeting had lasted past four a.m. on Friday, and Smith had no rowers available, the men decided to wait until nightfall to have new rowers take Andre to the *Vulture*, Since Smith knew Mr. Anderson only as a New York businessman, he felt no rush to return him to the *Vulture*.

The delay in leaving Smith's residence until after dark on Friday did not seem to matter. But as so often happened with Arnold's schemes, fate stepped in and changed everything. During the day on Friday, Patriot officers opened fire on the *Vulture* from shore batteries, without orders from Arnold, inflicting a good deal of damage. The sloop's captain ordered his ship south about ten miles, leaving Andre behind at Smith's home.

Benedict decided that Andre would have to make his way to New York by land, with Smith accompanying him part of the way. Arnold wrote a pass for him in case he was stopped by a Patriot patrol. Andre also had to change out of his British uniform, since they would be traveling by day.

While Benedict headed north to West Point on Friday, Smith and Andre started their ride south. About nine o'clock, they were stopped by a patrol of New York State militia. The captain of the militia warned them that they were entering a no man's land where bands of armed Loyalists called "Cowboys" roamed, eager to capture any Patriots, and other bands of Patriot militia, known as "Skinners," were eager to make prisoners of any Loyalists. They followed the captain's suggestion and spent the night in a farmhouse, and left again early Saturday.

When Andre and Smith reached the bridge over the Croton River, Smith suddenly announced that he was turning back. Forced to continue alone, Andre took the road along the Hudson and had reached within a half-mile of the safety of Tarrytown, when three armed men came out of the woods and ordered him to stop. Seeing that one of the men wore a Hessian soldier's green coat, Andre told them that he was with "the lower party"—meaning a Loyalist from New York. The leader, John Paulding, simply nodded and Andre, thinking he was safe, said, "Thank God, I am among friends, I am glad to see you. I am an officer in the British service, and have now been on particular business in the country, and I hope you will not detain me." 7.

Paulding suddenly grabbed the bridle of Andre's horse and ordered him to climb down. Too late, Andre realized he had ridden into a trap. If he had said nothing and simply produced his pass he probably would not have been detained. Instead, Paulding said, "We are Americans," and led him into the woods to search him for money. Andre tried to correct the situation. He showed them Arnold's pass and warned the Skinners not to detain him on the general's business.

Nothing worked for the desperate spy. They searched his clothes, his saddle and his equipment, then ordered him to take off his boots. They nearly missed the three wrapped papers in his sock, and, when they removed them, could not figure out what they were.

The Skinners figured they had caught a spy and decided they should take him to a militia officer for a possible reward. They ordered Andre to get dressed, tied his hands behind his back, and lifted him onto his horse. They led him to a guard post at North Castle and turned him over to Colonel John Jameson. One of the three militia men later recalled how suddenly Andre's mood had changed. "You never saw such an alteration in any man's face. Only a few moments before, he was uncommonly gay in his looks, but after we made him prisoner, you could read in his face that he thought it was all over with him." 8.

Colonel Jameson did not know what to do with the prisoner or the papers. He did not suspect that Arnold was leading a conspiracy, so he planned to send Andre to Arnold at West Point, along with copies of the papers; the original of the papers were to go to Washington, who was known to be coming from Hartford.

Major Benjamin Tallmadge, who was second in command at North Castle, knew that Arnold had been planning to meet a man named Anderson. He now figured that it was Anderson who was caught taking papers *away* from West Point, and he urged Jameson to have "Anderson" brought back to North Castle and not to tell Arnold. Jameson did not feel right accusing Benedict of being a traitor; he did agree to have Andre brought back to North Castle but also insisted on sending a note to Arnold telling him of the capture.

Benedict spent a quiet weekend at home with Peggy. They could feel good about their plan, especially after Smith sent word that Andre was safely on his way. General Washington, along with Alexander Hamilton and General Lafayette were expected Monday morning, but that should be an easy scene for Peggy and Arnold to play. However, the messages Jameson sent to Washington and to Arnold did not arrive until Monday and that was when the world of the three conspirators exploded.

Exposure and Flight

On Monday morning, Alexander Hamilton and another aide arrived at Benedict's headquarters and announced that Washington would be delayed and to go ahead with the breakfast without him. Breakfast had just started when Jameson's messenger arrived with the note describing Andre's capture. Arnold read the note at the door, swore the man to secrecy, and sent him to join the others.

Minutes later, Arnold rushed upstairs where he told Peggy that Andre had been captured. He had to try to get away to the *Vulture* ahead of Washington's men. Since there was no way to take Peggy and Neddy with him, Arnold had to tell her how to answer the questions they were bound to ask. They both seemed confident that she could manage her way out of the situation.

Peggy stayed in their room while Benedict limped downstairs, ordering that a horse be saddled immediately. He told Franks to inform Washington that he had been called over to the Point but would be back in about an hour. Riding at a reckless pace, Arnold took a shortcut down a steep incline that became known as Traitor's Hill to the Hudson River landing. His barge and eight oarsmen were as always ready. He ordered the men to row with greatest speed down river to the *Vulture*. Within a short time, Arnold raised a white flag and climbed safely on board the sloop. He offered his crewmen promotions and bonuses if they would join the British. All refused.

Less than a half-hour after Arnold fled his headquarters, Washington arrived at the Robinson House across from West Point. The commander had seemed in a good mood, joking with his aides when they chafed about a detour. "I know you young men are all in love with Mrs. Arnold," he said and told them they could ride ahead if they wished. 9.

After breakfast, Washington, Lafayette and Knox crossed to West Point, planning to meet with Arnold. Arnold, of course, was not there, and Washington was disturbed to see that the defenses were in a sorry state of disrepair. He returned to the Robinson House and went to the room assigned to him to rest. Minutes later Hamilton came in with the packet of papers from Colonel Jameson, including Arnold's assessment of West Point and Andre's letter to Washington in which he confessed his identity.

Washington read the documents in stunned silence. His bravest, most reliable officer had sold out to the British. Lafayette later recalled entering the room and seeing Washington sitting on the bed, holding the papers in trembling hands. "Arnold has betrayed me," he muttered. "Whom can we trust now?" 10.

Even in shock, Washington maintained his famous ability to act calmly. He ordered Hamilton and McHenry to try to catch Arnold before he reached the *Vulture*. But the traitor had too great a head start.

Once Arnold was safely on board the war sloop, he quickly relaxed enough to write to Washington, saying that "I have ever acted from a principle of love to my country. . . . The same principle of love to my country actuates my present conduct, however it may appear inconsistent to the world, who very seldom judge right of any man's actions." Benedict also tried to assure the commander that Peggy was not involved in the conspiracy and had no knowledge of it. He asked Washington to protect her "from every insult and injury that a mistaken vengeance of my country may expose her to. . . . [She] is as good and innocent as an angel, and is incapable of doing wrong." 11.

First Reactions

While Hamilton and McHenry tried to catch up with Arnold, Washington set to work to bring army regiments to the Hudson Valley, and had work crews begin to strengthen the fort complex. The commander-in-chief also questioned Benedict's aides – Varick and Franks – not because he thought they were guilty, but to gain any information they might have about Arnold's movements. Both men were placed under arrest, but Washington assured them that this was merely a formality.

The general also wanted to talk to Peggy, but soon after Arnold made his escape, she suffered through several hours of hysterics and sobbing, at times appearing to be quite out of her mind. She asked to see Washington, but when he entered her room, she hysterically denied it was the general. Washington quietly left.

Convinced of her innocence, Washington later told her through an aide, that "though my duty required that no means should be neglected to arrest General Arnold, I have the great pleasure in acquainting *her* that he is now

But I am mistaken if at *this time*, Arnold is undergoing the torments of a mental Hell. He wants feeling! From some traits of his character which have lately come to my knowledge, he seems to have been so hackneyed in villainy, and to be so lost to all sense of honor and shame that while his faculties will enable him to continue his sordid pursuits, there will be no time for remorse." 22.

In Philadelphia, Boston, and scores of smaller towns, people burned or hanged Arnold in life-sized effigy. He was shown seated, given two faces, with the devil standing behind him, shaking a purse at Arnold's left ear, while in his other hand was a pitchfork raised to drive Arnold into hell as a reward for his crimes. After being dragged through the streets, the effigy was hanged and then burned. Reaction was particularly vicious in his home state of Connecticut, where effigies were given humiliating treatment. In Norwich, mobs invaded a cemetery and destroyed every tombstone containing the hated name of *Arnold*, including that of his father.

Benedict's childhood was quickly reinvented to include countless tales demonstrating that he was in the clutches of the Devil from the earliest age. Rhymes and songs were used by parents to warn children of behaving like Benedict.

Throughout the rest of 1780 and 1781, a wave of patriotic fervor swept the country.

As soon as he fled West Point, Arnold sought ways to justify or explain his treasonous acts. He was not above using threats to make others appear in the wrong. In a letter to Washington, for example, received by the commander less than two hours after Andre's death, Arnold argued that Andre should not be blamed for decisions made by Arnold. But, if Andre should be held responsible, "I shall think myself bound by every tie of duty and honor to retaliate on such unhappy persons in your army as may fall within my power. . . . If this warning should be disregarded, and he suffer, I call Heaven and earth to witness, that your Excellency will be justly answerable for the torrent of blood that may be spilt in consequence." 23.

Throughout his life, Benedict insisted that he was in the right. Thus, he felt quite justified in threatening Washington. In a similar way, he knew how deeply Clinton was pained by the death of Andre, but he waited only a few days before pressing him to settle how much the British were going to pay him for his treason. Clinton was understandably annoyed at being dunned by his co-conspirator, but he paid Arnold handsomely within the next two weeks.

Benedict received just about everything he could have hoped for. In fact, no American officer made as much money during the war as he did. The initial sum Clinton had commissioned was 6,000 pounds plus 315 pounds—the 6,315 total being equivalent to between $60,000 and $80,000 in today's purchasing power. That was just the beginning. Arnold also received pay of 450 pounds a year as a cavalry officer, reduced to half for life after the war.

There were other sources of income: In March 1782, the King issued a warrant to his paymaster of pensions that "Our will and pleasure is, and we do hereby direct, authorize and command, that an annuity or yearly pension of five hundred pounds be established and paid to you unto Margaret Arnold, wife of our trusty and well beloved brigadier general, Benedict Arnold." As Van Doren discovered in Clinton's papers, Sir Henry had noted in regard to the pension that she had performed "services which [were] very meritorious." 25. In addition, each of Arnold's five surviving children with Peggy received annual pensions of 100 pounds. His three sons by Margaret Mansfield were rewarded with British army commissions: Benedict in 1780 at age twelve, Richard and Henry a year later when they were twelve and nine respectively. The total pensions paid to the family each year totaled 1,450 pounds, or about $20,000 in modern purchasing power. Finally, in 1798, the Arnolds received 13,400 acres of Canadian lands set aside for Loyalists.

Benedict may have done well in financial terms, but he had to be displeased with the negative reaction of the British army and people in New York. The British officers had been extremely fond of Major Andre and his execution was a shock; they could not help but associate Arnold's escape with Andre's death. Nearly all of the officers vowed not to serve under the turncoat.

In an effort to justify his actions and to persuade dissatisfied Patriots to join him, Arnold wrote two addresses to the American people. He was aided by Judge William Smith, a leading Loyalist. The first, "To the Inhabitants of America," was printed on October 25. In his address to the American people, he tried to argue that he was never a believer in the Declaration of Independence—although during his 1780 court-martial, he said he thought the declaration was "glorious." He also said that Great Britain's 1778 Act of Reconciliation gave Americans everything they had asked for, short of independence. That, combined with his belief that the French planned to take over when the British left, convinced him it was better to return to British rule. To the officers and soldiers of the army, he offered a bonus and good salaries for all who would join him in his body of cavalry and infantry. He said he wanted a chosen band of Americans to "share in the glory of rescuing our native country from the grasping hand of France as well as from the ambitious and interested views of a desperate party among ourselves . . . who have brought the colonies to the very brink of destruction." 26.

In the same month, Benedict also wrote to Lord George Germain outlining "The Present strength of the American Rebel Army, Navy, and France." After showing the weaknesses and resignations of the armies and navy, he assured Germain that with a few bribes he could quickly raise a force of up to three thousand former rebels to fight with a large British force, in which he hoped to serve as a major general.

All Arnold's efforts at persuasion had few positive results. Fewer than 100 Rebels chose to change sides. And he did not count on the negative reactions of the British officers, or the unwillingness of Clinton to make him a major general or to let him command a major attack on one of Washington's armies. Clinton did, however, encourage his new colonel to form his American Legion—a force of about 1,700 men, half of them British regulars and Hessians, the rest, Loyalists. Benedict set to work for the British with as much energy and skill as he had formerly used against them.

The Kidnap Attempt

While Colonel Arnold was planning a raid on Virginia, General Washington approved a plan to kidnap the traitor. The plan was the brainchild of Major "Light Horse Henry" Lee. Washington insisted that Arnold be captured alive; the commander wanted to make an example of him. Lee centered his plan around Sergeant John Champe, a powerful and ambitious member of Lee's cavalry.

The plan called for Champe to desert on October 20, and once approved by the British, join Arnold's Legion, and work his way close to Arnold. Champe played his part perfectly and carried out an exciting cloak-and-dagger scheme.

Champe studied Arnold's movements and planned, with accomplices, to seize him during his habitual midnight stroll in his garden. They would bind and gag Arnold and carry him into an adjoining alley, and from there to the Hudson River where another accomplice was waiting with a boat. If they were stopped they would say that Arnold was a soldier drunk on duty whom they were taking to the guardhouse. Once they were safely in the boat they would row across the Hudson where Lee would be waiting with a squadron of dragoons.

As so often happened in schemes involving Arnold, however, totally unforeseen circumstances changed everything. On the very day of the planned kidnapping, Champe's unit was ordered to board its transports. Lee waited nervously all night with no idea what had happened. Champe ended up serving under Arnold in Virginia for five months before he had a chance to escape back to the Americans. It is unlikely that Arnold ever knew how close he came to feeling Washington's revenge.

CHAPTER THIRTEEN

The Mystery of Peggy Shippen Arnold

PEGGY SHIPPEN ARNOLD WAS ONE OF THE MOST fascinating women of her time. Even in her late teens, she was known for her beauty and charm. Educated at home in the traditional subjects of music, art, literature, and household arts, she also received special training from her father that enabled her to converse intelligently on a variety of topics, including business and politics. All these qualities combined to produce a magnetism that kept men of all ages captivated, even years after her marriage to Benedict Arnold.

During her lifetime and in the years since, there have been countless questions about her role in Arnold's treason. This chapter reviews the evidence and opinions that have emerged over the 250 years since the betrayal. The weight of the evidence, much of it circumstantial, will show how deep her involvement was.

Early Opinions

Many of Peggy's contemporaries were certain that she was totally incapable of being part of a conspiracy. A half-century later, historians were still convinced that this

> flighty young woman would [never] be trusted with secrets by her husband or anyone else.... Perhaps a different wife would have kept the general on the straight and narrow. [He] had no counselor on his pillow to urge him to follow the rugged path of a Revolutionary patriot. 1.

The discoveries of Carl Van Doren in the 1930s began to change ideas about Peggy's role. He revealed, for example, that within two weeks of her marriage to Benedict in April, 1779, he made his first secret overture to the

British through shopkeeper Joseph Stansbury, who became the trusted go-between with British Major John Andre. It seems quite certain that the couple would at least discuss the matter before Benedict made the fatal move. Even with Van Doren's new evidence, however, later biographers concluded that Peggy's role was "a very controversial one." 2. As recently as 1997, biographer James Kirby Martin wrote that "historians have not resolved the extent of her involvement in her husband's perfidy, although Peggy certainly knew about his contacts with Andre." 3.

Although uncertainty about Peggy's involvement has continued, evidence of a partnership with her husband keeps piling up. For example, in Major Andre's first letter to Benedict, in which he explained the code system they would be using, he added that he wanted Peggy involved in the exchange of messages: "The Lady might write to me at the same time with one of her intimates—she will guess who I mean—the latter remaining ignorant of interlining, [and Peggy] will send the letter. . . . The letters may talk of the Meschianza and other nonsense." 4. In other words, Peggy would receive a letter from her friend, then write a secret message to Andre between the lines in invisible ink. The friend was Peggy Chew, who was Peggy's best friend and had acted in the Meschianza for Andre.

Arnold replied in his first coded letter: "Madam Arnold presents you her particular compliments." The conclusion seems unavoidable: Peggy was deeply involved from the very beginning, including her own secret message to Andre, which may not have been read by Benedict in every case.

Other Evidence of Peggy's Early Involvement

In late 1778, New York State made its offer of an estate and land to Arnold as a reward for his heroic actions in the state. Benedict immediately headed north to discuss the possibilities with General Schuyler. Peggy, who had not yet given Arnold her consent to marriage, was not thrilled by the prospect of living in the wilds of New York, where Indian tribes still held sway over large areas.

Benedict never made it to New York. He turned back largely because the

Pennsylvania Council filed eight criminal charges against him, charges that would be tried by court-martial. Timing became a factor at this point. When Arnold brought up the possibility of purchasing the handsome Mount Pleasant Estate a few miles outside of Philadelphia, Peggy's attitude changed completely; in fact, her wedding to Benedict took place barely two weeks after the purchase was made. It probably helped, too, that Arnold deeded the estate to Peggy and himself—plus her heirs—for life. Some writers have concluded that the purchase of Mount Pleasant was crucial in persuading Peggy's father to grant his permission for the marriage. Edward Shippen, however, had said that the decision was Peggy's to make; he did not have to grant permission.

The New York offer could have been perfect for Benedict. He might have escaped the clutches of Joseph Reed and his Pennsylvania Council. The estate and the possible sale of some 40,000 acres could have given his finances a big boost. Instead, he added a huge sum to his indebtedness with the purchase of Mount Pleasant. One is tempted to conclude that Peggy made good use of Benedict's desire for her to maneuver him toward the decision she wanted. Several authors have mentioned her strong romantic hold over him. For example, Willard Wallace wrote: "Demure and innocent before marriage, she soon evinced a capacity for passion that enthralled the vigorous Arnold." 5. There were surprising elements of her personality that have often been overlooked; for example, there was a sensuality about her that apparently was not shared by her two older sisters or many of her other contemporaries. As Wallace commented: "Perhaps it would have been remarkable if, with her background and her many Loyalist and British friends, she had not encouraged her discontented fiancé to take the decisive step that would bring him both revenge and vindication." 6.

In a letter to Peggy on February 8, 1779, he seems to indicate that he was happily giving up New York's offer. "Heavens!" he exclaimed, "what I must have suffered had I continued my journey—the loss of happiness for a few dirty acres. I can almost bless the villainous roads and more villainous men who oblige me to return." 7.

Another circumstance that points to Peggy's influence involves Benedict's first step in offering his services to General Clinton. How did Arnold know that Joseph Stansbury was a man who could be trusted with messages requiring the greatest secrecy? There is little doubt that he learned about the man from Peggy; she, in turn, was most likely introduced to him by Andre. Since Stansbury had performed charity work for Clinton, he might have attended social functions with Andre and Peggy.

Additional evidence pointing to Peggy's early involvement in the conspiracy has to do with the key plan of gaining control of West Point, then selling it to the British for a large sum. Modern authors have insisted that West Point was never mentioned before the late summer of 1780. However, Shippen family papers indicate that Peggy said she suggested the West Point scheme in May of 1779. Scholars insist that these statements are merely hearsay, since Peggy's letter(s) have not been found. 8.

In support of the Shippen family's contention, Andre wrote two months later in a coded suggestion to Benedict: "Permit me to prescribe a little exertion. It is the procuring of an accurate plan of West Point." 9. Another year would pass before Arnold would persuade Washington to give him command of West Point. By that time, all the conspirators were convinced that the complex of forts was the crucial piece in their scheme to bring the American Revolution to a speedy end.

Peggy and John Andre

During the British occupation of Philadelphia, Peggy had enjoyed a close relationship with British Captain John Andre, General Howe's aide de camp. Andre's charm and talents added liveliness to Howe's headquarters. In addition to his cheerfulness and skills, he wrote poetry and plays, designed scenery and costumes, and also acted and directed. He created an extravagant production as a special farewell to General Howe, who was being replaced by General Clinton. The colorful production, called the *Mischianza*, featured Turkish-style pantalooned costumes, including one that Andre designed for Peggy, which was so revealing that her father forbade her to wear it. Peggy was not used to being denied by her father or anyone else, but she chose not to attend the event, out of deference to him.

Peggy clearly enjoyed the months of British occupation of Philadelphia, especially the attentions of Andre and his fellow officers. Andre was a frequent visitor to the Shippen home. He escorted seventeen-year-old Peggy to social functions several times a week, sometimes with her two older sisters. He continued to write to her after the British left Philadelphia for New York. When Clinton replaced Howe, he retained Andre, promoted him to major, and made him his adjutant general, a position at which he showed great skill, especially in intelligence matters.

How close was Peggy's relationship with Andre? Van Doren, who made extensive use of British War Office records, concluded: "There is only the slightest foundation for the romantic story that Andre had been in love with Peggy Shippen, or she with him." 10. But there is an interesting circumstance supporting the idea of a love affair: Writing nearly a century after Peggy's death in 1804, her grandson Colonel Pownell Phipps wrote, "Poor Andre was in love with her, but she refused him for Arnold. [After her death] we found a locket with a lock of Andre's hair which we still have." 11. Keeping that lock of his hair for the last 35 years of her life suggests something more than a friendship. As far as Peggy's family was concerned, then, there seems to have been little or no question about how close she and Andre had been.

Whatever their relationship had been, it seems certain that, once she committed herself to Benedict, that commitment was deep and lifelong. In fact, they seem to have been completely devoted to each other. There appears to be no evidence to support the notion that behind her powerful efforts to make the West Point scheme work was a secret desire to be reunited with Andre in New York.

The Theatrics of Peggy Arnold

One of the difficulties in analyzing how deeply Peggy Arnold was involved in Benedict Arnold's treason is the confusion that Peggy herself thrust into the issue. From the moment Arnold's treason was exposed with the arrival of General Washington and the news of Andre's arrest, Peggy Arnold was never under suspicion. Washington did feel that those closest to Benedict—his two aides, Varick and Franks—and Peggy had to be interviewed for any information they might have.

After Arnold stumped upstairs to their bedroom to tell her the stunning news of Andre's arrest with the telltale documents, Peggy knew she had very little time to prepare for the questions that were sure to come. Washington arrived about thirty minutes after Arnold made his escape and was being rowed to the *Vulture*. All was quiet from Peggy's room until Washington and his aides left for the Point, thinking to meet Arnold there.

Peggy apparently started to go downstairs to Colonel Varick's room, where he was lying ill, as he had been the day before when she brought him tea. Varick, who was terribly fond of her, suddenly heard her scream for him from the top of the stairs. He instantly rushed up to her, and this is how he described the scene:

> With her hair disheveled and flowing about her neck, a morning gown with few other clothes remained on her—too few to be seen even by the gentlemen of the family, much less by many strangers. . . . She seized me by the hand with this—to me—distressing address and a wild look: 'Colonel Varick, have you ordered my child to be killed?' Judge you my feelings at such a question from this most amiable and distressed of her sex, whom I most valued. She fell on her knees at my feet with prayers and entreaties to spare her innocent babe. . . . I attempted to raise her up, but in vain. Major Franks and Dr. Eustis soon arrived, and we carried her to her bed, raving mad. 12.

For a time, she was quiet, Varick continued, then "she burst again into pitiable tears and exclaimed to me—alone on her bed with her—that she had not a friend left here." He tried to assure her that she had him and Franks, and that Arnold would soon return with General Washington.

"'No, General Arnold will never return!' she cried, sobbing and gesturing toward the ceiling. 'He is gone, he is gone forever; there, there, there! The spirits have carried him up there.'" 13.

Later, after dinner, Washington had a chance to walk in the garden and talk first with Franks, then with Varick. He assured them both that they were not under suspicion but he was anxious to hear what they knew of Arnold's movements in recent weeks.

When Peggy asked to see Washington, he agreed. She told Varick that there was a red-hot iron on her head and only the General could remove it. But when Washington entered her room, she exclaimed: "No, that is not General Washington! That is the man who was a-going to assist Colonel Varick in killing my child." 14. Without saying more, Washington quietly left the room. He had known Peggy most of her life and had always been fond of her, so this encounter must have been hard for him. Lafayette, who was deeply sympathetic to Peggy, remarked, "She looked on us all as murderers." 15.

The next morning, Lafayette and Hamilton visited her room to try to comfort her. In a letter to his fiancé Betsy Schuyler (General Schuyler's daughter), Hamilton wrote:

> She received us in bed with every circumstance that would interest our sympathy, and her sufferings were so eloquent that I wished myself her brother to be her defender. . . . Could I forgive Arnold for sacrificing his honor, reputation, and duty, I could not forgive him for acting a part that must have forfeited the esteem of so fine a woman. 16.

Historians George F. Scheer and Hugh F. Rankin speculated that Betsy Schuyler must have noticed "Peggy's cleverness in setting the scene [on her bed and still wearing very little]." 17. Was Peggy play-acting through all these histrionics? Few writers are willing to go that far. As Willard Wallace put it: "Whether she was play-acting at West Point cannot be determined for a certainty." 18.

A major reason for questioning Peggy's acting ability is the evidence of an earlier incidence of hysteria: Shortly before Peggy left Philadelphia for West Point, she dined at the home of Robert Morris. A friend of the Arnolds, arriving late, congratulated her on Benedict being appointed to a command far more prestigious than West Point. This was a reference to the mistaken announcement that Arnold had been named to command the left wing of the army.

Morris reported that Peggy immediately went into "hysteric fits. Efforts were made to convince her that the general had been chosen for a preferable station. These explanations, however, to the astonishment of all present, produced no effect." 19.

Many writers have concluded that the incident proves that Peggy was given to hysterics and her fits at West Point were merely an extension of that response. But that interpretation ignores how much was at stake for her. Months of planning and scheming had come to depend completely on Arnold being in command at West Point. Without that, their dream was shattered. It seems quite likely, then, that her hysterical fit at the Morris home was a genuine reaction to a great shock.

At West Point, on the other hand, Peggy knew that everything depended on her being in control of every situation. If her West Point hysterics were genuine, they were very effective. If she was acting, which seems probable, it worked perfectly.

Peggy could not have hand-picked a better audience for her acting at West Point. Hamilton, Lafayette, Varick, and Franks were all young—under thirty—vigorous men of action, who had spent most of the past four years living in military camps and waging war. And, as Washington had said, all the young men were already in love with her.

Twenty-three-year-old Alexander Hamilton tried to explain Peggy's appeal to his fiancé: When they went to her in the morning, he wrote, "she was still frantic with distress. . . . It was the most affecting scene I was ever witness to. One moment she raved, another she melted into tears. Sometimes she pressed her infant to her bosom and lamented its fate . . . in a manner that would have pierced insensitivity itself. . . . All the sweetness of beauty, all the loveliness of innocence, all the tenderness of a wife, and all the fondness of a mother showed themselves in her appearance and conduct. We have every reason to believe that she was entirely unacquainted with the plan." 20. Washington was no youngster, of course, but he did have a soft spot for the ladies, and he seems to have been as convinced by Peggy's theatrical display as the younger men had been.

The next day, Washington gave her the choice of going to her husband in

New York or to her family in Philadelphia. She chose to go to her family, and late in the day, she was on her way, with Major Franks as her escort. Her hysterics had apparently subsided.

Enter Aaron Burr

On the ride to Philadelphia, Peggy and Major Franks made several overnight stops. One was at the home of Mrs. Theodosia Prevost, said to be the wife of a British officer, but who two years later married Aaron Burr. This stop led to unusual testimony about Peggy and her role in the treason.

According to Burr, when strangers were present, Peggy had fits of sobbing. But when she was alone with Theodosia, Burr said, "Mrs. Arnold became tranquillized, and assured Mrs. Prevost that she was heartily sick of the theatrics...," She also spoke of her role in the conspiracy: "She stated that she had corresponded with the British commander [Clinton]—that she was disgusted with the American cause and those who had the management of public affairs—and that through great persuasion and unceasing perseverance, she had ultimately brought General Arnold into an arrangement to surrender West Point to the British." 21.

Burr's story is intriguing, but there are several problems with it. First, there is Burr himself. Many question his reliability, since his career is marked by countless self-serving statements, often of questionable veracity. He later became nearly as notorious as Arnold, when as vice president, he killed Hamilton in a duel, then fled west where he hooked up with another unusual figure—James Wilkinson—in a scheme that might have involved establishing an empire west of the Mississippi. That blew up when Wilkinson turned him in.

In the Prevost incident, the story did not come to light until after both Arnold and Peggy were dead. This delay was said to have stemmed from Burr's basic decency. The Shippen family denied any decency on Burr's part. Relying on family letters, they claimed that Burr had become Peggy's escort for part of the journey to Philadelphia:

> On the way he made love to this afflicted lady, thinking to take advantage of her just feelings of indignation toward her husband, to help him in his infamous design. Yet this is the

fact; if our tradition be true. And indignantly repelled, he treasured up his revenge, and left a story behind him worthy of his false and malignant heart...." 22.

There is an unusual addition to this already unusual Aaron Burr story: Benedict Arnold, in his *Memoirs*, written in the 1790s, stated that Peggy told him about her encounter with Burr as soon as she was reunited with him in New York in November, 1780. According to the diary, when Peggy and her escort reached Paramus, Major Franks turned her over to Aaron Burr, to escort her the rest of the way to Philadelphia. The *Memoirs* account continues:

> Aaron Burr [was] a friend of her childhood, under whose escort as an American officer, she was to proceed. Neither capacity prevented his endeavoring to seduce her on the way, and then, on being repulsed, circulating that she was party to my 'treason,' and that all her hysterics before Washington ... had been but acting, and that she had confided to Mrs. Prevost that she was tired of 'playing a part.'
>
> That Burr had the audacity to attempt the seduction of my wife in the very house of the woman he afterward married, and then call her as witness to a scandal he circulated about Peggy sufficiently characterizes both parties [Burr and Theodosia].
>
> But Peggy, frightened, and at a loss for a friend ... had unwillingly to accept Burr's protection for the rest of the journey, and only when safe in the arms of her father did she tell of Burr's insult and her rebuff. The father dared not challenge, and I [after] Peggy told me, could not. 23.

This entry in Arnold's *Memoirs* seems to confirm Aaron Burr's account, including the contention that Peggy was a major player in the treasonous scheme, and that it was her "persuasion" and "perseverance" that persuaded Arnold to take the fatal step.

The two accounts provide a very tempting "smoking gun" piece of evidence. However, I can't be sure that Benedict's diary is any more reliable than Burr's account in the Davis biography. Arnold's diary was first published in 1917 by Charles Scribner's Sons. After the book was out of print for many years, a facsimile edition was published in 2010, but with no new editor or copyright. The 620-page facsimile does seem accurate, although the narrative is often self-serving. Consequently I've used it only when it is verified by other sources. In addition, I have not found the 1917 original listed among the sources in any of the books used in preparing the present volume. The result is that I hesitate to present Peggy's encounter with Burr as *proof* of her leading role in Arnold's treason. But the two accounts do add intriguing possibilities to the growing body of evidence.

While Peggy's family was delighted to welcome her to Philadelphia, others were not. Authorities had already searched the Arnold household and one of the letters they discovered was from Andre to Peggy. It was assumed that the letter proved Peggy's complicity in the treason, and the government decided she was no longer welcome in the city. Joseph Reed's Executive Council resolved "that the said Margaret Arnold depart this state within fourteen days from the date hereof, and that she do not return again during the continuance of the present war." 24.

Accompanied most of the way by her father, Peggy went to New York to join her husband, arriving on November 14, 1780. The Shippen family tried every means available to have the ruling changed so she could remain in Philadelphia, but nothing worked. They assumed that Peggy had no desire to go to New York, failing to recognize her total commitment to her husband. (Hannah left Philadelphia at the same time, taking the three boys from Benedict's first marriage to New Haven. She always remained loyal to her brother and later joined him and Peggy in England.)

The Weight of the Evidence

No modern writers have concluded that Peggy Arnold was at least an equal co-conspirator with her husband. Carl Van Doren in the 1930s went farther than anyone since. He wrote:

> However beguiling she may have been during the warm days
> of courtship & honeymoon, she could hardly have done more

than confirm a powerful will like Arnold's in its own decision. Even if it was actually she who proposed the treachery—and there is no first-hand evidence that she did—the final responsibility must lie with the mature & experienced Arnold for undertaking to carry it out. 24.

If we consider the evidence—and the timing—some interesting conclusions become possible:

First, Peggy's "beguiling" ways were working on a man who was feeling harassed, isolated, and with Washington's reprimand, quite abandoned and defeated. For years his enemies had pounced on him at every opportunity, so that even his great battlefield triumphs became clouded by personal attacks and denial of recognition. During the year of court cases and hearings on finances, Peggy was always there—beautiful, warm, something like the "Beckoning Fair One" of the English short story, loving—but just out of reach during the months before their marriage. He might have become desperate and confused enough to think she was pointing in the right direction.

In the first three months of 1779, events moved him steadily to the frame of mind Peggy hoped he would achieve:

- Late Dec. '78 – Feb. 1779: New York State's generous offer; Benedict's trip aborted by criminal charges. Letter to Peggy—relief that he didn't trade happiness for a "few acres."

- March, 1779: Peggy thrilled by new idea of a Pennsylvania home—Purchase of Mt. Pleasant completed on March 22.

- April 8, '79: Peggy and Benedict are married.

- May, '79: Somewhere during these few weeks, Peggy has quietly urged Benedict to turn to her friends in New York—Loyalists and British officers who could make things easy for him. She provided the name of Joseph Stansbury and how reliable he will be. She might even bring up the idea for West Point as the least bloody way for him to become the peacemaker.

Of course, there is no "first-hand evidence" of her central role in bringing about the betrayal; Peggy was not likely to write her step-by-step plan to persuade him to move in the direction she wanted to go. Aaron Burr's account, supported by Arnold's version, would come close to first-hand evidence, but are these two sources reliable enough?

Later episodes add to the weight of circumstantial evidence. Her hysterics at the Robert Morris house demonstrated how heavily she relied on the West Point scheme. And the acting out of hysterics at West Point illustrated her masterful self control. She left for Philadelphia on September 27th; Arnold had made his escape on the 26th.

Over the next twenty years, as Benedict and Peggy tried to build a new life in England, she displayed some of her remarkable abilities. She managed their finances skillfully and when Benedict's business schemes failed—and later his health also failed—Peggy was always there to prop him up and restore his confidence. After his death in 1801, she performed financial wizardry to pay off all of their considerable debts in a very short time.

Reunion and Reactions

Benedict was thrilled and relieved when Peggy and Neddy arrived on November 14. He had just rented a handsome town house adjacent to Clinton's headquarters. The weeks since their frantic separation in late September had not been easy for either of them.

Arnold found that his reception in New York was not what he had hoped for. Some people were mildly curious about him, which made them polite, but only Clinton and Judge William Smith acted in friendly ways. But a major problem had been created by the execution of John Andre. People could not help but think that Arnold escaped with his life, while Andre paid with his.

Andre had been tremendously popular with the British army, especially the younger officers. Arnold must have been deeply hurt when he learned that the young officers unanimously refused to serve under him. The arrival of Peggy and their son helped improve the mood. She was well known to many British officers who remembered pleasant visits to the Shippen home. Loyalist and British women, not having been in Philadelphia, were polite but decidedly lukewarm. One Loyalist woman—Mrs. Rebecca Shoemaker—commented that "Peggy Arnold is not so much admired for her beauty as one might have expected. All allow she has great sweetness in her countenance, but wants animation, sprightliness, and that fire in her eyes. . . ." 26.

One area where the Arnolds did well was in the amounts the British were willing to pay for their treason.

How Treason Paid

Throughout his life, Arnold always insisted that he was in the right. Thus, he felt quite justified in threatening Washington over the trial and execution of John Andre. Similarly, even though he knew how pained Clinton was by Andre's death, Benedict waited only a few days before pressing him about money and rank.

General Clinton was irritated by Arnold's pushiness, but he was also a man of honor and he understood Benedict's need. In a similar way, he had earnestly wished that Washington would not have Andre executed, but he understood why Washington felt he could not counter his court's verdict. The military etiquette of the time also dictated that neither man could approve an exchange of Arnold for Andre. Consequently, Clinton wasted little time in addressing Arnold's needs.

Benedict received just about everything he could have hoped for. In fact, it's likely that no American officer made as much money during the war as he did. The initial sum Clinton had commissioned was 6,000 pounds plus 315 pounds for expenses—the 6,315 total being equivalent to between $60,000 and $80,000 in today's purchasing power. That was just the beginning. Arnold also received pay of 450 pounds a year as a cavalry officer, reduced to half for life after the war. He also received an additional 250 pound salary as a wartime brigadier general.

There were other sources of income. For a time, he was a favorite of King George. In March, 1782, the King issued a warrant to his paymaster of pensions that "our will and pleasure is, and we do hereby direct, authorize and command, that an annuity or yearly pension of five hundred pounds be established and paid to you unto Margaret Arnold, wife of our trusty and well beloved brigadier general, Benedict Arnold.". In addition, each of Arnold's five surviving children with Peggy received annual pensions of 100 pounds, thanks to Queen Catherine's fondness for Peggy. [Peggy bore a second son in New York, then five more in England—three sons and two daughters. One son and a daughter died in infancy.] His three sons by Margaret Mansfield were rewarded with British army commissions: Benedict in 1780 at age twelve, Richard and Henry a year later when they were twelve and nine respectively. The total pensions paid to the family each year totaled 1,450 pounds, or about $20,000 in modern dollars. Finally, in 1798, the Arnolds received 13,400 acres of Canadian lands set aside for Loyalists.

Efforts to Win Converts

Both Arnold and General Clinton had been confident that tens of thousands of disgruntled Americans would follow Benedict's lead in returning their loyalty to the King. Only a handful chose to become traitors. Instead a wave of patriotism swept the country, coupled with a hatred of the man who had betrayed them.

In desperation, Benedict tried to persuade people to join him. He wrote two essays to the American people and soldiers, explaining his reasons. Loyalist Judge William Smith helped him with ideas and wording.

In the first essay, which was printed in newspapers, he explained his treason as a reaction to the danger posed by France. He also accused Congress of "tyranny . . . and a total disregard of the interest and welfare of the people."

The second essay was addressed to "The soldiers and officers of the Continental Army who have the real Interest of their Country at Heart and who are determined to be no longer the Tools and Dupes of Congress, or of France." In the course of the article, he asked such questions as "What is America but a land of widows, beggars, and orphans?" 27.

Benedict's efforts were remarkably unsuccessful. People's distaste for Arnold's treachery translated into an urgent sense of unity and patriotic fervor, especially in the South. The Continental Army and local militia were eager to fight, in spite of ragged uniforms, and a shortage of food and other supplies.

Patriot Responses

The Patriots were blessed with outstanding leaders. After the disastrous loss in the August battle of Camden, Congress gave up on Galloping Gates and wisely let Washington name a new general in the South. He selected Nathanael Greene, only 38 years old, but highly regarded by the soldiers and officers.

Greene's first move was a daring one. Although his army was badly outnumbered by the British under Cornwallis, Greene decided to divide his army. Greene led one division in guerilla attacks on Cornwallis. Veteran Daniel Morgan led the other division. Both generals were aided by hit-and-run specialists Francis Marion (the "Swamp Fox") and Thomas Sumter (the "Caroline Gamecock"). Brilliantly orchestrated victories at King's Mountain, in October 1780 and the Cowpens, early 1781 drove the British and Loyalists out of the Carolinas and forced Cornwallis toward the Virginia coast and his eventual trap at Yorktown.

Benedict Arnold pushed ahead in spite of the disappointments. He formed his own American Legion regiment, with the rank of cavalry captain, plus the wartime rank of brigadier general. His regiment, in addition to deserters, included elements of: the 18th Irish regiment (mostly New York Loyalists); Colonel John Simcoe's Loyalist Queen's Rangers (mostly New York deserters); and Captain John Thomas's Bucks County Pennsylvania Volunteers. For his first raid against his former country, he had about 1,700 men. This included a few hundred British regulars, who were probably added by Clinton because he did not entirely trust his turncoat general.

CHAPTER FOURTEEN

Nil Desperandum: the Final Years

ARNOLD'S LIFE HAD CONSISTED OF a few flashes of brilliance, first in making money, then in battlefield glory. But each triumph was followed by criticism and a failure to achieve recognition. The disappointments were the product of his own character flaws combined with the attacks of his numerous enemies, who often picked on those personal weaknesses.

The Impact of Betrayal

The collapse of his treason was his greatest failure, and it cost him everything he had achieved as a leading patriot. The discovery of the plot left him as a minor footnote in the nation's history. Had he succeeded in selling West Point to the British, he would have gained far greater notoriety as a villain.

Writing in his journal at the time, Dr. Thacher declared: "He aimed to plunge a dagger into the bosom of his country." 1. Had he succeeded, the Patriot cause would have been desperate. With the British in control of West Point and the entire Hudson River, New England would have been cut off from the other states, and Washington's army would have been cut off from the French in Rhode Island. Combined with the low morale of the military and the weakness of the Congress, Arnold's treachery could have sounded the death knell of the Revolution.

There were, fortunately, several factors that could have saved the Patriot cause. First, news of Arnold's betrayal seemed to shock Americans into an urgent new unity. Second, new leaders, like Nathanael Greene and Daniel Morgan, stepped forward and led new offensives. And third, General Clinton became more cautious than ever. He had long been paranoid about losing New York and about confronting Washington; this made him unwilling to make a major push out of his New York base. In addition, he continued to distrust Arnold and that lack of trust grew steadily.

Benedict's American Legion in Action

Benedict urged Clinton to follow his plan for an attack on Philadelphia, but Clinton rejected it. Instead, he ordered Arnold to launch a raid on the Virginia coast to destroy American supply bases and take control of Portsmouth.

In typical Benedict Arnold fashion, he went about the assignment with great energy and skill. By mid-December, 1780, his 1,600-man force was ready to board transports. After a difficult passage the regiment entered the James River. Arnold launched successful raids on Richmond, Portsmouth, and smaller towns. He came close to capturing Governor Thomas Jefferson.

In the spring, Arnold almost became trapped at Portsmouth. Militia units swarmed the region, and Virginia governor Thomas Jefferson offered a reward for Arnold's capture. Washington sent Lafayette with 1,200 Continentals to Virginia, with orders to hang Arnold if they caught him. The commander also sought help from the French fleet.

Even with enemies all around him, Benedict held on at Portsmouth, determined to fight to the end if the American forces attacked. He vowed to take his own life rather than become a prisoner. Instead, Lord Charles Cornwallis, the handsome, popular commander of British troops in the South, moved into Virginia in May, relieving the pressure on Arnold. Clinton then recalled Benedict and his American Legion, and the disappointed turncoat was back in New York in early June.

The Raid on New London

The summer of 1781 was not a happy time for Benedict, although he came back with a considerable sum of prize money, his share of the plunder from raids in Virginia, making him, one observer commented, "as rich as a nabob." But he did not gain the military victories or fame he had hoped for.

Throughout the summer, Arnold had little luck gaining recruits for his American Legion. He was also increasingly annoyed with Clinton's lack of initiative and even wrote directly to the British war office in London with his ideas for an attack on Philadelphia. This idea fell through because Cornwallis was reluctant to move troops out of Virginia.

In early September, 1781, Clinton sent Arnold on an amphibious raid on New London, Connecticut. The idea was to destroy this base for American privateers and warships, and also to relieve some of the pressure on Cornwallis in Virginia. Neither Clinton nor Arnold was aware that Washington and Rochambeau had already started their race south to trap Cornwallis at Yorktown, while a French fleet planned to hold the British fleet at bay.

Arnold's raid on New London turned into a needless tragedy, one that reinforced people's view of him as a heartless villain. With about 1,700 troops, mostly British and Hessians, Arnold struck quickly, easily taking the town, destroying many of the ships, as well as a number of warehouses and the largest wharf. Two forts—Trumbull and Griswold—guarded the coast. Fort Trumbull's guns faced the coast, so it fell easily when Arnold attacked it from the rear. Other troops were sent to attack Fort Griswold—and that was when Arnold's skillful victory turned into a disaster.

From a hill above Fort Trumbull, Arnold saw that Fort Griswold was well defended. He sent an officer to the attacking force, ordering them not to attack. But the attack had already begun, with some 800 British assaulting the strong fort which had only about 150 defenders. After bitter fighting, the American defenders finally surrendered and threw down their arms. But the British continued firing and bayoneting for some time, killing 88 Americans and wounding 35 more before their officers gained control. Even though Arnold had tried to rescind the order for the attack, he had also ordered it, making him responsible for the massacre.

While the bloodbath was taking place at the fort, there was more horror at New London. After destroying about a dozen ships, Arnold's men were busy plundering and setting fire to shops, stores, and houses. A sudden shift in the wind sent the flames roaring through the town. Much of New London and nearby Groton were reduced to ashes, with more than 150 houses destroyed.

The American people were naturally outraged by the destruction and bloodshed, and just as naturally blamed Arnold. It was widely assumed that he had destroyed the town in a brutal act of revenge.

Benedict returned to New York, and soon realized that his raid would have no effect on the outcome of the war. It could not even relieve pressure on Cornwallis, since Washington and Rochambeau were closing in on the British at Yorktown. In fact, by mid-September—about a week after the New London raid—Washington's American and French armies were ready to lay siege to Cornwallis at Yorktown. As one American officer said, "We have him in a pudding bag now." Within a month, Cornwallis was forced to surrender, giving the United States the final stirring victory that guaranteed independence. The final peace accord did not come for nearly two years.

Arnold had returned to New York too late to travel south to help at Yorktown, but even after the surrender of Cornwallis, he refused to believe the British should give up. He asked Clinton for permission to go to England to present his ideas. Sir Henry agreed, but said Arnold would have to wait until the French fleet left so that a military convoy could be formed.

The convoy was finally organized in December, 1781. The Arnolds had a second child while in New York, so it was decided that Peggy, the two children, and several servants would sail in a private ship for greater comfort than a Man of War could provide. Arnold sailed in the convoy on the same warship as Lord Cornwallis, who had been allowed to return to England on the promise of not returning to the war.

The ships finally sailed on December 15. Winter storms created a rough crossing and Arnold's ship nearly sank. After limping to a port in the West Indies, Benedict completed the voyage on another ship.

The Search for a Fresh Start

The Arnolds arrived in London not knowing what to expect. The reception was mixed. Members of the Whig opposition party and people who felt kindly toward America were decidedly unfriendly. But what mattered most to Benedict and Peggy was that they were well received at Court and by government leaders.

Lord Germain was respectful and Sir Guy Carleton, his old adversary, was friendly. King George was very kind and asked him to write his views on conditions in America and the prospects for continuing the war. Peggy was greatly admired for her beauty and bearing. The Queen quickly became very fond of her and let the Court ladies know that she wanted them to befriend her. The Queen also directed the 100-pound pension for each of her children. Peggy had a total of five children, a daughter and three sons; another son and daughter died in infancy.

The Arnolds found a house on Portman Square and looked forward to a prosperous future. Benedict was only forty-three years old and Peggy was still in her early twenties; they felt they had a full life ahead of them. Benedict displayed his optimism by changing his family motto. The old motto was *"mihi gloria sursum"*—"Through glory yielded to me," a recognition that divine gifts created the Arnold family position. The new motto was *"nil desperandum"*—"never despair," a reflection of his determination (and ability) to overcome all obstacles.

In spite of the couple's optimistic beginnings in England, Benedict worried about their income. Their combined annual income of about 1,500 pounds was steady, but there was no way to increase it to meet the needs of his growing family. In addition, to Peggy and their four children, he was also responsible for three sons by his first wife as well as his sister Hannah.

Arnold tried several ways to increase their income. He presented a claim to the government for losses he suffered when American governments seized his assets. His claim amounted to about 45,000 pounds, estimated to equal about $3,000,000 in 21st century dollars.

While Benedict waited for the government's decision, he applied for a position with the private army of the East India Company. Within three days, he received an icy rejection from the company director. The director said that while he trusted Benedict, the majority of people did not. "While this is the case," the letter stated, "no power in this country could suddenly place you in the situation you aim at under the East India Company." 2.

In 1785, Arnold gave up his claims for compensation and decided to try his luck in Canada.

Canadian Interlude

Eager for a fresh start, Arnold bought and equipped a brig, the *Lord Middleton*, and set sail for Canada in October, 1785, leaving Peggy and their children in London. Determined to regain his past success as a merchant, he settled in New Brunswick, a bustling new town settled by thousands of Loyalists after the Revolution.

Over the next two years, Benedict's life followed a familiar pattern. At first, he enjoyed spectacular success. Shiploads of products from the West Indies brought high profits in New Brunswick and surrounding towns. He bought roughly 15,000 acres of land, built warehouses and stores, and was regarded as the most successful businessman in New Brunswick. He asked Hannah to come to Canada with his three sons and he later sailed to England to get Peggy and their children.

During the long winter of 1785-1786, Peggy became upset by the long silences with no letters from Benedict. It may have been during this time that he took a mistress. The affair, the only time that he was unfaithful to Peggy, produced a son named John Sage. The existence of the illegitimate son was not known until his will was read; the identity of the mother has never been known. During these months, Peggy wrote to her father expressing her worries about Benedict and at being "separated from, and anxious for the fate of the best of husbands." 3.

From the West Indies, Arnold sailed to England, then to New Brunswick with Peggy and the children, arriving in July, 1787. With his entire family in Canada, Benedict worked doubly hard to make a success of his far flung business dealings, and Peggy was content enough, giving birth to another son, George, in September, 1787; she also hoped that she could manage a trip to visit her family in Philadelphia.

A life of success and contentment, however, had always eluded Benedict, and his time in Canada was no different. He was not well liked, even by the Loyalists, in New Brunswick, and his reputation suffered further when the economy of New Brunswick and other parts of Canada suffered a recession caused by increased warfare between England and France. Scores of Loyalists had borrowed money from Arnold or owed him for purchases, and suddenly they could not pay him. Benedict's efforts to collect only served to antagonize his debtors. In some cases, he took debtors to court, winning most of the judgments, which did nothing for his popularity. In 1788, he sailed to England with a cargo. While there, days after he took out an insurance policy, his warehouse in New Brunswick burned to the ground, destroying the contents. Rumors spread that he had started the fire himself to collect the insurance money. His partner joined the chorus of accusers, leading Benedict to sue the man for slander. Arnold won the case, but people continued to believe he was guilty, and many began referring to him as the "Traitor."

To escape the growing hostility, Arnold moved to St. John. Peggy was finally able to make her trip to Philadelphia with her infant son. "My pleasure," she wrote, "will not be unaccompanied by pain; as when I leave you I shall probably bid you adieu forever." 4. After spending several months with her family and friends, she rejoined Benedict in St. John in July, 1790.

By this time, Arnold had decided that they should wind up their affairs in Canada and return to England. The move could not be soon enough for Peggy. She hated the hostility and the "succession of disappointments and mortifications in collecting our debts," she wrote to her sister, as she tried "to shake off that gloom that has taken possession of me and for which I have too much cause." 5.

The year 1791 was a time of almost constant frustration, disappointment, and fear. Benedict's arrogance in his efforts to collect debts added to the anger and hatred. The climax came when a mob surrounded their home and burned an effigy of Arnold in front of the house, calling it "Traitor!" The arrival of troops prevented further trouble.

Arnold tried to sell his extensive holdings but with little success. He finally gave power of attorney to two men, and set sail for England with Peggy and their children in early 1792. Two of his sons from his first marriage—Henry, age nineteen, and Richard, twenty-one-- stayed in Canada with Hannah to try to manage his business affairs. The oldest son, Benedict, entered the army to fight the French.

A Decade of Despair

There were few happy times in the last decade of Benedict Arnold's life. They did have a few close Loyalist friends and they were proud of their youngest children's progress in school. Lord Cornwallis became a family friend and helped his sons advance in their military careers.

For the most part, however, his desperate efforts to achieve success in the military or in business ended in failure and disappointment.

Within weeks of his arrival, Arnold fought a duel with James Maitland, Earl of Lauderdale, for an insult the earl had made in the House of Lords. Arnold fired first and missed, then was ashamed when Lauderdale refused to shoot. The matter was settled when Lauderdale apologized for his remark and Arnold accepted. This gentlemanly response led to widespread praise for Benedict and great relief for Peggy.

Hoping to take advantage of the favorable comments he had received, Arnold tried to gain a military position. Three months of appeals and letters, however, failed to produce results. As the disappointments increased so did his feelings of failure as a provider. Continued efforts to collect on the Canadian debts accomplished little except more costly lawsuits.

Feeling desperate again, he bought a ship and sailed to the West Indies in 1794 to renew his mercantile ventures. He soon ran into trouble and was taken prisoner by the French. Benedict showed a flash of his old bravado by making a daring escape, and eluding French warships in a rowboat to reach the safety of a British squadron.

Now in his mid-fifties, Arnold found that renewed fighting against France in the West Indies gave him a burst of energy. He served as a "gentleman volunteer" for the British commander, Sir Charles Grey, and was widely praised for his contributions. But he was also deeply disappointed when Grey refused to give him a military post.

In the summer of 1795, he returned to England, much to the relief of Peggy. His enterprises continued to do poorly and there were personal losses as well. His oldest son, Benedict, had been captured by the French and served two years in prison. As soon as he was released, he was sent to the West Indies as an artillery officer. England was in the throes of the long warfare against Napoleon and needed all the officers they could muster. Benedict suffered a leg wound, however, and, when he refused amputation, gangrene set in and he died in October, 1795.

The loss of his oldest son was a heavy blow for Arnold. Later, when their favorite son, Edward, went to India under the sponsorship of Lord Cornwallis, both Arnold and Peggy felt the departure almost as deeply as if he had died. And, in fact, they never did see him again.

The last few years of Arnold's life were a time of increasing disappointment, pain, and despair. He continued to try for a military appointment in 1796, 1797, and 1798, but his appeals were repeatedly turned down or ignored. He finally realized, as he confessed to Peggy, that his military dreams were over and the army was denying him even the chance to die a soldier's death.

There were a number of reasons for the lack of interest in Benedict. Much had changed in England in the nearly two decades since his treason. He was hated by most of the opposition Whigs and by the army's officers. The War Office was focused on the war with post-Revolution France under the leadership of Napoleon. In the late 1790s, England was worried about an attack on London, but the generals never considered Arnold as a possible leader of the city's defense.

In 1800, the stress began to take its toll on his health. He suffered from increasingly severe bouts of asthma, which troubled him day and night, making sleep almost impossible. One leg became badly swollen, probably with gout, and the pain in his wounded leg was now severe, making it difficult for him to stand or walk, even with a cane. Arnold's once powerful physique was also declining, and he became stooped with sagging shoulders and flabby skin.

Peggy was also ill, a semi-invalid with symptoms that were probably the beginning of the cancer that was to take her life in 1804.Through all the suffering, as well as business losses, she continued to support Benedict and keep him propped up. Peggy felt deeply for his misery. Early in 1801, she wrote to

Edward, "He is, at present, in the most harassed wretched state that I have ever seen him. Disappointed in his highly raised expectations, . . . and wishing still to do something, without the health or power of acting, he knows not which way to turn himself." 6.

Throughout Arnold's frenzied last years, a few others expressed sympathy for him. At the end of the Arnolds' stay in Canada, for example, Captain John Shackford had a chance to observe Benedict, who did not remember him from their previous association twenty years earlier. Shackford had been on the Quebec march and had been taken prisoner during the assault on the city. He wrote about seeing Arnold:

> I did not make myself known to him, but frequently . . . I sat upon the ship's deck, and watched the movement of my old commander, who had carried us through everything, and for whose skill and courage I retained my former admiration, despite his treason. But when I thought of what he had been and the despised man he [had become], tears would come, and I could not help it. 7.

Several years later, the French diplomat Charles Maurice de Talleyrand was staying at an inn on the English coast where, he learned, an American general was also staying. Talleyrand introduced himself and, during a rather strained conversation, asked the American if he could supply letters of introduction to his friends in America. Talleyrand recalled:

> He replied, "No," and after a few moments of silence, noticing my surprise, he added, "I am perhaps the only American who cannot give you letters for his own country . . . all the relations I had there are now broken . . . I must never return to the States." He dared not tell me his name. It was General Arnold. I must confess that I felt much pity for him, for which political puritans will perhaps blame me, but with which I do not reproach myself for I witnessed his agony. 8.

The testimony of Talleyrand, Shackford, and Peggy suggest that Arnold was painfully aware of how much he had lost. He could never set foot in his home country and, even after a fairly promising beginning, he did not feel welcome in his adopted country. Continued financial losses pushed him deeper into debt and depression, adding to the awareness of how much property and other assets he had left behind.

By January, 1801, as his symptoms worsened, Benedict seemed to lose the will to live. Desperate to provide for his family, his once sharp business skills were replaced by serious mistakes; sea captains he hired for his last privateers cheated him out of as much as 50,000 pounds. As Peggy commented, "There seems to be a cruel fatality attending all his exertions." 9.

In early June, he experienced several days of extreme agony and occasional delirium, then died "without a groan" on June 14, 1801, in their London home. He was sixty years old.

Peggy Carries On

Newspapers, both in England and America, paid scant attention to Arnold's passing—most providing only a sentence or two. The *European Magazine* reported that "Benedict Arnold had been a person much noticed during the American War." 10.

In the three years following his death, Peggy displayed her extraordinary devotion plus surprising business acumen. She wrote in careful detail to the children, including her stepsons Richard and Henry in Canada, as well as Hannah, describing his death and his love for all of them. Within a few weeks, she followed up with copies of his will and details of the serious debts he had left. In one letter, written at the end of July, she wrote "that there is but little probability of anything being saved to the family out of this wreck. I fear not even the Furniture, as the debts amount to upwards of 5,000 pounds." With determination, energy, and skill, the young widow, barely in her forties, sold off assets, and lived on a tight budget until she could write, in January, 1804, "I have paid Debts to the Amount of 6,000 pounds; . . . to accomplish this, I have been obliged to make a Sacrifice of many articles of comfort which I had ever considered my own. I sold my Furniture, Wine, Etc., and have not reserved even a towel or a tea spoon, that I have not paid for. . . ." 11. She even managed to set aside a sum for the use of "the best Children in the world," if needed.

Through the more than two years required for these tasks, Peggy suffered incredible internal pain, as the cancer destroyed her system. In a January 1804 letter to Edward she commented simply, "My health is but indifferent." She died August 24, 1804, at the age of forty four.

Epilogue

In the beautiful rolling hills of Saratoga National Battlefield Park an unusual monument draws visitors' attention. Carved in Vermont granite, it depicts a cavalry officer's boot strapped to a cannon barrel. On the reverse side, the inscription reads:

> In Memory of
> the "most brilliant soldier" of the
> Continental Army, who was desperately wounded
> on this spot, the sally port of
> BURGOYNE'S "GREAT (WESTERN) REDOUBT"
> 7th October 1777,
> winning for his countrymen
> the Decisive Battle of the
> American Revolution
> and for himself the rank of
> Major General

The monument, erected in 1887 by Civil War General John Watts de Peyster, includes de Peyster's name, but not the name of the "most brilliant soldier."

At the time of the momentous victory at Saratoga, the soldiers who won it would have been most pleased to see that monument on the battlefield with Major General Benedict Arnold's name featured in large letters. [de Peyster missed the fact that Arnold was already a major general in October, 1777.]

Throughout his career, no battlefield leader produced more excitement and loyalty than Arnold. After the treason, of course, America's greatest hero became the vilest of villains. In fact, General Nathanael Greene and other Patriots equated his fall with that of Lucifer as the ultimate fall from grace.

Even after that fall, however, many of his former troops could not forget how special he had been. One of those veterans, Private Samuel Downing, summed him up this way:

> Arnold was a fighting general, and a bloody fellow he was. He didn't care for nothing, he'd ride right in. It was 'Come on boys!' Twasn't 'Go on, boys!' He was a stern looking man but kind to his soldiers. He was as brave a man as ever lived! They didn't treat him right, but he ought to have been true. 1.

There is no way to excuse or forgive Arnold's teachery. No one made the decision for him and he fully deserves being consigned to the Hell reserved for those who betray their country and its ideals.

There remains, however, a feeling of tragedy about his story. The tragedy comes about because of Peggy and the deep passion they shared. The two seemed to go into their treasonous scheme with their eyes wide open. The trouble was that the vision of each was fatally clouded.

Benedict's vision was distorted by his all-consuming love for Peggy, combined with his desire to avenge the humiliations he had suffered over the previous months and years.

Peggy was a more than willing co-conspirator. She appeared to have a romantic image of her role in helping to heal her brooding, broad-shouldered, deeply wounded lover. The war for her was as a 17-year-old fawned over by young British officers, an enemy personified by handsome Captain John Andre, who was also in love with her. Peggy was sure that she had the charms and skills to strike a deal with those men.

In the comfort and warmth of each other's arms, then, everything seemed possible, and Peggy made it seem easy. She even provided the safe messenger and the idea of making West Point the prize.

The failure of their plan cost them dearly. They spent much of their final twenty years in increasing pain and disappointment. Nothing they tried ever seemed to work out. But they still had each other. Although Peggy destroyed most of Benedict's letters, and her family burned most of hers, neither one was heard to complain about their fate. Peggy did go through a long period of anxiety and depression during and after Arnold's capture by the French in the West

Indies, when she didn't know where he was, or even if he was alive. But they kept trying, and supporting each other, until their time ran out.

The tragic flaw in Benedict Arnold—the traitor within—was his willingness to risk everything in one bold act that would achieve fame, wealth, honor—everything he had always wanted. And key to this desperate undertaking was the partnership with the most beautiful, desirable, and intelligent woman in the world.

BIBLIOGRAPHY

Abbott, William. *The Crisis of the Revolution: Being the Story of Arnold and Andre.* (1899) reprinted Harbor Hill Books, 1976.

Andre, John. *Major Andre's Journal,* Tarrytown, NY: Wm. Abbott, 1930. Reprinted by New York Times and Arno Press, 1967.

Arnold, Benedict. *Diary/My Story: Being the memoirs of Benedict Arnold: The Late Major-General in the Continental Army and Brigadier-General in That of His Britannic Majesty.* New York: Charles Scribner's Sons, 1917.

Brandt, Clare. *The Man in the Mirror: A Life of Benedict Arnold.* New York: Random House, 1994.

Chernow, Ron. *Washington: A Life.* New York: Penguin Press, 2010.

Davis, M.L. *Memoirs of Aaron Burr.* New York, 1855, 2 vols., reprinted by New York Times and Arno Press, 1967.

Dell, Pamela. *Benedict Arnold: From Patriot to Traitor.* Minneapolis, MN: Compass Point Books, 2005.

Fitzpatrick, J.C. & Sparks: *Writings of George Washington.* Washington, D.C.: 26 vols. 1931-1938. vols. II-VI, XVIII, XX.

Fort Ticonderoga Museum. *The American Champlain Fleet, 1775-1777.* Ticonderoga, Bulletin of the Fort Ticonderoga Museum, vol. 12, no. 14, Sept., 1968.

Gould, Dudley C. *Benedict Arnold.* Middletown, CT: South Farm Press, 2006.

Ketchum, Richard M. *Saratoga: Turning Point of America's Revolutionary War.* New York: Henry Holt Co., 1997.

King, David C. *The United States and Its People.* Menlo Park, CA: Addison-Wesley Publishing Co., 1993.

Martin, James Kirby. *Benedict Arnold, Revolutionary Hero; An American Warrior Reconsidered.* New York: New York University Press, 1997.

Middlekauff, Robert. *The Glorious Cause: The American Revolution, 1763-1789.* New York: Oxford University Press, 1932, 2005.

Murphy, Jim. *The Real Benedict Arnold.* New York, NY: Clarion Books/ Houghton Mifflin, 2007.

Palmer, Dave R. *George Washington and Benedict Arnold: A Tale of Two Patriots.* Washington, DC: Regency Press, 2006.

Purcell, L. Edward & David F. Burg. *The World Almanac of the American Revolution*. New York: World Almanac, 1992.

Raphael, Ray. "America's Disastrous Invasion of Canada". *American History*, Feb. 2010.

Riedesel, Baroness Friederike von. *Letters and Journals Relating to the War of the American Revolution*, 2 vols. Albany: Joel Munsell. Reprinted by the New York Times and Arno Press, 1968.

Roberts, Cokie. *Founding Mothers: The Women Who Raised Our Nation*. New York: Harper Collins/Perennial, 2005.

Roberts, Kenneth. *March to Quebec: Journal of the Members of the Arnold Expedition*. Garden City, NY: Doubleday & Doran, 1938.

Scheer, George F. & Hugh F. Rankin. *Rebels and Redcoats: The American Revolution Through the Eyes of Those Who Fought It and Lived It*. New York: Da Capo Press, Inc. 1957.

Taylor, J.G. *Some New Light on the Later Life and Last Resting Place of Benedict Arnold And his Wife Margaret Shippen*. London: George White, 1931.

Thacher, James. *Military Journal of the American Revolution*. Hartford, 1862. Reprinted by New York Times and Arno Press, 1967.

Van Doren, Carl. *Secret History of the American Revolution*. New York: Viking, 1941.

Walker, L.B. "Life of Margaret Shippen, Wife of Benedict Arnold." *Pennsylvania Magazine of History and Biography* (PMHB). Vol. XXIV-XXVI (1900-1902).

Wallace, Willard M. *Benedict Arnold, Traitorous Hero: The Life and Fortunes of Benedict Arnold*. New York: Harper & Brothers, 1954.

Wheeler, Richard. *Voices of 1776: The Story of the American Revolution in the Words of Those Who Were There*. New York: Meridian, 1991.

Wilson, Barry K. *Benedict Arnold: A Traitor in Our Midst*. Montreal: McGill-QueensUniversity Press, 2001.

SOURCE NOTES

Chapter One: Early Patterns
1. Wallace, Willard M. *Benedict Arnold, Traitorous Hero*, p. 7.
2. Murphy, Jim. *The Real Benedict Arnold*. P. 19.
3. Wallace, p. 15.
4. Murphy, p. 37.
5. Murphy, p. 45-46.

Chapter Two: Ticonderoga and Crown Point
1. Martin, James Kirby. *Benedict Arnold, Revolutionary Hero; An American Warrior Reconsidered*. p. 68.
2. Wheeler, Richard. *Voices of 1776*. p. 26.
3. Wheeler, p. 23.
4. Martin, p. 82.
5. Martin, p. 100.

Chapter Three: The Wilderness March
1. Wheeler, p. 67.
2. Arnold, Benedict. *Diary/Memoirs*. p. 7.
3. Wallace, p. 65.
4. Washington to Arnold, Sept. 14, 1775, in Fitzpatrick, *Writings of George Washington*, vol. III, p. 491.
5. Van Doren, Carl. *Secret History of the American Revolution*, p. 207.
6. Scheer & Rankin, *Rebels and Redcoats: The American Revolution Through the Eyes of Those Who Fought It and Lived It*, p. 120.
7. Wheeler, p. 71.
8. Roberts, Kenneth, *March to Quebec: Journal of the members of the Arnold Expedition*, p. 337-338.
9. Arnold, p. 58-59.
10. Martin, p. 139.

11. Wheeler, p. 120.
12. Martin, p. 184.
13. Martin, p. 184.
14. Fitzpatrick, IV, p. 148.
15. Fitzpatrick, IV, p. 147.

Chapter Four: Quebec: The Forlorn Hope
1. Wallace, p. 79.
2. Wallace, p. 80.
3. Wheeler, p. 82.
4. Scheer & Rankin, p. 126; from a biography of Morgan, written in 1856.
5. Roberts, K., p. 537-538; Journal of Private George Morison.
6. Scheer & Rankin, p. 128.
7. Ketchum, Richard M. *Saratoga: Turning Point of America's Revolutionary War*, p. 35.
8. Wheeler, p. 115.
9. Wheeler, p. 115.
10. Ketchum, p. 36.
11. Ketchum, p. 36.
12. Martin, p. 203.
13. Martin, p. 244.
14. Martin, p. 184.
15. Martin, p. 233.
16. Murphy, p. 101.

Chapter Five: Meantime . . .
1. King, David C., *The United States and Its People*, p. 107.
2. Fitzpatrick, VI, p. 398-399.

Chapter Six: America's First Naval Hero
1. Martin, p. 248.
2. Van Doren, p. 111.
3. Both quotations in Wallace, p. 107.
4. Wallace, p. 111.

5. Martin, p. 249.
6. Murphy, p. 112.
7. Martin, p. 287.
8. Murphy, p. 113.
9. Martin, p. 288.
10. Murphy, p. 118.
11. Martin, p. 289.
12. Gould, Dudley C. *Benedict Arnold*, p. 16.

Chapter 7: Heroics and Politics

1. Martin, p. 301.
2. Fitzpatrick, VII, p. 251-252.
3. Thacher, James. *Military Journal of the American Revolution*, p. 158.
4. Murphy, p. 121-122.
5. Murphy, p. 117.
6. Thacher, p. 159.
7. Arnold, p. 248.
8. Fitzpatrick, VII, p. 490.
9. Martin, p. 321.
10. Martin, p. 320-321.
11. Murphy, p. 128.
12. Martin, p. 322.
13. Murphy, p. 129.
14. Wallace, p. 125-126.
15. Murphy, p. 134-135.

Chapter Eight: The Battle of Saratoga, Part I

1. Riedesel, Baroness Friederike von. *Letters and Journals Relating to the War of the American Revolution*, vol. I, p. 64.
2. Ketchum, p. 246.
3. Scheer & Rankin, p. 266.
4. Martin, p. 335.
5. Scheer & Rankin, p. 260.
6. Ketchum, p. 336.
7. Arnold, p. 284.
8. Ketchum, p. 344.
9. Ketchum, p. 344.

10. Scheer & Rankin, p. 276.
11. Scheer & Rankin, p. 276.
12. Wilkinson Memoirs, quoted in Scheer & Rankin, p. 279.
13. Wheeler, p. 222.
14. Wheeler, p. 222.
15. Martin, p. 383-384.
16. Ketchum, p. 366.
17. Martin, p. 382.
18. Ketchum, p. 368.
19. Riedesel, p. 214.
20. Murphy, p. 155.

Chapter Nine: The Turning Point, Part II

1. Wheeler, p. 234.
2. Ketchum, p. 375.
3. Wheeler, p. 223.
4. Wheeler, p. 235.
5. Murphy, p. 156.
6. Ketchum, p. 394.
7. Wood, W.J., *Battles of the Revolutionary War, 1775-1784*. Chapel Hill, NC: Algonquin Books, 1990. Quoted in Murphy, p. 162.
8. Murphy, p. 161.
9. Scheer & Rankin, p. 281.
10. Murphy, p. 162.
11. Ketchum, p. 417.
12. Ketchum, p. 411.
13. Both quotes in Ketchum, p. 431.
14. Arnold, *Diary*, p. 256-257.
15. Murphy, p. 166.
16. Martin, p. 407.
17. Scheer & Rankin, p. 410.
18. Martin, p. 403.
19. Martin, p. 383-384.
20. Ketchum, 350-351.
21. Martin, p. 409.

Chapter Ten: Twists and Turns

1. Martin, p. 416.

2. Martin, p. 416.

3. Van Doren, p. 172.

4. Martin, p. 425.

5. Wallace, p. 169.

6. Murphy, p. 176.

7. Murphy, p. 179.

8. Willard Sterne Randall, quoted in Murphy, p. 178.

9. John Richard Allen, quoted in Gould, p. 7.

10. Gould, p. 16.

11. Wallace, p. 172.

12. Walker, P.M.H.B., p. 35-36; 38.

13. Wallace, p. 174.

14. Van Doren, p. 192.

15. Dell, Pamela. *Benedict Arnold: From Patriot to Traitor*, p. 73.

16. Van Doren, p. 193.

17. Van Doren, p. 440.

18. Van Doren, p. 433.

Chapter Eleven: The Tortured Road to Betrayal

1. Wallace, p. 298.

2. Van Doren, p. 189.

3. Van Doren, p. 190.

4. Murphy, p. 196-197. Wallace, p. 186-187.

5. Wallace, p. 190.

6. Wallace, p. 191.

7. Gould, p. 64.

8. Wallace, p. 208.

9. Wallace, p. 216.

10. Murphy, p. 192.

11. Fitzpatrick, XVIII, p. 413.

12. Wallace, p. 215.

13. Gould, p. 50.

14. Gould, p. 57-58.

15. Van Doren, p. 194.

16. Wallace, p. 197.

Chapter Twelve: "Treason of the Blackest Dye"

1. Arnold, p. 263.

2. Wallace, p. 207.

3. Van Doren, p. 314.

4. Van Doren, p. 314.

5. Wallace, p. 228.

6. Andre, *Diary of John Andre*, p. 15.

7. Wheeler, p. 344-345.

8. Murphy, p. 212.

9. Wallace, p. 248.

10. Murphy, p. 212.

11. Murphy, p. 217.

12. Van Doren, p. 347.

13. Wheeler, p. 340.

14. Murphy, p. 218.

15. Murphy, p. 219.

16. Murphy, p. 219.

17. Andre's Journal, p. 108-109.

18. Andre's Journal, p. 110-111.

19. Wallace, p. 269.

20. Wallace, p. 269.

21. Wheeler, p. 352.

22. Arnold to Washington, Oct 4, 1780, in Sparks, *Writings of Washington*, VII, p. 541.

23. Wallace, p. 266.

Chapter Thirteen: The Mystery of Peggy Shippen Arnold

1. Ellet, Elizabeth, *Women of the American Revolution* (NY: Baker and Scribner, 1894, vol. 2, p. 216) quoted in Roberts, C. *Founding Mothers: The Women Who Raised Our Nation*, p. 129.

2. Wallace, p. 195.

3. Martin, p. 3.

4. Van Doren, p. 440.

5. Wallace, p. 196.

6. Wallace, p. 196.

7. Van Doren, p. 182-183.

8. Van Doren, p. 453.

9. Roberts, p. 129.

10. Van Doren, p. 198.

11. *Life of Colonel Pownell Phipps* (privately printed, 1894), in Taylor, S.G., p. 20.

12. Hart, A.B. *The Varick Court of Inquiry to Investigate the Implications of Colonel Richard Varick in the Arnold Treason*, quoted in Van Doren, p. 346.

13. Van Doren, p. 347; Varick testimony.

14. Van Doren, p. 347; Varick testimony.

15. Thacher, p. 471-472.

16. Scheer & Rankin, p. 384.

17. Scheer & Rankin, p. 384.

18. Wallace, p. 254.

19. Van Doren, p. 347.

20. Van Doren, p. 350.

21. Davis, M.L., *Memoirs of Aaron Burr*, vol. 1, p. 219.

22. Walker, P.M.H.B., p. 152-156, from Shippen Family Papers, *Burr Memoirs*.

23. Van Doren, p. 383.

24. Van Doren, p. 194.

25. Wallace, p. 261.

26. Van Doren, p. 387.

27. Wheeler, p. 351.

Chapter Fourteen: *Nil Desperandum*: **The Final Years**

1. Thacher, p. 476.

2. Murphy, p. 225.

3. Wallace, p. 291.

4. P.M.H.B., XXV, p. 168; Wallace, p. 294.

5. P.M.H.B., XXV, p. 456-457.

6. P.M.H.B., XXV, p. 488-489.

7. Wallace, p. 292.

8. Duc de Brogle, *Memoirs of the Prince Talleyrand* (5 vols., NY, 1891). Quoted in Wallace, p. 300.

9. Gould, p. 6.

10. Taylor. *Some New Lights*, p. 59-60.

11. Taylor, p. 63-66.

Epilogue

1. Gould, p. 6.

INDEX

A

B

Currency Act, 9

Y

About the Author

David C. King is an award-winning author of more than seventy books for both adult and young-adult readers. He specializes in American history and biography, but has also written about other cultures, including Rwanda, Kenya, Bosnia, and Taiwan. He has written books in association with American Heritage and with the Smithsonian Institution, as well as shorter pieces for The World Bank, UNICEF, UNESCO, and Lincoln Center. His most recent book, *First People: An Illustrated History of American Indians* (NY: DK Publishing, 2008-2009) has won four national awards.

King and his wife Sharon live in the Berkshire Hills on the edge of New England. They have collaborated on several projects, including a biography of Charles Darwin and an award-winning history of the Statue of Liberty.

MAKING
ALL THINGS
NEW

MAKING ALL THINGS NEW

Fundamentals and Programs of a New Catechesis

The Higher Institute of Catechetics of Nijmegen, Holland

Divine Word Publications
TECHNY, ILLINOIS

NIHIL OBSTAT: William J. Winter, STD
Censor Librorum

IMPRIMATUR: Vincent M. Leonard, DD
Vicar General-Chancellor,
Diocese of Pittsburgh

January 10, 1966

This paperback reprint authorized by Duquesne University Press,
publishers of the original hardcover edition.
First printing: August, 1968

Divine Word Publications is an apostolate of the
Society of the Divine Word serving the people of God
throughout the world by spreading the word.

Printed in the United States of America

TABLE OF CONTENTS

PART TWO

PROGRAMS

PREFACE[1]

RENEWAL, going back to the sources, up-dating, and adapting religious education and ways of worship to modern needs and modern mentality are in evidence everywhere in the Church of today.

Because of the differences among nations it is natural to have a variety of rites and liturgies and it is also natural to meet with various programs in the field of religious education. On that account we have witnessed the development of various forms of catechesis and the production, together with them, of a variety of catechisms.

However, amid that variety there is also a unity that is based on the fundamentals of Christianity. What Christ came to teach and proclaim—His word, His life, His sacrifice, His sacraments, His Church—and God's salvific work as evident throughout the Bible and continued in salvation history, these remain true and continue to speak to us and operate in us. Also human nature with its physical and psychological make-up is largely the same throughout this world, although there are, of course, also considerable cultural differences.

There are numerous elements all men have in common. Hence what has been studied intensely and intelligently, planned carefully and tried prudently in some countries for the necessary renewal of catechesis in the direction of an authentic religious *education* in the faith, rather than *instruction* can be of considerable help in other countries, to parents, teachers and priests who

[1] This preface has been adapted from that of the Dutch editions on which this book is based.

bear a special responsibility in that most important field. In fact, all members of Christ's Body share in His role of priest-teacher through baptism and confirmation, and all in various ways share in the responsibility of fulfilling Christ's will that His teaching and His life should be transmitted to all mankind.

For all these reasons it has seemed useful to make known to American Christians, and particularly to all religious educators (parents, teachers, priests), what has been done and published by the Dutch *Higher Institute of Catechetics.*

Some years ago the bishops of The Netherlands gave the Higher Institute of Catechetics the commission of revising the whole catechetical program of Catholic schools. The first part of this book is an attempt to trace the fundamental lines for such a revision. It is a first attempt. Hence it has still the nature of an inquiry; it is incomplete; it is a tentative effort. What we have suggested must be tested in catechetical practice. That is why we have asked and received the bishops' permission to make our project the basis of an experimentation.

The fundamental lines presented here have results from numerous discussions and studies during the last years. They are meant to throw light on the foundation which underlies the renewal that is presently going on in catechesis. We have done our best to make use of the ideas of renewal that are alive everywhere. This essay, we hope, will thus give food for thought and serve as an inspiration for renewal on a wider front.

There is need for further research, however. We invite religious educators to examine what is here presented and to make their own contribution to the much-needed renewal. This essay, then, must be looked upon as a starting point for a dialogue, a dialogue in which we wish all who are interested in religious education to take part.

The second part of the book contains programs for elementary and secondary schools. In these programs we have tried to apply to concrete practice what we have laid down in the first part of this book.

As we said already, the book is addressed to all who are active in catechesis, hence to priests as well as lay persons. The reading of some parts will not be equally easy for all, but we are convinced that, if we really wish to arrive at a true renewal, it is necessary to engage in more fundamental reflection. We have particularly in mind those whose function is to form catechists or to provide courses for catechetical renewal. It is our hope that our work will be helpful to them and that perhaps it will serve as a starting point for them. We think most specially of all who have a particular responsibility for school catechesis, such as principals and directors of schools.

The present strong tendency toward renewal we are permitted to greet as a manifestation of the Spirit in the Church. The Holy Spirit constantly desires to "change the face of the earth." May He also grant with respect to religious education what we ask for in the Sequence of Pentecost:

> Bend the stubborn heart and will
> Melt the frozen, warm the chill.

And may this work contribute its share to that achievement.

Doing away with the traditional catechism in the school does not mean that Catholics today need to know less about their faith. A solid "catechism" for adults must be prepared, offering them not only religious knowledge but also inspiring them to be Christians now in our time and our concrete situation. Catechesis in the school attuned to children and youths must be a preparation and introduction to this adult level of living the faith.

Nijmegen

W. BLESS, S.J.
Director of the Higher
Institute of Catechetics

13

The American edition of this work has been modified occasionally to eliminate points that are irrelevant to the U.S.A. The epilogue has been added especially to this edition. The book was translated by Reverend Walter Van de Putte, C.S.Sp., carefully revised by the undersigned, and submitted to the directors of the Dutch Higher Institute of Catechetics. The text was also sent to two American religious educators for their comments and criticism.

Duquesne University

HENRY J. KOREN, C.S.Sp.

PART ONE

FUNDAMENTALS

INTRODUCTION

THE renewal of school catechesis is not an isolated event. It is linked with many changes that are taking place in our time, changes in the conditions of life, in ideas and customs. We are witnessing the development of a new sense of life and a new image of man. The whole purpose of the catechetical renewal is to do justice to those tendencies. It follows that we must of necessity endeavor to get some insight into that new image of man if we wish to arrive at a correct understanding of that renewal.

School catechesis is both a proclamation and an education. It is a form of pastoral work that constitutes a part of the whole education given to children and youths. We are fully aware of the fact that we are presently in the midst of a re-orientation in the whole field of education and the whole field of pastoral care. And we must not divorce the renewal of school catechesis from that more general renewal, for the catechetical renewal cannot be rightly understood outside that context.

These considerations have led us to follow this plan in our exposition:

Chapter One is a description of our situation. Starting from a short historical survey, it tries to trace a few characteristics of man's image of himself according to the spirit of our time. At the same time the chapter discusses man's new way of living the faith as it is connected with that new concept of man.

Chapter Two contains theological reflections. It considers the modern view of Revelation as a salvific event and is thus led to a definition of pastoral care. After that, it tries to determine the place and role of catechesis within that pastoral function.

In the two subsequent chapters those ideas are applied to children and youths. Here we discuss questions about their growth to maturity, and questions of education and teaching. Chapter Three deals in a more general way with the development of the young human being and his religious education. Chapter Four pays particular attention to the contribution of the school as a whole to that religious education.

Chapter Five, which is the most extensive, deals with school catechesis in the strict sense. It can now be seen within the larger ensemble in which it has to function. Here we discuss the purpose, content and form of school catechesis, as well as the mentality and spiritual life which are presupposed in the catechist.

These chapters are followed by the Catechetical Programs established for children and youths in the twelve grades of Catholic schools.

CHAPTER ONE

THE SITUATION

THOSE who feel the need for a renewal of religious education are strongly influenced by their realization of the difficulties and the unsatisfactoriness of the methods that have been used until recent times.

On the other hand, it is a fact that suggested changes and renewals are only slowly working their way to the level of practical application. This is due, no doubt, to the heavy and time-consuming burdens of teachers, to the want of material that is ready for use, and similar reasons. There is, however, a more profound reason for the lag in catechetical renewal, namely, the fact that the renewal is not merely a matter of external adjustments, but is much more fundamental. What is required is becoming familiar with a new mentality, a new way of thinking, of seeing things, a new way of life. But before a Christian can confidently try to make these new ways his own, he has to overcome obstacles arising from the past and from the present. In our opinion, a brief historical survey can give him reasons to proceed with confidence. And, at the same time, it can orientate our search for the right approach to contemporary religious education.

1. *The Image of Man and the World in Former Times*

Medieval man lived in a strong, unquestioned and immediate bond of solidarity with men and things. His existence formed a global unity. For instance, he made no sharp distinction between thinking and feeling, between spiritual and earthly powers, between politics and religion, between faith and knowledge. All great events that lay beyond the reach of his power or his understanding, such as lightning, rain, sunlight, earthquakes, conception, birth, sickness, and death, he attributed to a direct intervention of God. This meant to him that God, as it were, actively operated among the created causes at work in the universe. Embedded in a system in which dependence on authority was generally unquestioned, he tried to satisfy his curiosity by listening to authoritative Greco-Roman authors, to Scripture and the tradition of the Church.

The great mass of uneducated people that could neither read nor write relied in all questions upon the authority of the ecclesiastical hierarchy, although even then there were already dissenting voices. This mentality continued to prevail throughout large sections of Western Europe and America till far into the nineteenth century and has not even disappeared entirely in our time.

On the other hand, a new mentality began to appear during the fifteenth century and, in the centuries that followed, it gained an increasing influence upon the whole of human life. The global unity of life and experience that characterized medieval man began to dissolve into distinct realms, and these various fields of values began to become independent. For instance, the fields of politics, economics, the natural sciences, art, education and the social order, became autonomous. Each field began to develop according to its own immanent laws. Man also became divided:

soul and body, intellect and feeling, man and his world were divorced from each other.

As mysteries in all those fields of life were gradually unravelled, there remained increasingly less room for God's activity as man had conceived it in earlier times. In direct ratio to man's depth of penetration into the laws of nature, every new discovery strongly suggested that man had less need of God. The religious dimension gradually lost more and more of its relationship with the ordinary, concrete life of man. Here also a dichotomy occurred: religion became a "private affair," lying outside profane and public life.

As Rogier has expressed it, "the Church became a sort of religious 'reservation' in a dechristianized community; yet her task was precisely to bring God's blessing to the world on the road to eternity." Speaking more concretely, Dondeyne adds:

> If we want to realize how true that is we have only to recall the three great events that are at the origin of our time and that still continue to determine its specific character. These events are 1) the formation of modern science through Descartes and Galileo, and later through Darwin in the field of biology; 2) the dissolution of the Old Regime and the birth of the democratic regimes of freedom; 3) the social breakthrough in the second half of the last century. When we consider these great upheavals, we must confess to our shame that the Catholic community reacted very slowly to them, that it showed hesitancy and fear, and that it had its eyes riveted more on the past than directed to the future.

It is quite evident that this hesitancy of the faithful to take part in those changes has affected the prestige of Christianity; especially because, as we have pointed out, these movements, which still dominate our times, contain authentic moral values. For a long time the Catholic community seems to have had little appreciation of those great moral values. . . . When . . . Christians reveal no openness to the values pursued by their contemporaries, a dialogue between Christianity and the world becomes impossible.[1]

In this way a profound loss of confidence in the Church has developed in the minds of many, perhaps especially in those who are well-educated and creative. This is true not only of unbelievers but also in some respect of believers.

2. Religious Instruction Around 1900

Quite naturally the catechists were children of their own time and their religious instruction reflected the characteristics of that period. They too were influenced by the divorce between soul and body, mind and sentiment, the profane and the sacred. Thought, striving and feeling were dissociated. And so we see that religious instruction as given around 1900 showed the following characteristics. It was:

Intellectualistic. Because the mind was conceived as an isolated faculty, teachers were greatly concerned with presenting Revelation as a system of truths expressed in clear definitions which crystallized centuries of thought.

Moralistic. Beside this very abstract dogmatics, catechists taught an extremely concrete morality that was as clear as the dogmatic sector of instruction and that gave a detailed description of all that was commanded and forbidden. Little account was taken of the growth of the pupil's personal conscience. The clarity of that morality was accompanied by a training of the will that often led to vigorous Christian conduct.

Devotional. The rationalistic and voluntaristic character of that religious instruction left the emotional life isolated; but it was

[1] Albert Dondeyne, *Faith and the World,* Pittsburgh, 2nd impr., 1964, pp. 22–23.

often taken care of separately in a carefully tended life of prayer and in countless devotional practices. These had great warmth but not infrequently only little theological depth, so that there was a danger of yielding to sentimentalism. Prayer and devotion were a source of a strong spirit of faith and of a generous spirit of sacrifice.

Closed. An iron wall separated the life of faith from secular life. If there were any communications they had a moral character. Morality governed good and evil in ordinary life; a good intention gave a value before God—the value of love—to each and every deed. But there were no categories to express in the light of faith the values proper to many other constructive elements of man's life. The Christian often lived in two worlds. The possibility of a dialogue between the churches was still beyond the range of vision.

Many of our readers are no doubt acquainted, through personal experience, with the sort of religious instruction that was given in those days. If we now in a painful way experience these characteristics as shortcomings, it is due in great part to the manifold changes that have taken place in our time. It is certainly not our desire to pronounce judgment on that which the past generations have achieved through great generous efforts. We merely wish to reflect on the tasks that lie before us because of this changing world.

3. *The Present Image of Man and the World*

During the last decades we have been both witnesses and actors in a shift that is as radical as that which took place after the Middle Ages. But the present change is not one that affects only a small upper layer of the population; it confronts everybody.

It is not easy to reveal the structure that underlies the phenomena of our time and point out its essential characteristics, but it is useful for our present purpose to make an attempt. We shall, therefore, try first to indicate two fundamental characteristics and then speak about them in a more concrete fashion.

Unity in Diversity. The autonomy of diverse fields of life established in the preceding period continues to exist. Human life is broken up into many functions. At the same time, there is a growing urge to bridge the gap between those fields, to see connections and to establish bonds between them. We can say, therefore, that there begins to be a unity in diversity.

Dynamism. In the past, concepts, essences, laws, the whole of reality were conceived as strongly static, and unchangeable. Today we have attained to a vision of and an interest in growth; we are attentive to the dynamic aspect of all that exists.

As a result of those changes, man experiences the relations that make him a man in a totally different way than was the case in the past. He experiences primarily their growing unity. If we may permit ourselves to schematize those relations, we could say that man experiences a growing unity, first, in himself between the soul and the body; then with the world that surrounds him and in dialogue with which he develops himself; then with his fellow-men whom he experiences as essentially connected with his own being-a-man; and, finally, with the ground of being in which he is rooted—however one may conceive that ground of being, as a personal God or as an impersonal All. Let us now consider those various relations a little more profoundly.

A Growing Unity in Himself. When man asks himself, "Where do I come from?" the horizon appears to recede. The hypothesis that man sprang from the animal kingdom hundreds of thousands of years ago is gaining in probability. The history of life and the billions of years during which the cosmos has been in existence constitute a phase in the development of man. This history shows him how manifold were the elements from which his unity finally resulted and how profound the relationship is that binds him to the world. Even when he looks at his own life, he is aware that he is a historical being that realizes itself in a succession of moments.

This image of man which has been formed through the collaboration of numerous sciences, makes it increasingly clear to him that man is not composed of loose building-blocks but that every aspect of his being can be understood only in the context of the whole, of the human person. In other words, the human person is placed at the center, as the only gate giving access and understanding to everything that exists. Thought, striving and sentiment are interwoven and rooted in the unity of the person. Man is a besouled bodily being.

If man wishes to inquire about himself, the primary condition and requisite is veracity. This veracity includes both distrust of loose speculations and respect for the unique and irrepeatable aspects of each man. Man, in his search for value and truth, wants to stand on the firm ground of sober, controllable evidence and of his personal experience. The latter implies that in his personal conduct he wants to be guided by what he himself can experience as true.

A Sense of Responsibility for this World. Modern times have witnessed the enormous development of the natural sciences; science has encountered man's labor on a large scale and multiplied its production a thousandfold. Nature, in the sense of the impersonal part of creation, on which medieval man was so greatly dependent, is now seen as raw material upon which man can put the imprint of his talent. Modern man is busy creating a "second" nature, one that refers to him as its creator. With passionate eagerness man labors at the construction of a single world in which all human beings can find a fitting dwelling-place. The possibility of such a world has suggested itself in the enormous technological development of the West. He is increasingly inclined to view the wealth that has thus been produced in the West as an injustice in reference to the poverty that is found elsewhere.

The man of today is not so much aware of being the passive subject of evolution as of being its guiding agent. This brings with it great responsibility, a responsibility which is often terrifying in the literal sense of the word.

Work is seen as constituting an essential element of human life: man is a being who is called to "make himself" in this world and through his busyness with the world. Thanks to mechanization every man can now have leisure time for "re-creating" himself. This "free time" is necessary; not merely so that he may restore his energy after physical or mental exertion, but also in order to avoid the danger of one-sidedness involved in his quest for controlling the world. He must be able to relax and take time off from his quest. He uses this time to admire and enjoy things, to be free for his family and for religion.

It is evident that modern technological culture also has its dark side. It increases the temptation to let oneself be immersed in material comfort; it also forces man to give his full attention to external things and subjects him to ever new impressions. These impressions are thus often registered in a superficial way and, on that account, man does not easily have an opportunity to look for more profound connections or for a synthesis; he is not prompted to ask himself what the meaning of human existence is.

A Sense of Human Fellowship. As a result of mechanization, countless persons have lost contact with their old spiritual and social bonds and certainties. Man becomes more and more isolated; he becomes fundamentally insecure and uncertain in his attitude to life. Many human relations have become businesslike and functional. Society is now something the ordinary man is no longer able to survey and understand. He feels that as a person he hardly counts and experiences a growing loneliness of heart.

Moreover, man now realizes that all life is a living together with others, that human existence, by its very essence, requires personal relations with other men.

From this realization and the above-described insecurity springs the sense of human fellowship. This sense finds expression in countless ways. There is a growing awareness that all men, irrespective of position, economic condition or color, are essentially equal in value, that being-man implies a solidarity which binds Christians and non-Christians together.

All this is not limited merely to our own immediate surroundings. Modern means of travel and communication have so greatly expanded our horizon that man can rightly be called a cosmopolitan, an inhabitant of the world. Closed groups are opening up. Whether we wish it or not, we come in contact with other cultures, philosophies of life and religions.

Nearness to the Ground of Being. Reflection upon the three relations we have described make man conscious of this fourth relation. Our present purpose makes it necessary to treat this relation more extensively and we shall do it immediately from the Christian standpoint. We will see then how much the contemporary life of faith is rooted in our modern image of man.

4. *Christianity in Our Time*

When we try to characterize the kind of Christianity contemporary Christians seek, we may point to the following distinguishing marks:

A Personalistic Christianity. Today, the person is central also in the way the life of faith is experienced and lived, that is, faith is seen as a personal giving of oneself to Jesus Christ.

Formerly there was great stress on knowing doctrines and observing commandments and precepts; now there is greater stress upon a more personal life of relationship with Christ and through Him with the Heavenly Father.

At the same time there is a corresponding shift of emphasis in the life of faith from the previous devotionalistic practices to a life in which the core of faith is experienced as and lived in a more personal responsibility before one's own conscience.

A Biblical-liturgical Christianity. Because man feels it necessary to go to "the heart of the matter," he wants to return to the sources of our Christian existence as these are found in Holy Scripture. Study of the Bible has been helped by the development of modern historical science with its respect for sober facts and love of exactness. We are increasingly aware of the fact that our own human existence is involved in a salvation history of which the Bible speaks to us.

The liturgy wants to renew itself and looks for forms that will enable us to celebrate together this salvific dimension of our life. We desire a liturgy which expresses the new awareness of community and our greater ecclesial consciousness and which, at the same time, fosters that consciousness. We realize that a constant dialogue with the laity is necessary if the renewed liturgy is ever to attain an authentic living form.

An Earthly Christianity. We no longer live in two worlds, the world of faith and the world of ordinary life. For us there is only one world, of which faith gives us its deepest meaning. This implies that all human values have a salvific dimension. Work and leisure have a Christian value; and they stand in the perspective of the universal resurrection of men. From this standpoint Christianity offers inspiration to man's efforts to build a world that is a suitable dwelling-place for all.

An Open Christianity. The world has become one and in it the Church is in a diaspora situation. The non-Catholic Christian and the unbeliever have now become our neighbors. On that account there is a growth of the ecumenical movement and a sense of sorrow at the sight of the division of the churches. At the same time, there is a growing awareness of the solidarity that binds all men together.

Our eyes are opened and enable us to see the irreplaceable contributions that can be made, not only by other Christian churches but also by non-Christian views of life, toward a broader understanding of God's salvific intentions.

A Christianity of Fellowship. The Christian commandment of love is made central. We once more look upon the virtues and the commandments as concrete applications of the *one* commandment of love. At the same time, we are becoming increasingly conscious of the fact that love for our fellow-men does not merely tend to transcend the boundaries, such as social position or color of skin, that encircle various groups, but it wants to break down all walls of separation. All men are essentially equal in value, as children of one common Father.

CHAPTER TWO

THE PASTORAL WORK OF THE CHURCH

In Chapter One we mentioned that in our own time there is a growing unity within the diversity of fields of life. This tendency is active also in the pastoral endeavors of the Church. Her various activities are viewed increasingly in their interrelations. Catechesis is also involved in that development and we are presently in search of a pastoral catechesis.

The "return to the sources" of Christian life and the growth of Church consciousness have led to a renewal of theology which shows more clearly that Revelation has the character of salvation history and, at the same time, sheds new light upon the function of the Church and her pastoral task in that salvation. A better understanding of what salvation history is and of the mystery of the Church also shows the precise role and task of catechesis. We realize better now that catechesis should not be isolated from the other pastoral activities and that it can function properly only within the framework of the Church's total pastoral task.

Until recently this point was given insufficient attention. That is why we wish to say a word first about the pastoral work of the Church in its totality. It is not our intention to deal fully with this work in all its forms; we shall confine ourselves to the aspects that must be taken into consideration in order to determine the place that catechesis occupies in the total pastoral work.

We can look upon pastoral work as a confrontation of man with God's offer of salvation, through which this work aims at awakening and nourishing man's faith. This suggests to us the following plan for the present chapter. In the first part we will examine God's offer of salvation with which pastoral work wants to confront man. God's offer is a divine initiative of love inviting us to enter into communion with Him. The second part considers man's faith as a response to God's invitation; this is what pastoral work aims at. In the third part we will study pastoral work itself more thoroughly, paying particular attention to its various forms and their mutual relations. Here we will see the place and function of catechesis and what connection it has with the rest of pastoral work.

We realize that this threefold division is somewhat artificial, but use it merely for the sake of clarity. In reality God's offer of salvation, our response to it and pastoral work are intermingled and interwoven. Together they constitute God's saving action with respect to man.

1. God's Initiative of Love

Revelation must be seen as the execution of an initiative of God's love toward men. This loving initiative becomes concrete in an "event," a salvific happening: God deals with us and speaks to us for our salvation. We should not look upon Revelation as an isolated, abstract communication of a salvation doctrine, a system of revealed truths. Neither should we see in it only a revelation through words, as God's speaking to us, in the narrow sense of this term. In the past such ideas have sometimes led to a too intellectualistic proclamation of Revelation.

The verbal revelation, as God's speaking to us, is always accompanied by an "event," by God's action. That is why contemporary theology speaks of a "revelation by reality." The verbal revelation is an accompanying explanatory aspect of that revelation by reality; it does not contain the whole reality of salvation. Moreover, the revealed words are incapable of fully expressing that which the whole reality of salvation places among us. Although the verbal revelation is an essential aspect of Revelation, *it is only the integral saving "event," God's action together with His words, that constitutes the whole of God's Revelation.*

This saving "event" takes place in concrete history; for through His actions God enters into human history and, as a consequence, makes history together with men. This is the reason for speaking of Revelation as *salvation history.* We ourselves are taken up in that salvation history; we stand in the midst of it; it is being fulfilled for us, in us, by us and around us. Hence the saving "event" does not consist only in Christ's and the prophets' speaking to us about God's loving initiative, but that "event" is essentially the historical accomplishment of God's loving initiative within the course of mankind's universal history.

That is why Holy Scripture and especially the Church Fathers designate Revelation by the Greek word *"mysterion"*—from which we get the term "mystery" and which is translated into Latin as "sacramentum." It means that God's action to save men is accomplished in an earthly historical visibility. Hence the expressions "Revelation is a sacrament," a *"mysterion,"* and "Revelation is sacramental" mean that it is an earthly historical event in and by which God manifests His salvation to us and accomplishes it in us. This event contains a mystery, a hidden reality, namely, God's plan of salvation for us, which is revealed and accomplished in us precisely in and by that event. By definition, therefore, Christianity as a revealed religion is *the unveiling and making real of God's "reality of salvation" in our earthly world.*

God's saving action does not take place alongside of and apart from profane events, but *in* the universal history of mankind. In the Old Testament, the history of Israel was the *privileged* place of God's salvific action. In the New Testament this place is occupied by the history of the new Israel, the Church. But for those who are able to see things with the eyes of faith, the whole of human history has a salvific dimension. God's action is also realized in profane events but remains unnoticed and anonymous there for those without faith. However, it reaches its apex of visibility and efficacy, its fullness and coronation, in sacred events and finds its authentic interpretation through the preaching of the word which awakens and nourishes our faith precisely by that act of interpretation.

The salvation that God offers us is a communion of love with Himself. God's saving action consists in His communicating Himself ever more fully to all creatures and particularly to us human beings. "I am your God; you are my people." Or, expressing this in other words: God more and more takes up the whole of creation in Himself. This divine self-communication is in the process of fulfillment everywhere and also in us. It is the Godward dynamism of all creatures. This Godward movement is realized gradually in the course of time and thus brings nearer the definitive Kingdom of God, God's dominion over creation and mankind, so "that God may be all in all."

The center and core of that salvation history is the historical "event" called "Jesus Christ," with its preparation in the Old Testament and its unfolding in the Church. Salvation attains its fullness in Christ; God's plan of salvation for men is fully expressed in its actualization in this one man: Revelation is complete; God has fully shown what He intends for all of us. In and through the Church that salvation placed in Christ, that salvific plan already actualized in Him, is progressively realized in all its fullness in all mankind. This is the beginning of the new heaven and the new earth that will be completed at Christ's return.

To show this more clearly, let us briefly survey salvation history in the past and the present.

A. God's Saving Action Under the Old Covenant as an Ascent to Christ

The writers of the Old and New Testaments, and especially the Latin and Greek Fathers, view the Old Testament Revelation as a history in which a continued revelatory activity finds expression. The Old Testament is really a historic drama between a faithful God and the ever unfaithful People of God, the chosen people. In this way the total history of this people is a gradual revelation of who and what God is.

Thus, the story of creation does not intend to give a scientific account of the origin and development of the world. It wishes to show the beginning of salvation history—as a reflection upon Israel's own existence—and wants to stress the fact that Yahweh is the God of Israel, who, with creation, began an initiative of salvation that will show itself henceforth in the course of history. Thus the creation of the world for man, and of man for God, is the start of a salvation history that is directed in a creative way by Yahweh Himself. From creation, history then proceeds through the period of the patriarchs to the time when Israel became a people with, as its high point, the legislation on Mt. Sinai.

The Old Testament Revelation is really a salvation history in which the historical drama of grace or election and sin becomes the "expression apparatus" of Revelation.

The "Covenant"—the term which designates that historical drama of salvation—rests entirely on God's grace. Man has only to respond with fidelity to that Covenant, but he fails over and over again. The reality of God's salvation becomes ever more manifest in the development of the Hebrew history of the Covenant. There is an increasing awareness of man's impotence and a growing religious consciousness of the fact that what is impossible to man left to himself, is possible, yet only through God.

From this there develops a desire for the creation of a "new heart" which God Himself must place in man. The Old Testament Revelation culminates in that desire. And at the same time there is an increasing realization that the election of the people, which is constantly followed by this people's unfaithfulness and its consequent temporary rejection by God, will become a redemptive "rejection" of the Just Man, the "servant of Yahweh," prefigured in the "parable" of Job, the innocent sufferer. The Old Testament Revelation is thus interwoven in the dramatic history of a people. It is the historical symbolization and realization of God's loving initiative and, at the same time, a first prophetic beginning of an eschatological event. In other words, the historical course of the Jewish people is itself the mysterious, sacramental manifestation of God's efficacious, merciful love for His people.

In this salvation history verbal revelation always goes hand in hand with God's activity. The prophets, the authors of the sacred books, the whole community of believers constituted by the Jewish people express in words, under the direction of the Spirit of God, how the vicissitudes of that people have a salvific meaning: they are an immediate expression of God's love and they are, at the same time and for that reason, a foreshadowing of a more profound and more universal saving event in Christ.

We thus reach the second, the completive stage of Revelation.

B. Christ, the Fullness of God's Saving Action

That which had begun in the Old Covenant attained its fundamental fulfillment only "when the fullness of time came" (Gal. 4:4). Here we find the mystery, the "sacrament," that is, the

35

divine gift of salvation in an externally perceptible, tangible form that makes the gift visible in the full sense of the word: God Himself enters history. This is Revelation, *tout court.* The whole New Testament is centered on this one fact of salvation; He has appeared; He has made Himself visible. Revelation is God Himself, living and acting, who has appeared in the shape of man. God who of Himself transcends all worldly events—"In the beginning was the Word" (John 1:1–3)—now is, at the same time, "one-who-was-made"—"the Word was made flesh and has dwelt among us" (John 1:14).

"He who is" has now become a part of history, a tangible reality in our earthly reality. Here, then, we face a particular human life, a man who appeared in this world at a definite point of time and, like all other men, finally disappeared. Here a divine reality enters and penetrates into the web of earthly events. This is the whole meaning of the prologue of St. John's Gospel: the eternal life that was in the Father has manifested itself in Jesus Christ. St. Paul says explicitly: "Obviously great is the mystery of godliness [i.e., Christ] who was manifested in the flesh" (1 Tim. 3:16).

Revelation is therefore the manifestation of Christ, His being, His word, His actions. St. Irenaeus sums it up, saying "The Word was made flesh in order that in the flesh of our Lord the light of the Father should come to us."[1]

The Incarnation, the whole life of the man Jesus, His sufferings, death and resurrection place the transcendent mystery of God as His salvific action in the realm of temporal and earthly visibility. The Word of God became flesh: His earthly life runs its course in words and deeds that spring from His human existence. His speech makes His action fully human, conditioned by circumstances of place and time. And, at the same time, He stands above time; His verbal revelation indicates the divine dimension of His activity. What Christ does and says speaks to

[1] *Adv. Haereses,* IV, 20, 2.

us of the divine: His word makes explicit and unfolds the very mystery of His manifestation. The divine has become "our" reality in the manifestation of the man Jesus and has thus revealed itself under visible signs in our earthly world. This reality of Revelation we call the "Mystery of Christ."

This Mystery of Christ is the full Revelation of the secret of salvation that remained hidden for centuries and has now been unveiled (Rom. 16:25–26). This secret of salvation is the divine decree, God's plan of salvation for men, His initiative of love. It stands fully unveiled in the "event" of Christ. God reveals His plan of salvation for all men by realizing it in the one man, Jesus of Nazareth. In the things that happen to this one man, God's plan for all of us becomes fully visible. The concrete history of Christ's life, of his death and resurrection, constitutes God's salvific action for that man; but it is, at the same time, the "Book" in which God has written a full account of His plan for us.

What took place in Jesus of Nazareth means more than the unveiling of that plan of salvation; it also lays down the foundation of its realization in us. For Jesus has saved us by accepting the salvific action of the Father in His regard, that is, He has made it possible for all of us to obtain access to communion with the Father. For the communion of the man Jesus with the Father is rooted in His communion with the Father as God the Son. Jesus is thus the only man who could open that gate for us. It is only through Him, who is always with the Father, that we have access to the Father. That is why Jesus not only makes the salvation of communion-with-God possible for us, but it is also through Him that the Father fulfills that salvation in us—according to the measure of our acceptance. God's plan of salvation aims at bringing the universe and mankind together under one Head in Christ (Eph. 1:1), and thus leading us to a community of love with Himself.

The Son in God's eternal Now turns to the Father in the Holy

37

Spirit's dynamism of love. But in His life history as man Christ manifests and achieves that communion with the Father in an earthly visibility. This He does in the power of the Holy Spirit. He thus carries mankind and the whole of creation as His Body, along in His ascent to the Father through the dynamism of the Holy Spirit.

Our participation in that ascent of Christ is brought about by the Holy Spirit who was given us through the event of Redemption. It is in this that God's plan of salvation is realized in us. This participation is still in the process of gradual achievement in the Church until the final fulfillment comes at Christ's return.

From all this, it follows that Revelation was closed with the visible departure of Christ from this world. For God's plan of salvation for all of us became perfectly manifest in its realization in Jesus. Hence the verbal revelation, as a constitutive element of the total sacramental Revelation, is also closed, though it still continued, because of its character as verbal revelation, in the preaching of Jesus' official witnesses until the death of the last apostle. The two statements, "Salvation is accomplished" and "Revelation is completed or closed" mean the same thing because Revelation is precisely accomplished in the salvation event itself.

In the light of Christ's fullness of Revelation, the Old Testament Revelation itself becomes a part of Christian Revelation. Hence Revelation essentially means that the divine realities become visible in Christ; it is "fulfilled" in the historical Christ; it is "begun" in the Old Testament. That is why the New Testament calls Christ the "author and finisher of the faith" (Heb. 12:2). In other words, it is He who begins and closes Revelation; He is Revelation pure and simple.

We see then that the Word-made-flesh is the core of the event of salvation: it is the personal contact in Christ between humanity and the Godhead. This contact fills all reality with God's saving action, for we must not conceive Christ's humanity as being apart from the rest of mankind and other creatures. The whole of created reality stands in contact with that humanity of Christ and thus undergoes also the influence of its divinization. Christ's influence, then, extends to all creation, to all men and to all fields of human life. In other words, through Christ's salvation, all creatures and the whole of human existence are a divine offer of salvation: God meets us with His salvation in and through everything that makes up our existence. Or, again, Christ's salvation, His ascent to the Father, makes our whole life and everything it contains a possible ascent to the Father, a possible participation in His ascent.

This possibility becomes a reality through the "Yes" of our faith; thereby the offer of salvation is changed into a reality of salvation. But man's "Yes," his active acceptance of God's offer of salvation in Christ, is itself also a saving operation of God because our own inmost freedom is also encompassed by God's almighty power. For it is in the power of the Holy Spirit that we achieve that surrender of faith and thus actually participate in Christ's ascent to the Father.

Thus we come to the third phase, the unfolding of Revelation —after it had been closed in Christ—in the mystery of the Church.

C. The Sacramental Church as Mystery of God's Saving Action Among Us

The salvation God offers to men is a divine initiative that is realized in a historical time. That is why Holy Scripture and the Fathers speak of an "ordinance of salvation," of an "economy of salvation." This means that God Himself, in an earthly and historical visibility, continues among us the salvation that was once fully given, as a progressive manifestation of God.

The first Christians clearly realized that the salvation offered at this moment to man was based on fundamental historical facts of salvation: "He suffered under Pontius Pilate." If we wish to get the right approach to the Mystery which is the Church, it is most important that we start from the fact that Revelation is fulfilled, that salvation is accomplished. Holy Scripture insists as much as six times upon the impossibility of repeating the "event" of Christ: "Once and for all" we are saved; "He dies no more"; "Christ was offered once to take away the sins of many" (1 Pet. 3.18; Rom. 6:10; Heb. 7:27; 9:27; 9:28). The constitutive, decisive phase of Revelation is over.

But this does not mean that, with respect to modern man, every present or future moment of time does not contain a true opportunity for salvation or an occasion for loss of salvation. On the contrary, precisely that already accomplished salvation makes every moment of time *now* a moment of salvation, in which something divine manifests itself and a perspective is opened toward the eschatological event.

There is, nevertheless, something that is proper and particular to the period of time in which we are living, between the closing of Revelation and the *parousia,* the second coming of Christ; there is something proper that precisely finds expression in the *sacramentality* of the Church. It is in and by it that the salvation that was achieved comes to us.

Hence the question concerning us here is: How are we, people of the twentieth century, presently confronted with a reality of salvation that came about in the past?

Jesus Christ, the fullness of Revelation, is unthinkable without His Church, without the People of God assembled by Him. Called by God to be the representative of fallen mankind, the Christ had to acquire for Himself, in and by His human life, this fallen race as a saved People of God.

This means that Christ by His death, as sorrowful fruit of His sacrifice, actually accomplished the redemption of fallen mankind. He actually acquired for Himself His Church, the saved human community: "Christ dies in order that in His death the Church might be born."[2] And this is done in such a way that Christ is Himself the eschatological community of salvation, the Church, in His accepted sacrifice, in His glorified body. The "body of the Lord" is the Church. In Himself, the glorified Christ is at the same time "head and members."

The Church is the earthly manifestation in historical visibility of that reality. She is the earthly visibility of the Heavenly Lord. This means therefore that she is, in a mystical way, "head and members."

The sacramental way of making Christ the Lord visible as the Head of the People of God is achieved in the hierarchical structure of the Church. In this respect the Lord stands, in His representatives, in a state of serving sovereignty with respect to the faithful. But, on the other hand, the whole community of the faithful, the People of God is the earthly sacramental way of making Christ visible in His capacity as "representative People of God." In this regard the faithful themselves are the Church. Thus the Church as a whole—in her apostolic function and community of faith—is the "sacramental or mystical Christ." In and by the visible activity of His Church, the Lord finishes, by sending the Holy Spirit, the salvation of which He as historical Messiah has laid the foundations. Of this finishing activity of the Lord, the Church is the visible presence in our world. She is the fullness of Christ; being herself filled with Christ, she fills all her members.

The Church is the prolongation, the permanent presence of Christ's task and function in salvation history. She is His presence in history.

The heavenly body of Christ is the permanent, eternal sign of our salvation. For the time being, until the *parousia,* that heavenly sign still remains invisible for us, human beings dwell-

[2] St. Augustine, on John's Gospel, Tr. 9, no. 10, P.L. 35, col. 1464.

ing upon earth. That is why our Lord gave to that permanent sign of our salvation an earthly visibility in the earthly, visible Church. It is precisely through this that salvation is made manifest as being *for us* and as *offered to us*. The visible Church is sacramentally and therefore only inadequately "the body of the Lord," or salvation as visibly directed to men.

The Church, then, is here on earth "the sign that is raised among the nations," the great salvific sign of the Redemption that is accomplished for us and of Christ's final victory, she is a sign of victory but one that is wrapped in the earthly form of weakness. Especially in this respect do St. Paul's words about all Christian life apply to the Church: "God's power is accomplished in weakness."

The Church, as the earthly representation of the heavenly sign of salvation, also bears salvation within herself. She represents Christ and is, as such, "the daughter of God the Father." Endowed with power on Pentecost, she is animated and moved by the Spirit of Christ and thus participates in His dynamism of love toward the Father. In her is actualized the supreme worship of the Father in a visible filial religiousness.

Passing through a diversity of contrarieties, misfortunes, infidelities, crises and darkness, the community of faith which is the Church arrives at a more mature response to the divine invitation. The bonds that connect her with concrete circumstances of persons, place and time must therefore also be seen as the full incarnation of the Church as the sign of the Lord. She embraces all human values and needs them.

Revelation, as God's realization of man's salvation, reached its fullness in Jesus Christ, and it is transmitted in the Church in a living way through the operation of the Holy Spirit. This living tradition is not a new revelation, but it brings to us the Revelation that was completed and closed.

The Christ "event," the mystery of Christ, is prolonged in the Church by the operation of the Holy Spirit to enable all to enter into the salvation and the glory that was revealed and foreshadowed by Christ in His resurrection.

Hence also the preaching of the word is not a new verbal revelation, but an announcement of the word, a guide which, explaining and detailing, points to a sacramental Church in which we can enter with faith, hope and love in order to come into contact with Christ. The act of faith, then, is directed to Christ's presence among us, namely, in the sacramental Church.

Thus, the question, "How are we *now* confronted with the reality of salvation that was established in the past?" receives an answer: "By and in the Church this confrontation takes place."

When we say that tradition brings us the "closed" Revelation, this expression must be understood in the sense that the history of the Church at the same time unfolds that closed Revelation. The fullness that is contained in the mystery of Christ is gradually disclosed in the Church by the Holy Spirit. The salvation that was given us in the historical "event" of Jesus of Nazareth, unfolds in all its inexhaustible riches in the Church. Every new human life unfolds a new facet of that event. On that account we can speak of a growth in the Church, a growth that springs from the Revelation that was closed in Christ. For this Revelation is understood in ever new ways; and, in the ever varying ways of making Christ's mystery present in each new man, mankind, through the Church, grows toward its final fulfillment. In that whole development the Church is led infallibly by the Holy Spirit who animates her.

It follows that we must look upon the Church's proclamation of the word as a guide that wishes to give meaning to the life of modern man in the concrete modern situation and to see his existence as God's saving action. This the Church does by witnessing to the historical event of Christ; and she confronts our own life with that of Christ, with His actions and words, and thus makes us see God's salvific plan for us in our own day. In this way she awakens and nourishes faith in us, through which God's invitation to salvation becomes fruitful in us. That is why she constantly recalls what happened to Jesus of Nazareth, for Christ's life, death and resurrection give meaning, significance and value to our own life with all its vicissitudes.

Our whole life, like the life of Christ, is thus realized in us by God as salvation, according to the measure of our acceptance. Our own life, too, is an ascent to the Father, but it is this only because and insofar as it is one with that of Christ. That is why God's saving activity in our whole existence should not be divorced from the liturgy and its sacraments: they actively bind us to Christ and lead God's salvific action in us to its apex, its crowning and fulfillment.

D. God's Signs of Salvation in Our Time

We can, therefore, distinguish the following aspects in God's offer of salvation. They should not be separated from one another and it is only when they are taken together that they constitute God's integral invitation. In view of the sacramental structure of the Church, we can describe those aspects as signs in which God's saving action is accomplished in man.

1. All creatures and the whole of human existence are a sign of God's saving action. For, on the basis of the sacramental structure of Revelation, by which the divine manifests itself in shapes and forms of our earthly reality, we believe that earthly realities are visible, tangible and audible manifestations of divine realities of salvation.

All creatures and the whole existence of man are God's offer of salvation, a divine invitation to man to live Christ's mystery in his relations with God, with his fellow-men and with the world.

2. The proclamation of the word is that by which the mystery of Christ is made known by the Church: the mystery of Christ as it has been deposited in the New Testament under the inspiration of the Holy Spirit and was prefigured and prepared in the Old Testament.

This proclamation of the word constantly throws light upon the whole of human life in its salvific dimension.

3. The sacraments are signs of salvation given immediately by Christ. Through them, He manifests Himself in forms that belong to our human, earthly reality, and through them He enters into the seven most important events of life that encompass the general situation of man.

The sacraments are life's seven moments of salvation; in them God manifests Himself through Christ in forms that belong to our earthly reality. God Himself thus enters really into the human situation and thus renews the face of the earth. The seven sacraments are God's success where man would always fail in the fundamental tasks of his life. Therefore, the sacraments are a "mystery" in the full sense of the word, that is, efficacious means of making visible a divine reality of salvation in and by the sacramental celebration of the mysteries of Christ's life.

This shows that they are the high points of God's accomplishment of salvation in human existence, for they embrace the whole human situation. They are high points of both the offer and the acceptance of salvation with respect to visibility and efficacy.

But here again those sacramental signs must be clarified and explained by the proclamation of the word in the light of Christ's mysteries. That is why the proclamation of the word has a proper place within the sacramental celebration of those mysteries.

We see, then, that all the aspects we are able to distinguish in the whole Christian world of signs compenetrate and always accompany one another.

2. Faith as Man's Response to God's Saving Action

In those signs, God meets us with His salvation. This divine offer of salvation becomes fruitful in man's faith; in his response by faith that divine offer becomes actual salvation for man, the possibility of salvation becomes a reality. This, however, does not mean that God acts on one side and that man, on his side, can by his own power respond to it. Man's response is also wholly God's saving action which pervades the inmost depth of our human freedom.

God has gifted us with a new heart that enables us to give a consenting response to that divine initiative of love. Here God meets man, not by forcing or overpowering him, but by inviting him. It is with freedom that we are asked to respond to His call. Christ's salvation and revelation are not forced upon us; they are offered to us.

Man, however, does not give his response as an individual but as taken up into the community, as a member of the People of God. The People of God gives that consenting response to the whole of the divine event of salvation by *believing.* The term "to believe" we take here in the biblical sense, as including hope and love. It therefore means much more than merely accepting the verbal revelation, for it implies a loving surrender to the Person of Christ, to His Word and to the salvation that He has already given, with everything that this loving surrender involves for our life as a whole.

The act of faith is thus directed to a being present of Christ's reality of Revelation in our own day, that is, in the sacramental Church. In and by that reality, the encounter takes place with Christ's reality and in Him with the triune God. Hence the Church is for us a breakthrough and a visible manifestation of a divine reality which we attain sacramentally in grace.

The Church, the sacraments, and the believers' life of faith, thanks especially to the sacraments, contain the reality of Revelation as an ever-actual reality. Hence the historical course continues after the closing of revelation; but in that historical course of the Church, it is always Christ's mystery that reveals itself in our time and in shapes and forms that belong to our own earthly reality. Thus even today we can come into personal contact with the divine by our faith in the sacramental mystery of Christ, as it is actually made present in signs.

This life of faith, in the course of centuries, takes on the way of life and thinking proper to the diverse forms of culture. The Church, since the Ascension, is on her way, through the centuries, to the final and completed revelation of the Lord in this world. That is why the way the Church views her saving role in this world is also determined by the cultures of particular times and peoples. Here we touch upon the historicity of the Church.

The first great adventure of the Church was undoubtedly her encounter with Greco-Roman culture. At that time, for instance, she expressed her living experience of the sacraments in the language of the mystery religions of that time. In the Middle Ages she expressed it anew in the Aristotelian doctrine of matter and form. This shows that the Church's proclamation and religious experience of the faith bears the stamp of particular times. In our day we see how the Church is freeing herself from the time-bound forms that were connected with the Counter Reformation; at that time she was chiefly motivated by her aversion to the Reformation and, more broadly, to the life and thought of the world in general.

As the Church reflects upon and speaks about herself, she becomes ever more aware of her own essence. A one-sided vision of the Church as a hierarchical structure is now gradually making room for a more complete view of the whole People of God. And in her attitude toward the world the Church is gradually moving from "closedness" to a state of openness. In the religious self-experience of her own mystery the Church today, in addition to her sacramental celebrations, assigns much importance to the word.

Moving away from a static concept of salvation, the Church gives increasing recognition to the process of growth and dynamics. This new attitude manifests itself, for example, in questions concerning the concept of sin, the valid and the sacramental marriage, and the recognition of authentic religiousness in non-Christian religions.

We saw already that the Church is the Lord Himself in earthly visible form but that she is the visible sign of the Lord in the form of earthly weakness. The Lord asks us to accept also that earthliness, that weakness, in our faith in Him. We must break through our human smallness and narrowness to attain the freedom of the children of God. If man wishes to accept freely the divine offer of salvation that extends to the whole of human existence, his response must likewise embrace that whole existence. To believe means to accept the change of life that is offered by God and to remain faithful to it through life and death. Such an attitude of life demands an ever repeated "conversion," a breaking through our human cloisteredness and, as a consequence, an ever-growing faith. In the whole of life and in every new situation of life there lies a divine *offer* that demands a *response* from us and *in which we can experience God's nearness.* This we shall develop more fully in Chapter Five.

It is the pastoral work of the Church that awakens and nourishes man's belief as his response to God's salvific action.

3. The Pastoral Work of the Church

In the first section of this chapter we considered God's offer of salvation and described the signs in which this invitation is manifested to men. In the second section we spoke about faith as that in which this offer becomes fruitful in man, changing it into actual salvation by man's acceptance.

However, if man wishes to come to the faith and grow in it,

he must come into contact with the divine invitation; he must be confronted with it in the concrete situation in which he lives. Now to confront man with God's saving invitation is the task of the Church in her pastoral activity. Since it is a task proper to her as Church, in it, therefore, she is guided by the Holy Spirit.

All believers ·confront their fellow-men with God's saving action. For by their words and deeds they give more or less express testimony of their faith. Hence pastoral work is an *activity of the whole People of God.*

On the basis of these considerations we can define the Church's pastoral work in the following words: *The pastoral work of the Church is the endeavor of the People of God, under the direction of the Holy Spirit, to confront men in their concrete situation with God's offer of salvation in Christ, and thereby to awaken and foster their faith.*

As this confrontation takes place in diverse ways, we can thus distinguish various aspects in the Church's pastoral work. They are the following.

A. *"Incarnated Pastoral Work"*

By this term we mean the witness of an authentic life of faith that is incarnated in the whole of human existence. In this form of pastoral work we can discern the following elements:

1. The spiritual inspiration that comes from believers because, by their authentically Christian lives, they are living witnesses to the Lord and a sign for others.

This witness implies giving a Christian meaning to their whole existence, to their family life, their work, recreation, joy, suffering and death, especially on the basis of an active participation in the Church's liturgical life and great willingness in hearing the word of God.

2. A sense of responsibility, too, belongs to an authentically Christian life. In the measure of his possibilities, i.e., his education, abilities and position in social life, the believer considers himself responsible for the creation of a community that is worthy of man on the level of both family and society at large. He wants the Christian view of man and the world to be constantly more embodied in society. Priests, religious and lay people have their own particular tasks in this respect.

3. This express engagement for the benefit of others means, in many cases, that guidance and aid is given to lead those for whom we are responsible to an authentically Christian life.

This responsibility resides primarily in the whole community of the People of God. However, within this community we can distinguish various structures in which particular men have a responsibility for others. Thus parents have such a responsibility with respect to their children, teachers toward their pupils, priests toward the faithful, bishops toward priests and the faithful. Here, then, there is question of a greater or lesser participation in Christ's pastoral function that continues to live in the Church. That is why the authority on which we base ourselves in guiding and accompanying others has the character of a service: "I did not come to be ministered to but to minister."

This "incarnation" of pastoral work safeguards the preaching of the word against the danger of becoming abstract and degenerating into mere doctrine, and it prevents the liturgy from becoming ritualism and magic.

B. Liturgical Pastoral Work

The Church of God when celebrating Christ's mystery, as she does in the sacraments and her whole worship, honors God in the most perfect manner. At the same time, God's salvation is made present among us in a visible and most efficacious way.

Liturgical pastoral work also has the task of educating the

faithful and guiding them into an active participation in the celebration of the sacred mysteries, for instance, through liturgical initiation. It aims at making the faithful realize that they constitute a community in Christ, being assembled around Him in liturgical celebrations, particularly in the celebration of the Eucharist, which is the supreme sign of our common union in Him as well as a new source of divine life. The liturgy lights up in a very special manner the transcendence and mystery characteristic of Christian life and of the proclamation of the word.

C. Catechetical Pastoral Work

This form of pastoral work encompasses not only catechesis proper, but also the task of awakening the right attitude for the reception of that catechesis. By catechesis we mean enlightening human existence as God's saving activity, by giving witness to Christ's mystery in the form of the proclamation of the word, for the purpose of awakening and fostering the faith and stimulating men to live a real life of faith. Catechesis is the proclamation of the word of God, the dissemination of the Glad Tidings: "Go, therefore, and make disciples of all nations" (Mt. 28:29); "He who hears you hears me" (Lk. 10:16); "Faith then depends on hearing and hearing on the word of Christ." Or, as another translation expresses it: "Faith arises by preaching, and preaching takes place as a commission given by Christ" (Rom. 10:17).

However, catechesis will have that dynamic power only on condition that, on the one hand, it announces the Glad Tidings as giving meaning to the whole of human existence as it is concretely lived and, on the other hand, that it is truly a witnessing and not an abstract information about Christian "doctrine." The catechist, the herald of faith, must speak "in the power of the Holy Spirit."

This proclamation of the word frees the other pastoral ac-

51

tivities of the Church from their ambivalence and vagueness, and serves as a norm manifesting their meaning.

Precisely because catechesis throws the light of God's salvific activity on human existence, it needs the support of another element of catechetical pastoral work, namely, that of disposing people for a right listening to and understanding of the Glad Tidings. Hence it is not directly a question of an explicit and express proclamation of God's word; it is much more a calling forth of fundamental questions regarding the meaning of man's life in general. This other element of catechetical pastoral work is concerned with those existential aspects of the formation of personality and of human existence that consciously or unconsciously influence the growth to maturity or self-determination in surrender to God's love. They are essential aspects of the human situation, which spontaneously lead to questions that catechesis can answer only on the basis of Revelation.

These questions, ultimately, are all different expressions of man's need of salvation, a need that, of course, can be answered effectively by God alone. We can mention as examples the questions about human freedom, fellowship, responsibility and expectation.

In this way a preparation is made for a fully human encounter with Revelation. However, we must not conceive that creation of a proper disposition as a phase that precedes the actual catechesis. It is rather a permanent substratum of the whole catechesis from early childhood to maturity. The themes as well as the methods will vary according to the psychological development and the social situation of those who are to be catechized. With respect to children those fundamental human questions will be primarily implicit, but, when the catechesis is directed to older and mature people, they will be brought up explicitly. That permanent substratum makes catechesis to be true to life, "incarnate."

Wherever the Church appears—and, after all, she appears only in living human beings, in priests and in lay people—she must be a sign that is itself full of the reality it signifies; otherwise she will lose the power to attract men. It is precisely this element of personal involvement that will make the preaching of the truths of faith and the administration of the sacraments have that originality by which the word of God will touch men. The witness must speak from the heart, from his deepest conviction.

This personal involvement in Christ's mystery also confers on the whole of man's existence its Christian authenticity. Thus all forms of pastoral work become a showing forth and a passing on of one's own deepest conviction.

D. *Mutual Relations of the Various Aspects*

The various aspects belonging to the Church's pastoral work cannot be separated from one another. They are so closely related that it is impossible to leave out one aspect without doing harm to the organic whole of pastoral work.

It is in the liturgy that we find the strongest expression of the fact that Christ is engaged in saving men. That is why catechesis needs a living liturgy to which it can direct attention and in which it must culminate. Otherwise there is real danger that catechesis will not do much more than give a historical account of Christ's life.

The liturgy needs the proclamation of the word to become clear in the light of the historical mysteries of Christ and also to show its relevancy for man's ordinary daily life. Without the proclamation of the word, the liturgy remains incomprehensible; it becomes a stranger to life and will easily degenerate into ritualism and magic.

Both catechesis and the liturgy help to throw light upon earthly reality in its salvific dimension. And all other forms of pastoral work likewise either are based on a constant proclamation of the word and liturgical life or make use of them.

All this clearly shows the central place that catechesis has in the totality of pastoral work.

The Church's pastoral task does not consist merely in awakening faith and making it grow, but it also implies helping this faith find a proper form in our modern time. For, it must be granted, we think, that all too often today the life of faith is a stranger to the reality of human existence. What we need is a proclamation of the faith that throws light upon the whole of human existence. The proclamation of the integral mystery of Christ in the Church must give meaning and significance to the whole life of man in our time. It must give meaning to his joys and sorrows, his work and leisure, his success and failure, his hope of salvation and liberation, and to his death.

In order to achieve this, one of the things needed is that the catechetical task of the Church be incorporated into the other pastoral activities. We shall make an effort to do this in the way the renewal of school catechesis in its diverse forms will be outlined in this work.

CHAPTER THREE

PASTORAL WORK WITH
CHILDREN AND YOUTHS

THE Church's pastoral work concerns all the faithful. Men differ greatly in virtue of their disposition, circumstances, vicissitudes of life and personal response to God's offer of salvation. Hence different approaches and adjustments are a necessity in pastoral work. It stands to reason that particular pastoral requirements correspond to the various stages of life which the faithful pass through. Here we shall deal in greater detail with the period of life which begins when, at the age of six or seven, the boy or girl is ready for school and which lasts till about the twelfth year. We refer to human beings in this period of life as *children*.

Our attention also extends to the period that lies between the years of this "childhood" and the attainment of maturity. All who are in the latter period we here designate as *youths*. The present chapter deals with the pastoral work for children and youths.

Because children and youths are immature, they naturally need the support and guidance of the adults who are responsible for them. This need is present in all elements of their existence but varies in duration and intensity. Since pastoral work with children and youths is characterized by the fact that it takes place in an educational framework, this pastoral work is also called "religious education" or "education in living the faith."

1. The Responsibility of the Adult Members of the People of God

In Chapter Two we said that Revelation is not forced upon but *offered* to men. The God of love respects man's freedom. We also stressed the fact that, although God offers salvation to all men, He nevertheless directs His invitation within the compass of the Church which is the People of God. How does that invitation come to those who grow up as children of Catholic parents? The People of God, in its leaders and its adult members, is responsible for the task of letting the children and youths who live in its midst share in the salvation offered by God. Brought into the world through the procreative love of their parents in a Christian marriage, and raised on the basis of that love, the children come in contact with the mystery of salvation. The parents, to the extent that it is dependent upon them, desire that the fruit of their Christian love should share in salvation. For this reason they present the child for baptism, by which it is visibly incorporated into the People of God. This step is a Christian act of love of neighbor, for in it they enable others to share in the good they themselves possess. Through this step, as well as by the many actions that are its prolongation and consequence, the child and the youth are *offered* salvation—it is not imposed upon them. All these actions together are God's salvific gift as it is made present in and by the Church and which appeals to man to give himself to His divine love.

Children and youths are attended upon and sustained in order to make it possible for them, as they grow up, to give their *own* fully human response to God's appeal and accept what is offered them for their salvation. The possibility that some might reject the offer belongs to the tragic dimension of human life to which every man is exposed. This possibility must therefore also be accepted as a risk in the religious upbringing of young persons. In this way, then, the growth to maturity of Christian life acquires the character of a choice.

2. Rendering the Unquestioningly Accepted Faith More Profound

When youths feel the need of opposing their elders to some extent and of freeing themselves from their control in order to gain autonomy, the values of life which they had accepted without question now become a subject for argument in their relations with their educators. There exists then an opportunity for the youth to let his growing freedom mature into a more conscious acceptance. This opportunity is lost if he is at this moment subjected to pressure; on the other hand, it would not even arise if he had not previously been given the experience of living these values in an unquestioning way. A further and a serious complication is the fact that the values of life always and everywhere take on a concrete form and that the youth is faced with the task of preserving these values while, at the same time, perhaps he may have to help in giving them a new concrete form.

What is said here in general about values is particularly true of religion, which occupies such a unique place among those values. Just as God ceaselessly offers His love to man, even when he turns away from that divine invitation because of a misunderstood desire for freedom, so must the People of God prepare and continue to help those who are not yet mature so that they themselves may find salvation.

Education in living the faith takes place within the whole of education. In fact, for a Christian, this authentic religious education is the heart, the core, of the whole of education. The possibilities, difficulties and demands of education are the theme of the special science of pedagogy. In no way must we neglect the insights that have been acquired by and systematized in that

57

science, but we must transpose them to the very distinctive frame of the life of faith.

Briefly stated, this frame comes down to the following: In the Church, both educators and their pupils—by which term we here mean all who receive an education—as believers, are orientated to the encounter with the Lord, who comes to meet them as Savior and, through life and death, leads them to the Father. Educating children and youths in a living faith has to bring them into contact with Christ's invitation to follow Him, within the compass of the People of God, through life and death. They must be given the best opportunities to become acquainted with that invitation; they must be sustained so that they will give their own response to it with increasing awareness. Since it is a matter of an engagement of the whole person, authentic religious education must help children and youths to discover a Christian attitude of life and live accordingly.

Education in living the faith, like all education, aims at maturity. Christian maturity, which is the object of authentic religious education, includes taking a personal stand leading to their giving themselves to this God of love. This personal decision is sustained by and culminates in the act of faith by which one commits oneself to Christ in the Church, and opts for a scale of values in which the Christian values are supreme. The giving of oneself that is already contained in this commitment finds expression especially in the acknowledgment of one's sinfulness and need of salvation and in the acceptance of Christ as the Lord.

While education in a living faith confronts children and youths with sinfulness, salvation and grace, it is itself involved in these. Religious educators may, and in a certain sense must, believe (since it is concerned with the truth) that God's Spirit works in them, in their pupils and the world. Yet they must also take into account the imperfection and sinfulness that exists in themselves, in their pupils and in the world. Reflection upon authentic religious education would become unrealistic and hence useless if it failed to acknowledge that, inevitably, this education is only partially effective. For, as a matter of fact, even those who earnestly pursue the Catholic ideal are imperfect and many educators do not take the ideal seriously enough. Moreover, the children and youths are also influenced by other persons, the communications media and the general tone of social life in which there are many deviations from and conflicts with the Catholic ideal.

3. Education in Living the Faith Must Permeate the Whole Education

We said above that authentic religious education takes place within the whole of education. It is not something that is extrinsically added to education but the whole education must be orientated and permeated by it. This is the case when education supports and stimulates the pupil to realize an existence that is guided by the right scale of values and that finds expression in a Christian attitude of life. Hence, explicit discourse about faith is only part of such an education.

This place and function of authentic religious education in the whole of education implies that all educators who deal with children and youths help in educating them in a living faith. We said already that the parents, as members of the Church, bring the child into this world in virtue of their Christian marriage and in this sense they stand at the beginning of this education. When they present their child for baptism, the priest administers this sacrament unless special circumstances demand that it be administered by someone else. Hence the priest, too, stands at the beginning of authentic religious education. Later, when the child's life broadens and it steps beyond the family circle, teachers and other guides of youth also become responsible for the still immature person and have their share in his education. Hence all these are called to contribute to this person's upbringing in a living faith within the field of their particular responsibility.

It is beyond the scope of this work to present here a precise and complete definition of each one's particular responsibility. We shall deal only with what pertains to education in school. All those educators act on behalf of the People of God which, as a whole, bears responsibility for the children living in its midst. It is only within this community that the children can develop into full-grown Christians.

That which holds good for education in general applies also to authentic religious education, viz., deliberate pedagogical intervention is meaningful only when it takes place within a simple, matter-of-fact "togetherness" of educators and pupils. In this togetherness children and youths are involved in the life of the grown-ups and this, especially, orientates them toward their own maturity. Hence the everyday life of faith, as practised in the life of the educators, is a fundamental condition and the principal factor of authentic upbringing in the faith, insofar as this education is imparted by the educators. As examples we may refer to the life of prayer; the contact with the priest and adult faithful in the liturgy, especially in the celebration of the Eucharist; the Christian attitude in the adult's daily life; and, above all, his behavior with respect to life's more striking events such as the experience of joy and guilt, failure, sickness and death. It is only against this background that pedagogical planning and, in particular, catechesis become meaningful.

4. The Pupil's Stage of Development Must be Taken into Account

Because education in a living faith takes place within the whole of education, it is necessary to take account of the developments that are taking place in children and youths. Obviously, this education must be adjusted to the real possibilities that present themselves to pupils. For this reason it is useful to be familiar with the stages of development that as a rule occur in children and youths belonging to our civilization. Circumstances, however, can change unpredictably and exercise their influence upon that development so that a survey of that development is subject to constant revision. Moreover, the nature and tempo of development of children and youths differ in individual surroundings and are co-determined by their personal talent, experiences and decisions.

All education demands that educators should as much as possible address themselves to the individual personality of each pupil. Hence such a survey of development can offer no more than a schema which the educator must make concrete in a critical way and in openness toward the unique character of each young person. This means that the educator must be on guard against pre-conceived ideas and must be willing to listen and attune himself to his pupil.

It would be useful for authentic education in the faith if we could describe the development of religious life. But religious life depends in great measure on the character of that education; and the latter has precisely become a matter of debate and is evidently undergoing a change. When we read the reports of conversations with children on religious subjects, as they are published in studies of the psychology of religion, the question constantly arises whether the deficiency of the children's ideas does not show a catechesis that is insufficiently religious, insufficiently Christian and too little attuned to the nature of the child. With respect to the process of religious development we cannot do much more than make conjectures along the lines suggested by the general course of development toward maturity and in constant reference to the important role which education plays in all development.

61

5. Education Through Identification and Aid in Growing Self-Responsibility

When we refuse to reduce religion to a mere assent to a number of truths and the exercise of a number of practices, but see it as a personal orientation toward God who reveals Himself in the whole of existence and therein comes to meet man as his Savior, it becomes clear that authentic religious education must foster that dialogue between God and the child or youth. At the same time it must exercise great discretion with respect to the developing person.

This dialogue takes place in the actual life of the child or youth, and of necessity involves relations with the world and with its fellow-men, especially educators. In a not too unfavorable educational situation, the child has spontaneously accepted bonds with educators, particularly with its parents. That which the child takes over and assimilates in this spontaneously accepted solidarity regarding manners of conduct, ideas and mentality constitutes the unconscious or scarcely conscious foundation of the child's actions and omissions.

Because this assimilation takes place spontaneously, it also penetrates deeply; for here there is no critical consideration or choice. This foundation of action and omission is laid so imperceptibly that it is difficult at a later time to account for one's fundamental attitude. Hence both correction and personal acceptance of this attitude are hardly possible unless the education is carefully directed to maturity. Accordingly, during education, a twofold influence is exercised: on the one hand, the pupil is given the possibility of identifying himself with the educators whose lives serve as examples of human existence and, on the other hand, the educators prompt their pupils to become aware of and to take a personal stand with respect to the values exemplified in the lives of the educators.

Spontaneous acceptance through identification can occur in

greater or lesser measure during man's entire life. In early childhood, when the field of experience is still principally confined to the family and the child does not yet have much consciousness of its own self, the parents' example exercises great influence. Expansion of the field of experience, especially during the school years, gives access to ideas and ways of conduct that differ from what the child has encountered in its contact with its parents. The tension that arises from those new experiences, acts as a stimulus for a mental awakening and critical reflection, which appear especially in the period of youth.

On the other hand, it is remarkable that again and again a new spontaneous identification can take place, both with older persons and persons of the same age, with persons living in the neighborhood and with others who are known only through communication media, or even persons who are more or less legendary.

It is important that educators should take account of the identification occurring in the children and youths entrusted to their care because it is especially in this that one must look for the motivation of their conduct and ideas. No general rules can be given regarding the nature of that identification; outstanding personalities, even in the children's and youths' own group, an impressive teacher, an athlete, television or movie star, or historical figure can serve as a model for them.

The tendency to imitate others, the desire to "belong," especially with those of their own age, and a barely conscious resonance with the things their heroes stand for, all these play a role in those identifications. The influence of their models is certainly one of the most crucial factors of development. It is tragic that men make an evil use of the youth's sensitivity to impressive examples. His or her enthusiasm for particular film stars, musicians or dancers, is sometimes exploited for commercial interests so that there arises a danger of superficiality and lack of sensitivity to higher values. On the other hand, that sensitivity to the power of example gives educators their principal means of fostering the proper development, as we already pointed out, particularly with respect to religious life.

Children, until puberty, are sensitive to the power of example that is given by great figures of the past, when it is presented to them in attractive story-telling. Older pupils are less affected by figures of past ages because they are more attracted to persons of their own time whom they can learn to know very well. It is an established fact that they can be affected by persons animated with high ideals if these persons approach them with simplicity and authenticity. Youths test the appeal directed to them by the criterion of authenticity. Whether or not in their development they will continue to orientate themselves by examples of Christian existence, will depend to a great extent upon their contact or lack of contact with men whose lives are an eloquent witness to such an existence.

Educators should not content themselves with striving to give the young valuable opportunities for identification. They must also help them to develop the self-responsibility which comes from reflection upon the things that were spontaneously taken over or spontaneously rejected through identification. This reflection must be made in function of a human existence; that is why it must avoid a cold analytical hyper-reflection that knows no diffidence when faced with the mystery of existence and that kills affectivity and spontaneity.

Hence reflective growth of self-responsibility should not be conceived exclusively or even principally as "thinking things over" but rather as a more thoughtful and selective engagement in experiences that are recognized as valuable. There is a danger, particularly with respect to religion, that conscientious educators might be too eager to achieve too much too quickly. This undue haste produces an inauthenticity which arouses opposition or disturbs personal contact with the young.

In individual cases it is possible to find the right balance through prudent experiments guided by careful observation and a relatively broad understanding of the whole process of development. When a particular procedure for a particular group of children or youths is proposed, the educators will feel a need for more information about the characteristics proper to the developmental stage of these groups. More detailed descriptions therefore will be given later when we discuss catechesis in the various types of schools. In the following pages we will limit ourselves to a general survey of the developmental process.

6. *General Survey of the Process of Development*

The description of the stages through which man's development must pass is inevitably somewhat static. So-called established facts must be understood in connection with the whole course of development. Of this course we shall try to outline the principal characteristic traits.

To designate the transitions of the development from beginning to the end we speak of "tensions." This term expresses the dynamic contrast between two poles together with the strain to bridge the gap between those two points.

Tension between the spontaneous security of the young child and the requirement of independence and self-commitment of adulthood. The human being who develops from childhood to maturity stands between these two poles of the developmental process, not as an object that is moved from one point to another, but as a dynamic tension between the unfinished fullness of his origin, on the one hand, and the call and challenge of adulthood on the other. His development is not a continuous process following a definite course in virtue of a blind law, although a role is played in it by the laws governing physiological growth. When we look at a young person's development within the whole of his human existence, we see it as a *self-*

65

development that is goaded and directed by manifold influences.

The call for the young person's development comes from society by way of institutions such as schools and professions; it is also imposed by the expectations and the demands he experiences in his contact with teachers, with companions of his own age and others he happens to meet. For example, we estimate the age of children and youths and accordingly expect them to be able to do a number of things; but with respect to other things we realize that they need our support.

This appeal to the young person to "grow up" is sometimes experienced as demanding, but most of the time he readily accepts the invitation. His readiness arises in part from his desire to share in the privileges of older people. The strongest motive, however, is a tendency to self-development aroused in him primarily by the love that his educators manifest for him and to which he responds largely without even being aware of it.

Over and over again new experiences, new possibilities and new tasks present themselves to him and they are for him a source of surprise and confusion. So great can be the confusion that his progress may bog down; but usually the young person quickly proceeds further, sometimes searching artlessly, or again conquering with full deliberation.

This "being in the making" imposes special demands upon the young person. He constantly meets those who are younger than himself and looks down upon them, even though they are what he was only a little while ago. He also meets older persons, to whom he looks up, who surpass him and stand before him as examples. Thus he must constantly loosen the bonds that bind him to the present in order to advance and meet what is new. He is goaded in this process by competition with those of his own age, among whom he must constantly try to hold his own.

This progress does not occur in equal measure and with the same regularity in all realms of life. In the family, that rivalry with and emulation of older brothers and sisters can be felt strongly; but, on the other hand, there may also exist a strong link with the past because of the contact with younger children and the relative stability of the milieu. Marked changes in development occur when the child begins to go to school and later again when it changes from grade school to high school.

Transitions from one grade to the next within the same type of school also mean a change in the course of development; they clearly mark and affect this course. However, these transitions from grade to grade within the same type of school are less disruptive, for principally they mean the attainment of a higher status. The case is different when the younger person goes to a higher type of school, for he then loses the prestige he had as a member of the highest class in the school he has now left.

With respect to leisure hours, the way the young person develops through contact with other children or youths differs greatly from pupil to pupil; here there is no regular process, for several age groups often play together and, even in the pursuit of hobbies, sports, and diverse cultural activities, the age group is relatively less important.

Aptitude and various circumstances will influence the development in all these realms of life. Sometimes the course of this extremely complex process is regular and rather peaceful. But there is frequently an alternation of peaceful phases and times of confusion, unrest, anxiety, loneliness, aggressiveness, etc. Even at an early age stagnation may manifest itself. Sometimes it will appear only in one or the other field, such as the experience of one's bodily being and sexuality; but also the whole development can run aground, as in the case of quasi-maturity.

It is amidst the ups and downs of that development that growth toward a mature life of faith must be achieved. Here also we may expect the provisional and unstable features characteristic of the person who is still unfinished and developing: his surprise and confusion, his clinging to and rejecting things, his search for new experiences and his fear of the unknown. All this we can expect when there occurs a genuine development in which the whole person is involved. If we reduce authentic education in living the faith to an exercise or drill in modes of behavior and the acquisition of knowledge, we shall notice the characteristic repercussions of change only in the pupil's attitude toward his teachers, but we shall find scarcely any—if any— authentically religious development.

Tension between the security and safety of the young person in the family and the requirements to hold his own outside the family. Religious development is conditioned by the development that takes place in other fields of human existence. For example, a development must take place in the young person's relations with his fellow-men, so that the shelteredness of the family can be gradually left behind and all kinds of contact established with other men. Life is, to a great extent, full of relations with our fellow-men. It is in these relations that we learn who we are, new perspectives open before us, and we also meet our limitations. Kindness and goodness, selfishness and hatred, are experienced and awakened in our contact with other men. As a young person experiences and becomes better acquainted with the human condition in such relations, he will also be able to experience and respond to God's invitation with fuller awareness and appreciation.

The more he discovers the wretchedness of guilt, the need to be forgiven, gratitude for kindness and the broadening influence of love, the more fully also will he be able to enter into the sublime dialogue that God wishes to conduct within him. All this the educators can prepare by the way they approach their pupils; but it is principally through the contacts brought about by the children and youths themselves that it becomes a personal acquisition.

The young person who struggles to satisfy the demand that he become independent is easily hampered when we confront him too emphatically with his need of security. This is his vulnerable spot and if we fail to respect it we can expect an aggressive rejection. The aspects of religion that are related to security, such as being a child of God, being sheltered in His forgiving love, and divine consolation, undoubtedly mean a great deal to him, but more as something that he spontaneously lives by than by way of explicit reflection.

The development of a complete personality in genuine human fellowship is endangered when there is a one-sided emphasis on achievement. Daily life, the natural rivalry between young people, and most school activities stimulate them to know and do things in view of achievements. The youth's future success in life depends very much on such achievements recorded and established in diplomas; hence it is understandable that educators attach great value to such performances. However, it can give rise to one-sidedness in the development of their pupils, accompanied by expressions of dissatisfaction, emotional outbursts and a search for means to satisfy their underdeveloped emotional and affective life.

The great role which our Catholic schools play in educating the young in the life of faith makes it imperative that we be particularly on our guard against transferring to education in the faith the general tendency of schools to stress achievement.

Tension between spontaneous solidarity with the world and with others, on the one hand, and mature solidarity in distinctiveness on the other. In this broad survey of the young person's development we must pay special attention to the image of life with others in the world that those young persons will form under the guidance of their educators and the influence of their many impressions and experiences. For their whole way of living the faith will be marked with this image.

The young child still lives in an uncritical solidarity with the world and with its fellow-men. The child directs its attention mainly to other persons and things. It has little awareness of what is taking place within itself. It also relates everything to what it can picture and connect with previous experiences. Its expectations help to give shape to its experiences, which thus are clearly stamped with the mark of the individual subject. In this respect the child is sometimes said to be egocentric and to have a magic and animistic world image. The use of such terms, without sufficient reflection of the appropriateness of the comparison, runs the risk of comparing children to grown-ups who belong to so-called primitive cultures. However, with due reservations, it may be useful to describe some traits that are typical of childhood by means of those terms. The significance of the fairy-tale in childhood and during the first school years, the belief in Santa Claus, the extraordinary ideas children have about natural phenomena are examples of what we have in mind here.

The practical demands of daily life and constant contact with objectivizing thinking in causal terms, especially in school, make the child place itself at a greater distance from the world and from its fellow-men. In this way it can gain a more objective view and the possibility of abstractions is created. The absolutizing of that objectivizing knowledge, which readily arises in our society under the powerful influence of technology and the scientific way of thinking, has led many to the view that the child's development must be orientated to this kind of attitude. This view, however, is one-sided and incomplete. It is true indeed that that attitude manifests itself at the end of childhood. The child then discovers the distinction between what is really perceptible, what is only conceivable, and, on the other hand, that which is merely imagined. The latter not infrequently becomes the victim of misappreciation.

The disillusionment that takes place in the loss of the child's world, with its mixture of phantasy and reality, easily leads to a contempt for the way it used to live; in this reaction disappointment, protection against a secret desire to return to its earlier shelteredness, and perhaps even resentment can play a role. In such a case the child's access to its own feelings, strivings, surmises and the like is impeded. It is led to confine reality to that which can be touched and handled, to that which can be calculated; but access to the non-transparent aspects of existence is in danger of being blocked, so that the intuitive feeling for mystery is greatly jeopardized.

In education we make efforts to prevent this danger by carefully developing affective life; for instance, by stimulating expressions of emotions and by giving an esthetic formation to the pupils. The children themselves find a living experience of and outlet for their feelings and strivings in their play. But their playing does not always develop sufficiently to let those needs be satisfied; moreover, it frequently happens that the strong emphasis placed on achievement in sports quickly eliminates the world of the imagination.

In a healthy development of the total personality, the acquisition of objectivizing thought fulfills only a partial function and is not the apex of the person's complete development. The child's thinking must be able to go beyond objectivation, and this can be done only if its life of emotions and aspirations is also properly developed. Then it becomes possible for the child to discover values that lie outside the reach of the grasping and calculating mind. Only then can it experience a new solidarity with the world and with its fellow-men, which is an enrichment of the child's original solidarity with them.

These ideas point to a necessary condition for the development of the life of faith, for we experience and encounter Christ through the world and our fellow-men, or rather in them.

With regard to this development, a crucial stage is reached when a sense of critical realism makes its appearance in the higher grades of primary education. The attention of the children then runs the danger of being directed one-sidedly to the elements of religion that can be observed, sharply formulated and clearly defined in regard to conduct in the ritual life and in the religious and moral practices of a Christian. This kind of orientation can take place even when the teachers in no way aim at such one-sidedness and impoverishment; for, in modern life, children are strongly influenced by this way of looking at reality; they aim at what can be observed; they gather factual knowledge and are interested in achievements. Puberty and adolescence can be a help in correcting such one-sidedness in the development of personal life; but if the educators wish to foster such a favorable course they must themselves, already during the pupil's years of childhood, avoid as much as possible shocking ways of disillusioning the child and a too one-sided way of evaluating things.

That is why we must not allow religious impressions and moral demands to overstimulate the feelings and aspirations of young children. Such a stimulation is an obstacle to the child's awakening thought and observation. The feelings that are so difficult to control when the child is confronted with the demand that it should grow up and adjust itself to the world of adults, would take up too much of the child's attention. For, the child must learn to dominate its desires and aspirations. It must learn to attune itself to the demands of the factual world. It must dare to meet the new and the unknown at the price of what it formerly took for granted and which was a source of security in its little world. For this reason the child must be protected to some extent against its emotional life, so that it does not become the slave of impulses and emotions. This requires that the child be approached in a peaceful, well-balanced manner. Unfortunately, this balanced approach is often lacking.

If children, because of the infantile way they have been catechized have strongly connected religion with their childlike way of experiencing things, the transition to a higher development is thereby rendered more difficult; it will also be accompanied by a more violent and stronger defense against the things the child has to outgrow. That is why we must use discretion in the religious formation of young children so as to facilitate their development. With respect to older children, while it is necessary to recognize their need and desire for factual knowledge, we must keep open the pathway for their appreciation of affections and aspirations, for the recognition of everything that is contained in human existence, even if it escapes the grasp of rational thought. This requirement demands that the pedagogical framework be integral, that it leave room for the experience of kindness, respect and admiration, that we avoid attributing excessive value to achievements and show appreciation for the value of play and expression.

The schooling that follows the lower six grades is one in which knowledge and abilities are greatly stressed. This brings with it the danger that the one-sidedness of the objectivizing attitude will become fixed. In this case the pupil's personal development will stagnate; the young person will not be sufficiently prepared for the love that pertains to marriage, for personal participation in social life, for the recognition of religious values. It is an important educational task to create opportunities for a many-sided development during the time of puberty and adolescence. Here we see clearly that a good religious education requires the framework of an education that is good also in other respects.

Tension between the experience that is acquired spontaneously and a life in which memory achievements and remembrance foster the interior enrichment of the young person. The small child learns a great deal. This learning takes place either spontaneously or through the care of its parents; but the child is not at all, or scarcely, aware of the fact that it is learning things. Intentional learning takes place mostly in school. The more a child is given the impression of the supreme importance of factual knowledge, the more it will tend to gather facts and memorize things in an attitude of neutrality rather than personal commitment.

Remembrance relates to experiences in which we have been so involved that our involvement causes those experiences to be preserved. An education that tries to avoid a one-sided orientation toward factual knowledge should cultivate remembrance especially with respect to the higher values of human life (Chapter Five).

Tension between the child's experience of freedom in its world of play and in the use of its leisure hours. By "leisure hours" we mean the time that remains beside the work we do for a salary or wage and beside every other kind of work that is similarly obligatory, such as that of a housewife or pupil. All sorts of things take place during such free time: eating and sleeping, helping others in or outside the home, taking part in religious celebrations and in activities we perform purely because we like such things.

Schools are often praised because they give children and youths a sense of having to perform a task and thus condition them to work. Underlying this praise, however, may be a one-sided view that considers work the principal task of life. A more balanced view, in which the significance of leisure hours is recognized, will make us reflect also upon the great educational significance of free time during the years of childhood and youth.

We usually designate as "play" any occupation of young children who do not yet attend school; but that term covers a wide variety of activities. The child engages in those activities because impressions have awakened corresponding tendencies in it. The child then does one thing or another and in that being-occupied it unfolds its human existence. When a child begins to go to school, it meets restrictions concerning its free time. Conse-

74

quently, it perceives more clearly the contrast between the time when it "has to do things" at school and other times when it is not so bound. It thus understands better the experience of being-free, and a way is opened for experiencing freedom *for* something. Only very gradually will the child learn to use its leisure hours on the basis of previous reflection, careful resolutions and self-chosen tasks. Even then in the background there remains the feeling that this is the time in which it could do what it liked.

To some extent leisure hours remain the playground of that seminal form of liberty: the freedom of having and following a notion, a hunch, a whim. We could say that leisure hours must not only give an opportunity for the whole gamut of human behavior that lies between the extremes of deep rest and high scientific, artistic or religious activities; but within leisure time there must also be room for all the diverse forms of human self-realization belonging to the various levels of freedom: the varieties that lie between doing anything one feels like doing and activity deliberately chosen for the most noble purposes. When we are fulfilling an obligatory task, our different activities are constantly bound by that obligation; however, the balance needed in our various uses of leisure hours must arise from our own freedom. When we consider leisure hours in this way, we see that they have a special significance for young people as a field in which they can train their awakening freedom.

Tension between proceeding from moment to moment in immediate reaction to impressions and impulses, on the one hand, and conduct in which one deliberately advances toward the future with the help of past experiences. The acquisition of a time perspective, such as we here have in mind, is an aspect of development that we must consider very important for religious and moral growth. It concerns a condition of freedom that, in part, presupposes a certain maturation but is also determined by culture.

75

An education that one-sidedly stresses learning things by rote but, at the same time, neglects personal remembrances places the pupil outside his own personally "lived" time, for what he learns by rote has no relation to his own life as he lives it in his personal history. Circumstances of time that are so bewildering and complex to young people that they offer no perspectives, make them afraid of looking ahead; as a consequence, they remain anchored in a disorderly, precarious and uncertain present.

It is clear that educators must give attention to that problem. What they are able to expect from children and youths in that respect will vary greatly according to the talent and character of the pupils. Looking to the future and backward to the past depends on the pupil's intellectual ability and on whether he is principally attentive to varying impressions or more inclined to thoughtful introversion. The extremes must, as much as possible, be avoided here; namely, that, on the one hand, children and youths live superficially and without reflection, from moment to moment and that, on the other, they excessively cling to remembrances or are so intensely orientated to the future that they fail to live in simple surrender to the present.

Hence in life there should be room for simple and relatively carefree joy as well as mature deliberation, responsibility and expectation. An education that orientates the young person to this kind of life contributes effectively to his growth toward Christian maturity which, after all, is characterized by hopeful expectation and confident commitment to God.

CHAPTER FOUR

THE SCHOOL AND PASTORAL WORK
WITH CHILDREN AND YOUTHS

WE have seen that education in a living faith is a task resting upon all educators. Hence a school that is truly pedagogical is also involved in the pupils' authentic religious education. We stated also that education in living the faith must permeate the entire education and cannot be exclusively concentrated in religious instruction and confined to explicit expressions of religion. The whole of education therefore must be animated by education in the faith. By this we mean that every teacher approaches his pupils from the standpoint of a Catholic image of man, that every teacher teaches from the standpoint of that vision of human life, so that the pupils are helped to arrive at an appreciation of things in conformity with a Christian life. A school that strives to accomplish this can be called a Catholic school.

The efforts that have been made for the renewal of education have given the educators a keen awareness of the powerful influence the school exercises upon the whole personality of young people. If we wish to prevent this influence from becoming harmful, we must avoid a one-sided stress on knowledge, proficiency and achievement; we must aim rather at educating the pupils in a way that is helpful for their growth to maturity.

77

Since education in living the faith must be interwoven with the whole of education, the school is also involved in that task. In this respect, however, we are not thinking primarily about the time that is specifically set aside for religious instruction, for religious instruction can take place meaningfully only within the context of an integral education in a living faith.

This education within the framework of the school depends upon those who function in it as teachers. In order to fulfill that religious task, they must do their share in the work of letting the mystery of Christ manifest itself to the pupils in the way that is proper to the school environment; they must help the pupils to notice that mystery and respond to the call thus addressed to them. This manifold task is achieved in education; hence the teacher, the subject matter, the method of presentation, and the circumstances in which instruction is given, all play a role in this task.

1. The Teacher

The teachers' influence on authentic education in living the faith is exercised not only by their relations with their pupils but also by their relations with each other. The teaching staff must appear as a truly collegial corps. With respect to the teacher's relations with the pupils, it must be evident to them that he is orientated to them with sincere respect, interested in their growing personality, and capable of stimulating and correcting them with patience and gentle considerateness.

A more complete description of the relations between teachers and pupils is possible, of course, but what we have said sufficiently indicates that those relations should contain an opportunity for the pupil to encounter Christ; for children and youths ought to be able to encounter the Lord in a particular way in their contact with teachers. No teacher should yield to discouragement because he is aware of his deficiencies in that great task; such defects are inevitable.

Because we have mentioned this task, teachers should not get the impression that a new and exceptional burden is placed upon their shoulders. We are merely applying to them specifically the responsibility of every Christian to make Christ present to his fellow-men. On the other hand, however, it is true that children and youths, because of their dependence on others and their great impressionability, must be approached with special care by ·the teachers. The words of Christ regarding scandal given to children (Mat. 18:1–10) make it unnecessary to develop this point further.

This making-Christ-present to the children evidently does not mean that the teachers must have recourse to saccharine piety or indiscriminately peddle religious ideas and motives. Authenticity and discretion are indispensable conditions for being a good witness to Christ. Likewise, neither is a sort of uniformity demanded from the teachers. Each of them must bring Christ to his pupils in his own way and according to his own possibilities, by living a good life marked by authenticity and simplicity.

Obviously, also, adults have their weaknesses, they pass through times of crisis and confusion and commit faults. Although one must avoid exhibiting those shortcomings and burdening his fellow-man and particularly children with them, it would be incorrect anxiously to strive to hide such weaknesses behind a façade of quasi-perfection. The sham that underlies such a camouflage is even more harmful. Moreover, great harm would be done to children and youths if they were given the erroneous impression that a sort of perfection can be attained in which no weakness, confusion or faults ever appear. They would be prevented from frankly confronting their own imperfections and would fall either into insincerity and make-believe or discouragement.

No doubt, the teacher is called to set before the child or youth his own example of a good life, but he must at the same time dare to be truly human and ready to acknowledge his weakness and his need of the Lord's forgiving love. It is evident that such an attitude will at the same time prompt the teacher to exercise gentleness and considerateness toward his pupils' faults.

What is said here is not a plea for loose indulgence, for such laxness does not deserve the name education. The teacher must, evidently, remain himself in his relations with his pupils and also must give them clear guidance. In this respect the diversity that is found among his pupils makes great demands upon the teacher's ability to be a guide.

2. Subject Matter

Any subject matter of teaching is part of the passing on of culture and as such can contribute to the pupil's development as a human being. This humanization is necessary for education in living the faith. In it, the teacher must bring to the pupils' more or less explicit attention the sign of Christ's mystery that is contained in this culture. However, the teacher should be discreet in speaking deliberately about the more profound significance of that culture; otherwise there is danger that the religious way of thinking that is imposed will prevent the pupils from paying attention to the merely relative significance which cultural values have in themselves. The danger of overstressing the Christian significance of culture is not at all imaginary and hypothetical; hence one must use great prudence in this respect.

Keeping this reservation in mind, we may say that especially in subjects directly related to human life, such as history, an opportunity is offered to call attention to this religious significance. In this connection it is proper to recommend that explicit attention be paid to Catholic social training, particularly in secondary schools.

In the entire program of studies that fulfills a function in educating pupils in the faith, it is evidently necessary also to have special times for an explicit discourse about religion. But it is also evident that this proclamation of the faith must not be added to the program as though it were an appendix, as a thing that stands isolated. This proclamation of the faith is necessary in order to create the framework within which the whole transmission of culture can acquire meaning for authentic education in the faith. At the same time, those topics which are not made explicit or are only casually referred to with regard to religion must be dealt with explicitly in a "religion course."

Hence, though there is a danger that the proclamation of the faith within the framework of the school might degenerate into a mere course alongside many other courses, this proclamation has its value within the program of Christian education.

3. Didactics

The relations between teachers and their pupils are formed to a great extent by their being occupied together with some particular subject matter. It is also true that contact with the cultural goods transmitted through the school is established in great measure through the teacher. To make sure that instruction functions within the whole of education, the teacher must present the matter in such a way that the pupils really assimilate it and are not merely gathering scattered intellectual information.

A well-conceived and richly varied method of teaching is indispensable to awaken the pupil's interest and to prompt him to become personally involved through examining things, practice and application. Such a pedagogy requires that the teacher possess a profound knowledge of the subject and of the means by which it can be acquired. He also needs to understand the pupils, their potentialities and difficulties. But he needs, above all, to be animated by the desire to help young people through his teaching in their ascent to maturity. This animation gives inspiration and power of conviction to his instructions.

When instruction takes place in this manner, the development of the pupils' human existence is truly fostered. What this kind of teaching includes we can describe somewhat in the following particulars:

a. When the pupils are brought into contact with cultural values through interest and personal commitment, they also become involved in the wonder, the efforts of seeking and the surprise of discovery, through which the cultural heritage is enriched and grows from generation to generation. Respectful interest in that which has true value can thus be fostered.

b. The desire to explore, so characteristic of young persons, can be broadened through contact with the explorations of the most brilliant representatives of mankind; it can lead them from one discovery to another.

c. This kind of teaching tries to promote, as much as possible, the active participation of the pupils by creating interest, by the stimulus of cooperation with fellow-students and by relationships with the teacher. A call is thus addressed to the pupil in his growing sense of responsibility. A more thorough result can be expected from this approach than from the use of compulsion and from motives that stand outside the process of learning itself. In this way a possibility is created for experiencing and accepting personal responsibility for the fulfillment of a task.

d. In this manner of teaching, the human relations in which the pupils find themselves, especially within the school itself, are recognized and fostered. For cooperation and mutual help constitute an essential part of this teaching. In this way learning and being-occupied with cultural values become a very special way of being together with one's fellow-men.

e. The clear pedagogical orientation of this kind of teaching helps the pupils to discover their own potentialities and responsibilities. It is a preparation for, and a discovery of, the place each one is called to eventually occupy in the community; it is the discovery of a personal destination.

All this is not intended to advocate any particular method of pedagogy. We have merely sketched a form of teaching so strongly oriented to the development of *the whole man* that it can make a real contribution to authentic education in the faith. It is a pleasure to find that, in the present renewal of education, efforts toward such responsible methods of pedagogy are in evidence everywhere. A climate will thus be formed within which a renewal of catechesis will finally be made possible.

4. The Sphere of the School

Quite rightly, school authorities make high demands regarding the buildings, furniture, and environment that serve the purpose of education. These factors are determined, among other things, by the requirements of hygiene, as well as by those directly connected with teaching, such as good blackboards and proper facilities for storing teaching materials. Moreover, the building and furnishing requirements are affected by the intention of creating the proper atmosphere for the students in order that they may have a maximum of receptivity and the best possible orientation toward the goal intended by the school. That which relates to this sphere especially deserves our attention here.

The pedagogical purpose can be realized only when the pupils can associate with one another and with the teacher in a restful and relaxed way. In order that a human being be interestedly and devotedly occupied with acquiring and assimilating cultural values, he must be open for the true, the good and the beautiful. He cannot acquire and assimilate such values if he is tense and restless, when he is preoccupied with feelings of insecurity, anxiety, agitation, repugnance and boredom.

Obviously, the teacher cannot completely prevent such feelings either in himself or in his pupils, but he can strive to make the circumstances as favorable as possible for the assimilation of his teaching. To this end he must create an atmosphere that is in harmony with the character of his pupils, adapted to the subject matter and capable of fostering the desired openness. With respect to children, we can characterize this atmosphere more or less by saying that they must feel at home, secure and sheltered. With respect to older pupils, the differences between boys and girls, and those that exist between various types of schools make it impossible to offer a general characterization.

The atmosphere is, in great measure, determined by the teacher, but what he strives to accomplish can be greatly aided by the educational environment he creates for his pupils.

In an atmosphere in which the teacher's balanced way of acting is coupled with a refined and well-cared-for environment the resulting picture of man's nobility can become a sign pointing to the mystery of Christ as it is to become incarnate in this world.

5. The Interplay of the School and the Family

Because the school has to fulfill such an influential role in education, a close cooperation ought to exist with those who are primarily responsible for the education of the young person, viz., his parents. Although there is still much uncertainty regarding the manner of realizing that cooperation, all accept its necessity.

We must now ask ourselves what form that cooperation between the school and the parents must assume regarding education in a living faith. With respect to Catholic schools, the above-described Christian orientation can be demanded unqualifiedly. The fact that parents send their children to this kind of school implies that they accept that kind of education at least in principle. However, we must take into account the fact that there is great diversity among parents in regard to their life of faith. Thus it is impossible to formulate in a universally valid and concrete way to what extent education may or must be explicitly religious.

In the case of parents who lead an intense Christian life, the school might assume a less explicit religious function. However, there will be hardly any objection on the part of such parents when the teachers speak about religion and the children participate in liturgical celebrations as a school unit, as long as the school does not take over the things for which the parents themselves are responsible. A discussion between such parents and the school authorities will make it possible to find an acceptable balance. We can say, in general, that the school should be discreet and reserved.

The problem is more difficult when the parents are careless in the religious upbringing of their children. Especially in these cases there is a danger that the school, because of its concern for those children, would want to exercise a profound influence on the religious upbringing of these pupils. The latter are then placed in a tension between the milieu of the home and the school environment and this tension is not without danger for the religious development of the child. For religious life must be rooted in the whole personality; understanding and expression must, as much as possible, spring from, and be linked with, a way of life that is deeply imbedded in the personality.

In such cases—and they are not at all infrequent—if the teacher is not very discreet, there is a danger that he will provoke resistance if the pupils strongly identify themselves with the home, or that he will impart only superficial knowledge and practices of religion because the pupil's religious basis is too narrow. That is why the concern for those pupils, in itself perfectly just, demands careful reserve: the school is called to co-operate with religious upbringing but, at the same time, it must take into account the religiousness of the pupils that depends on the family milieu.

It frequently happens that the pupils brought together in one class come from homes that vary greatly regarding religion. Hence, it is impossible, even in the case of an individual school, to determine precisely what is to be done with regard to authentic education in the faith. It is also impossible then to establish a policy that is perfectly attuned to the needs of individual pupils.

However, besides those evident disadvantages, there are also advantages in this situation. The mingling of the students can bring about mutual influence that is beneficial to all. Those who have, as it were, spontaneously grown up in a Christian family are thereby prompted to become conscious of their Christianity. Others who have undergone few religious influences can, if the whole atmosphere of education evokes a certain solidarity, receive impressions from their fellow students that may affect them more deeply than impressions that come from adults. However, the teacher's flexible adaptation to the particular needs of a class is a necessary condition for such favorable results.

CHAPTER FIVE

CATECHESIS OF CHILDREN AND YOUTHS
IN THE CONTEXT OF THE SCHOOL

IN the last chapter we spoke about the whole of pastoral work in the context of the school. Our attention will now focus on the specific form of pastoral work with which we are particularly concerned in this book, namely, catechesis within the context of the school.

Previously we tried to indicate the place of catechesis in the Church's pastoral work, especially in education to a living faith. For catechesis must always function within that larger ensemble if it wishes to be wholly successful. In the following pages we will always presuppose that organic solidarity of school catechesis with the other forms of the Church's pastoral activity, as these unfold in and outside the school, especially in the home and in the church edifice.

1. Definition of Catechesis

On the basis of our reflections in Chapter Two regarding the Church's pastoral functioning and in particular regarding the place and task of catechesis within that pastoral function, we are able to arrive at the following definition of catechesis. By catechesis we mean: *Throwing light on the whole of human existence as God's salvific action by witnessing to the mystery of Christ through the word, for the purpose of awakening and fostering the faith and prompting man to live truly in accord with that faith.*

Let us explain this definition.

1. Catechesis is concerned with "throwing light on the whole of human existence." Catechesis speaks about the whole of human existence. It is concerned with the life of children and youths, as it is lived in the school, family, church and anywhere else. It deals with everything these young people do and go through, with all they encounter and their reactions to those things, not only in prayer and liturgy, but in their whole life of study, play, recreation and, eventually, work. The whole life of those children and youths, as it is for them now and as it is directed to the future, their joys and sufferings, hopes and anxieties, successes and failures, all the things that occupy their attention and all that inspires them belongs to the domain of catechesis.

However, catechesis looks at all this in a special way, namely, in its salvific dimension; it illuminates all this as God's salvific activity. Hence its object is man's concrete existence in its most profound dimension. Catechesis really wants to help those young people so that they may discover that dimension of their existence and thus be confronted with the person of Christ who encounters them in and by everything that is contained in their life. For it desires to help the people of our own time to understand their own individual and social history of life and existence as a salvation history.

2. How does catechesis do this? By "witnessing to the mystery of Christ through the word." For it is a question of giving an authentic meaning to human existence, a meaning as it is given

by God Himself in Christ and as it comes to us guaranteed by the tradition of the Church. Catechesis wants to give meaning to human existence as the realization of God's salvific plan for us which is revealed in the mystery of Christ. Christ's life gives meaning, significance and value to our own life.

That Christ has saved us means that our life is God's offer of salvation, that our life can be an ascent to the Father. How our life is all that we see in Christ's life. That is why we must announce and proclaim Christ's salvation and recount His life as the original form of all God's salvific action in respect to men and, therefore, as enlightening human existence.

Catechesis is a question of giving witness, that is, communicating to others what we ourselves experience in a life of faith and what the Church as a whole is conscious of concerning Christ's mystery. Now there are many ways of giving witness: by our presence and our Christian conduct, by our participation in the celebration of the sacred mysteries. In catechesis we have a special form of witness, namely, by means of the word. Catechesis is a proclamation of the word.

It is the nature of man that the humanization of action takes place in speech. Speech gives a human meaning to action. That is why the proclamation of the word is the means *par excellence* for imparting Christian meaning to man's existence. It is God's word that illumines and clarifies our existence.

The expression "through the word" is used to distinguish the catechetical witness from witness through other forms of pastoral work. Nevertheless, this expression must be properly understood. In the transmission of ideas and sentiments, catechesis, of course, makes use of other modes of expression than the spoken word. Yet, more important is not to interpret the term "through the word" as verbalism, a hollow and empty use of words. Catechesis does not mean isolated words, words divorced from the whole person and life of the catechist or from the life of the Church in her entirety. Catechetical speech must remain organically connected with all the rest of the Church's pastoral functions.

3. What is the intention of catechesis as that enlightening witness? It wishes "to awaken and foster the faith of the pupil and prompt him to live truly in accord with it."

School catechesis is aimed at the faith of children and youths in their whole life of faith. In this faith, insofar as it is an activity of man, we can distinguish three aspects: a vision of faith, a personal commitment in faith and living one's faith.

By *vision of faith* we mean faith insofar as it is a supernatural knowing and seeing, a seeing through and beyond the surface of events and recognizing God's hand in them. This vision sees God as working with us through and in everything that constitutes our life. It is awakened and fostered by the proclamation of Christ's mystery. It is the Christian vision of life and of all reality.

We must *personally commit* ourselves to God whom we thus discover in our whole life. For believing is more than seeing; it is a personal surrender, the commitment of our whole person to the person of Christ who comes to meet us in and by our whole existence, but especially in sacramental celebrations.

An integral faith, however, also includes *living according to faith*. A person's commitment to Christ must be given an authentic expression in the whole of his life, in his conduct and activities. To believe means actively responding to the divine invitation in Christ; it means an active response by positively striving to possess Christ's attitude of life in all our actions and omissions.

However, these three aspects are misunderstood if they are seen simply as three successive stages. The vision of faith grows with our believing commitment and our living according to faith, for it is only by seeing that we shall love. Vision of faith,

personal commitment and living the faith are interwoven; they condition and presuppose one another.

This brief summary will be made explicit as we proceed. We will first look at catechesis from the standpoint of that which it wishes to produce in the pupil, namely, faith. Next, we will give attention to the person of the catechist and his task; finally, we will deal with the actual course of catechesis.

2. The Pupil

Before we can discuss catechesis from the standpoint of its purpose, which is the faith of the pupil, we must first present a more complete exposition of faith as man's response to God's offer of salvation (cf. Chapter Two). This will be done in Section A. Section B will be devoted to the conclusions to be drawn from this exposition with respect to catechesis. These conclusions, finally, we will try to apply to the situation of faith in our own time; this is the subject of Section C.

A. FAITH

God's salvific activity brings about an encounter between God and man. This encounter, God's offer of salvation, attains complete fruitfulness in man's response of faith. However, faith includes more than accepting doctrinal truths. It is first of all a loving surrender to the person of our Lord Jesus Christ, the fullness of Revelation; but this commitment implies the acceptance of certain truths.

Man's believing response is also itself God's salvific action; it is His gratuitous gift of grace. It is, at the same time, a totally free action of man; thus it is not only a gift that is received but also a human task, a project of man. Finally, faith, as man's encounter with God which results from Revelation, blossoms in a lasting union with the Lord. These three aspects of faith, a gift of God, a task for man and union with God, we shall now examine more fully.

A Gift of God

Faith is a gift from God. God offers man communion with Himself. This communion has a very special character; it has a depth of its own when compared with communion among men, for it is a communion of man with the One to whom man owes his whole life and his salvation.

The initiative for that communion between God and man comes entirely from God. It rests on God's self-communication in Christ, the Lord who has made Himself present among us. Faith is an encounter with God, and the Lord comes to us in order that we may know Him. He desires to take man unto Himself: He offers him His presence, His friendship, His life.

To believe, as a communion-of-life with God, includes *knowing* God. God's communication of Himself to us as knowing beings is, at the same time, a revelation.

Already in human faith we experience a communion with persons, not only in the sphere of sentiments, but also through knowledge; and here we mean by knowledge not purely conceptual knowledge but the intellectual unfolding of one's being. In other words, intuitive elements also are involved in this faith.

Because of its supernatural character, Revelation demands even more that God make known something about Himself. For His plan of salvation, His nature in which He gives us a share, and our salvation in Him are things that are naturally unknowable by us. God actually communicates Himself to us in history and, for that reason, it is necessary to become acquainted with salvation history in Israel, in Christ and in the Church. In this salvation history the proclamation of the word plays an increasingly larger role: as interpretation of history, as the giver of meaning to religious celebrations, as the content of our prayer, and as expression of faith in daily life.

The cognitive aspect of faith is not side by side with communion with God but is contained in it. This knowledge itself creates communion. Hence the factual data of that knowledge must be so transmitted and imparted that they always function in and lead to communion with God's personal self-disclosure. And this God is not only a Thou but a mystery. He completely transcends man and the created order. We cannot accept Him without recognizing His transcendence. To believe means to enter into communion with the mystery which God is.

The content of Revelation is concerned with the invisible reality that lies beyond visible reality and is the latter's deepest ground. It deals with God's salvific action in us and in the whole of creation. It is the mystery which God Himself is and which we can approach only "in faith": "Faith is the proof of the reality of the things we cannot see" (Heb. 11:1).

A Human Task and Project

Faith as man's response to God's self-disclosure is entirely God's gift and, at the same time, a wholly free action of man. That is why to believe is a human project and task, for it consists in a commitment of man's whole person to Christ in the community of His Church. This commitment surpasses every kind of commitment to men, although it implies, of course, also a commitment to men.

That human task includes not only an acceptance of the Lord, but this genuine adhering to God demands an ever renewed "conversion." It means an ever renewed turning away from human pettiness in order to turn Godward once more; it means overcoming our self-love in order to be open in love for God and men.

The whole of Revelation proclaims this attitude of mind whenever it speaks about faith: "The time is fulfilled, and the kingdom of God is at hand, *repent* and *believe* in the Gospel" (Mk. 1:15). And this conversion is necessary, because man is not an innocent being but one who constantly experiences that cleavage within his own existence.

The situation, in virtue of which man cannot begin with himself and from his own existence but must depend upon grace that comes from the saving Christ, is traditionally called "original sin." Our life in a sinful world and also our own sinfulness demand a constant conversion because man must over and over again free himself from his selfishness.

To be converted means to accept fully in one's whole life and in every situation that Christ is the Lord, to acknowledge Him as God, as Lord and Master over life and death. This, evidently, is of decisive importance and significance for all expressions of life. This conversion is for man truly "the foundation and root of all justification" (Council of Trent).

Conversion, by which man commits himself to the living God in the person of Jesus Christ, coincides with God's gift of grace by which He begins to fulfill His promise in the believer. God makes him just, that is, gives him purification and a new life, friendship with God and the assistance of the Holy Spirit. As St. Paul expresses it: "Having been justified therefore by faith, let us have peace with God through our Lord Jesus Christ, through whom we also have access by faith unto that grace in which we stand, and exult in the hope of the glory of the sons of God. And not only this, but we exult in tribulations also, knowing that tribulation works out endurance, and endurance tried virtue, and tried virtue hope. And hope does not disappoint, because the charity of God is poured forth in our hearts by the Holy Spirit who has been given to us" (Rom. 5:1–6).

A Lasting Union With the Lord

To believe is more than simply to accept the Lord and to be converted. It must unfold into the full human response, viz., an unconditional personal commitment to Christ of our whole existence with all that belongs to it. This commitment signifies a lasting union with the Lord, a dialogue with God in friendship, a new form of life. All that we do or abstain from doing then gives evidence of that union with the Lord, and, at the same time, makes that union more real. To that loving surrender in faith essentially belongs the love of our neighbor, hence the whole moral life.

In this way, faith gives a totally new dimension to life and man's world; it makes them a new life and a new world. And it is the power of the Holy Spirit, who is at work in us, that makes us accomplish that commitment of faith. The Spirit of the Father and of the Lord Jesus makes man participate, by this personal commitment, in the mystery of Christ; and it thereby makes man share in Jesus' ascent to the Father.

God offers His gift to man. No true faith is present unless man enters into and responds to that offer by actively making himself willing to receive Him. Divine faith means "come to know and . . . believe the love God has in our behalf" (1 Jo. 4:16). Thus it is, at the same time, the resolution of living a life of communion with Him in His Christ.

To believe is a response of the whole person. That is why faith, in the New Testament, is often described as all-embracing, hence as implying hope and love. When we make a distinction between faith, hope and love, faith refers more to knowing, though without losing its connection with hope and love. We must always remind ourselves of the bond between that faith and the whole of human life.

Our faith, which hopes for the things we do not as yet possess, finds its actualization in the exercise of Christian love of neighbor.

St. Paul very rarely uses the word "love" to express our relations with God (Rom. 8:28; 1 Cor. 2:9; 16:22; Eph. 6:24), but he uses it constantly to express God's attitude toward us. To this love of God for us corresponds the faith of the Christian, a faith that is active through love of neighbor. "We have heard of your faith in Christ Jesus and of the love that you bear toward all the saints because of the hope that is laid up for you in heaven" (Col. 1:4–5).

The fullness of believing is a permanent commitment to the Lord, a definitive conversion, a life of willingness to become like to Christ. It is "putting on the new man" and growing to the mature measure of the fullness of Christ: "until we all attain to the unity of the faith and of the deep knowledge of the Son of God" (Eph. 4:13). This includes also the eschatological aspect of faith; we have here no lasting dwelling but hope for a heavenly glory where our faith shall unfold into vision.

It is evident that Christian faith, as we have described it, cannot be the fruit of one act of the will by which we definitively choose Christ. There is question here of a constantly renewed choosing of Christ, especially whenever there is a change in the Christian's situation of life. Faith always remains a project; it has to be fulfilled in a process of growth.

B. CATECHESIS AS AWAKENING AND FOSTERING FAITH IN ALL ITS ASPECTS

Catechesis must respect all those aspects and stages of faith; it must respect them with regard to God but also with regard to man.

Toward a Personal Encounter

Catechesis must, in the first place, foster the encounter between God and man. That is why it must constantly strive to make possible the encounter with the living God, in Christ; it must enable children and youths to experience and understand Christ's call in their own situation. To accomplish this purpose it is necessary that the catechist should constantly try to free himself from the conceptual and notional level, from the level of knowing *things,* and pass to the level of the knowledge of a *person.* In catechesis, children and youths must constantly be confronted with the personal God, the God of the reality-of-salvation: Christ, who lives in the Church (the life of the faithful), Christ who speaks in the Church (hierarchy, authority, guidance, proclamation of the word), Christ who acts in the Church (the sacraments). This kind of personal catechesis is at the same time connected with, and invokes, the other aspects of the Church's pastoral function.

Toward a Personal Commitment in Faith

Children and youths stand at the threshold of their life, and this beginning already bears in itself the promise of a fully human development. They are persons in the process-of-growing. In and through His People, God offers them the gift of faith; and they can, within that community and borne by it, gradually reach the stage of a personal response. Their growing personal commitment does not become more total but it does become more fully human, more complete in terms of a greater freedom and a deeper understanding.

Young children, secure in their dependence upon adults, can attain to a childish and artless, but full, gift of themselves to God. As they grow up and become youths, there appear greater possibilities for a more fully human commitment because:

97

1) according as their intellect develops there is also a more mature understanding.

2) according as they become more independent, they ask more questions and develop their growing need for reflection.

3) crises arise during the process of growth; some of these occur in every youth because they belong to the ordinary development of man; others are personal and result from the individual's own experiences. Such crises prompt them to take a stand and thus give rise to new opportunities for a more deliberate choice, hence for a more self-chosen commitment.

As the child and the youth become more independent, an ever-more-conscious personal choice (commitment) is also necessary, for theirs is the growth toward the fully human self-commitment of adults, which contains a deliberate fully human choice.

When the catechist is looking for possibilities to stimulate the child and the youth, through the *religious* proclamation of the word, to a fuller self-commitment, he must avoid "adapting" himself to them too much. Otherwise he would offer them too little inspiration and would not sufficiently satisfy their most profound desire to "grow up." A certain challenge to rise to a higher level is necessary if we wish to help them to arrive at an ever fuller self-commitment.

Toward Living the Faith

Catechesis has as a further task the stimulating and helping of children and youths so that their religious self-commitment will develop into a permanent union with the Lord, and will find an authentic expression in their whole existence through a Christian attitude of life and Christian conduct.

This task implies that the catechist makes the pupils realize, through his proclamation of God's word, that Christ makes an appeal, not only to their mind and memory, but to their whole personality and particularly to the supernatural possibilities that are given to them. Christ invites them to believe, to have confidence and especially to have an effective love for God and men. Christ asks us to respond ever more fully to our vocation of being children of God, which He Himself has made possible for us through baptism.

God's word continually puts man before a dilemma, a for or against. It constantly asks for an answer, a "Yes" or a "No," a commitment or a refusal. The catechist must respect the modality of the answer, but his aim must be to make the children and youths in the community gradually reach the level of the personal response.

This task requires, first of all, that the catechist himself personally believe in the supernatural possibilities of the child, and he must show this by constantly inviting, encouraging and helping the pupils on their way. Secondly, he must respect the individual rhythm of the spiritual development of children and youths. For their receptivity to the Glad Tidings depends upon their own psychological structure and also on their social situation, their milieu, the spirit of the time, and other factors. The catechist does not catechize a universal child or youth, but individual children and youths of this particular time and this particular environment.

C. CATECHESIS IN OUR TIME

Opportunities and Dangers

Man has an inborn need of the transcendent but of himself is incapable of meeting this need. God has taken the initiative of coming to fill this need. However, in spite of his need of the transcendent, man is simultaneously inclined to close himself against it. This is due to a variety of causes springing from his own disposition as well as from outside. Every age, including our own, has its particular form of "closedness" to the mystery.

Our time has undergone an enormous process of technical evolution, which has affected our image of man. Technology has given freedom to that which is properly human in man, for by it man's dependence on nature has been greatly overcome. Thus man can now more fully devote himself to togetherness and fellowship.

Yet, there is also a certain ambivalence in that technical progress. For instance, we notice a certain tendency to divinize man. His power over matter threatens to make him place his ultimate end and highest good in himself and, at the same time, close himself to God. Similarly, man's dignity is sometimes put in jeopardy because his essence is considered to lie in his relation to matter. Thus he shuts himself up in his world and closes himself to God.

For medieval man, God shone through nature. The universe was a sign of God's power and majesty. But in our time man has created an artificial milieu for himself; a world that places itself between nature and man, an environment that speaks of nothing but man.

The way to God through nature has become much more difficult, but the way to Him by way of man and through man is now more open. There exists now a better chance that man himself will be more clearly seen as a sign of God. But, just as nature formerly was able to lead man to God, although there existed also the possibility that man would remain stuck in nature and make nature his god, so it is now with respect to man.

Our civilization with its manifold comforts and many wonderful possibilities brings with it the danger that man might no longer consider the deeper questions of life. On the other hand, it also offers man the possibility of being more authentically human together with his fellow-men.

Modern youth shares in this civilization and its mentality. People nowadays think much less in absolute terms about many things, and consequently they run the danger of falling into complete relativism, agnosticism and scepticism. But there is also a bright side, namely, that they will relinquish a too rigid and undifferentiated view of their fellow-men and approach them with more openness. This openness offers many possibilities in authentic religious education for seeking God together with others. Moreover, the individual person has much more opportunity to be himself, and thus also find God in a more profound way. At the same time, however, more is demanded from man's personal understanding and decision, for the support that was formerly given by many accepted frameworks has fallen away.

This is why the catechist must give a very personal and existential catechesis; he must foster the pupils' personal judgment and personal responsibility and offer them a deeper understanding of their own existence. In this matter he finds support in the contemporary attitude that is beginning to see many things regarding religion in a way that is both more pure and more profound; this brings with it an opportunity for living one's faith more consciously and responsibly, and in a more authentic way.

The tension which modern man experiences between his world and the realm of religion need not remain a tension that will lead to a separation of the two; it should, on the contrary, find a solution in a higher integration, in a new discovery of God's presence, in a faith that is more profound. This solution is principally a question of developing a vision of faith regarding everything that motivates and inspires modern man in his endeavor to build a livable, habitable human world for all, and in his striving for a true and universal fellowship of men. It requires a more profound view of our earthly existence but also a new understanding of Revelation.

To care for the "conversion" of children and youths means to see to it that they have the opportunity to grow toward a personal, conscious and free acceptance of their Christian project of life. They must gradually learn to accept their life with all it contains from the standpoint of a Christian vision: as a gift of

God and, at the same time, as an invitation and project to translate that Christian outlook into a personal commitment wholly inspired by that vision. Of course, we must in all this take into consideration the possibilities that children and youths have on account of their age, talents and development.

This approach will prevent that mentality frequently met with nowadays, a mentality usually expressed in the words: "I am a Catholic, but why? I have never asked for it!" Such persons have not been given a sufficient opportunity to develop a conscious personal decision; they have not learned how to give a Christian meaning to their everyday life. And the reason for this failure is that Christ has not become a reality for them because they lacked a vision of faith about their whole existence, because they were unable to find Christ everywhere in their lives. They are bitterly sceptical about the faith, which they view as a collection of revealed truths lying completely outside the world of their own life. For they never learned to see their own lives as a religious reality; they looked upon their world of faith as something far removed from their daily reality. Their scepticism extends also to the practice of faith; they can think of it only as an ethics of duties and not as a loving response to God's invitation. They have never learned gradually to discover the inviting God in their everyday life. And, not having seen Him in that way, they have not learned gradually to respond to that God.

Such a gradual personal response and position, however, can be securely developed only when the faith was spontaneously accepted during childhood. Children and youths must have an opportunity to experience the faith as the silent sustaining basis of life. If we force too much consciousness of this basis upon them at an early age, there is a danger that we will force its development and cause it to stagnate. Its growth demands patience and gradualness. Let us explain this more fully.

A Dynamic Catechesis

We saw at the beginning of this chapter that catechesis essentially is a clarification of existence. It makes human existence "transparent" as a salvation history. Catechesis essentially wishes to assist the child in arriving at a Christian vision of its own life. Thus it follows at once that we must avoid saturating them with endless proclamations of the faith. For we are not proclaiming the Gospel in a vacuum, but we announce Christ's mystery as the giving of meaning to fully concrete human lives, viz., those of the children and youths entrusted to our care. We must avoid flooding them with our witness. Otherwise we shall create a distaste for faith and religion; and the greater part of what we offer will not only remain un-assimilated by the pupils but will exercise a harmful influence upon the development of those young people and will prevent them from arriving at an authentic life of faith.

We must therefore witness in a measure and on a level that can truly be meaningful for the life of our pupils, as this life is lived today and as it is directed to the future. But this does not mean that we must present only a portion of Christ's mystery to pupils at a particular age. Christ's mystery is a totality, a living unity; we cannot leave anything out without mutilating the whole. It follows that in catechesis there must always be a confrontation with the totality of Christ's mystery. At the same time, in this confrontation there must be room for growth. It is neither wise nor prudent to confront pupils in their early years with Revelation in the depth and fullness corresponding to the needs of adults.

The pupils' lives are precisely a growing-up, and it is within the context of this growing-up that catechesis helps them to discover the dimension of salvation. Hence catechesis should grow, together with the growing person, and must differ according to each stage of this growth. Each age and each degree of talent and development requires its own catechesis.

Thus it is clear why we must radically abandon the more static idea that formerly dominated catechesis, an idea that rested on a static concept of man and the world, on a static image of man as well as a static theological vision of Christianity. For man is a growing being, a being-in-the-making. The child is not a pocket edition of an adult, but he is a man who is on his way to maturity. And, with respect to faith, we are never full-grown; we remain always on the way in our relation to God.

Our catechesis must therefore be dynamic, which means, within a proclamation of the totality of Christ's mystery, it must grow with the growing life of the pupil, in which it desires to let God's salvific action shine forth.

3. The Catechist and His Task

In Section II, after examining the purpose and goal of catechesis, namely, the faith of the pupil, we drew conclusions regarding the nature of catechesis. In this section we will direct our attention to the consequences flowing from that consideration with respect to the person of the catechist. His function and task demand a *special spirituality*. It is this spirituality, proper to the catechist, that we should like to describe here.

At the beginning of this chapter we gave a definition of catechesis. We can now, in harmony with it, summarize the function and task of the catechist in the following words:

The catechist is a believer who by his word gives witness to Christ's mystery and thus illuminates men's earthly life, in order to help them to achieve an authentic religious self-commitment.

In the following pages we shall first explain this definition. After that, we shall discuss a few questions concerning the cooperation between the school and the family and conclude with a consideration of the task of the priest in the school catechesis.

A. "THE CATECHIST IS A BELIEVER, WHO BY HIS WORD GIVES WITNESS TO CHRIST'S MYSTERY"

The task of the catechist places him in the heart of the Church, of the community of the faithful gathered around Christ; and it is from this center that he must proclaim Christ to children and youths. That is why we define the catechist's function more precisely by saying that he must be a *witness* to Christ's mystery, a witness in imitation of Christ and in virtue of the commission given by Christ himself.

Jesus Christ "is the faithful witness" (Apoc. 1:5), who by His life and words has revealed the Father to us: "All things that I have heard from my Father I have made known to you" (Jn. 15:15); "He who has sent me is true, and the things I heard from him, these I speak in the world" (Jn. 8:26). Christ sealed that testimony with His blood and, by rising from the dead, His testimony acquired eternal value.

In turn, Christ gave His apostles the commission of carrying that testimony farther: "As the Father has sent me, I also send you" (Jn. 20:21). And to enable them to fulfill that task He gave them a share in the Holy Spirit who animated Him: "You shall receive power when the Holy Spirit comes upon you, and you shall be witnesses for me . . . to the very ends of the earth" (Acts 1:8).

The catechist who gives witness as a believer proclaims the living conviction of the Christian community of believers in which he is personally involved. Hence he speaks out of his most profound conviction. This witness extends to the whole Christ-consciousness which the Church has by the power of the Holy Spirit when she celebrates the liturgy, when she speaks from Holy Scripture and when she acts.

It follows that the witness is personally involved, as believer, in that which he proclaims. On the other hand, his testimony also transcends him because he must be the faithful herald of the whole faith-consciousness of the Church. Let us enter a little more deeply into those two aspects of the testimony.

The Catechist's Self-involvement in What He Proclaims

The catechist addresses himself as a believer to fellow-believers whom he wants to lead further into the mystery of Christ, in which he himself believes and according to which he lives. Hence he is not one who, merely possessing a thorough knowledge of revealed truths and being familiar with religious matters, tries, on this basis, to convince the children who are entrusted to him. He is himself on his way to God: he is certain, as faith alone can make one certain, and yet is, at the same time, always in search of truth and values.

Nowhere does the teacher stand so much on equal footing with the pupils as here. He himself stands in the attitude of a hearer and recipient before Christ's mystery which he cannot completely fathom but which discloses itself increasingly as he tries to respond to it in a more complete personal commitment. This believing openness toward Christ and this believing self-commitment to Him must resound in the catechist's proclamation of the word.

This openness and self-commitment are necessary because he must, before all else, confront the children and youths with Christ Himself, and because they will be able to arrive at an authentic religious life only when that same openness is awakened in them and confirmed by a believing self-commitment to Him. It is by his own loving faith that the catechist ignites the faith of his pupils.

The testimony of the catechist's own Christian life must form the background of the testimony of his words. The better a man he is, the more fruitful his work as a herald of the faith will be. He himself must strive to become a mature believer. It is precisely this that enables him to create a situation in which his pupils can graft themselves onto the mystery of Christ.

An adult's proclamation of the faith which is not in harmony with his life is no witness; it is, at most, giving information about the content of faith. Such an instruction remains outside, or is kept outside, a believing approach to its content. In the past there was certainly a one-sided emphasis on the transmission of knowledge; insufficient attention was paid to the question how this transmission of knowledge should have functioned in an authentic education in the faith, that is, should have aimed at a believing self-commitment.

The personal involvement of the catechist in what he proclaims presupposes that he is truly God-conscious. By this we mean that he is conscious of the fact that he is placed in a personal relationship with God, with the three Divine Persons.

A confrontation with the signs of God's salvific activity, as these have been described in Chapter Two, can lead us to an encounter with God, and we shall thus experience God. It is from this experience of God that our God-consciousness grows. The more we learn to discover and discern the signs of God's salvific action in our life and increasingly respond to them, the more, and the more strongly, our God-consciousness will develop. It is this God-consciousness that gives its vivifying power to the witness of the catechist.

Faithful Herald of the Whole Faith-Consciousness of the Church

The personal faith of the catechist does not stand detached from the faith-consciousness of the whole Christian community. As a catechist, he is one who "is called"; he does not speak on his own authority but must faithfully proclaim the living tradition, as it is constantly vivified in the whole Church by the Holy Spirit.

If he wishes to be able to accomplish this, he must—besides

participating as intensely as possible in the life of the People of God—constantly study so as to deepen his knowledge of what the Church communicates, in virtue of her faith-consciousness, concerning the mystery of Christ, basing herself upon Scripture and tradition, the liturgy and the living testimony of Christians. This study and knowledge do not yet, of themselves, guarantee that the catechist will give a true proclamation, but they are indispensable.

The Glad Tidings which we proclaim are unchangeable; we proclaim Jesus Christ and Jesus Christ is the same yesterday, today and forever (Heb. 13:8). The revelation of Christ took place in human words and deeds which were very simple and direct, in the language and according to the mentality of the hearers of those days. Because of the expansion of the Church and her progress through history, there is, however, a question that comes up again and again as to what those words and actions of Christ contain and signify in the constantly changing circumstances of country, people and time.

Now, the believing community, in which the Spirit of the Lord is present, has been able to express in sharp formulae her intuition of faith. These formulations we call "dogmas." They are truths that are so closely connected with the Person of Christ and His mission that the acceptance or rejection of what they intend to say are crucial for the right understanding of Scripture and tradition; and thus our faith also either stands or falls with this acceptance or rejection. Those formulae help the catechist to become more conscious of the life of faith. They also help him to distinguish that which is essential for the life of faith and what is accidental.

However, those dogmas themselves must always be seen in the light of the new understanding of Christ's mystery which the Holy Spirit awakens in every age in the Church in connection with the ever-changing way men experience their world, their fellow-men and themselves. Fidelity to the faith-consciousness of the whole Church requires that the catechist keep in touch with what is alive in the whole Church at the moment and that he try to find out what the Holy Spirit in our times says to and through the People of God.

Hence he may not close himself to the renewals and currents which the spirit of God awakens in the Church; he may not cloister himself in a way of looking at and living according to Christianity that no longer suits our times. He must speak in accord with the Holy Spirit as He expresses Himself in everything that motivates and occupies the Church at this particular moment. For it is the Holy Spirit who gives testimony of Christ and continues His work.

The catechist's duty to let his proclamation of the Gospel be stamped with the life of the whole People of God demands of him a well-developed Church-consciousness. This Church-consciousness is linked with God-consciousness.

Every man experiences God's saving action in an individual way but it is always the same God that men encounter. By this common experience of God there arises in believers a consciousness of belonging together and, as a consequence, there develops also a Church-consciousness. This consciousness binds them together in one community of faith. God's salvific action creates a Church, His revelation brings together a People of God. It is to this People of God as a whole that God gives the guarantee of His Spirit. In this Spirit who is the soul of the Church, Christ is with us until the end of time. That is why a well-developed Church-consciousness is essential for a catechist. He must realize, when he proclaims the Gospel, that he is connected with the whole People of God, for only thus has he the guarantee that he gives a truly faithful witness to Christ's mystery.

The Witness of the Catechist

The two aspects of the catechist's witness of which we have spoken belong together. It is a question of faithfully proclaiming the living conviction of the whole People of God, but with a personal involvement. We do not mean an artificial enthusiasm or external show of piety, but a living and true testimony that springs from a profound understanding of faith and that is daily renewed by reflection, meditation and practice. The catechist must constantly ask himself in what measure he himself is affected by that which he proclaims, to what extent he himself is involved in it.

It remains a great task, however, day after day to give witness by words to the mystery of Christ. It concerns that which is highest in human life, and expressing that mystery demands more from us than transmitting intelligible truths that can so easily remain at the periphery of our life.

We shall inevitably fall short, for we are not always able to integrate that which we present to others. But this fault becomes serious only when the contrast between what the catechist teaches and what he practices comes to look like a divorce, namely, when he no longer tries to practice what he preaches to his pupils. The entire high calling of the catechist is then reduced to a joyless life, meaningless in his own eyes and also without much significance for others because they find it difficult to separate the message from the person who brings it. It is precisely our own involvement that makes a truth be a witness and thereby a message, an invitation.

It is especially children and youths who are strongly influenced by the person who approaches them. That is why it is so very important in catechesis that the proclamation and the one who makes it should as much as possible be identical. This, of course, does not mean that the catechist may not at times experience personal difficulties with his own faith. Our faith is always a searching faith; and this fact need not detract in any way from the honesty and truthfulness of our catechesis.

B. THE CATECHIST "ILLUMINATES MEN'S EARTHLY LIFE IN ORDER TO HELP THEM ACHIEVE AN AUTHENTIC RELIGIOUS SELF-COMMITMENT"

The catechist assumes responsibility for the development of his pupils' life of faith. Hence in school catechesis there is question of a pedagogical relationship within the context of the Church. It is the task of the catechist to help his pupils arrive at a positive response to Revelation. He must stimulate them to assimilate Christian values. He must sustain their efforts to become aware of their own particular place in the Church and attain to a fully-human religious commitment of themselves to Christ in His Church.

We see, then, that the function of the catechist is a serving function, not only with respect to God, but also with respect to his pupils; for he serves God by serving his hearers. The catechetical witness described in the previous section is not concerned with a reality foreign to life; it concerns the whole concrete life of the pupils and is directed to their religious commitment in that life. The object of the catechist's witness is precisely the salvific dimension of human life; in other words, with respect to our present concern, he must give witness to this dimension in everything that constitutes the concrete existence of his pupils. Because we already spoke about this matter in the introduction to this chapter and in Section II, we shall confine ourselves here to some consequences affecting the attitude of the catechist and his relationship with his pupils.

Human Relations with the Pupils

Because catechesis aims at awakening and fostering the faith of the pupils, it is clearly and decisively important that they have the right disposition so that they may listen to and accept the witness of the catechist. Now, this disposition will depend in great measure upon the attitude which the pupils adopt toward the person of the catechist. When they accept the catechist as a human being, they will have more openness and readiness toward his spoken message. Hence it is the teacher's human relation with his pupils that merits his first attention. He must let himself be guided by deep respect for the personality of his pupils. What we have said concerning this in Chapter Four regarding the teacher in general applies particularly to the catechist.

Since it is faith that is aimed at, there should also exist a religious atmosphere. The climate of the catechist's being together with the pupils must tend to create an atmosphere within which prayer can arise with a certain spontaneity. Such an atmosphere cannot be forced, cannot be created artificially; it must result from our whole conduct and from what we say and the way we say it. Section Four of this chapter will develop this more fully.

A Dialogue with the Pupils

The faith of the pupils awakes and grows by a confrontation with the God of salvation who is active in their lives. Our proclamation will contribute to that confrontation by shedding the light of faith on the pupil's whole life. This means that our catechesis must essentially take place in a dialogue with the pupils themselves, hence it must not degenerate into a pure monologue. Thus we must listen to them with faith so as to discern the operation of the Holy Spirit in them. The particular form of that dialogue differs according to the age and degree of development of the hearers, but the catechist must address himself always to the situation in which his pupils live and to everything that occupies their attention and inspires them.

In this dialogizing relationship of the catechist with his pupils, he should respect the awakening and growing life of faith of these young people; and this respect implies that the catechist does not impose his own vision on them. However, he should illuminate reality in such a way that the children and the youths themselves discover the dimension of salvation, hence that the pupils are confronted in their own lives with Christ, the God of salvation. The catechist must, therefore, avoid forcing anything while, at the same time, trying prudently to stimulate the pupils to that of which they are capable.

The catechist's activity rests on his faith in the supernatural potentialities of the child and youth, in the connatural knowledge of the Savior that is germinally present in them through baptism. In every baptized child the Spirit cries, "Abba, Father" (Gal. 4:6). It belongs to the essence of catechesis that the pupils be invited, encouraged and helped, not only to let the Spirit cry out in them, but so that they themselves, by and with the Spirit, cry out to the Father; for "the Spirit himself gives testimony to our spirit that we are sons of God" (Rom. 8:16).

Penetrating to the Fundamental Questions

Illuminating human life as God's salvific action means primarily a faith-inspired interpretation of life in its essentials and fundamentals. It implies that we break through the surface of daily life and reach the underlying problem of each man as man, so that we penetrate to the fundamental questions about the meaning of life and make the pupils conscious of the need of salvation, as these questions and this need arise from the pupils' own situation. This penetration is necessary if we wish to prevent our witness from remaining on the surface of life. We spoke about this already in Chapter Two in connection with catechetical pastoral work.

The form which this contact of our witness with the existential substratum of the pupil's life will take varies according to their age and degree of development. The fundamental questions

113

will sometimes appear only implicitly. But it is always necessary to use ideas that are based on the pupils' concrete existence, so that they possess a living value for them. In this way we shall avoid using empty terms and words for which the pupils have no corresponding experience and that, on this account, have little content for them.

The Salvific Meaning of Earthly Values

Catechesis is primarily concerned with the more profound questions of human life, with the foundation and meaning of our existence; but this does not mean that the whole of earthly life in all its variegated fullness cannot be given a religious meaning. All earthly values have a Christian significance.

If the catechist is to be able to give such a meaning to those earthly values, it is necessary that he himself in his own life increasingly discovers the inner relation between the life of the Church, with her explicit religious values, and his life in the world; this life has its own values and signs, and these, on their own level, are not less important; they are taken up into the plan of salvation.

Salvation history and the history of mankind do not run their course merely side by side, but man's final end lies in the extension of the immediate purpose of his life. This idea and living according to it belong to every authentic religious existence. The catechist, however, must be able to express that idea in words. He must be able to explain to the pupils how he himself looks upon the intimate bond between earthly values and those he lives by in the Church. Concern for the truth, which characterizes the catechist, demands fidelity not only to the Church but also to today's world and its values. There can only be an encounter between the Church and the world if both are respected as well as cleansed of all impurities, and if we free ourselves from everything that can obscure an open-minded view of the Church and the world.

It may be useful to conclude this section by summarizing the qualities that ought to belong to the catechist's witness:

a. It must be *truthful*. His testimony must never appear as something artificial. The catechist must realize that the power of his witness does not come from himself but from the Spirit who works in him, that he possesses this treasure of faith from which he must speak in "an earthen vessel" (2 Cor. 4:7). And he knows that this contrast between the two is part of his testimony: for "strength is manifested first completely in weakness" (2 Cor. 12:9), or, as another version phrases it, "strength is made perfect in weakness."

b. Obviously, it is also necessary that the catechist speak with great *boldness*. St. Paul frequently mentions his boldness and practiced it vigorously.[1] The catechist must not be discouraged by his want of faith, of practical faith. For he does not rest on his own excellence but on the Spirit who works in him.

c. His own deficiency will make him very *modest* and *discrete*, and therefore also very *patient* in his proclamation. He should abstain from forcing others to accept or do anything to which the Spirit does not lead them; he must avoid putting human pressure upon them.

"Though we walk in the flesh, we do not make war according to the flesh; for the weapons of our warfare are not carnal,

[1] "Having therefore such hope, we show great boldness. We do not act as Moses did, who used to put a veil over His face" (2 Cor. 3:12). "I myself, Paul . . . who to your face indeed am diffident when among you, but when absent am fearless towards you! Yes, I beseech you that I may not when I come have to be bold with that assurance wherewith I am thought to be bold, against those who regard us as walking according to the flesh" (2 Cor. 10:1 ff.). "Do not, therefore, be ashamed of testimony for our Lord, nor of me, his prisoner, but enter into my sufferings, for the gospel through the power of God." (2 Tim. 1:8). "I charge thee . . . preach the word, be urgent in season, out of season; reprove, entreat, rebuke with all patience and teaching" (2 Tim. 4:1–2).

but powerful before God to the demolishing of strongholds, the destroying of reasoning—yes, of every lofty thing that exalts itself against the knowledge of God, bringing every mind into captivity to the obedience of Christ" (2 Cor. 10:2–5).

C. COOPERATION BETWEEN THE SCHOOL AND THE FAMILY

Religious education is primarily the task of the parents, who in this are aided by the school and other educational agencies. The whole of religious education is accomplished within the Church community, but as youths grow toward a more adult existence within the Church, the school and other educational agencies must gradually withdraw into the background.

Family life is by far the most decisive and important influence for the young child. With respect to older children, it is particularly beneficial for them to come into contact with grown-ups who make their faith and religion more explicit. The school can come in here to supplement what the family is unable to give, that is, it can help in creating a certain distance from the matter-of-fact accepted religious attitude, for the school has a less emotionally-charged relation to the pupils than their parents have to them. The child also needs this more objective approach in order to mature. But this more objective approach must continue to function within the framework of the faith, of increasing knowledge about the personal God. The more instructional contribution of education in the faith takes place in great measure in and through the school.

Let us remark here that, with respect to the young child in particular, religious education and religious life as found in the home must be the norm for what the school can give to the child. Otherwise it is not at all rash to expect that undigested conflicts will arise. As the child grows older, the school takes on a more distinct and independent place beside the family also in the matter of religion. This is an opportunity for the pupils to arrive gradually at a personal position also with respect to the meaning of life.

It is certainly desirable for a sound religious education that the cooperation between the school and the family should become more intense, in the sense that the school limits itself to its own task and gives back the primary responsibility to the parents. We must look for means to achieve this purpose gradually.

That is why we believe, among other things, that parents should have a greater share than until now has been customary in the child's initiation in the sacraments of the Eucharist, confession and confirmation, in making the child familiar with Holy Scripture and also in other aspects of catechesis.

Good relations and communications between the school and the family also merit attention. For instance, it is desirable that parents be informed of what the school is doing in the matter of religious education. Meetings of parents and teachers, preferably according to the grades of the children, are a suitable occasion for speaking with the parents about the character formation of the pupils, and should not be limited to mere information about their achievements.

We shall give more detailed suggestions concerning the cooperation between the school and the family in the programs for individual types of school attached to this book.

D. THE TASK OF THE PRIEST IN SCHOOL CATECHESIS

Besides the parents and the school, the priest has his own task in the catechesis of children and youths, for our school catechesis must be integrated into the whole of the living parish community for which the priest is responsible.

Is it not true that, within our strongly organized Catholic school system, we have not become sufficiently aware of the fact that it is the Church community that catechizes? Too often schools function as independent institutions, without a living bond with the Church community. This problem is particularly urgent where there are regional or interparochial schools.

With respect to the primary school, in order to bring about a catechesis that functions truly as a part of the whole Church community, a close cooperation must exist between the pastor and assistants and the teachers. As the priest is ultimately responsible for the catechesis, his principal task consists in fostering the catechetical renewal and helping to give it shape. He must inspire the teachers in their work as catechists, by giving them guidance, by deepening their religious knowledge and understanding, and especially by taking care of their Christian attitude of life and spiritual outlook.

One of the best means to foster that end is regularly held conferences and discussions between the priests and the teaching staff of a school or of schools that are similar. On such occasions there could be a discussion of the topics which the catechists will develop until the next conference. The priest could explain the theological, biblical and liturgical background and interconnection; the teachers could discuss together the proper pedagogical and didactic aspects of those questions. Also questions of a more general nature that are connected with education, especially education in a living faith and pastoral work, can find a place in those discussions; for instance, there could be questions about the cooperation with the parents, the religious mentality of the children and their sacramental practice.

This cooperation must not consist exclusively in jointly organizing the catechesis. There should exist, above all, a living bond between the priest(s) and the teachers. The priest should try to perform his priestly task also in regard of the teachers, although he must take care to respect their spiritual freedom; hence it is more a matter of providing the teachers with a considerable amount of adult catechesis than of giving them spiritual guidance.

A situation in which the priest's closest collaborators are most neglected by him would be intolerable, although that sometimes happened in the past. In fact, with respect to the catechesis of the children in primary school, the teachers are the priest's closest collaborators. They should therefore have a great openness, confidence and Christian commitment, both with respect to the priest and toward one another.

Besides the priest's responsibility with respect to the teachers of catechesis in the school, there is also his task of being himself a catechist for the children. For, in virtue of his priesthood, he is the herald of the Good News *par excellence* and for all. Particularly with respect to the higher grades of the primary school, it is desirable that the priest together with the teachers continue to take care of the catechesis. In the lower grades, his catechetical activity can have more of an incidental character; he can, for instance, visit the various classes from time to time, talk with the children or pray with them, exercise a priestly function on festive occasions, etc. Especially when the pupils are being prepared for the sacraments, the priest has a particular place in those classes.

Although in this way the priest may appear less frequently as catechist in the school, this does not at all mean that his over-all responsibility for the school catechesis has diminished. It merely acquires a new form, one that is more adapted to his possibilities and his pastoral functions. Through that kind of cooperation with the priests, the teachers as well as the pupils will become increasingly aware of the fact that they form a part of a larger community of faith and that the priests stand by them in this community.

Because one priest cannot do everything and because not every priest is equally adept in all his functions, it may be desirable to appoint a priest with special talent to be director of catechesis even for the primary school. He should be exonerated from other duties, at least in part, so that he could devote himself fully to catechetical work in several schools.

In high school, especially in the upper grades, the priest has a more important task in the direct catechesis of the pupils. For such students have a greater need of more profound reflection. This need requires a more complete training than the lay catechist usually possesses, so that the priest is a much more suitable catechist here.

Nevertheless, it would be desirable that laymen, in addition to the priest, continue to give religious witness in high school, especially to older pupils. In this way the Church appears much more clearly to the students as the community of all the faithful. Moreover, because laymen stand in a different relation to the world than priests, particular aspects of Christ's mystery will show to full advantage in their testimony.

The fact that the priest catechist, in the eyes of the youths, is clearly set apart from the other teachers although he acts as a teacher, is not entirely disadvantageous. The advantage is that the appearance of the priest-teacher automatically gives a special character to catechesis within the context of the school. It constantly confronts the pupils with the fact that the proclamation of the faith, which may not be absent from authentic religious education in a school, is not just another course of instruction in ordinary school matters.

4. Catechetical Procedures

A. THE TIME AND DURATION OF THE CLASS

The purpose of catechesis makes it mandatory to impose certain demands, within the limit of possibilities, with respect to the time to be devoted to catechesis. Catechesis has a right to the most suitable period, regardless of when this period occurs in the various academic schedules of courses. On the other hand, its very purpose also demands that we avoid doing harm to it by unduly multiplying the hours of religious instruction. If, for instance, we try to dispose a child or youth to make an act of faith, excessive repetition will be harmful and merely do violence to him. Children and youths do not have an unlimited capacity for explicit acts of faith.

In the upper grades of high school, where a more complete explanation of some aspects of the mystery of Christ is desired, it may often be desirable to have two connected academic hours on the schedule for religious instruction.

Regarding the question of the number of hours to be devoted to catechesis, we prefer to discuss this matter in connection with each type of school. Suggestions for each will be made in the Programs appended to this book. All we want to say here is that, in determining the number, we recognize that the religious renewal requires that the catechesis of children and youths be complemented by religious instruction given to them when they are adults. Moreover, certain limitations are imposed by the very fact that school catechesis has to deal with young persons whose capacity for assimilating instruction is limited.

B. THE ATMOSPHERE OF THE CLASS

We spoke already of the climate, the educational atmosphere, that is necessary to foster the growth of faith. But a more restricted sense can be given to the word "atmosphere" as applied to catechesis.

The requirement that the catechist's own life of faith be able to influence his pupils, in addition to the content of the catechesis, demands a special atmosphere for religious instruction; this instruction has a character that differs entirely from any other class. This atmosphere is not one that consists only in a good understanding, in mutual sympathy, between catechists and

121

pupils; it is rather, as we have said already, a matter of a religious attitude; hence we could speak here of a religious atmosphere.

The atmosphere of catechesis depends primarily upon the catechist's own interior disposition. This disposition first and foremost determines his way of living the faith and the impressions he makes. A religious atmosphere is possible only when the catechist lives in a religious attitude of self-commitment to God. Such an atmosphere cannot be created artificially by a number of tricks. True, external means can be useful for improving the atmosphere, but only on condition that the proper interior disposition of the catechist lies at its foundation.

Of course, concerning this atmosphere, we also depend upon the spirit that is prevalent in a particular class; and this spirit can only partially be brought about by the catechist. This is particularly true when the catechist is not the regular teacher of the class but appears only once a week.

There is also a problem of discipline. Religious instruction is impossible without a minimum of order. Catechesis even requires a particular atmosphere of peacefulness. On the other hand, it is necessary to be flexible in this matter; for instance, we must readily listen to spontaneous remarks and try to incorporate them into our teaching. And in religious instruction there is really no room for punishment.

It is only when there is a background such as we have just described that it makes sense to give further specifications regarding the place where school catechesis is given, the arrangement of the room and the organization of the lesson.

Religious instruction in school naturally lacks the explicitly religious atmosphere of liturgical celebrations and sacred environments; on the other hand, it has its own possibilities and advantages:

a. The possibility of more perfectly adapting the teaching to a definite group, to particular situations of young people.

b. The possibility of an exchange of ideas in which the catechist seeks, together with the pupils, for a greater consciousness and better expression of Christ's mystery; a common search for its content and its meaning for life, as well as the justification of this meaning.

c. The possibility of making use, with due moderation, of a greater number of forms of expression and other didactic means, for the transmission of faith.

On the other hand, when instruction is given in a classroom, we miss the advantage of sacred surroundings; if, then, we wish to benefit by the advantages of school catechesis, we must try, as much as possible, to create in the class, the atmosphere that is in accord with the purpose we want to achieve.

The blackboard must be clean of all the writing or drawings left from previous classes, for these things distract the pupils. We should also remove maps and pictures pertaining to other subjects. However, it is useful to place before the class something that is distinctly religious and that can make them see the complete "otherness" of religious instruction; for example, a beautiful copy of the Bible placed on a stand or a religious picture related to the mystery with which we intend to deal. Special exhibits for catechesis can also prove useful; older pupils can gather the materials for such an exhibit and arrange them gracefully.

A special room set aside for catechesis, as is done in some high schools, offers, of course, more possibilities. However, the ordinary classroom has its own advantages, too, for it suggests less an element of separation between the life of faith and other aspects of life.

The religious atmosphere of catechesis also depends on the way the lesson is organized, the matter one deals with, how the lesson is started and whether one tries to promote a certain climate by means of prayer and the singing of a hymn. Such means can raise the lesson above the ordinary work attitude that characterizes a school. Catechesis requires an atmosphere of restfulness and peace, in which the pupils feel that performance and achievement are not the important point, but that it is a question of standing before God with faith and of listening to what He has to tell us; a question of a personal encounter with God.

The catechist must appeal not only to the mind of the pupils but also to their heart. However, he must avoid, particularly in respect to young children, so playing upon their emotions that he forces religious experiences upon them and makes them perform religious acts that are not sufficiently spontaneous. This danger is not purely imaginary, for one can make children do almost anything. With respect to pupils who have reached puberty, it is necessary to deliberately strive for reserve, that is, it must be possible for them to "stay out of range." Here the teacher must be satisfied with explicitly manifesting his own faith.

C. THE CATECHIST MUST TAKE AS HIS STARTING POINT THE PUPILS' OWN WORLD OF LIFE

The purpose of catechesis requires great discretion on the part of the educator. He must take account of the possibilities of young people according to their personality development, and especially their religious development. Yet in a school we find assembled in one class pupils that differ greatly in that respect. The religious environment from which they come can vary considerably and there may exist a similar diversity in their own religious development. Also, although we must not exaggerate the group-spirit of a class, the interest of one class as a whole in what we present to them may be distinctly different from that of another class of the same grade.

If, then, it is necessary to let ourselves be guided by what is important for and is needed by particular students, it is evident that it is impossible to stick strictly to a sharply defined program. The various programs that we shall offer later in this book must leave room and must create room. There must remain a possibility of growth. A program that aims at educating to faith must show great openness and flexibility.

When we are dealing with a large class of pupils, we can only partially take care of their individual needs, even when we know those needs quite accurately. As a general rule, however, we should avoid addressing ourselves to the elite of the class; we shall often do better in the context of a school if we address ourselves to the average student. Pupils who are weak in their religion sometimes are hardly ready for catechesis. They barely rise above the environment from which they came; and they will probably lose all contact with the catechist if he aims too high. Pupils with a more religious attitude, however, will be able to benefit by a prudent religious approach that is closely connected with the life of young people and that now and then offers them a perspective toward something that is more deeply religious. Such an approach can even help them to insure the authenticity of the religious dimension in their life because it illuminates the bond which religion has with their ordinary life.

Another general rule which holds good for school catechesis, is that it is fruitfully and safely possible to reflect upon the faith only when and to the extent that this reflection can be based upon a corresponding religious experience. Otherwise we talk without reaching the students, and what we tell them remains for them a theory with no connection to their experience. Children and youths already have many religious experiences al-

125

though these are often diffuse. It is the task of the catechist to make those religious experiences reappear; only then should the catechist offer reflections upon them.

It is often remarked that it makes no sense to speak to youngsters about certain mysteries of the faith because they are not ready for them. But one must be very prudent in this matter. In catechesis we constantly deal with mysteries that are unfathomable even to adults, yet this is no reason for not speaking about them. There are no mysteries that are destined for children and others that are for adults; the whole mystery of Christ is for all men. However, everything depends on the way we confront our hearers with a particular aspect of Christ's mystery. And this way is sometimes poorly adapted to them. We must approach this mystery starting from the world of the child or youth. Our speaking about this mystery to them must not be in dry, abstract formulae but should be based on the way of thinking and the ideas that are found in the Bible, a way that is more existential and more personalistic.

Especially with respect to children and youths, we must leave implicit the aspects of the mysteries that are not yet suitable to their age and stage of development. This we must do out of respect for the mystery itself and also out of respect for these youngsters. Even their becoming acquainted with the mystery of Christ may show a gradual development similar to their whole progress toward maturity.

D. CONTENT AND FORM OF CATECHESIS

The Various Dimensions of Catechesis

Catechesis, as a genuine part of the Church's pastoral work is the proclamation of the mystery of Christ. This proclamation is a call, an invitation, to enter into the salvation mystery that was realized by Jesus Christ. But the question is, how can we now, in this time, enter into contact with the divine reality of salvation?

In Chapter Two we have shown how God's gift of salvation that reached its fullness in Jesus Christ is passed on in the Church by the action of the Holy Spirit. This act of faith to which the proclamation of the faith unites men is directed to the actual presence of the reality of Christ's Revelation in our own day, viz., in the Church.

In and by that reality man encounters Christ and, in Him, the Triune God. The Church, then, is for us a visible manifestation of a supernatural reality which, in our faith, we attain sacramentally, that is, in signs. The encounter that was realized in the risen Christ between sinful man and the heavenly Father is continued in a visible, historical community of men, viz., the People of God, the Church.

It is the task of catechesis to direct children, youths, and adults by proclamation and witness to the sacramental Church, in which we in faith, hope and charity must enter, so as to encounter Christ who is the fullness of salvation, *our* salvation.

That is why catechesis wants to direct us to an active participation in the celebration of the sacraments, as the Christ-given immediate signs of salvation. The sacraments are truly "mysteries" in the full sense of the word, that is, they are effective manifestations of God's reality of salvation, in and by the sacramental mystery celebration of Christ's mysteries.

This implies that catechesis must constantly announce the mysteries of Christ's life, as they are written down in the New Testament under the inspiration of the Holy Spirit and as they are announced and prepared in the Old Testament. For Scripture is the place where we see clearly expressed how God and Christ act with men. And in it we again understand better how God and Christ are still working in our own lives.

But the task of catechesis is not fully defined by that, for salvation is not offered to us solely in the sacraments and in Holy Scripture. The whole of reality in which we live is redeemed and, therefore, laden with salvation. "God became man, in order that man should be divinized." God shows Himself really as being at home in our earthly reality, in order that we may be at home in the divine reality.

To believe means to give myself to God who continues to reveal Himself constantly in my life, to God who is concerned with me. God's salvific action is thus the most profound dimension of our human existence, a dimension that can be perceived only with the eyes of faith and that contains an invitation to live the mystery of Christ in our relations with God, with our fellowmen and with the world. It is therefore also the task of the catechist to illuminate the salvific dimension of man's life. This throwing light on daily life should not be counter-opposed to what takes place in a *biblical* and *liturgical* catechesis but arises precisely through this catechesis.

Catechesis must show how God Himself enters through the sacraments into the human situation, how He comes and meets man as his Savior and Helper precisely at those moments when man most strongly feels the need of salvation. The proclamation of the faith on the basis of Holy Scripture is not merely a confrontation with God's entrance into the history of man. It includes, at the same time, an invitation to us to become involved in the still living and actual reality of that entrance, which is such that now we can go through life together with God.

The Bible and the liturgy, however, are not the only ways to discover the divine dimension in our daily life. It would be an impoverishment if we left entirely out of consideration God's presence and action in the human existence of the Church, of the People of God. Besides the biblico-liturgical dimension, catechesis has also a *historical* dimension, the history of the Church as the People of God.

Hence the content of catechesis is constituted by the mystery of Jesus Christ, as it continues to live in the Church. It is therefore not the proclamation of a *doctrine* but of a continuing "event" in which we are intimately involved. The content of the proclamation is the Glad Tidings of our salvation. If this message is to show to full advantage, it must as much as possible be preserved in its original form. The form of catechesis is therefore not wholly free; it does not depend solely on the inventiveness of the catechist or the personal ideas he has about it, but the form itself of catechesis is contained in Revelation. The mystery of Christ has come to us in the shape of "Good News" and under the form of a word spoken to us.

Education Toward Consciousness of God, of the Church and of Sin

The various dimensions of catechesis are all directed to one end, viz., to educate man for belief in God's salvation. This means that the catechist must help the child and youth in the development of their faith. It is not primarily a question of transmitting a *doctrine* but of educating them to a certain consciousness. Catechesis aims at making these youngsters conscious of the reality in which they live. To educate them in the faith means, therefore, concretely to educate them toward God-consciousness, Church-consciousness, and consciousness of sin, and an awareness of all this in its mutual interconnection and its centeredness around a connecting bond with our Lord Jesus Christ.

Catechesis must educate youngsters toward *God-consciousness*. It aims at making children and youths constantly more conscious of the fact that they stand in a personal relation with God, the God whom they experience in their own life, who meets them in everything they go through. It is for this purpose that catechesis wants to illuminate their life and show it as a salvific activity

129

of God, in order thereby to bring them face to face with Him who holds their whole life in His hand. Here it is not a question of God in general but of the Father toward whom they are on their way and with respect to whom their heart is restless until it rests in Him. It is concerned with the Son, their Fellow-man who shows them how to be man and so to come to the Father. It is a question of the Holy Spirit, in whom they cry with a heart full of desire, "Abba, Father," the Spirit by whom they are one with Christ in faith and are solidary with all men who place their hope in Him.

In this solidarity we have already reached *Church-consciousness:* a consciousness of being united with all the faithful who are borne by the Holy Spirit. Every man has his own personal relation to God, but the experience of God that is common to all believers binds them together into the People of God. The one God removes the walls of separation and makes all men, His children, to be brothers and sisters around His First-born, Christ.

God-consciousness implies Church-consciousness. In constant connection with their relation to God, catechesis will also make children and youths sensitive to the fact that they live in the community of the People of God. This awareness cannot be attained in one lesson; it is something that must be present throughout the whole catechesis. Again and again an appeal must be made to that consciousness, so that they will gradually realize that they share in the common responsibility for the Church and will discover the place they occupy in her.

Church-consciousness brings with it *consciousness of worship.* The faithful experience a need to be strengthened by one another's faith and to express that faith to one another. They want to come together to commemorate and take part in celebrations around their eldest Brother, Jesus Christ, and to continue what He has delivered to them. Authentic education in the faith is therefore at the same time an introduction to the liturgy of the Church.

God's salvific action demands a fully human response, a total gift of self to God and a total commitment toward one's fellow-man and the community. According to the measure in which man becomes conscious of that task, he also realizes how greatly he falls short of fulfilling it. And, thus, he develops his *consciousness of sin.* The unfolding of conscience and the development of sin-consciousness stand, therefore, wholly against the background of a growing God-consciousness and Church-consciousness. Only to the extent that man sees what God is and what God does for him, will he hear God's call for his response and become aware of his guilt in relation to God. God's infinity reveals the infinity of sin.

It would not serve any really useful purpose to reserve a special place in catechesis for a systematic explanation of sin on the basis of a theological formula. Such a theological and juridical approach leads easily to a formalistic and pharisaic attitude of life. It is much better if sin-consciousness is awakened as interwoven with the whole fabric of authentic education in the faith.

Who God is and what sin is, is fully revealed in Jesus Christ. His whole life was a revelation of God and at the same time a stand against sin. In and through confrontation with Jesus we gradually grow in our awareness of God's greatness and the abyss of sin. That is why the catechesis of Jesus Christ must dominate the whole of education in the faith.

Education to sin-consciousness takes place, therefore, in the whole of catechesis, for catechesis is a constant proclamation of Jesus Christ as coming to our encounter, as saving, redeeming, re-creating, and bringing salvation. In the light of this loving Revelation of God in Jesus Christ, man sees and recognizes ever more how his life is spoiled by moral evil, and he hears an ever more pressing invitation to free himself from that disorderly situation. To live Christ's mystery, to accept Christ, means to become ever more Christlike in the struggle against evil, by a life of love toward God and neighbor, as is exemplified in His own life: "Have this mind in you which was also in Jesus Christ" (Phil. 2:5).

The Formation of Conscience

God meets us with His salvation in everything that we go through and experience in every situation of life. He invites us to give Him a believing response in every concrete situation. The "instrument" that enables us to discern in every situation what response God here and now expects from us, the interpreter that expresses God's concrete will for us, we call "conscience."

The usual definition of conscience as "the judgment about our own good or bad conduct" needs some clarification. It is true that conscience is primarily a knowing that rests on understanding, but our knowledge and judgment are at the same time influenced by our affections. Conscience is not mere thinking, reasoning and pronouncing judgments; it is also intuitive knowledge in which affective elements play a role.

In modern thought about man, affective life is again taken into account in the appreciation of morality. Affectivity connects us with the outside world. Hence no education is possible that does not constantly appeal to our affectivity. Only that which attracts or repels us is real for us; our affectivity makes the outside world become really present to us; it makes us discover the world's values or lack of values.

The "voice of conscience," then, is influenced by our affective atmosphere. The way we morally evaluate ourselves depends upon our condition, our affective disposition. That is why a true *metanoia* (conversion) is necessary for a pure judgment of conscience, for this judgment requires purification and honest inquiry. Since the function of conscience is closely connected with our affective life and our passions, the task of conscience consists precisely in creating order in that life. Man's consciousness strives for order and unity, and conscience is the organ of this human unity; it creates order in the chaotic multiplicity of tendencies which man experiences in himself.

Conscience makes man capable of being personally responsible for his conduct. It is toward that self-responsibility that children and youths must grow, and this requires that they be given opportunities to do so. Hence, all education must, as soon as possible, become self-education.

In the past there has sometimes been a wrong appeal to God's will: "God wills it that way; hence it is good; so do it that way." We should say instead: "This is good, that is why God wills it." Hence we should not be content with external motives such as reward and punishment. Values must speak for themselves. God does not impose His will on reality from without; His will lies within reality itself. God speaks in the value that lies in men and things themselves. The voice of their own value is God's voice. Yet it is true that if we wish to recognize the ultimate true value of men and things we must be enlightened by Revelation. The Gospel has a critical function with respect to our value judgments of men and things. We have a constant need of an ever renewed *metanoia* or conversion of our vision and must constantly test our views according to the standard of the Glad Tidings.

Children and youths are continually in contact with concrete reality. Their mind and conscience are formed through innumerable experiences. They must learn to ask themselves: "What is expected of me by my concrete life?" For it is in that life that God's will is to be found. If God is represented as a purely external authority and one has recourse to this alone, there is a danger that conscience will not be able to grow since it does not learn to conquer and master reality. Then children and youths may still adjust themselves to the demands but they assume no responsibility: "If God didn't ask this, I wouldn't do it."

Conscience is not primarily an organ for judging what is evil, but one by which I here and now recognize and fulfill the good that is to be done. The Lord is holy and He wants us to be holy. This is His great plan of salvation for men: "Be holy as I am holy." This holiness of the living God, that was revealed in all its splendor in Jesus Christ, is the firm pivot of my conscience. The holy living God speaks here and now directly to me. His law was not only engraved on stone but lives in the hearts of all men, it is the hidden presence of God in us.

From this presence we may not divorce conscience. Conscience is a voice within us but, at the same time, transcending us. The Holy Spirit lives in our hearts, and in our conscience. It is He who enlightens our mind and moves our will to what is good and even to what is heroic. Through Him we already possess the holiness of God, but as yet only in capacity, as a taste for what is good and holy. This capacity comes alive by being confronted with the values of the world and of men around us. It is in the encounter between myself and these values that I hear God's voice.

Hence conscience may not be isolated from the religious foundation which gives it a divine dimension. Conscience is the organ for the good, still more for the holiness, that consists in love. It is the instrument by which God's Spirit makes me see God's will: what does God want of me at this moment in the present situation?

But this means also that man must learn to have an eye for the situation, for the possibilities and opportunities that the situation contains for the realization of what is good. With respect to the formation of conscience, this means that it is absolutely necessary to explain at once to the awakening conscience of youngsters that moral goodness has its foundation in the earthly reality of things and men themselves. On the other hand, however, we would render a disservice to them if we did not also, just as early, orientate that goodness Godwards.

"Do not extinguish the Spirit, but test all things; hold fast that which is good. Keep yourselves from every kind of evil" (1 Thes. 5:19).

Education in Prayer

Catechesis aims at fostering the dialogue between man and God. God offers His salvation to man, and man hears the call to respond to God's offer. Man's response to God's loving initiative must encompass his whole life.

This means that man must try, in his whole life and in all his actions, to recognize God as His God, that is, to adore, love and thank Him. But all this must be coupled with a profound awareness of his personal insufficiency and his need to be supported by God's help. A very special and profoundly human form of that human attitude toward God is prayer. In it man tries to express his sentiments of gratitude, reverence, love and adoration toward God. But the disorderly and spoiled situation in which man finds himself makes him also implore God's assistance.

Prayer is a vital expression of our religious life. That is why the catechist must take great care of it during the whole course of educating his pupils in a living faith. In their ordinary life youngsters learn to pray mainly by taking part in the prayers of adults. Religious instruction, however, offers an opportunity to the catechist to pray together with his pupils and to adapt the prayers to their religious capacity. This does not at all mean that he must content himself with childish prayers.

In this respect he should avoid stereotype formulae so that prayer will not be experienced exclusively as a duty. On the other hand, prayer must not depend solely on whether we feel a need for it or not; it is essentially an expression of our personal relationship with God.

In order to prompt pupils to genuine prayer, the material environment is important but the spiritual atmosphere has an even greater role: peace, quiet, cheerfulness and sympathy, educating them to a sense of admiration and making them sensitive to the meaning of symbols. Youngsters depend in this respect mainly on their home environment, which can be scrupulous, devotion-minded, weakly religious or genuinely Christian. Yet the attitude of the catechist can be either a help or an obstacle.

The child and youth pray to God in the way they have learned to know God. The best chances are had by those who grow up in a well-balanced family where they have acquired a wholesome idea of God, that is, where they realize God's majesty but also look upon Him as a Father.

The content of prayer must be truthful. It should, as much as possible, be biblical and liturgical in text and inspiration. On the other hand, we must take account of the realism of youth and, hence, make use of their own experiences as a starting point. Even more than in other fields, we must here show great reserve; we may not force ourselves upon our pupils. The older they are, the more we must respect their growing personality and freedom.

Prayer formulae are a necessity but contain the danger of degenerating into a sort of magic or mere words. When formulae are used they should at least awaken a certain atmosphere of prayer. This applies also to religious songs. Improvised prayer offers more opportunity to teach the young that prayer is a conversation, a being-together with God. Nevertheless, we must at the same time try to preserve a certain true style of prayer. It should not be turned into a discourse or a sermon. External posture and gesture merit more attention than they sometimes receive. It is possible by way of the spontaneous postures and gestures that belong to the youngsters' own world of expression to make them discover the riches of the universally used religious postures and gestures.

Special attention should be given to a form of prayer that has been called "catechetical celebration." Here, by word and action, in a sacral atmosphere that resembles a liturgical gathering, a biblical or historical event is represented to make the pupils relive a mystery and in which all of them can take part. Many things can lead to such a celebration, for instance, jointly admiring something beautiful and thus being naturally led to prayer. In its most classical form, suitable for older pupils, the catechetical celebration is a sort of service of the word with songs, readings and prayer. The form must be adapted to the environment. The school environment permits less in this respect than a church or chapel.

Conversation and Story-telling

The religious attitude of both the catechist and his pupils makes conversation between them a natural method for engaging in a common exploration of faith. He can, for instance, start from some actual event in order to draw attention to a general question man must face. This question must then be proposed to the pupils in such a way that it stimulates them to think and reflect. The catechist should not be satisfied with a mere "yes" or "no" or let the pupils give a particular answer because they know that it will please him. At the same time, they must be confronted with God's word in such a way that they are prompted to look for an answer in terms of faith.

The older the pupils, the greater the possibility of giving the form of dialogue to the whole instruction, although difficulties will frequently arise because of the number of pupils and the seating arrangement of a particular group. This sort of dialogue requires that the catechist have sufficient knowledge of the rules of a good conversation, for these are generally applicable also to catechesis. It is true, however, that here, even more than elsewhere, we must show respect for the opinion of others and must not seek any other clarity in our conclusions than a clarity that is wrapped in the mystery of faith.

Precisely because catechesis does not aim merely at instruction and clarity of understanding but wants to create a disposition to a way of believing in which the whole personality is involved, story-telling can be a useful method. For a story has the riches and concrete coloring of real life; sentiment can have an important place in it, and full scope is given to the personal dimension. In catechesis, personalistic examples are always preferable to examples taken from things.

At the same time we must avoid overburdening a story with all sorts of incidental details and strive to make the dominant idea stand out clearly. The amount of development to be given to a story depends on the power of imagination and the intelligence of the pupils. It must, however, be always illustrative. Repetition *within* a story can serve to make a particular idea stand out strongly. Repetition *of* a story is useful for younger children to make them gradually familiar with it. The development of a story must always be inspired by the religious attitude that should be the soul of the whole catechesis.

It may happen sometimes that the suggestive power of a story is weakened if, after telling it, we make applications of it or begin to moralize about it. It is much better to preface the story with a certain framework within which it will become meaningful and then, by judicious selection and development, make that meaning stand out clearly. Sometimes it might be useful to return to the purpose of the story in a subsequent lesson and in a wider perspective.

The Function of Memory

Learning things by heart was for a long time considered one of the most important methods of assimilating a particular subject matter. In recent times the esteem for memory achievements has greatly decreased. The reason might be that the abundance of impressions with which everyone is presently bombarded prevents the concentration that is required for memorizing.

Moreover, the significance of ideas and views has been relativized by the numerous changes that have occurred, so that we are not sure which things deserve the troublesome labor of memorization. Again, the knowledge gathered in diverse fields has grown to such proportions that we are forced to have recourse to books of reference and documentation. Finally, there is the fact that we feel a strong need for knowledge that is critically assimilated and that can also be used in a new context.

All this, however, should not make us conclude that the function of memory has but little importance. The preservative function of memory is necessary for human life. By it, the rich treasure of experiences that is gathered in the course of life creates the indispensable background of our thoughts, aspirations and our conduct. Moreover, we need to have at our disposal skills and knowledge, which become our possession through systematic exercise and repetition. Finally, we need knowledge which, by ever more profound study, brings up questions and insights that make it possible for us to proceed in an intelligent and prudent way.

That is why education certainly should not neglect the enrichment which memory brings with it to the pupils. But this must be done in diverse ways according to the particular nature of the respective data. With respect to some subjects, manifold repetition is in order; regarding other subject matters, the emphasis must be placed on studying the data in their structure and relations with other data. Regarding religious instruction, particular importance must be attached to the enrichment of the memory that arises from deep-felt experiences. Repetition plays no essential role in this; one single striking experience can become unforgettable. In such cases it is not a matter of knowing things, of getting a mental grasp, it might be better to say that it is a "knowledge of the heart." The privileged field of such "knowledge of the heart" lies especially in fellowship with other human beings; it is a knowledge that transcends the mere recording of facts. For instance, we recall some startling encounter, some experience we lived through together with others; we recall a word spoken by a person we loved. To indicate the special form of memory activity that takes place in such cases we use the term "remembrance."

The above-mentioned distinctions should not be conceived as complete separations: intentional learning must be based on experience, experience can become remembrance, and the passage to remembrance can also find a place within the frame of intentional learning. However, it is very important for systematic education to take those distinctions into account; otherwise we shall almost inevitably use, too one-sidedly, intentional learning through study and repetition. There is then a danger that all knowledge might be reduced to "having a grasp of things." Life can become distorted by such mistaken views, for what is truly human cannot be caught in such a cognitive "grasp." This point is very important with respect to religious instruction.

If, in the present renewal of religious instruction we want to minimize memorizing, this is done for the purpose of limiting as much as possible and counteracting the tendency to objectivize religion. While fully recognizing the importance of memory also for the growth of religious life, we want to stress particularly the value of "remembrance." Children and youths need the support of memory in order to understand and acquire an over-all view of their religious life. Otherwise their religious experiences are too ephemeral to permit steady growth.

The principal means, however, to contribute to that growth is not learning by heart data and ideas that can be manipulated; it is rather acquiring that very personal knowledge that we have called "knowledge of the heart." The only purpose of religious education is deepening and interiorizing the life of faith. And this aim will not be attained by feats of memory. A dangerous malformation takes place when children and youths learn to look upon religion as the "subject matter" of one of their many courses, and connect it with a system of credits, rewards and punishments.

Religion must speak to the whole man; hence religious knowledge must be that fully human knowledge in which there is "remembrance." Then I do not learn to know the Church as I learn to know and look upon a purely human organization; but I learn to know Holy Church which I, together with my fellow-believers, form and constitute in Christ. Or to give another example, I do not learn to know the Bible as a collection of more or less wonderful stories, but as the word that God directs to me. Of course, "knowing" plays a role also in religion. It helps us to remain linked with the past which, as tradition, has a fundamental significance for the life of the Church. But this "knowing" must remain within the framework of God's salvific action toward men: it is not concerned with *thinglike* facts that we record and assemble in an attitude of neutrality, but with a matter that is of the greatest conceivable *personal* importance, viz., the salvation of each one of us and of all together.

The catechist who tries to educate youngsters on the basis of these ideas will place everything he says and does in religious education within the context of this personal reference to himself and his pupils; his actions and words will thus acquire the character of being an authentic witness. In his speech and conduct

141

he will bring into relief, and repeatedly return to, that which can most effectively give young people access to a more fully conscious Christian life. By emphasis and repetition within the context of a witness, he will call forth and strengthen experiences that can acquire the character of "remembrances." This result will scarcely ever be achieved when the pupils merely memorize theological formulae. An appealing prayer, a deeply religious song, a striking text from the Bible presented to young people in a devout atmosphere, are obvious means of support for "remembrance." This sort of thing is not learned by "exercise"; but, by doing such things in perfect simplicity before them and letting them do those things with us, we discreetly get them personally involved in religious life.

By a well-planned program we must strive for a progressive initiation of adolescent pupils that corresponds to their growing development. Only by paying attention to that shall we be able to forestall the dislike and boredom that inevitably result from monotonous repetition. Such a kind of repetition would be out of place for them. For youths the repetition should consist of a returning to fundamental experiences arising from a more profound and richer religiousness.

This kind of progress can be compared to a rising spiral—and, evidently, it should occur not only in youth but throughout man's entire Christian life in his repeated participation in liturgical celebrations. This progress is fostered only when we enable youths to have experiences that can become "remembrances." Thinglike formulae that have been learned by rote are static and will probably stand, inertly, outside the development of the gradually unfolding personality. How else can one explain the fact that so many adults become stagnant with respect to their religious knowledge and that they have never gone beyond the knowledge which they learned in childhood without ever really penetrating into it and assimilating it?

Those who are afraid that the youngsters who are going to be educated according to the new catechesis "will no longer have to know anything," are causing themselves useless concern. In reality, the educator's task of giving the pupils the knowledge that is suited to them has become more difficult and more delicate. Making children learn formulae by heart and repeat things, and telling them to recite their lessons are rather simple tasks. But educators have another duty. Authentic education in a living faith aims precisely at a kind of knowing which affects the whole personality, a knowing which must mature in accord with the young person's unfolding toward a full human stature.

Audio-visual Aids

Jesus Christ, who became man for our salvation, is the sign *par excellence* that is placed among us, human beings, to direct us Godwards. But by the Incarnation everything human and all creation have become a sign of the divine reality. In those signs we are confronted with God's mystery. This confrontation imposes its own demands on the audio-visual aids used in catechesis.

What we said above about atmosphere and experience applies here also. The aids we use, such as pictures, drawings, records, photographs, films and music, should serve as positive helps to bring out the sacred character of religious instruction. We should never yield to the temptation of using visual aids to make a mystery understandable, as if it were a question of knowledge through which we can master and manipulate things, when it is really a question of personal relationship. We must always choose the aids in such a way that they can serve as signs of the mystery. That is why it is desirable to practice moderation in the use of those aids. In other words, the aids themselves should be simple so that no affluence of detail diverts attention from the principal point; there must also be moderation in the use of those means so that children will not be swamped by visual and auditory impressions. Yet, particularly with young children, a repeated use of the same pictures, records or films can provide an opportunity to assimilate the matter more profoundly.

It is useful to make a distinction between documentary material that gives information about facts and illustrative material that is aimed at imparting a more profound sense of the mystery to youths. If these two kinds are thoroughly mixed, the result is always an emphasis on the documentary character and a diminution of the illustrative function.

With respect to both types of materials, it is essential that they be truthful. But the truthfulness that tries to bring the mystery nearer to us is different from that which tries to make us become familiar, let us say, with the milieu in which Christ lived. The truthfulness of the illustrative material tries to create the right atmosphere in which we can take up in ourselves and assimilate Revelation. This means that the illustrative material must have a sacred character. Nevertheless, even the documentary material used in catechesis has another meaning than when the same aids are used to acquaint pupils with the geography of any country. The documentary material about the Holy Land gets its value for us from the fact that Christ lived there.

The audio-visual aids must be correct from the esthetic and psychological standpoint. With regard to the latter, this is not the same as saying that we must adapt ourselves completely to the spontaneous taste of the child, for we have the educational task of providing an orientation for these young people. There are still educators who do not sufficiently exploit the possibility of letting the youngsters themselves make their own materials. This can be done both in regard to documentary matter (for instance, letting them construct a model of the temple) and in that of illustrative material (for instance, an exhibit illustrating the love of neighbor). There are great possibilities here, especially for older pupils.

Activities

If we wish to help our pupils to reach religious self-commitment within their personal possibilities, we must incorporate their own activity, their personal work, as an important means to this goal. This can be done not only in conversations with them and seeking, together with them, for a better appreciation of the mystery, but also through projects that they can execute individually or in groups. It is true that catechesis cannot make use of all the activities that are customary in profane subjects. On the other hand, children and youths need active methods to make them assimilate the content of our catechesis.

The first kind of activity that demands our attention in catechesis is *exploration.* Here children and youths as individuals or in groups try to get acquainted with some biblical event, a liturgical subject or an expression of Christian moral life; for this purpose they seek information; they make inquiries, visits, excursions. Such an exploration could precede the study of the subject in class for the purpose of gathering materials and fostering the pupils' interest.

The situation is different regarding activities that are usually grouped under the heading *forms of expression.* They comprise drawing, painting, molding, dramatizing, dancing, singing and many forms of verbal expression. In this respect it is not enough to have pupils draw pictures of a religious subject, for this will not produce anything worthwhile if such an activity has not been preceded by some real experience. We must first discuss the subject with the pupils approaching them also through the heart, for it is only when they are touched as persons that they will be able to assimilate properly what has impressed them; only then will they hold fast to those impressions precisely by giving expression to them.

We can say in general that in catechesis preference must be given to the kind of activity which provides more opportunity for assimilating in a religious way the materials offered to the pupils. The activities should help them to attain a more profound faith, for the chief purpose of those activities is *not* to make them remember things. That is why we should not content ourselves with projects that aim principally at making the pupils record facts and gather bits of information. The activities should offer them an opportunity to see for themselves how they are personally involved in the mystery of faith. The activities must prompt them to go beyond merely reproducing what has been offered them during class. For they are not meant merely to give the catechist the means for determining whether his instruction was sufficiently clear and whether the pupils have assimilated the essential points of his teaching.

The pupils' activities should provide freedom for personal assimilation. That is why they must be given some leeway with respect to their choice of means. We thus speak of "free expression." This freedom makes things interesting for them, stimulates a more personal reflection and will result in a more profound assimilation.

It is proper to the child to imitate others, and by imitating others he can attain to experiences of his own. Hence it is not at all wrong if children are influenced by examples. Mutual help among children can stimulate the less active; however, we must see to it that they do not content themselves with mere copying.

On the other hand, there is a need for constant guidance. Both the assignment and the guidance should take care that a certain tension be created between what we give as a starting point and the religious discovery the pupil should make. Otherwise, things degenerate and the pupil limits himself to a purely profane activity. Occasionally a youngster may also need our help, namely, when he is on the wrong track and there is danger that he become fixed in the wrong way. But such help must be patient and discreet.

The series of activities should speak to all the faculties of the child and youth, so that they may become involved in religious instruction with their whole being; otherwise, some of their faculties could become atrophied with respect to religious matters. On the other hand, children do not have equally great potentialities in every field and each pupil will naturally seek to express himself in the way most suitable to him.

This presents an extra difficulty, for the catechist himself also has his own preferences and talents. He is not to be blamed if he pays special attention to the things with which he is more familiar during the time the pupils are entrusted to him. However, he must allow those pupils who have different talents full freedom to use their own potentialities.

We should avoid judging the effectiveness of religious activities by a pupil's ability to draw, by his talent for dramatization, etc. That which looks pleasing can be poor in religious value, and a crude result may have been a great help to the child in arriving at a deeper understanding. The religious value in individual cases is something that in great measure escapes our observation.

Generally speaking, the young child who is still weak in verbal expression preferably expresses himself through action, in bodily expression, in gestures and postures (pantomime), in drawing, molding, and dramatizing. However, we should also try to stimulate them by asking them questions and letting them tell stories. Older children and youths do not so readily make use of drawing and molding, for they have become too critical of the products of such activities. Hence bodily expressions are less in evidence. They prefer verbal expressions; for instance, a recital, writing a composition or a poem. It is advisable also to utilize their interest in music and photography by asking that they use them to express their religious ideas and sentiments.

Actualization

The purpose of the entire catechesis, and of all the subsidiary aids, is to make the pupils interiorize what they learn in prayer and religious celebrations and to make them realize in their own lives what through catechesis they have learned to understand more profoundly and have made their own in personal experience. Because this "interiorization" has already been discussed we have merely to add a few words about the actualization of the catechesis.

The catechist—while avoiding moralizing—should show children and youths how to live their Christianity also in their profane existence. They should especially show them how they can realize the Christian love of neighbor on their own level by readiness to help, by forbearance, by willingness to give up certain things. In the case of older pupils, he must point out the possibilities of taking part in charitable and apostolic work and should help them to do this.

In this way catechesis can impregnate the whole life of the pupils and make it become an authentically Christian life, a life that is a light for all those with whom they come in contact.

5. THE RESULTS

In describing the catechetical method, we have tried to show that the aim is not to make the pupils realize definite achievements. That is why it appears preferable not to give them some kind of examination to test their religious knowledge. On the other hand, the pupils need more or less concrete points of orientation. For this reason we should strive to find some primarily religious high points; for instance, a special religious celebration, a particularly fervent reception of a sacrament, or the celebration of major liturgical feasts. And especially with respect to older pupils, one could still say that it would be useful to give them the opportunity to express orally or in writing what they know about the faith. However, this expression should not take the form of a display of intellectual acquaintance with religious knowledge but should be in a much freer form in which the pupils can express their personal attitude.

This whole catechesis is strongly orientated toward the person with his religious potentialities. That is why, though we can draw up a certain program, we should at the same time employ it with freedom, according to the interest shown by the pupils, for this interest is a manifestation of their needs. This, of course, does not imply that we should limit catechesis to the rather peripheral questions that they often ask. On the contrary, we should find out whether their direct questions are not perhaps the manifestation of other questions that lie at a deeper level. Hence our intent is to arouse those questions which are truly alive in the pupils. We must also appeal to them in a way that makes them assimilate and appreciate more profoundly the answers to these questions given by Revelation which they have discovered together with us.

The entire catechesis must be characterized by patience. For we do not have coercive power over these young people; and it is impossible to force their genuine growth. By reverting to the same mystery of faith, at different times, in different contexts, we must patiently work toward the goal: that they gradually develop an appreciation of spiritual life.

The sacrifice which the catechist is called to make consists in this: the results of this authentic religious education cannot be rigorously observed or verified. Particularly the catechist who is also engaged in "ordinary" education should constantly remind himself of this characteristic property of catechesis. Failing to do so, he might permit his catechesis to degenerate into mere instruction, the dispensing of religious information.

PART TWO

PROGRAMS

CHAPTER SIX

THE NEW CATECHETICAL PROGRAM FOR CHILDREN IN CATHOLIC PRIMARY SCHOOLS (GRADES ONE TO SIX)

1. *Introduction*

We wish to preface this part by remarking that it is important for every teacher, and for every priest who deals with pupils of the primary school, to become acquainted with the *whole* program. A religious educator who wants to limit himself to his "own" class will not be able to apply his "part" of the program properly. It is only when the teacher has a clear over-all view of everything that takes place throughout the whole process of primary religious education that he will be able to effectively fulfill his task for the children of a particular grade.

The catechical programs for primary school children that we offer in these pages are an attempt to concretely apply the ideas we expressed in the preceding *Fundamentals for a Renewed Catechesis*. As we pointed out, these fundamental considerations are in many respects tentative. This is even more true of these basic programs.

They must be seen as a continuation of a dialogue about catechesis in the primary grades. It is a dialogue in which all who are interested in catechesis are invited to participate. But it is our opinion that such a dialogue can be fruitful only if those who engage in it have made a thorough study of the first five chapters of this book. It is our hope that many priests and teachers will be willing to cooperate by study and practice in order that we may arrive at a worthwhile renewal of catechesis for the primary grades. We were greatly encouraged by the fact that our project for the renewal of catechesis received the official approbation of all the bishops of the Netherlands.

In the following pages we will first summarize certain points of the preceding chapters that are directly relevant to these programs.

AUTHENTIC EDUCATION IN THE FAITH

Education in a living faith is not something that stands apart and is, as it were, accidentally added to education; the whole of education must be directed by and permeated with religious formation. Authentic religious education is orientated toward Christian maturity. The whole People of God, in its leaders and adult members, is responsible for the development of children and youths toward Christian adulthood, for the whole People of God is called to make others share in the salvation that is offered to it.

The parents, in virtue of their Christian marriage, stand at the fountainhead of religious education. The authenticity of the life of faith in the family that is embodied in great mutual love and openness toward others, in a life of prayer and true participation in the liturgy, is of vital importance for the growth of the child toward a Christian personality.

The priest who is responsible for religious life in the parish, hence in every family, through his pastoral activities exercises from the beginning at least an indirect influence upon the religious life of children. When the child, at a later time, broadens its life beyond the confines of the family, then teachers, instructors, leaders of youth and others who are responsible for young

154

persons participate in their education. All of these, then, must make a contribution to education in a living faith within the province of their particular responsibility. It does not belong to the framework of the present survey to determine more accurately those individual responsibilities. We believe, nevertheless, that something more should be said about the task of the school regarding the authentic religious education of children.

The school plays a very important role in the education of primary school children; it is equally evident that it also has great significance with respect to their education in the faith. In order to achieve this it is important that every teacher approach his pupils from the standpoint of a Catholic view of man and instruct them from that standpoint, so that the children are assisted in their endeavor to arrive at value judgments that are in harmony with a Christian existence.

This point applies to the relations among the teachers themselves as well as to those with their pupils. Their collegial spirit is a necessary condition for making the school a Christian environment. The teacher's relations with his pupils must show that he approaches them with sincere respect and interest in their developing personality, that he knows how to stimulate them and correct them with patience, mildness and understanding. In this way these children will encounter the Lord in their teachers. It is not necessary to insist that making-the-Lord-present does not consist in offering them a saccharine pietism or in becoming a cheap peddler of uncalled-for religious reflections and motivations. Truthfulness, sincerity and discretion are indispensable conditions for a good witness to the faith. A school in which this aim is pursued deserves to be called a Catholic school.

No one should be discouraged because he fulfills that task imperfectly; this is inevitable. Moreover, when we speak here of the teachers' task, they must not get the impression that an exceptional burden is being placed on their shoulders. It is merely a question of specifying the general responsibility of making the

Lord present to one's fellow-man that belongs to every Christian. On the other hand, educators must approach children and youths, who are so dependent on others and so pliable, with particular care. The words about scandalizing little ones make it unnecessary to develop this point further (Mat. 18: 1–10).

CATECHESIS

Authentic education in the faith entails, from time to time, that particular attention be given to the life of faith. It is this we call "catechesis." As has been said in Chapter Five, catechesis may be defined as "illuminating the whole of human existence as God's salvific action by witnessing to the mystery of Christ through the word, for the purpose of awakening and fostering the faith and prompting man to live truly in accord with that faith."

Who Should Give This Catechesis?

Catechesis is first of all the task of the parents. They are the first educators of children; they form the first ecclesial community in which children experience the mystery of God's love and live accordingly; it is in the family that children receive the first explanation of such a life. This will take place principally in the form of an occasional catechesis as suggested by particular occurrences and questions asked by the children. But the Catholic school has also an important share in this catechesis. It must exercise this function with the maximum of intimate cooperation with the parents; otherwise, there is the danger that the results will be only mediocre.

Beside the parents and the school, the priest, too, has his own specific task in the catechesis of children. For the school catechesis must be taken up in the whole of the living parochial community for which the priest is responsible.[1]

If, in the primary school, we wish to give a catechesis that

[1] Cf. p. 118.

functions as an organ of the whole Church community, a close cooperation must exist between the pastor (priests) and the teachers. The task of the priest—who is ultimately responsible for catechesis—consists principally in this, that he fosters the catechetical renewal and helps to give it shape. Moreover, he must inspire the teachers in their work as catechists and hold conferences with them, as we have explained in Chapter Five.[2] Besides his responsibility with respect to the teachers of catechesis in school, he has also his own task of catechizing the children. It is most desirable, especially with respect to the higher grades, that the priest together with the teachers should continue to take care of the catechesis. In the lower grades, this function can have a more incidental character, as we have explained.[3]

The priest's over-all responsibility for the school catechesis, however, has not diminished, but merely acquired a new form, one that is more adapted to the possibilities and other pastoral tasks of the priest. Because one priest cannot do everything and not every priest has equal ability for every sort of function, it may be advisable to appoint a priest, who has a special talent for the work, as director of catechesis and to relieve him in whole or in part of other duties so that he can take charge of catechesis in several schools.

The Program

As we see in the descriptive definition of catechesis, it has for its object man's concrete existence in its deepest dimension. Catechesis wishes to be of real help to children and youths so that they may discover that deepest dimension in their life and thus be confronted with the Person of Christ who comes to their encounter in and through everything that is contained in their life. Thus the starting point and the content of catechesis cannot

[2] Cf. p. 118.
[3] Cf. p. 119.

be a dogmatic thesis or proposition (the old catechism) which we must explain to children, nor is it a definite program that has to be taught at all cost. This is true even if we were able to make such a pre-established catechetical content more or less intellectually digestible through didactic means.

The starting point of catechesis is the life of the child in the family, in school, in play and recreation, in his prayer and participation in the liturgy. That is why we try, in the programs here offered, to trace the religious line of growth in children from the age of six to twelve.

Hitherto catechesis as taught in the primary school often gave the impression that it was something standing outside the life of the child and the world in which it grows up. That is why religion frequently failed to give sufficient support to the child's life of faith both in its early stages and later on. If we wish to give catechesis a true to life character, so that it can exercise a formative influence upon the life and the personality development of children and youths, we must take account of the results of modern psychology regarding their development and of the image of the changing world in which that development takes place.

Themes of Catechesis

We must constantly remind ourselves that a catechesis that is true to life can only take place against a background of an education in the faith covering the whole life of every day. If we deal with a particular theme in separation from this background, almost inevitably it will remain more or less at the periphery of the child's life. In such a case they will accept it indifferently as merely some kind of information or as the subject matter of one course similar to other courses offered them in school. The themes catechesis presents to the children must be such that they will awaken experiences in them or make their experiences more intense. Appropriate for this purpose are:

1. Topics spontaneously brought to the attention of the teacher by one or more children, while many others show their interest in them. It is not possible to construct a whole catechesis on the basis of such suggestions. At times it will even be necessary to gloss somewhat over remarks made by the children because they may not be suitable to the group.

And yet the contributions of children contain precious suggestions for a living instruction; this, however, requires flexible adaptation and a talent for improvisation on the part of the teacher. But it can be done, if the teacher knows in general lines what can be useful for the children and the way some themes should be presented to them.

Themes such as death and suffering, perhaps also God's pardoning love, can be best introduced on the occasion of something that has happened and of remarks made by children that awaken the attention of the class. Only the teacher who is free enough to put aside the idea that he is obliged to deal with this or that particular subject matter will be able to follow the direction of the children's suggestions.

2. Events or impressions that speak to the children and contain a religious element offer a second type of suggestion for the choice of a particular theme. For instance, it stands to reason that great religious feasts must play an important role in that teaching; but shocking events that took place in the immediate surroundings or that have been broadcast over radio or television should also be seized upon for that purpose. There is, in addition, the change of the seasons; they too can be an occasion, especially when there is an evident connection, for instance, between Spring and the Feast of Easter.

3. Only in the third place should we speak of topics that are chosen for catechesis without being suggested in these ways. By this we mean that, especially in lower grades, we must

avoid trying to cover a fixed program. It seems best, in our opinion, to give the teacher a number of projects in which he can find suggestions and material for a truly religious instruction. He can then make his choice according to the circumstances. He can stop a certain project when it seems, from the children's reactions, that they are not sufficiently ready or disposed for it—he could then postpone it for a later time. He can also stick peacefully to one subject or theme as long as the children's interest remains fully alive.

Is There Room for Separate Bible Classes in the New Program?

The programs we present have the character of a liturgical-biblical catechesis in which Holy Scripture is worked in throughout. Moreover, the children of the Sixth Grade (11–12 year olds) are put in contact with Holy Scripture, though it is only as a first reconnoitering. For it is only at this age that children begin to have a feeling for a historical perspective.

Until recently many schools had Bible courses that were distinct from other religious lessons; this is evident even from the fact that there were so many "Readings in the Bible" for various classes. The children had lessons in salvation history and sometimes had to learn these lessons just as one learns secular history.

This led to duplications and surfeit. There were duplications because many stories were repeated in the separate Bible classes as well as in the other religious courses. This led to satiation; students in higher grades got the feeling that they were "overfed" and "already knew all that." The main objection, however, is that this made the children prematurely conscious of things for which they were not yet sufficiently ready.

The new programs we offer try to avoid those duplications and super-saturation. Thus we do not propose separate Bible courses. On the other hand, something valuable seems to be lost if primary school children are no longer made familiar with the world of the Bible, if they are not introduced to the many wonderful stories which, of course, they are still unable to fully comprehend but which, nevertheless, give them some glimpse of the mysterious world of God's conversation with men. Even if they do not fully appreciate the historical perspective, they are enriched by that history.

We know that children develop with the help of many stories they hear or read, for by them they are confronted in a childlike way with the world and history of adults; so also must they be given an opportunity to look in a *childlike* way at the history of salvation. But in that case, certain conditions must be fulfilled. Salvation history should not in any way be presented as a history that has to be "learned." We must not expressly confront children with Salvation history as catechetical instruction, for this would be to ask too much of them.

The children's contact with the world of the Bible is perhaps best accomplished by telling stories from the Bible. "Story telling," as parents and teachers know, plays an important role throughout the education of a child. Why, then, not make good use of it in religious education? Yet, there is great diversity in the upbringing of children and many lack the necessary background for understanding the religious elements of such a story. In any case, the story-telling should not be too explicitly or too emphatically "pious." The fact that we are telling a story provides ample opportunity to adapt its content to the children.

In telling the story or reading it, we could sometimes use the Bible itself, but the use of a Bible history may often be preferable because the story is then told in words that children can better understand. However, let us then use a good "children's Bible" that is exegetically correct and which, especially, captures the atmosphere of that mystery world. Such a children's Bible should as much as possible leave God's words intact but should not hesitate to adapt it somewhat when necessary.

Accordingly, there should be no more Bible "lessons," Bible "learning," and particularly, no Bible "classes," but instead a

161

telling or reading of Bible stories to the children, preferably during the last half hour of the school day.

We suggest that in the Third and Fourth Grades (8–10 year olds) preference be given to matter taken from the New Testament; the Old Testament could be used in the Fifth and Sixth Grades (10–12 year olds). With older pupils, we could, beside reading such texts to them or telling stories, let them read such stories in silence. This would work out well particularly in schools in which children are regularly given such tasks.

If we follow this method we shall retain what was good in former Bible courses and eliminate their defects. Education in high school is thus given full opportunity for a more deliberate confrontation with Holy Scripture, and this is made possible because there has been no premature exposure to Scripture as such in the primary school.

The Time and Duration of the Class

If we wish to give an authentic catechesis, that is, really foster a life of faith, we must avoid unduly multiplying the class hours and forcing religion upon children. The same rule also applies to the teacher. He is called to give witness of his faith, to testify to the highest values in life; and speaking about this is certainly more difficult and strenuous than merely transmitting some tangible truths that lie at the periphery of our life. It follows that, on this account alone, daily catechesis is decidedly too much.

The question of the duration of the lesson also needs to be considered. In practice it is always necessary to start from the children's world of life; hence we need sufficient time to introduce the subject to the children. A session of half an hour is often too short to develop a religious subject properly. Moreover, it is extremely useful to give the children ample opportunity for religious expression. That is why it is preferable to limit the time of formal instruction and to allot more time to self-expression during the class.

A longer session—which, of course, should never be "filled" with talk by the teacher—evidently requires great energy on the part of the catechist. Therefore it might be best to provide for both long and short sessions on the program.

It is in view of all those considerations that we make the following proposal:

For Grades I and II (6–7-year-olds): a half-hour class twice a week. One half-hour seems sufficient for those grades, even when children are given the opportunity for self-expressive activities; for these will not take up too much time. These classes are given by the teacher.

For Grades III and IV (8–9-year-olds): one lesson of a half-hour and another of three quarters of an hour, per week. It does not seem too great a burden to give a longer class once a week. Once every two weeks the half-hour class could be used for telling or reading stories from the Bible, as we explained above. These classes also are given by the teacher.

For Grades V and VI (10–11-year-olds): one half-hour class by the priest, one half-hour by the teacher, and a one hour class by the teacher. The half-hour class given by the teacher could be used for telling stories and reading from the Bible. The full hour should be consecrated to instructional catechesis.

These suggestions deviate considerably from the regulations that govern the existing programs. It is not our intention to try to eliminate such programs entirely. We are merely seeking a way of making better use of the time that is available within these programs. Those who think that our suggested times are too short can lengthen the sessions for each has his own responsibility to see that the religious topics are well treated.

It remains true that those who follow our proposed program

will have more "free time" in comparison with the former programs. This is now available for regular discussions between priests and teachers. We have pointed out above how imperative such discussions are for the renewal of catechesis. There are other uses to which this time can be put:

1. It leaves room for "casual" catechesis. By this we mean that the teacher now has the time for occasionally indulging in a spontaneous and free conversation about religion with the children.

2. If from time to time we want to have a longer religious celebration, especially that of the Eucharist, we can do so without upsetting the school's schedule.

3. There are more opportunities for free expression of religious experiences in all its forms.

4. The priest has a chance to visit classes which he does not teach and to talk briefly with the children.

To conclude this introduction, we wish to repeat what we said in the beginning: it is our hope that many priests, as well as lay people, will help us search together for the best way to arrive at a renewed catechesis for our children.

2. *Program for the First Grade* (Six-year-olds)

The child who enters the first grade usually has had some religious experiences. It has heard about Jesus, Mary, angels and saints. Probably it has been to church with others on one or more occasions. It says its own childlike prayers and has had experience of important Christian feasts. It has also a beginning of a moral life, which manifests itself in efforts to "be good," and it has some idea of evil.

We can say that a child has a general openness toward God and religion. It wants to join others in what they do. It has some little thoughts about religion and sometimes attempts to give meaning to what it sees and experiences. It does not consider those things critically, however, but accepts them in a matter of fact way.

In Dialogue with the World

The world in which children grow up has a salvific meaning. Hence we can say that children awaken in a Christian sign-world. The child is involved in this world and strives for ever richer and more numerous relations with it. The child is in a dialogue with this Christian sign-world, and this dialogue is essential for its own development. Especially for the young child, this dialogue is greatly dependent upon its educators. If they want to help the child in that dialogue, they must take account of the way the child experiences the world, of what this world is to the child.

This means that educators must have an attentive eye for the way the child experiences its contacts with parents, brothers and sisters, with other members of the family, with teachers and playmates. The dwelling, clothes, food, playthings, the street in which it lives, plants and animals—all these have a place in the child's world. We can only guess about the way the child experiences these things, and yet, if we look and listen carefully, we can come very close to the child. We should, of course, pay particular attention to the specific religious impressions that children receive from people who are praying, persons wearing religious garb, from the crucifix, religious pictures, statues, and churches.

We propose the following as the starting point of their catechetical program: The religious development of a child is accomplished within its dialogue with the world, in which the child depends on adults for guidance and support. It makes little sense to proclaim or announce to children religious truths, if the child's world does not offer any dwelling place for those truths. If these are nevertheless proposed to them they will remain outside the child's life so that there is great danger that the religious dimension will be divorced from the whole of a child's development.

From September to Advent

The child entering primary school is between the ages of five-and-a-half and seven and is going through a period of transition. It is still somewhat a toddler. In its religious expression it still depends largely on *doing things together* with adults. This should serve as a warning; we must use great discretion in our catechesis and must remember that there is, for the time being, but little possibility for explicit proclamation of the faith to the child. Especially during the first months of the first grade, it is preferable to continue the "casual" catechesis used in the home or in the kindergarten. We could, until Advent, use the time of catechesis for an exploration of the world as it is accessible to the child, of everything a child is able to observe in its surroundings.

In this way we confront the children with the *signs* in which God's salvific action is accomplished in men and which alone makes possible the personal encounter of a human person with the invisible but living God.

By *signs* we mean here not only, nor primarily, the explicitly Christian signs, like the word of God or the liturgy. All creatures, and in fact the whole of man's existence, are signs of God's salvific action. In other words, by them, God is ever more fully revealed and His salvific action is ever more completely accomplished in men. We may say in general that all creatures and the whole of man's existence are an offer of salvation, a "divine invitation" to men to live their life of relations with God, with their fellow-men and the world, in a Christian way. We say explicitly a "divine invitation" to indicate that God, at the same time, offers men the possibility of giving a believing response.

Naturally, we must bear in mind that children can realize this only in their own childlike way.

It makes sense, therefore, and we can truly speak of catechesis when, together with the children, we look, filled with admiration and wonder, respect and gratitude, at the world in which our life is cast. We thus confront the children with the mystery that lies in all things. Little children are particularly interested in small things such as flowers, birds and fish.

In this exploration of the world, we are dealing with real experiences in which the child can be wholly involved. If we confine ourselves to "mere talking about things and men," we risk falling into verbalism and arousing inauthentic feelings. We must also give children as much opportunity as possible for exploring their world through motor activity. In this way their bodily being will continue to play its indispensable role in their experiences.

Quite clearly the richest possibilities of experience lie in the domain of human fellowship. Although the child must still pass through a long process of social development, nevertheless, other human beings play a prominent role in its dialogue with the world even at this stage.

God is at work in the world that we thus explore together with the children. Now we ought to do our best to let this real world gradually manifest to the child its profound significance as a sign of salvation. Precisely the history of salvation that culminates in Christ has made it really possible for us to discover this sign of salvation with the eyes of faith. These children already know the Person of Christ; hence we can easily let them hear how Jesus saw this world as the expression of the Father's love and care. We can show Him as being full of the beauty of creation, as telling us that the Father gives all these things to us. The Father cares for us as for His children and makes others take care of us.

In this exploration of the world we must avoid prematurely

introducing God; otherwise the proper value of the world will be too quickly passed by; so that the question regarding the origin of the world would not unfold spontaneously and thus our premature answer to that question would become a mere cliché. It is not even necessary to always make an explicit reference to God. For only gradually can the more profound significance of the world become evident to the child.

While striving to make the children appreciate and admire this world, we must avoid blurring or hiding its negative aspects. Such insincerity and untruthfulness could lead to a shocking disillusionment. The concrete reality that awakens our authentic admiration also has a threatening aspect, as we see, for instance, in the powerful natural phenomena of water, wind and fire combining into a thunderstorm.

The same approach applies to everything in this world, to our fellow-men, to animals, plants and the material objects we use. We must keep in mind that children grow up in a world in which men are also led by other judgments than those of admiration. The pragmatic attitude that belongs to the struggle for life makes us experience reality, not only as something useful, but also as putting obstacles in our path.

Moreover, children meet with vicissitudes such as pain, sickness and sorrow. We should not attempt to gloss over or forget those things when we try to awaken admiration in our pupils. He who has a solid attitude of faith can look realistically at the world and still remain sensitive to its truly beautiful aspects and able to communicate this sense of beauty to others.

The Personal Religious Experience of the Catechist. We have already noted the particular importance of respecting the sign-value and sign-influence of everything with which children are confronted. This means that the catechist, in exploring this world together with the children, must remain very sincere. He himself must try to develop a truthful and genuine spirit of wonder and admiration, respect and gratitude concerning everything that exists around him. His own attitude will then, as it were, of its own accord be transferred to the children, though each will assimilate it according to its particular disposition and talent. It is this involvement of the person that makes catechesis a witness. We cannot talk children into dispositions and attitudes; we can awaken these in the child only through our personal experiences as individuals and as members of a group.

Teaching Children to Pray. The attitudes of genuine wonder and admiration, of respect and gratitude that are aroused in the children through personal experiences can be the starting point for an occasional, very gradual, education in prayer. It is not meaningful to make the children learn to pray with prayer formulae from the beginning of the school year. This remark is in line with what we have said about explicit proclamation. True, the children can without much difficulty learn a number of prayers by heart. It is true also that the texts of those prayer formulae, which they do not yet understand, can enable them to express their childish religiousness. Yet there is a great danger that the child will merely stammer words to which no religious disposition corresponds. When, on the contrary, the children, together with the catechist, explore the world in wonder, a kind of religious disposition begins to arise in them; we can then really help and support the children in giving expression to their experiences in a simple prayer and, thus, deepen and fix those dispositions and attitudes.

There are many possibilities for that sort of prayer. We can link it with Bible texts or liturgical texts, we can borrow fragments from our prayer formulae. The prayer can take the form of verse or that of a litany. It can be sung and be supported by gestures and bodily postures. Even gestures can, by themselves, be a prayer.

Needless to say, in our joint exploration of the world and the resulting education of the children in prayer we must avoid any kind of moralizing. Moreover, when dealing with children of the first grade we must also avoid explicitly connecting God with their conduct, for otherwise we may easily disturb the proper development of their moral life. Again, we ought to respect the feelings of the children during this phase of transition. They are vulnerable and can easily fall victims to anxiety and insecurity.

The Danger of Forcing Children. In connection with all this, a number of questions come to mind: Is there not a danger that we shall do violence to the child's affective life if we use this method of catechizing? Is it not possible that this method will produce a certain artificiality? The children of that age (six-year-olds) have a great tendency to identify themselves with others; can they really retain the little autonomy they have with respect to what the adult catechist tells them? Does not the catechist force the child to engage itself in a religious way, and don't we easily forget on such occasions that the children cannot all have the same kind of involvement?

These are honest questions and they certainly merit our attention; they also contain as many warnings. In discarding the strongly intellectual approach that was customary in the catechesis of the past, we must be on guard against playing excessively upon the emotions of the children.

First of all let us repeat it, it is very important that adults should know how to create for the children a proper atmosphere of security and belonging to the community in which they live. Secondly, when the adult wishes to bring out the religious dimension of the world he must do this with *discretion;* he must always avoid forcing children to become involved. Only when proper discretion is used may we hope that the child will be attracted by this dimension. It will then gradually discover that its life is truly directed to God.

It is only when a particular "sentiment" has been somewhat awakened in children that one can try to make this sentiment more explicit. And then, we must also keep in mind that not all children will reach this stage at the same time. Hence discretion remains very important if we wish to avoid talking children into inauthentic religious sentiments.

Advent and Christmas Time

The solemn Feast of Christmas, with its very distinctive ecclesial character coupled, moreover, with a most intimate family celebration, forms a natural starting point and supplies the content of the catechesis that takes place during the weeks before and after Christmas.

However, it would not be wise to confront first-graders with the depth and fullness of the mystery of the Incarnation as it is presented in the liturgy in accord with the needs and the capacities of adults. It is true that Christ's mystery is a totality, a living unity. We cannot take anything away from it without seriously maiming it. Thus, in catechesis, we must always confront the children with the totality of this mystery; but there must also be room for *growth* in that confrontation.

Hence in the catechesis for first-graders, we shall pay no explicit attention to the coming of Jesus Christ as Savior of all mankind or to His return at the end of time. But we shall simply tell about Jesus who was sent to this world by the Father to let people know how much He cares for them. This same Father chooses a woman, Mary, to be the Mother of Jesus. The message of the Angel is also a good occasion for learning to pray the Hail Mary meaningfully. The Story of Christmas itself with its whole entourage of angels, shepherds and magi can also be presented in the perspective of Christ's coming.

During the first weeks after Christmas it is better not to spend too much time dealing with the childhood of Jesus. It is preferable to let the adult Christ appear before them as soon as possi-

171

ble, for He lets us see in words and deeds how good the Father is and what loving care He has for men. In these stories we can let them understand a little that this is true not only of Jesus as He lived in Palestine, but that it is still true of the way the Lord now lives among us.

Lent (Preparation for First Communion)

With Lent there begins the actual, though still remote *preparation for First Communion.* As is well known, there is a growing tendency to put off First Communion until the second year of the primary school. This we readily prefer because it is becoming increasingly evident that the child's development is slower today than in former times, so that it is only in the course of the second grade (seven-year-olds) that we can speak with certainty of a true "maturity for school" or of "reaching the use of reason." However, since it is still customary in many places to admit children to First Communion at the end of the first grade, we consider it necessary to present here a simple form of preparation that is adapted to the children of that grade.

This preparation consists of a very elementary "introduction" to the celebration of the Eucharist together with others. We can start from the "coming together" of all God's children in God's house, for this coming-together is the first thing that strikes the children. We come together to pray and sing to celebrate a feast together with Jesus in honor of the Father. Jesus gives us there bread from Heaven.

This we can let the children see in the scene of the Last Supper in which Christ had a meal with His apostles, a meal over which He presided and during which He distributed the Sacred Bread. (In the second grade those essential elements of the Eucharistic Celebration are taken up once more but, then, within the structure of Holy Mass.)

Just as it is in the case of the mystery of the Incarnation, here too, it is not possible to give the children a full and deep realization of all the aspects of the Eucharistic Celebration. This is why we do not explicitly present the aspect of sacrifice. Sacrifice, sin, salvation, love, community, these are ideas children find difficult to grasp. They have some experiences along those lines, it is true; but they are not yet ready for reflective consciousness, for this demands a level of abstraction which is still impossible for such children. To confront them prematurely with such ideas in an explicit fashion can act as an impediment because the children are given more than they can assimilate. There is then a great danger of verbalism. This is particularly true with respect to the much-used words sacrifice and love; hence we should make spare use of those words in our catechesis. We can, of course, use those elements of these ideas that are within the reach of children. For example, gratitude appears to be one aspect of love that children more easily experience and appreciate when we present it to them. For this aspect is one for which children first develop sensitivity and it is also one of their earliest experiences.

The Time for First Communion. Although it might be easier to have the same time appointed for the children's First Communion throughout the country, there are also advantages in the existing divergence of practices.

When the children are allowed to make their First Communion at the end of the first grade, the summary preparation we have suggested will certainly suffice, but then it will be necessary to follow up this preparation with a more expanded version in the second grade. If the children make their First Communion at the end of the second grade the proposed Eucharistic catechesis in the first grade retains its value as a preliminary acquaintance with and introduction to participation in the Eucharist.

Moreover, with the idea that the parents themselves will take an increasingly more active part in preparing their children for First Communion, the program we have proposed for the first grade offers the necessary background and support to the parental efforts. And, on the other hand, it also leaves sufficient room for further development according to the needs of each child and its power of assimilation.

Passion Tide

The last two weeks before Easter are so filled with the thoughts of the Passion, the Cross and the Resurrection that our catechesis must pay attention to them.

And yet we find it necessary to recommend that the catechist use great moderation and sobriety when telling the story of Christ's suffering, death and resurrection. Jesus had come into the world to let us see that God is the Father. Many believed in Him and were glad because of what He came to tell. Others did not believe in Him. These became angry because so many followed Jesus; so they decided to kill Him. Jesus then performed His greatest miracle to let people see that all He had told them was true and that He had really been sent by the Father. He rose from the grave. The teacher should put the principal emphasis on the resurrection.

Easter Time

In many schools the immediate preparation for First Communion begins directly after the Easter holidays. The catechist should therefore return to the topic of the Last Supper and the resurrection. Jesus told the apostles to always do again what had been done together at the Last Supper, namely, to hold a holy banquet together for the honor of the Father. If they did that, He, Jesus, would always again be with them and would do those things with them. He would distribute the Bread as He did at the Last Supper and it would again be His Body. All those who wish to belong to Jesus have a meal with Him in honor of the Father in Heaven. By having a banquet with Jesus we belong ever more to Him and become ever closer to one another.

After this we can give a brief outline of the structure of the Mass:

a. We come together around Jesus in God's House.
b. If sometimes we have fought with others, we ask forgiveness.
c. We listen to Jesus's words.
d. The table is prepared for the meal.
e. Prayer of Thanksgiving; the catechist says a few words about the Preface, the Consecration and the end of the Canon.
f. Communion: Our Father and Holy Communion.
g. Thanksgiving.

During the weeks after the children's First Communion it is certainly necessary to return again sometimes to that great event. We could have a celebration of Holy Mass for the class in which, if possible, the parents participate. It is also useful to give some attention to teaching the children how to participate in Holy Mass when they do not go together with others, for they will sometimes go to Church unattended. This could be done with the help of a simple children's prayer book.

Until the End of the School Year

Holy Mass must influence ordinary daily life. Hence we can now say something to the children about loving their neighbor: Jesus, who takes such good care of us, also likes us to be good toward one another. This point we must develop in a concrete way; otherwise, our advice will remain pure verbalism for our pupils. "Love" mostly means to them "being sweet" and they fail to understand the true meaning of "love." But beautiful stories about people or children who are good to one another exercise a strong appeal. However, we must avoid all moralizing in this respect.

This whole preparation for and follow-up after First Communion is certainly not overburdened. Some might even say there is not sufficient subject matter for that catechesis and might ask themselves how they can "fill" the time appointed for this catechesis. We should realize that time is needed for carefully preparing the children for the liturgical solemnity. However, the principal reason for offering such a moderate program is that it is very important that everything be done in a very peaceful way. There should be no tension or exaggeration. The time of First Communion must be a time of peace and quiet.

3. *Program for the Second Grade* (Seven-year-olds)
Introductory Remarks

Eucharistic Catechesis. Here also, as we said with respect to the children of the first grade, it is the Eucharist that is central in the year's program. The program we now present is intended as a development for the children who made their First Communion during the first grade. We also mentioned that many children do not reach "school maturity" in the first grade. That is why many prefer to put off First Communion until the children are in the second grade. But whenever children are admitted to First Communion during the first grade, we must content ourselves with giving them a most simple and most elementary preparation. This preparation necessarily demands some completion during the second year. Children require constant accompaniment and assistance in order that they may continue to participate meaningfully in the Eucharistic celebration in their new situation and according to their increasing development.

The program we offer for the second grade can, we believe, serve as a means to deepen the eucharistic catechesis of the children who received Communion in the first grade and also as the immediate preparation for those who will make their First Communion in the second grade. With respect to those who have already made their First Communion, the catechist should give some attention to the eucharistic community and eucharistic prayer when he deals with community and prayer during the first three months; this should serve as a means to maintain contact with the great day the children already celebrated during their first grade catechesis.

A Realistic Catechesis. Throughout catechesis, and especially in that of the sacraments, we must do our very best to be "realistic" in our way of proclaiming the Faith. A personalistically conceived catechesis is of the greatest importance in this matter.

By this we mean a catechesis that transmits Revelation in terms of personal relations and is oriented toward the encounter of the pupils with God as person to Person. This personalistic approach is essential for an authentic catechesis. For it is not a question of presenting Revelation to the children as a way of living a good life (which tends to happen when we one-sidedly stress the moral character of Christianity), as a doctrine or system of truths we must learn (intellectualistic catechesis), or as an ensemble of rites (ritualistic catechesis, which often degenerates into a magical presentation of the sacraments and of the whole liturgy). But it is a question of gradually educating children to authentic faith in Christ, that is, to their personal self-donation to Him. This personal commitment must find expression in their whole life.

This brings up another feature that is equally essential if we wish to give a realistic character to our catechesis. The personal encounter with God in Christ takes place in and by everything that belongs to our existence. To believe means, therefore, not merely to accept divine truth and reality as it comes to us

177

through Holy Scripture and the sacraments. For the whole realm of reality in which we live is redeemed and hence is a bearer of our salvation. "God became man in order that man might become divinized." God shows Himself as "at home" in our earthly reality in order that we may feel at home in divine reality. To believe, then, means to give myself to God who continues to reveal Himself in my life, who is continuously occupied with me and calls me in and through the whole earthly reality that makes up my human existence.

That is why the catechist must accompany the children in exploring and discovering human existence and its values as they stand revealed in a vision of faith. This, in catechetical language, we called "illuminating man's actual existence in its salvific dimension." This kind of catechesis should not be opposed to biblical and liturgical catechesis, but is achieved with the latter's help.

Influence of the Milieu. Now, one condition that must be fulfilled if we wish to accomplish this aim in children, and certainly in small children, is to create an opportunity for them to get a living experience of all those things together with others, to mingle with those who already have such living experiences. Then everything else, such as doctrine, rites and moral life, also falls more easily and more perfectly in its place. Where there is a wholesome Christian milieu there is a minimum of difficulties. But the catechist has to be concerned also with a large group of the faithful, even within the Church, who have no living faith. His difficulties are increased by the fact that in most of our parochial schools children come from most diverse religious environments.

Regarding the preparation of children for the sacraments in general, and particularly in preparing them for First Communion, the question arises: how does the child experience those sacraments when it does not live in a home in which faith is

178

a living reality? How does such a child discover that Jesus lives, and that it belongs to a living community of faith?

Not only the child's family but the larger milieu in which it finds itself can play a role as a possible basis for a true and living religious experience. That is why the school functioning within a larger community of faith can make an appeal to the child's still unawakened religious potentialities by means of an authentic religious education. This appeal will have more chance of success if the catechist is able to involve the parents in this task.

In sacramental catechesis and very particularly in eucharistic catechesis, we must link the children's education in living the faith with their social experiences. This we can do by making them attentive to their experiences in the family, in class, in their play with others, and in their observation of other human beings. In this way a foundation is laid for a living experience of oneness with Christ and with others. The whole catechesis thus acquires a more realistic character.

Until Advent

From the beginning of the school year until Advent we aim at making the children somewhat aware of the way the eucharistic community is anchored in the ordinary human community. In other words we help them to look at the values of the human community with the eyes of faith.

This community consciousness is certainly not yet very strong in primary school children, but we can do something to educate them in that spirit. To what extent we should speak explicitly about it and explicitly work in that direction is a question to which it is difficult to give a general answer. There is, on the one hand, the danger of verbalism or of talking children into it, but there is also the real danger of asking too much of them and overemphasizing things from the affective standpoint. That is why it seems better to link our catechesis as much as possible with the children's own experiences, experiences that are still clear in their memory, or experiences that we can bring to their awareness by accompanying and assisting them in observing human relations.

We can, as a starting point recall the experiences the children had during their recent vacation. There are pleasant and unpleasant memories, but they are always in connection with other people. Would it have been possible for any child to have a pleasant vacation if it had been left all alone? No, we need other people. From thinking of those experiences it is only a short step to home and family, for many memories about vacation are at the same time experiences about the family. Next, we focus attention also on the human community as it expands for the child. After one year in the primary school, the special character of school has already become clearer to the child: we come together here to learn, to work, to play, to sing.

Outside the school also, children begin to seek one another's company more than in the first grade. They gather in the street or elsewhere to play together.

We look also at the world of the grown-ups, where people gather to do something together. At home, in the factory—everywhere, people always need one another. There is still another place where people come together, namely, the church: from all the houses, all streets, we come together in the church to pray.

In what we have proposed thus far there is no intention at all of approaching the children in a theoretical or thematic way. Although the children become mature for school during the second grade, their power of abstraction is still very weak. The terms "community," "sacrament," and "Church" remain mere words for children. Conceptual knowledge, after all, remains difficult until children reach the age of puberty. Children are most receptive to concrete events, to actions done by persons. That is why it is important, whenever possible, to let the children see that what we proclaim to them is a reality for the adults with whom we live. This is true of everything we have said until now; it is also true of what follows.

Training for prayer, which must find a place throughout the education in a living faith, can be fostered within the framework of catechesis by favorable circumstances but especially by awakening the right interior attitude.

Man's bodily being plays an important role here, for bodily postures and gestures, words and songs, quietly watching something and listening, all these constitute means of expression for praying man. This we try to make children accomplish and experience. Both their own prayer and the sight of a fellow-man at prayer are means that make children get such a living experience.

Advent and Christmas Tide

The catechesis of Advent and Christmas Tide can now be placed into a somewhat richer perspective than was the case in the first grade.

Jesus is coming in order to go to the Father, together with all men who dwell together, live together, work together, pray together and who are always in need of one another.

What happened around Christmas can now also be told with more details than in the first grade, but always within the perspective we have outlined above. This we can let the children see in the announcement of the birth of St. John, the joyful annunciation to Mary and in the story of the birth of St. John. Zacharias and Mary are, moreover, true examples of prayer.

From January to Passion Tide

During the next three months we begin with Christ's historical appearance in Palestine. We are not concerned here with all sorts of picturesque and exotic details; what interests us is the discovery of men's reactions and attitudes toward Christ. We

181

thus try to develop in the children themselves the various attitudes toward Christ that must find expression in our Christian life and that receive particular relief in the Eucharistic celebration.

In this connection we must avoid excessively isolating and emphasizing Christ's *historic* words and actions; that is, we must constantly place ourselves with great naturalness *in* that actuality: Christ did not speak only at that distant time; He speaks now; He did not act then only; He acts now.

Christ and the Father. Here we take as our starting point the theophany, the visible manifestation of God at Christ's baptism in the Jordan. Now we can speak a little more explicitly about Christ's relations to the Father and of the Father to the Son, of which we previously spoke several times but only implicitly. Yet we have no intention here of using this divine manifestation as an occasion for expounding the doctrine of the Blessed Trinity. However, it is evident that we must gradually confront the children with the reality of three distinct Divine Persons, if we want the children to arrive ultimately at a sound Christian idea of God.

The relation of the Father and the Son that is indicated in what took place at the Jordan and on Mt. Thabor becomes increasingly real for us in the words and the attitude of Jesus Himself. All these words and deeds are, moreover, a constant invitation to us to enter into the relationship He has with respect to the Father: "My Father is also your Father." The Holy Spirit as a person, no doubt, remains much longer beyond the reach of the children. Hence the revelation of the Holy Trinity cannot be presented in a fully explicit way to those children.

The Life of Jesus. We now try to prepare the children for all the principal moments of Holy Mass on the basis of the life of Jesus. For, making use of the Gospels, we can show the children how people everywhere come to see Jesus and how they always come together and surround Him They come to listen to His words of peace and joy and to see how He does good to people. They come to listen to what He says about love and the attitude of forgiving, which people should have toward one another and which is the best way to honor God. He Himself sets the example for all that. They come to see how He prays to the Father and ask, "Lord, teach us also how to pray that way." They come to eat together with Him and then to listen to His words and to thank and honor the Father together with Him.

Celebration of the Eucharist. After that, during the fifth month of the second grade (until the First Sunday of the Passion) we can give a catechesis about Holy Mass and its most important parts. Of course, we do not mean a purely analytical, schematic explanation of the Mass, but teaching the children how to participate actively in the Eucharistic celebration.

This, we believe, is now truly possible because of the fundamental Christian attitudes that have appeared in the previous considerations of coming-together around Jesus. This education in participation in the Eucharistic celebration can, after all, take place only if we educate the children in the fundamental Christian attitudes. But it is not enough to confront the children with the events recorded in the Gospel. They must also be confronted with the actual living celebration of the Eucharist of grown-ups, for this concretizes for them the *here and now* coming-together-around-Jesus. If we isolate the children from that, it is not possible to educate them for an active participation in the Eucharistic celebration. This remark calls attention once more to an aspect of catechesis we have stressed before, namely, that it is much more important to introduce the children into the living Christian world of grown-ups, of which the Eucharist is the apex, than to fill them with theoretical explanations.

Catechesis needs a living liturgy to which it can point and in which it must culminate. Otherwise, there is real danger that it will become an almost exclusively historical study of the life and deeds of Jesus Christ; or, on the other hand, liturgy might remain incomprehensible, have little viability and would easily be reduced to ritualism and a sort of magic.

The parts of Holy Mass we wish to deal with in this grade are the following:

1. The coming-together around Christ. This presupposes that there be great harmony among those who come together. A feast is often an occasion for doing away with divisions, for pardoning one another. This reconciliation often comes about by the fact that they now matter-of-factly accept one another, invite and greet one another. This pardoning receives even explicit attention in Holy Mass.

2. Listening to Christ's words. Listening is much more than simply hearing things and committing them to memory. It also implies being ready to fulfill what has been proclaimed.

3. The preparation of the Eucharistic Table. This preparation makes an appeal to all of us to be willing to cooperate actively with everything that is going to take place. It is also for us that this Table is being made ready; and for us, too, there is a place and there is bread.

4. Together with Christ and with all men, we now thank the Father in whose honor we have come together around Christ. In fact, we must always thank the Father and honor Him for all that He does for us. But we are weak human beings; that is the reason our thanksgiving and our honoring are so weak and so defective. That is why we all come together around Jesus. With Him we can thank the Father in the right way.

5. Together with Him, we also pray the Our Father, the prayer Jesus taught us; after that He offers us the Heavenly Bread. This Heavenly Bread is His own Body. We now belong to Him more than before. And we also belong much more to one another, because we have all been fed by that one same Bread, which is the Body of Jesus.

6. Together, finally, we thank Jesus for everything He has given us. He has received us in the House of the Father and at His Table. He has forgiven us our faults; He has spoken words of life to us. He has helped us to thank and honor the Father. He has given us Himself in the Heavenly Bread by which He shows us once more that He wholly belongs to us and we belong entirely to Him.

Passion Tide

In January we began with the Christian reality as it has come to us through the Gospels. From there we proceeded to the liturgical life of the faithful, as being an actualization and prolongation of that evangelical reality. We now return to the Gospel and show how that liturgical celebration, which we constantly repeat, took place for the first time at the Last Supper. Here we have another opportunity to shed light on all the aspects of the Eucharistic celebration of which we spoke above.

During the institution of the Eucharist, Christ constantly referred to the events of the following day, namely, His arrest, His passion and death. It is our opinion that it is still quite difficult for these young children to understand very much about the connection between the Last Supper, and the Sacrifice of the Cross and Holy Mass. However, the very special atmosphere of the Last Supper, the seriousness and the sorrow, but also Christ's sureness and resoluteness in spite of the events of the following day that stood clearly before His mind, already contain in germ the fuller vision and experience of the Eucharist that the children can attain at a later time.

The resurrection as a proof of the truthfulness of Christ's word should also be explicitly emphasized during this year.

Paschal Time

Now begins the final preparation for First Communion, or, in the case of those who made their First Communion during the first grade, we can now give a more complete Eucharistic catechesis.

Jesus is risen, He lives. He stands in our midst. He knows all of us. He is interested in us. He invites us. The apostles now recall also, after Christ's resurrection, what Jesus had asked of them during the Last Supper: they should constantly assemble around Him to have a supper with Him for the honor of the Father. For this celebration they preferably chose Sunday the day on which Jesus rose from the dead.

Here also we start from the Christian signs that mark our life, and especially Sunday as the day of our Lord. We next pass on to the liturgical signs that are immediately related to the Eucharistic celebration: the priest's vestments, the chalice, the paten, the altar bread; the gestures and postures of priest and faithful during the Eucharistic celebration; the most important prayers and songs used on that occasion.

All these liturgical signs and symbols form a world of their own and they present quite a problem for the catechesis of children. For this liturgical world often remains vague and incomprehensible to modern children. That is why those signs are frequently interpreted by them in a fanciful way that reflects only partially, or not at all, what they are supposed to convey. Children must be guided and aided so that by means of the liturgical signs, such as persons, objects, postures of the body, they may penetrate to the deep meaning that lies behind those signs and symbols.

Here we should like to call attention to a kind of liturgical initiation that does not deserve this name. We might too easily imagine that the child is initiated in the liturgy once it knows the names of liturgical objects, vestments, etc., and can mention or recognize the successive parts of the Mass and other liturgical functions. But what really matters is that the children learn to discover the deeper meaning of those signs. Those visible signs are bearers and effecters of our salvation; hence it is important to confront the children with those signs in an atmosphere of profound respect and great faith and with constant reference to what Christ did during His life in Palestine.

The End of the School Year

Throughout the year we have emphasized men's relations among themselves and the place Christ acquired in their midst by coming into this world. This permanent union with one another and with Jesus is repeatedly given its highest expression in the celebration of the Eucharist. This union continues even now although Christ no longer lives visibly among us.

He still has the same eagerness to gather all men around Him and bring all into one fold of which He is the shepherd. There are several parables of our Lord that are most suitable for developing that idea, which, in fact, coincides with that of Church-consciousness.

Jesus is the Good Shepherd: He knows His sheep and His sheep know Him. They listen to His voice. One sheep was lost; then there is the joy of the Shepherd and the other sheep when it is found again. Here, moreover, we have an excellent occasion for explaining more fully that Christ always remains ready to pardon us for our faults. There are also sheep that do not belong to this fold, who do not yet know the voice of the Shepherd. We can thus initiate the children in the missionary idea which is an essential aspect of Church-consciousness.

The parable of the banquet with its emphasis on the pressing, wholly undeserved, invitation addressed to all men, can serve as a good finale of this catechetical program—though we should not insist too much on the eschatological character of that invitation.

We also recommend helping the children, at the same time, to make use of their own little prayer book. At the end of the second grade they can read fairly well and they are in other ways also much more mature than first-graders. Hence there should also be some development with respect to the prayers, songs and pictorial illustrations that help them to participate in the celebration of Holy Mass.

The Child's Confession

Hardly anyone is ignorant of the fact that today there exist many problems regarding the practice of children's confessions. While a complete account of those problems is not our intention, we will present a brief description and justification of our own position regarding that matter.

As must have been noticed, thus far we have not yet said anything about confession as the sacramental experience of penance, guilt, sorrow and pardon. We should like to advocate an expression of penitence that is adapted to those children and that can gradually develop into an adult celebration of that sacrament.

With respect to the children's moral formation, it seemed preferable to us not to devote separate time to it in the first two grades but to speak of it only occasionally. Special attention must be given all the time to God's forgiveness both when we speak about Jesus' life and deeds and in liturgical celebrations.

That is why we thought it advisable to conform to the growing custom of postponing the sacrament of confession in the form used by adults until later. These are the reasons:

1. The confession of the primary school child (six to eleven-year-olds) is a confession "of devotion"; hence it is not required for First Communion.

2. There are many other means to obtain forgiveness that, until now, have been too much neglected. As a result, confession has often been looked upon as the only means to forgiveness and even led to neglect of the duty to ask and receive forgiveness from men. Children can obtain direct forgiveness from their parents and other educators and from one another. These are true possibilities of pardon within the Church, they do not take place outside of Christ. Moreover, they are well adapted to the life of children because they are firmly situated within the child's own possible experiences.

3. Besides, there is also a growing appreciation of other liturgical forms of forgiveness outside of confession; for instance, at various moments of the Mass. To experience this forgiveness together with adults also presents good opportunities for the children. The renewal of the liturgy tends to give those moments the character of a more living experience.

4. The auricular confession, as it is practiced in the Church, brings with it particular difficulties for the child:

a. Reflection upon the past generally lies beyond the mental ability of the child. The child finds it very difficult to relive again its guilt-feelings of the past.

b. Children cannot understand why they must still ask pardon from God for something that was already forgiven by others.

c. Even if the child were conscious of guilt at the time of confession, it experiences difficulty in giving verbal expression to this.

d. The child learns by doing things together with others, by imitation. This is true also of religious acts. But in auricular confession this possibility is excluded since the child is alone in the confessional.

e. A mooted question is that of the child's ability to sin. And even if it can commit sins, there still remains the question whether it is good to make the child explicitly aware of sin every time. After all it is important to avoid, as much as possible, fostering a tendency to anxiety about God who will punish.

Besides the already mentioned possibilities of receiving pardon outside sacramental confession, we can also ask ourselves if there is not perhaps a solution for our problem in the *common celebration of confession* that is used more and more, for example, in the Netherlands. At first, there is only a general confession that the children make together; but at a later stage the children begin to make a more personal confession. The general confession is often followed by a general absolution; in the second case the children who wish to do so make an individual confession, and thus the common celebration ends for them in a personal confession. These experiments certainly contain much that is good, although the definitive form has not yet been found, nor is there general agreement as to whether we can speak of a sacramental confession in the first case (where there is only a general confession and general absolution). But this should not prevent us from giving our cooperation to those experiments and helping to make them something valuable.

However, we should like to make an observation regarding special celebrations for small children that consists *exclusively* of penance, sorrow, guilt, sinfulness and pardon. It is possible that in this form of celebration the children are confronted with evil and sinfulness even more than in the ordinary confession, against which there are so many serious objections. Hence would it not be better to omit these special celebrations and to incorporate the dimension of guilt and sinfulness, and particularly that of pardon, into other religious celebrations? In this way they would become an integral part of a larger whole, so that their experience functions within a larger context. For instance, they could be incorporated into the Eucharistic celebration, when the whole class goes to Holy Mass together. But this can also be done in celebrations that serve as a preparation for Christmas, Easter and other important religious events of the year.

With regard to their frequency, we should take for our standard the normal frequency of confession that is found in adults because, generally, it is not possible and, in most cases, it is not wholesome to prompt little children to a more intense religious experience than that of their own Christian milieu.

In the program of preparation for First Communion that we have presented for the first and second grades, there are various times that can be used as an occasion for speaking about mutual pardon in the community of men, and in the celebration of the Eucharist. In the third grade, when more explicit attention is given to the moral formation of the children, it is also possible to bring that matter into greater relief in other celebrations.

In the fifth grade, confession is dealt with extensively in the catechetical program.

4. Program for the Third Grade (Eight-year-olds)

Introduction

The children of this grade have become truly ripe for school. They are less dependent on others; this they express by daring and doing many things, though with little reflection. They are eager to learn, remember things well and ask, as it were, to be introduced further into the world. That is why education at that level begins to be more instructional. This might tempt us to change our catechesis into a more intellectualistic instruction, in which we explain the deeper foundations of our faith and their interconnections, and also present to the children the formulae in which those things are expressed. Undoubtedly, the

191

children of that age can, with a little effort and help, learn the necessary formulae by heart; but this does not mean that these formulae will thereby become a living reality for them.

Concerning the measure in which the primary school child is able to arrive at a deeper understanding of the mysteries of faith, we believe, as do many others, that such a child is not yet sufficiently mature to engage in theoretical reflection in any field, including that of religious matters. Conceptual knowledge and abstract thought remain difficult for children who have not reached the age of puberty; and with respect to religion there is also the danger that that kind of knowledge will lead to a split between knowledge and life.

The Child and the Adult. These children, however, are receptive to religion. But because the child is a human being in its own particular way, its personal religious life and experience will also differ radically from the religious life of adults. As a matter of fact, children and adults can be considered more alike one another in their ideas and experiences of any other realm than the realm of religion. It is possible that in the past this fact has not been sufficiently taken into account. The reason may be that, unfortunately, the religiousness of adults is often so little involved in their personal existence, so exteriorized into mere matters of knowledge and the fulfillment of certain duties, that it seems to be something that can easily be imparted to children.

The docility of children in many respects, together with their sense of the wondrous, too easily hold out false hopes for good results. Especially today, when the distance that lies between children and adults has grown, the child's own way of being has become more manifest; hence children must be given the opportunity to arrive in their own way at the assimilation of religious matters.

Play and Duty. We believe that what psychology says about the significance of play for the child, that play makes it enter into communication with an exciting world which invites the child's exploration, has particular importance for our catechesis. Only those who realize the perfect earnestness of children's play will be able to accept the role of play in the religious field. Both their acting together with grown-ups and seeking their own forms of expression must be given full opportunity. Stories, free expression, and religious celebrations adapted to the child offer rich possibilities to that end.

Being-busy-in-play should not be placed too early in the framework of tasks and duties, for there is a possibility that the systematic interest that follows upon and from play has not yet sufficiently matured. In this case the child will experience that duty as something foreign to him; he will do what he is asked to do, but without interior participation, hence personal involvement and personal assimilation will be absent or will be disturbed.

Education to a Sensibility for Symbols. We have thought it necessary to give this, perhaps lengthy, consideration, in order to understand and handle better the program for the third grade we are now ready to present. Various aspects of authentic education in the faith are intended for this grade. First of all, because the child of that age does not yet think as realistically as it will in later years, we think that now is the best time for a more explicit development of the child's sensibility toward symbols and consequently also for initiation in the liturgy. Although liturgy and symbolism are not fully understood by the children of the third grade, these seem to be better disposed for a liturgical initiation than those of the fifth and sixth grades (between the age of ten and twelve), for the latter are perhaps less receptive to the referential character of things.

An education and cultivation of sensitivity to symbols concerns something essential to our faith. It aims at making the child attain—eventually—to a personal attitude toward each of the three Divine Persons by and in the whole visible and tangible world. This shows, at the same time, that our interest is not confined only to liturgical and biblical signs as means for establishing and maintaining our relationship with God. All creatures and everything that pertains to human existence are a sign of God. When we foster the child's sensitivity toward that, we virtually foster also its sensitivity for liturgical and biblical signs, and vice versa. This is an education for an incarnate life of faith. The consciousness of the bond with God must permeate and embrace everything.

When we give explicit sacramental catechesis, it must be done in a concrete fashion; in other words, our catechesis must seek help from the liturgical symbolism that is based on a universally human experience of symbols, as well as on what is prefigured in the Bible. With respect to the latter, we give preference in this grade to the actions, words and miracles of Christ, for in them we are permitted to see a pre-realization of the sacraments.

Moral Education. The child constantly comes in contact with concrete reality in its playful discovery of the world. We now try to help the child to become receptive to the divine that is revealed in all concrete reality, by putting the child in a sacral atmosphere.

This means that this kind of education in a living faith is, at the same time, a moral education and a formation of conscience, for in that reality God's will in our regard is made plain also. In the past, educators have not infrequently made bad use of an appeal to God's will when dealing with children; "God wills it that way; hence do it that way; therefore that is good." However, the proper way of putting it is: "This is good, that's why God wants it." Hence we must not be satisfied with external motives such as reward and punishment. Values must speak for themselves. God's will is not imposed upon reality from without, but it is imbedded in reality itself. God speaks in and through the values that are proper to men and things; we hear God's voice in the voice of those values themselves. It remains true, of course, that, if we wish to get an authentic view of what ultimately constitutes these values of men and things, we need to be enlightened by revelation. The Gospel exercises a critical function with respect to our value judgments about men and things, and our view of the world must constantly be renewed in the light of the Gospel.

Children and youths constantly encounter concrete reality. Their minds and consciences are formed through endless experiences. They must learn to ask themselves: what does life demand of me?, for therein lies God's will. When we present God to them purely as an external authority and appeal to this alone, there is a danger that conscience will not develop properly, for this method does not teach them how to connect God with reality. In such a case the child adapts itself to what we want but does not assume any responsibility. It says: "If God didn't ask this, I wouldn't do it."

Good and Evil. Conscience is not primarily an instrument that enables us to judge what is evil, but it enables us to discover and fulfill here and now the good that ought to be done. Hence when we educate children in morality, we do not at all intend to play immediately upon the child's eventual experience of guilt and put that experience explicitly in a religious framework. The child experiences a world in which good and evil are at war with each other but in which it is the good that triumphs, thanks to God's power and assistance. The child is involved in this world—its interests in those phenomena clearly show that this is so—but it does not directly place the little experiences

195

of daily life in a religious perspective. Now, if we moralize too much with respect to the child's own life, there is danger that we shall make the child oversensitive and anxious. On the other hand, we can also help the child to learn to realize that its feeling for what is good is in harmony with that which God also prefers.

Until Advent

At the beginning of the third grade we present creation as it meets us and as it appeals to us. In this way we intend to confront the children with creation, according to the perspective we have outlined above as a sign of God's own reality and hence as an expression of God's call to us. This we do in several stages:

1. Full of admiration and respect we look at the beauty and greatness of creation: the seas, the mountains, the sun and rain, the power of growth of plants, animals and men. Actually it is a question of attentive contemplation in an atmosphere of prayer. Here the children's exploring spirit, their self-activity and self-expression must be given full opportunity. However, if we confine ourselves to physical nature, everything might still remain too much outside the child's world, for the modern child is growing up amidst the achievements of technology and a wealth of comforts. That is why it is well to make the children see the beautiful things men have made. It is not a good thing to introduce a distinction between God's creation and the creations of men; we can, at the most, let them see that God in His creation offers great possibilities and powers to men and that He meant it that way.

2. Besides the fact that all this is beautiful in itself, as we have just explained, we can now point out to the children that we also have need of these things. We cannot do without grain, water, light, heat and all sorts of things that men have made.

3. When you make good use of creation you thereby honor God. Respect for creation means that you use it the way it was meant by God. Yet, if we were to express that in this theoretical way, the third-grade children would find it difficult to understand what we mean. Hence we should work this out by means of examples and stories.

4. There are also things we use particularly to honor God Himself, things we consider very beautiful: flowers, light, gold, silver, fragrant incense. This we can explain by analogy with the honor and respect that are given to men.

5. But the most beautiful thing God has given us is that we "are together with others." He has given us fellow-men. In the third grade there is as yet no question of a true community-feeling of the children. Nevertheless, they are gradually arriving at a period of their life when there are more possibilities for appealing to the children's strong sense for "belonging," their desire not to stand alone. On this foundation we can continue to build: we need others and they need us. We belong to others and others to us.

After showing the beauty of being together with other human beings and, also, the need of this togetherness, we can make the children realize that men deserve more respect than all other creatures.

The catechist will notice that here, as also later in the course of the program, various divine commandments will come into view, though they are not explicitly mentioned. It is precisely our desire that, as much as possible, reality itself should be allowed to speak to the children and exercise its appeal to them. If we began with commandments as preconceived laws and

197

truths, this would make it difficult for children to still be receptive for the truth that lies in reality itself and for the call which that truth addresses to us and in which that which God desires comes to us.

Around the beginning of November it is useful to speak about some of the saints. They belong to us (the community-feeling must be extended to the saints). Saints are truly good people, full of respect and gratitude toward God. This they showed precisely because they made good use of creation and especially by their great respect for their fellow-men.

We are now fully into autumn, even closer to winter. This is a useful starting point for calling attention to the transitoriness of all things. However beautiful the world of men, animals and things, it is a fact that all things are passing. In the fall, look at the trees, how they lose their leaves; look at the flowers, how they fade. Look at men, how the little baby becomes a child, a grownup, an old man or woman. But this is no reason for being very sad, for after this life there begins a new life: and in it there will be no more sorrow; no one will be old or need help; no one will be sick or sad. We speak here about Heaven, but do not yet emphasize much the eternal being-with-God.

Advent

At the beginning of Advent it is important to point out the contrast between living as children of light and living as children of darkness. In all of us there is some light and also some darkness. But those who live as children of light try to look at and live their life the way we have described above: in joy, peace, gratitude and respect toward God. It is a great gift of God if we receive the strength to live that way. Darkness will prevail if we are not grateful for creation, not joyful to be with our fellow-men, but merely sad because all things pass away. This sadness, however, is not always the people's fault. For there are people who have never heard anything about the things we know. They don't know God; they don't know that He is a good Father for men; they don't know that there is a Heaven where we can be happy forever. There are others, however, who know that but give no thought to it; and there are those who do not act in accordance with what they know.

Now Christ came to bring the light, He was Himself the light of the world. The light shone in darkness so that men could once more see well where they were, how beautiful everything was and where they were going. Here we can make use of the various symbols of light that center around Christmas; the Advent wreath, the Christmas decorations, the Christmas tree, that is, the tree of Christ.

After Christmas

In connection with various things that happened in Christ's life, we make it ever clearer to the children that He is the light of the world, that He brings light among men and in the hearts of men, and that they thereby become joyful. He brings light especially by giving pardon to sinners.

Meanwhile Ash Wednesday draws near. Since we are dealing here with children who are a little older, it certainly makes sense to pay some attention to this day, although they are not yet ready to grasp the deep symbolism of that celebration.

The Forty Days of Lent

During this forty day period we should like to give the catechesis of baptism, for it is through baptism that Christ's light began to shine in us.

Here we must not go too fast but must give the children as much opportunity as possible, so that the various symbols of baptism can really speak to them. A purely intellectualistic explanation, even if it is done with the help of films and records, makes the children approach baptism from the outside so that it easily remains lifeless for them. They should, on the contrary, be so confronted with the symbols that they become aware of what it means to be baptized.

It is of little importance whether the children can describe in exact order all the successive actions that take place in the administration of baptism. It is much more important for them to become personally aware, by means of the operation of the symbol, of the work that was begun in themselves by baptism. To achieve this end, it is also helpful to make use of celebrations. However, being present at a baptism can perhaps be more fruitful for children of the sixth grade.

Passion Tide

During this time we can develop a little the idea of the conflict between the children of light and the children of darkness, of whom Jesus became the victim. The children of light are people who believe in Jesus. They have accepted the light. The children of darkness do not believe in Jesus. Their unbelief reaches its highest point on Calvary: Jesus dies, everything becomes dark and it looks as if darkness has conquered. But the light is victorious in spite of everything. Behold the splendor of Christ's resurrection!

Paschal Time

After the Easter recess we can speak about living as children of the light according to the example of Mary and the apostles. In this grade we can also pay more attention to Pentecost and the coming of the Holy Spirit. We shall always represent the Holy Spirit as the Spirit of Jesus: His light, His power, His love. "To live as children of the light" is in reality a brief outline of Christian moral life, especially of love of neighbor. Now is a suitable time to present this, for children of this age (nine-year-olds) begin to be more open for the rules of community life. Let us remark once more that we do not begin with the commandments but start from reality itself.

During these months we take as our starting point: spring, the new light, the new life of flowers and plants. Jesus invites us to His table with all the other children who want to be children of light; there we listen to Jesus who is the light of the world. We give thanks for the light that He lets grow in us. Jesus gives us His own Body by which we receive the power to live as children of light. What does it mean "to live as children of the light?" This we can show in the life of others, in the life of Mary and the apostles.

Mary was the only one who from the very beginning was wholly open to accept the light of Jesus. She was full of the light. The apostles, who had first been so proud to belong to Jesus, had evidently not received much light. Perhaps they were too convinced of their own excellence. After Christ's death, they had fallen back into darkness. They were frightened, small men, who did not dare to go outside. The resurrection revived their hope. Then came the Holy Spirit. They received the Spirit of Jesus: fire and light, power and love.

Only now did they become truly children of light. They regularly celebrated the Eucharist so that by receiving Jesus' Body once again they might be filled with His Spirit, His light and His love. They tried to live as children of the light: they gave everything away; their life was wholly given to the service of others. They were not afraid of death. Their life was a life of being good to others and of prayer. By the fact that they spread Christ's light ever more, a growing number of people believed in Jesus and these, too, received the light.

When explaining all these aspects of the life of the apostles, we must so present them that a call goes forth from them to the children themselves. We, too, must try to live always more and more as children of the light. The Holy Spirit, the Spirit of Jesus came into us also at our baptism. From Him we received power to become ever more truly children of the light. We are constantly strengthened by the Body of Jesus so that we may become more and more closely united to Jesus and to one another. And if we have not lived as children of the light, we can ask pardon. Then will Christ's light grow in us.

We recommend that the catechist should not confine himself to dealing with the Eucharist and to connecting the various catechetical aspects with it. We suggest that, toward the end of the school year, a beautiful Eucharistic celebration be held in which the various aspects stressed in the catechesis can now be really "lived" by the children.

5. *Program for the Fourth Grade* (Nine-year-olds)

Introduction

Religious education must be attuned to the pupils' real potentialities. That is why it is useful to survey the development which children and youths usually undergo in our cultural environment. Of course, unpredictable circumstances can arise and influence the development of the children; hence such a survey needs constant revision.

Moreover, both the nature and tempo of development vary according to the milieu and are, at the same time, influenced by personal talent, vicissitudes and decisions. All education requires that the educator direct himself as much as possible to the personality of each pupil.

It follows that, when we sketch the characteristics of a particular phase of development, these have significance only as general starting points which must, over and over again, be critically examined with openness for what is appropriate to the individual child. Hence the educators must be on their guard against prejudging matters; they must be willing to observe and listen. It is with this reservation in mind that we present here and elsewhere the "psychological characteristics" that can serve as starting points for the various grades.

Childlike Realism and Objectivity. It is an almost universal opinion that the pupils of the fourth grade are growing toward a sober, realistic attitude and that they begin to feel the need of an explanation of what they hear and see. They gradually begin to think in terms of causality; they have also more interest in the interconnection of events and are no longer captivated only by isolated details. This critical, more realistic view of life and the world is accompanied by a shallow emotional life, although they see the sorrow and need around them and ask questions about it. There is a decrease of the spontaneous religious receptivity of the first years. All this demands earnest reflection on the part of the catechist so that he may arrive at an attitude that is carefully attuned to the child.

We saw that the children of the lower grades are capable only of a minimum of reflection. There was little possibility of influencing children by offering theoretical subject matter but it was possible to influence them directly and integrally through personal witness. The child had to discover the place of religion in its whole milieu and, in this discovery, prayer played an important role both as an experience and as a measure of interiorization.

In the higher grades—beginning with the fourth grade—the teacher's personal witness continues to hold first place; but the child, now, somewhat more independently begins to discover the religious dimension in persons, things and events. Hence, in addition to the need for integral education, there is here also a growing need for being approached more by way of understanding. With respect to didactic means, however, the manner in which these are used has primary importance. For everything must remain specifically directed toward authentic education in a living faith. That is why in the catechetical use of didactic means more attention must be paid to living the faith than to having knowledge about matters of faith; this is in contrast to what was done formerly in the field of religious instruction.

Materialism and Humanism. Many catechists eagerly make use of the growing child's typically more critical and realistic attitude to give their pupils a so-called contemporary view of the world and also of religion.

Undoubtedly, it is an advantage that our time has given us a deeper and broader understanding of biology, physics and other sciences and that, as a consequence, many people now have realistic views of the world; thus primitive, magical and mythical fancies and explanations have less chance to obscure religion. Those who had looked upon religion mainly as an answer to questions not yet solved by natural science sometimes viewed the progress of science as a diminution of "religion" and a sign that man was independent of God. For, in former times all events that lay outside man's control and understanding were attributed by man to God's direct intervention; for instance, lightning, rain, the sun, earthquakes, conception, birth, sickness and death. This direct intervention was conceived as if God's causality was at work as a cause amidst created causes.

Many people have become insecure as a result of the scientific explanation of those "divine" operations; they experience the new view as a painful absence of God from this world. Nevertheless, we may expect that in the long run this more realistic view will serve as a means to purify religion. Man participates in God's creative work; God continues His creative activity through man. For this reason it is in his creative dealing with his fellow-men and the world that man depends on God. And it is this point that we are able to understand better in modern times.

However, in the meantime, man's consciousness of his own power presents a real danger for many. For they are tempted to remain on the level of natural science and neglect human values or, respectfully recognizing human values in a humanistic fashion, leave out of consideration or deny transcendental reality.

It is especially the first of those two dangers that threatens school children when their still primitive ideas and experiences are too brusquely confronted with an arrogant rationalism that disregards man's inmost being and personal relationships and reduces everything to calculative aspects. Only when man recognizes the limited significance of the method of natural science will "scientific" thinking serve as a means for purifying religion and thus be a blessing for man. Too often, that which should be an enlightenment and an introduction to man's magnificent achievements serves to strip man of his dignity. This kind of "thinglike" approach to man constitutes a great danger for authentic religious education. Only an education and instruction in which as many human values as possible are made accessible can form the basis of a fully human life of faith.

However, the incorporation of integral human values into our education in a living faith is only the first part of our task. We must also illuminate all those values in their salvation aspect. Otherwise we remain stuck in pure humanism. The world of faith is not another world added to our world, but there exists only *one* world, of which faith offers us the most profound meaning.

Some might think that we are devoting too much time to those considerations, but in our opinion we have here one of the crucial points regarding the modern problem of faith. Of course, it is necessary to give children an up-to-date image of the world; but, if we do not simultaneously educate them into a more purified image of God, we run the risk of ending in materialism and humanism.

Critical Attitude Toward Themselves. Let us add one more psychological remark that is important for the catechetical approach to children of the fourth grade. Not only do these children look more critically at their environment—their parents, educators and events—but they are also becoming increasingly critical of themselves, especially concerning the way they express themselves and their achievements. This fact has consequences for the children's religious expressions; they become more exacting in the demands they make of themselves with respect to mimicry and gestures. And not every defective drawing can still serve as a religious expression for them. More attention must now be given to the perfection of their religious expressions and it must be done in accordance with their own capabilities.

Education in Church-consciousness

In this grade we want particularly to educate the children in Church-consciousness. Of course, within this Church-consciousness, attention is devoted also to the development of God-consciousness and sin-consciousness because, after all, those aspects are indissolubly connected. During this year we speak less about the sacraments. The Eucharist and baptism have already been dealt with extensively in the lower grades; they will be taken up again in the fifth and sixth grades, where confirmation and the sacrament of penance will also be considered. Implicitly, however, the various sacraments are included in the program, principally against the background of the Church which we now wish to make more real in the life of the children. One important reason for not speaking again explicitly of the sacraments is that we want to avoid the children's obvious reaction of "We had this already." To avoid such a rejection we must constantly provide education in a living faith with a new and fresh approach.

One can say that the children of the lower grades live almost entirely in the "now," they hardly look forward or backward. But around their ninth and tenth year they begin to acquire some idea of a past and a future. This gives us an opportunity for putting their life in a somewhat broader perspective. It is now reasonable to say something about growth and even about the purpose of life.

This is also connected with their growing experience of pain, want and sorrow in the world that lies around them. For in this experience lies the foundation of a desire for another life where we can be perfectly happy. Because they do not yet have much capacity for authentic love as orientated to the other person, we do not yet present Heaven so much under the aspect of a personal union with God. And because their concept of sin is still undeveloped, we put little stress on the idea of being delivered from sin.

The social consciousness of these children is also growing, at least in the sense that they gladly do things "together" and wish to "belong." Few things are as fearful to them as the feeling of standing alone. They crave being with someone who gives them security. This gives us the opportunity of presenting Christ as our guide upon whose support we can count. That is why we try to let children in this grade experience that we are *together* on the way; that we are on the way under a trusted *guide;* that we are on our way to the *Father* under this guide.

Until Advent

Most children have had some experience of travel or camping during their vacations. We try to connect our catechetical program with those experiences. What do you do when you are going on a journey? Where are you going? Someone must know the way, must guide and direct us. Our whole life is in reality a wonderful journey through a wonderful country. We are allowed to enjoy this wonderful country: it is for this that it has been given to us. But everything is not equally beautiful. For amidst all this beauty we constantly meet less satisfactory things, things that show defects and that disappoint us.

We could perhaps let them recall that they could not always do what they pleased. Here again is an opportunity for attending to their moral formation. We are on a journey together with all other men, but this journey does not last forever. Look at the passing of the seasons. So everything passes, and so does our life. Where does that journey end? With the Father who is waiting for us; in the house of the Father in which there will be no more sorrow, no tears, no hunger nor any want.

Is it true that people are on their way *together?* How can we recognize that they belong together, that they help one another? We see this at home; and when the occasion offers, we see it in the care of the sick and of those who are aged. We need our fellow-men in our journey through life, we need them to provide food and shelter, clothing, protection and care.

But we also need guidance. This we receive from our parents and other educators, and in religion guidance is given us especially by priests. All these make present among us the guide who is Jesus Christ Himself. He has said: "I am the Good Shepherd." Thus He calls His fold together in church every Sunday through His priests.

It is not enough to make the children understand all this in an intellectual way. Knowledge and explanation cannot make these things real for them; we must make them experience such things, make them feel that men need one another. And we can try to make them feel that people come to Church because they need Christ, the Guide, and that the priest takes the place of Christ. One can organize a celebration in which the children are greeted by the priest who receives them in the church as the good shepherd, and who shows them all the things men need on their journey of life to the Father's house: the baptismal font, the altar, the confessional and the pulpit.

In this way we try always to show Christ and the priest as being one; this we do in all our lessons as well as in celebrations: he, too, is the Good Shepherd who knows us and calls us by name, who rejoices with all the others because the sheep that was lost is found again. There are other sheep that do not belong to this sheepfold; but they are also called and the shepherd thinks of them and our attention should likewise go out to them (Mission Sunday).

Around the Feast of Christ the King we examine that in which Christ's kingship consists: He is the King of all the saints who have already arrived at the Father's house and are now with the Father. They are all the men and women who made a good journey of life and meant much for others. Christ is King also over all those who have died and are, full of longing, waiting for the moment when the Father will let them come to Him. Christ is King also over us who are still on our journey and are so greatly in need of a Leader and a Guide.

Advent

Some data of the Old Testament can suitably serve as a preparation for Christmas. It seems to us that those facts can help us to make the children realize and appreciate better Christ's kingship and leadership. Bu it is not the intention to put those events in a large historical context. We merely wish to show the children that the people needed a Guide and a law in order that they might be able to live together in solidarity. Those ideas can eventually be more fully developed through biblical stories and readings.

A long time ago there lived a people for which God had a very special preference. It was His people, the People of God. He Himself was the King of that people. This was hard for those people, for they didn't see God. They wanted a leader whom they could see, who cared for them, who pointed out the way to them, who told them how they should live together. So God then appointed Moses as their leader.

Moses went to the mountain and received the law from God's

own hand. Something about the commandments could be given in this connection. However, it is preferable to reduce them to the two most important commandments, namely, love for God and love for men. Moses died. The people wanted a king, like other peoples. "We have a law," they said, "but we have no king, no leader." God gave them David as king. But David, too, however great he was as a king, was only one who took the place of God; the real King had still to come. Isaia and several other prophets foretold the coming of the great, the true King. People began to look more and more for that King who was promised them by God.

When John appeared at the Jordan, people thought: "He must be the King who was to come." But John said: "After me comes He who is greater than I." God sent an angel to Mary to announce to her the coming of the King. His name is Jesus, the Savior, He is Emmanuel: God with us.

After Christmas

We can begin with the Epiphany, the search for the King. Many expect the King but not all look for him with the same intention. Most wanted a king who would free them, who would chase away their enemies. Perhaps we could here give the children a brief outline, in most simple terms, of the political situation. Herod also thought that there would be an earthly king and he felt threatened.

Only a few people understood exactly what was the intention of the great King who was to come, namely, that He came to bring men to the Father, to show the way on their journey of life to the Father's house.

Jesus begins to appear in public. He does great things and people run out to listen to His words. Immediately they ask themselves, "Is He the one who is to come or must we wait for another?" In the synagogue of Nazareth Jesus proclaims very clearly: "The Spirit of the Lord rests upon Me. I am the one

210

sent by the Father." But the son of the carpenter meets with ridicule.

Others believe in Jesus. Ever larger crowds come to listen to what He has to say. "I am not come to abolish the Law of Moses but to fulfill. In the Old Law it is said . . . , but I say to you. . . ." What He tells us is beautiful. He helps the sufferers, the sick, the poor, the oppressed, and even works miracles for them. People become enthusiastic and want to proclaim Him their King. But Jesus withdraws because He knows that they have not yet understood everything and because they look upon Him especially as an earthly king, a king with armies, who will go to war against the enemies and the oppressors.

The Period of Lent

During these Forty Days we can speak very explicitly about faith in Jesus as the Guide, the King who leads to the Father those who believe in Him. If it is true that children are scarcely able to take a personal stand, this means that they believe especially on the basis of what their educators believe. Although the child begins to be more critical in its attitude toward adults and also with respect to its educators, it takes over much from their attitude, and more from this than from what they say and explain.

Hence it is not our intention to make the children learn the historical facts of Christ's life as neutral spectators. We must not be content with making a sober and objective analysis of people's faith and lack of faith in Christ. What we want is, together with the children, to look with faith at Christ and listen to Him so that our life of faith and that of the children may grow and become more profound. Thus we must more fully unfold the various attitudes and aspects of faith, as they are manifested in various persons who believe in Christ. We must create opportunities for the children to identify themselves with believers in Christ.

By "believing in Christ" we do not mean in the first place believing that He tells the truth. To believe is much more, it is to give ourselves, to commit ourselves completely to Him with our whole person. It means not only that we *see* something in Him, but that we commit ourselves entirely to Him and choose Him as our ultimate support.

Slowly there formed a small nucleus of men and women around Jesus who said that they firmly believed in Him. After the miraculous catch of fishes, several men left their possessions and followed Him in His journeys through Palestine. These were the apostles. Jesus was fond of them though He also knew their faith was not very strong and not very pure. Because of this He had a special name for them: "you of little faith." There were others who believed much more strongly in Him, for example, the centurion who came to ask Jesus to cure his son who was ill; the sick woman who touched His clothes to be healed.

Christ began to announce with increasing clearness what He intended to do, viz., to lead men to the Father: "I am the way, the truth and the life. No one comes to the Father except through Me."

Then came the multiplication of the loaves and, on this occasion, Jesus spoke of the Living Bread which is nothing but Himself: "I am the Bread that has come down from Heaven. He who eats this Bread shall live forever." After that many no longer wanted to listen to Him. Even His disciples began to doubt. A great tension developed between the people who were for Jesus and those who were against Him. Some even made plans to kill Him.

Jesus took three disciples with Him to Mt. Thabor. There they were witnesses of what the Father said about Jesus: "This is my Son in whom I have put my delight, listen to Him." Shortly after that, Jesus questioned the apostles: "What do people say that I am?" And after hearing the answer, He asked much more expressly, "And you, who do you say that I am?"

On a certain day they were so close to Jerusalem that they could see it lying before them. Jesus wept over Jerusalem. People did not believe in Him; they did not believe that He had come to show them the way to the Father. He knew about the plots that were being made to kill Him. And yet He said: "Come let us go to Jerusalem."

Jesus addressed Himself to all who were with Him: he who wants to go with Me to the Father must also in all things fulfill the will of the Father, just as I am doing. This biblical passage lends itself particularly as an occasion for explaining the Christian way of living one's daily life.

Next, we follow Jesus to Bethany where the resurrection of Lazarus takes place, which results, a few days later, in Christ's joyful entrance into Jerusalem. Those who believe in Jesus seem to have won the upperhand. But suddenly things go in reverse. Jesus is taken prisoner during the night. To the question of Pilate whether He is king, Jesus proclaims openly: "Yes, I am a king, but not one of this world." During His suffering and death Jesus is abandoned by everyone except Mary, John and some women. Under the Cross, after Christ's death, the centurion openly expresses his faith in Him. Christ is truly and everlastingly King. This He shows by His resurrection.

Paschal Time

In this period of the school year we wish to let the children see how the faith of the apostles revives because of Christ's resurrection. This is brought out wonderfully in the stories of the resurrection. After that we give a brief outline of the growth of the young Church. Those who believe in Jesus Christ now definitively cling to Him to go with Him to the Father.

Accordingly, throughout the year we try to emphasize the "essence" of Church-consciousness, namely, that we are on the way to the Father together with one another and with Jesus Christ, because we believe that Jesus is our Lord, our Shepherd, our King who was sent by the Father. This ecclesial consciousness has its apex in the celebration of baptism and particularly of the Eucharist. Our bond with Christ means also that we have a bond with one another, and this solidarity brings with it a mutual love in everyday life. Other aspects of the Church, such as the hierarchical structure, acquire meaning only against the background of this essential feature. We must particularly avoid giving the children an exclusively institutional idea of the Church.

After the Ascension

The catechesis of the Holy Spirit is one of the most difficult in educating children in a living faith and hence requires a gradual initiation. The children of the intermediary grades manifest a great desire for action. This tendency, however, is not yet clearly orientated to being-good-to-others. Furthermore, they also have as yet little awareness of their own powerlessness.

For those two reasons the internal operation of the Holy Spirit still means little to them. That is why it is better for the time being to show what animation by the Holy Spirit does to the Church, as it expresses itself, for instance, in missionaries who go to proclaim the faith.

Pentecost and the preaching of Peter lead to the conversion of many. The Church is born. Now does the journey with Jesus to the Father really begin.

After this, we try to explain various aspects of the young Church and place them at the same time in the actuality of the Church in our own day.

We speak of the mutual love in the early Church and of love in the Church today.

We tell how the apostles travelled throughout the world and became bishops of various large cities. We speak of the Church of today with her hierarchy and gatherings of bishops in world-wide councils.

We narrate the spread of the Church, speaking about Stephen, Paul, Barnabas. Parallel with it, we mention the spread of missionaries over the whole world in the Church of today. The Church of today, too, has her contemporary martyrs.

But Jesus remains the Guide, the King. He leads the Church by his Holy Spirit, who prompts people to help Jesus. This they do by helping others according to each man's particular place in the Church.

6. *Program for the Fifth Grade* (Ten-year-olds)

Introduction

The children of this grade belong to the older pupils of the primary school. They matter of factly live a life of their own among their seniors; being less dependent than younger children, they can and want to go their own way. Society accepts and sanctions their living to a great extent outside the concerns and cares of the adult world; they thus have full opportunity for developing their own life. Of course, they come constantly into contact with the world of older people. The child observes what they do; it thinks about it and speaks about it when it has an open contact with its educators. In this open contact, the ten-year-olds find themselves cooperating with the educator and they discover here a wonderful world of transition between their peer-world and the world of adults.

One easily understands, in this connection, that the child is most itself when, together with other children, it is outside and beyond the direct supervision of educators. At home it is subject to educational demands, but it is unquestionably accepted the way it is and cloistered in the security from which it emerged into consciousness. The home is primarily the background and starting point of the child's development. In the school, the child is brought face to face with the thought of the future. This con-

215

tact, of course, is adapted to its capacity; nevertheless, it is demanding, it imposes duties, it appraises the child in view of the task it will have to fulfill later. But when the child is outside together with other children, it finds itself in an uncomplicated environment: somewhere between houses in the city or, in the country, out in the open where there are no houses, the child finds its own playground. Here it can measure its powers and courage with other children, experience feelings and ideas together with others and give expression to them.

What is astonishing about the play of these school children is the fact that they can play in-between and around adults without being aware or concerned with what these adults think about it, and without forming any direct connection with the way of thinking and acting of grown-ups. There are, of course, constant conflicts with the adults and these, no doubt, contribute to the gradual development of a process of *interiorization* in the children.

The play-world of the child gets its own tension, for there is a playful dealing with older people and their world; the child weaves a fanciful web around this world. But again and again this world shows its real face in a more or less unexpected manner and in this way is discovered by the child. The child's world and the world of adults are thus constantly brought into contact with each other; but there is a difference: grown-ups and children meet one another only sporadically and superficially in the same world. It looks in fact as if children pay attention only to external and perceptible things, for personal togetherness, which demands communication within a world that is more or less the same, still offers too many difficulties to them.

Taking its cue from the adults' expression of religion, the child begins to have an inkling about God's presence through experiences that lie beyond its everyday life of play and work. For instance, during early childhood and even long afterwards, all sorts of natural phenomena can make a profound impression and open up that perspective: the gale and the storm, the clouds, the boundless blue sky, the heavens studded with stars and the moon. Similarly, meeting with phenomena of life such as conception and birth, growth, old age and dying can lead to religious thoughts, as also the often astonishing phenomena of plant and animal life. Particularly the sometimes startling discovery of being an "I," a "self," can be a strong incentive for the awakening of religious life.

This growing awareness makes the young school child vulnerable to stunning emotions that can lead to anxiety. The way a child develops during those years, also with respect to religion, is strongly determined by its educators. However, we must recognize that those children can already have their own personal attitude toward God. Although they are not yet able to express this attitude, we must respect it as a mystery of God's dealing with these young people. Educators can help children to discover God in the signs offered by creation and the events of salvation. If the children receive little support from their educative environment, there is a danger that they will find it difficult to assimilate the above-mentioned religious experiences or even that these may not occur. In that case the children might experience the real world as a source of anxiety, and this, in turn, may prompt them to seek a kind of magic security which would prevent the development of a sound religiousness.

Older children lead a life of their own among adults but are, at the same time, constantly in contact with them. They already begin to notice that everything is not perfect with mankind. They discover sinfulness in the world and observe the failures of adults.

They also become aware of a certain division and opposition that exists within themselves. They see that their sentiments, ideas and words can be better than their external conduct. That is why the time is approaching for confronting them with the

217

fundamental questions of man's fall and salvation. Starting from their own concrete observations and experiences—of which they become conscious under the guidance of their educators—the children can now gradually begin to understand that every human being meets with guilt and suffering, that man is in constant need of salvation and that Christ came to meet man in that need as a Savior. Terms like "salvation" and "need of salvation" often remain mere words for children. It is certain that they cannot feel or understand their full meaning. The deepest dimension of those realities lies on a different level than that of the children. Hence it is important to ask ourselves what our own concept is of the reality of "salvation." People are still too often thinking only of "slavery to the devil" when they hear the word "salvation"; and this bond of slavery is then broken by Christ's death on the Cross, through which "the gate of Heaven has been opened." They then forget that the whole of Christ's life, all His words and deeds, are "saving." Christ meets men with understanding, support, encouragement, consolation and pardon.

On the other hand, throughout our life we remain marked with insincerity and powerlessness, and this we experience in all our actions. Children, too, already experience this want to some extent; hence they are sensitive to the aspects of Jesus' saving words and deeds that we have mentioned above.

The question that now comes up spontaneously is, What are we supposed to do in order to share in Christ's salvific action which is still at work among us? The sacrament of penance naturally enters in here as the principal experience of the encounter between man-in-need and the saving Christ. Thus we try to gradually understand better what it means to accept our task of living a Christian life: it means that, in spite of our fundamental insufficiency, we continue to strive for a life of love of God that is expressed especially in the love of our

218

neighbor. Christ has not left us to ourselves in this life task. He has given us His Holy Spirit, the source of all love. "And hope does not disappoint, because the charity of God is poured forth in our hearts by the Holy Spirit who has been given to us" (Rom. 5:5). Confirmation is the outstanding sign of this gift of the Holy Spirit.

Today there are a number of bishops—for instance, in Holland—who want to postpone Confirmation until the children are in the fifth and sixth grades (ten or eleven-year-olds). Where this practice exists, the last three months of the fifth grade should be consecrated to an extensive catechesis about Confirmation.

The Place of Conversation in Catechesis

These, then, are the general outlines of our program for the fifth grade. What we have said here can also serve as a guide for the way we can best approach the children of the higher grades of primary school. This approach consists in thinking together with the children about Christian life in this world, and this thinking would seem to be most advantageous if it were done in the form of conversations with those children.

Because of this, it is very important that children should feel that catechesis is "different" and allows more freedom than other classes, even with respect to their relationship to their teacher. Many things that are more or less pushed into the background in other classes can then manifest themselves. Experience teaches that many questions come alive when there is a free and open atmosphere. It is very advantageous for education in a living faith when the children realize that the teacher or priest is frank and open with them, that what they bring up is recognized as valuable and honestly and openly discussed. This is wholly in accord with the spirit of true catechesis, for nowhere are teachers as much on equal footing with the children as here. The teacher, too, stands in an attitude of listening and receiving before the mystery of Christ. He too cannot completely fathom it, but the mystery constantly unfolds itself more fully for him as he tries to respond to it in a more complete religious self-commitment. It is precisely this that is proper to an authentic education in the faith.

Until Advent

Together with the children we try to penetrate a little more deeply into human existence so that we may understand better our task of being Christians.

These children observe the world of the adults though they do not give constant attention to it. They feel that they are no longer little children but "big." This could be used as an opportunity for examining with them the various things one can become in life, by looking together at the world of adults. Whatever we become in life, we stand always in the service of the other. What is always most important is *to be good to others.* This makes it possible that one who has a very simple and lowly position can mean more as a human being than another who occupies a high position. But it is also possible that the latter understands very well his position and realizes his great responsibility, while the one who has a low position does not realize it.

When are we really good to another? This depends first of all on our intention. The children are gradually learning to understand that it is the *intention* that strongly determines the character of their actions and that we should not judge actions merely by their results. They tell us explicitly that they did not do this or that "on purpose." However, they must develop that idea; we must assist them in developing that natural feeling for the role of intention. This is necessary, for the categorical way in which demands are often expressed in the educational milieu makes it appear to the children that it is the performance, the achievement, that is the one and only criterion for judging whether their conduct is good or bad.

Besides having the proper intention, it is also important to acquire an "eye" for the *situation,* for seeing the possibilities and opportunities for doing good that a situation contains. It is precisely in the situation that God's intentions become clear to us. God speaks to us through the values proper to men and things. We must not look upon that divine speaking through circumstances as something that stands alongside God's expressing Himself through Revelation. The latter is precisely a light that is shed upon my dealings with men and things, and it is only in the situation—a situation seen in the light of Revelation—that God's will becomes known to me.

That is why we must see in conscience, as formed by the Gospel, the "instrument" that enables us to discover the good we must do here and now and thus to listen to God's voice in this particular situation. The question that must gradually dominate the life of a Christian is this: what does God expect from me at this moment, in this or that circumstance? This means, regarding education, that we must from the beginning discover what is good in earthly reality and must relate it in this way to God.

What we have just said brings up the question, When is our intention good? This question demands great honesty on our part. The children are already somewhat aware of the dividedness and ambivalence that exist in themselves. A good intention, in addition, demands perseverance, particularly when we happen to be misunderstood or our actions are misjudged. Moreover, however good our intentions may be and however much people may desire what is good, even saints show that they are not always able to come up to expectations. Man is weak because he shares in the wounded and disfigured condition of the whole world. He cannot do things alone but needs God's help. This presents us with a threefold catechetical task:

221

1. We must dispose the children for the salvific action of God.

2. We must try to make them mild in judging the faults of their fellow-men and honest in their judgment of themselves.

3. We must make them realize the significance and importance of the prayer of petition with which they have been familiar for a long time, making them more conscious of that need on the basis of the universal human situation.

Needless to say, the moral education of children must make them appreciate the value of moral conduct with regard to relations with other human beings; and they should not confine this value to a number of commandments, regulations and prohibitions. Only then can we have a morality that is authentic. With respect to relations with other human beings, the moral life of ten-year-olds is principally shaped by their educators and by companions of their own age. These children are open to honesty and truthfulness, comradeship, helpfulness and fair play.

It is useful to consider human relations, not only in the light of the children's own world of life, but also in that of biblical characters of the Old and New Testament and especially in the light of Christ's own life. As we said before, God speaks through values that belong to men and things, and this speaking is not something that stands juxtaposed to God's speaking to all of us through His Revelation. God's will stands revealed to us only when a situation is illuminated by Revelation. For this reason it is beneficial to let children see how various persons of the Bible tried to make their lives respond to the call of God that came to them in their whole concrete life and in diverse situations. We feel sure that many beautiful examples can be found in the Bible for the children of that age, examples that can help acquire the proper understanding and feeling regarding their own Christian task of life. This is catechesis in the full sense of the word. Moreover, when we present those personages to the children, we can easily make our reflections in the form of a conversation with the children, a value we have already stressed. We could ask, for instance, "What did Abraham think when he heard that . . . ?" Or, "What was the intention of Peter or John when he asked Christ . . . ?"

Advent

During this season we want to let the children see that Christ is the Messiah, the Savior who comes to meet and help us in our weakness. We must open ourselves to His salvation, in the sense we explained above.

John the Baptist announced the coming of the Messiah; he pointed out, at the same time, the attitude with which we must go to Him; he put great emphasis on acts of penance and not merely on good intentions. We must constantly renew our attitude toward Christ.

The creature who was best prepared for the coming of the Savior and most open to Him, was Mary. We must see how she, too, searched and groped trying to discover in varying circumstances what God expected from her.

This year we explain the joy of Christmas especially in view of the salvation Christ brings. "I proclaim good news to you of a great joy which will be shared by the whole people: today, in the city of David, a *Savior* has been born to you, who is Messiah and Lord" (Lk. 2:10–11). The whole catechesis of Advent contains opportunities for the fostering of and education in Christian hope: an expectation and confidence, not a forward-looking expectation like that of the Jews of the Old Testament, but of men who *have been* redeemed, who know and believe that Christ the Savior is here and now concerned with men. This idea can find expression, for instance, in the prayers we say together during this season. Certain hymns are also particularly suited to express our confidence.

After Christmas and Preparation for Lent

At this time we wish to put Christ's life and preaching at the center of our attention so that we may more clearly see our Christian task of life. Most striking in Christ's life are the miracles; in these He very clearly manifests what He wants and the spirit that animates Him. His miracles are not arbitrary deeds nor are they witchcraft. Hence our catechesis must avoid picturing miracles as something sensational or magical. We must bring out the fact that Christ was prompted and moved by the suffering, wretchedness and anxiety of people, that every miracle was, therefore, a sign of God's offer of salvation in the form of a response to a profound human need.

This, too, is what He teaches, for instance, in Matthew 25:31–46: "When the Son of Man shall come in his majesty . . . the king will say to those on his right hand, 'Come, blessed of my Father, take possession of the Kingdom prepared for you from the foundation of the world; for I was hungry and you gave me to eat; I was thirsty and you gave me to drink; I was a stranger and you took me in; naked and you covered me; sick and you visited me; I was in prison and you came to me . . .' 'Amen, I say to you, as long as you did it for one of these, the least of my brethren, you did it for me.'"

We must try to see the needs of our brothers, of those who suffer from hunger and thirst, who are strangers, are naked or in prison. We notice that Christ says explicitly: "As long as you did it for one of these, the least of my brethren, you did it for me." By our attention to our fellow-men, we show that we truly belong to Christ, that we truly believe in Him.

Here, however, we must explain to the children how the human situation described by Jesus can be transferred to us and our own times. This we must do especially by taking examples from the children's own lives. In other words, it is important not merely to recall the needs of people who are far away, in distant missions, or in some foreign country where people suffered some disaster; we must also show the children the difficulties that exist in our own midst.

The second commandment is similar to the first. Even the liturgical service of God must yield in the face of the need of our neighbor. The sanctification of the Sabbath yields before the need of a sick man.[1]

Jesus also tells us the conditions for a true love of neighbor. It demands discretion and true respect for the other. There must be a pure intention; we may not seek ourselves while practicing charity toward others.

In contrast to the Pharisees, Jesus holds that all men are equal before God and that all men are our neighbors. He also extends this explicitly to sinners by His word and example. In fact He came precisely to save sinners. We too must be merciful, even toward those who have wronged us.

The Forty Days of Lent

The children of the fifth grade are capable of participating religiously in Lent though, of course, in their own childlike way. The catechesis during this important season of the liturgical year should not be an isolated event but must be connected with the liturgical celebrations of the season and their rich symbolism.

[1] "It came to pass on another Sabbath . . . a man was there (in the synagogue) and his right hand was withered. And the Scribes and the Pharisees were watching whether he cured on the Sabbath, that they might find how to accuse him. . . . He said to the man with the withered hand, 'Arise and stand forth in the midst.' And he arose and stood forth. . . . I ask you, 'Is it lawful on the Sabbath to do good . . . to save a life?' " (Lk. 6:6–11). Luke describes a similar scene when, on another Sabbath, Christ cured a woman who had been ill for eighteen years: "The ruler of the synagogue . . . said, 'There are six days in which one ought to work; . . . and not on the Sabbath.' But the Lord answered, 'Hypocrites! does not each one of you on the Sabbath loose his ox or ass from the manger and lead it forth to water?' " (Lk. 13:10–17).

The celebration of Ash Wednesday, either together with adults or in a celebration adapted to the children can, if it is well prepared, be a fruitful starting point for our catechesis during Lent. The attitude that is expressed in that celebration can then repeatedly be taken up in the catechesis and especially in prayer.

In connection with the children's awakening ability to share in the spirit of Lent, it is well to point out to them what constitutes the significance of those days. This liturgical season aims at making the adult Christian reflect once more upon what he is. Holy Church, of which the Christian is a member, gives him powerful support in this and a rich atmosphere by means of her proclamation and liturgy. Moreover, she invites him to take a greater part in common prayer and in active love of neighbor. This personal commitment to which the Church invites the Christian and the proper climate she offers him aim at a *metanoia,* a conversion, of the Christian, that is, a renewed personal choice of Christ in His Church. This conversion finds expression especially in the encounter of repentant man with the forgiving Christ in Confession.

We need not mention that all this is still far above the capabilities and possibilities of children in the fifth grade. That is why we spoke only of an "awakening" of such a possibility. For this reason we propose that during Lent all this be offered to the children in a way that is adapted to them and that can terminate in initiation into making a personal Confession.

During the first three months of this year we try, together with the children, to enter more deeply into human life, to discover in it what God expects of us, especially what He expects of us with respect to our fellow-men. Next, we let them see how Jesus perfectly fulfilled that task of life and how He asked others to do the same, if they wished to belong to Him. Jesus is holy and demands holiness. But Jesus is also the Savior. He understands our weakness and gladly forgives us.

Hence at the beginning of Lent, it is reasonable to make the children realize again, and now more fully, what it means to belong to Jesus: we must try to be like Him. He was good for all people, for the poor and the rich. He cured the sick, made the lame walk again and gave sight to the blind. He made all men happy. He was friendly to sinners. He even forgave those who had caused Him pain.

We can point out that this following of Christ demands much from us. To accept our Christian task of life frequently demands that we deny ourselves certain things, that we overcome ourselves.

After all this, it is possible, it seems to us, to make the children realize a little that they do not always accomplish that task of life. This is due in part to the fact that we do not always see well and understand what is expected of us, or that we are not yet able to do it; but it may also be due in part to the fact that we do not want to do it.

It is important that the children should learn to see the difference between thoughtlessness, a mishap, defect and guilty deficiency. The negative reaction of adults to a child's clumsy actions or to a misunderstood behavior, perhaps even their impatience because of a defect the child is born with, frequently make children experience feelings of guilt for which there is no real foundation. It is essential, therefore, to constantly explain to them the importance of personal intention with respect to their actions and omissions.

As the awareness of guilt increases there grows a need for forgiveness. It is preferable to have the children seek forgiveness first from those whom they have offended. That is why we have not explicitly related their moral life to God during the previous years. Even now, we must avoid divorcing pardon by God from the pardon that is granted by others. When others forgive me, this pardon takes place within the Church; hence this forgiveness does not lie outside of Christ and the Father.

First Personal Confession. After giving attention once more to interpersonal forgiveness, we now begin preparation for the child's first personal confession.

In our opinion, the most important point here is to pay attention to the *fundamental attitudes* of the penitent. This can best be obtained by having children see the attitudes of the sinners who came to ask Christ for forgiveness or seeing what Christ said about this. We can take as an example, the parable of the Pharisee and the tax collector or that of the prodigal son, the story of the lame man who was brought before Jesus after being lowered through the roof or that of the murderer on the cross. Christ and His Father are always ready to forgive us when we acknowledge that we are sinful. In this preparation for the child's confession, the emphasis must be placed especially on pardon.

The effects of confession we can also illustrate best by examples from the Bible. The parable of the lost sheep, showing especially the protection and security of the stable and the joy of the shepherd when the lost sheep is found again, the change in the lives of Zaccheus and Mary Magdalen after they had received pardon from their sins; these stories are effective for our purpose. Of course, we must also give some attention to the external manner of going to confession, but surely it is not on this that we should put the main emphasis.

Generally the direct preparation for the personal confession is best done in a common celebration, after which the young penitent enters the confessional, makes his own confession of sins and receives an individual absolution. It is well to conclude this celebration with a common prayer of thanksgiving. The important fact we should also emphasize is that this sacramental reconciliation is not an ending but a turning point, that it is a new beginning which will require frequent renewals.

Every sacrament is a gift of God, but it is also at the same time a task for man. Here the task that should perhaps be stressed most to the children is the duty of pardoning others. This we can make the children realize well if we use the parable of the ungrateful steward and the Our Father.

Passion Tide

Choosing Christ or choosing Him again is not easy. Christ Himself accepted His task of life consistently. He clearly saw the situation into which He had come. If He continued to be good to people in word and deed, He knew that this would mean death for Him; the Pharisees would not rest until He was dead. In the Garden of Olives Christ passed through that ordeal with full consciousness.

All the disciples abandoned Christ. Many people expressly turned against Him. Men are that way. So are we; we are weak, ungrateful, hesitant, self-seeking, and easily influenced by others.

Mary alone remained faithful and stood under the Cross in that hour of greatest abandonment, precisely at the time when Christ was giving the greatest proof of His Love.

After Easter

Because Jesus consistently accepted his task of life and thus fulfilled His Father's will in everything, He entered into His glory. This is revealed to us in His resurrection. In the power of the Holy Spirit, He saw that divine Will in the needs of men and read it in the situation in which He was placed. To us He has given the same task: Do as I have done. I have given you an example. Then you too will be glorified as I am glorified.

Christ has not left us behind as orphans. In the first place, He has given us to one another. He has gathered us in a large family. He has made us children of the same Father, of His Father (through baptism). That is why, every Sunday, the family of God comes together with Jesus to give thanks to the Father; we must show gratitude for that salvation which He gives us in Jesus Christ, His Son. Together we confess our guilt: together we eat the same Bread. There we find the power to make true also in our own life what Christ has so clearly asked of us in the first celebration of the Eucharist: "Love one another, as I have loved you." (Eucharist means thanksgiving.)

It is the Holy Spirit, the Helper, living in the Church and in each one of us, who is every Eucharistic celebration will fill our whole life more and more. This Holy Spirit was promised us by Jesus: "It is good for you that I go. . . . I will ask the Father and he will give you another Advocate to dwell with you forever. . . . If I do not go, the Advocate will not come to you; but if I go, I will send him to you" (Jn. 14:15).

In a catechesis of *confirmation* we try now to make the children realize their place in the Church. They are growing older and have a growing responsibility toward others.

The texts and rites of the administration of that sacrament provide an occasion for developing more fully the deep significance confirmation has for our whole life. By the imposition of hands the bishop confirms that the Holy Spirit is given to us, by which we, as children of God, actually belong to the Church of Christ.

These sacramental gestures and words of the bishop contain, not only an offer of salvation, but also a call to respond more fully henceforth to the gift of the Holy Spirit. The imposition of hands and the anointing with chrism are the signs expressing that. The imposition of hands signifies giving power in the Holy Spirit. The chrism fills the confirmand completely with its perfume and the odor spreads all around. One thus receives the Spirit not only for himself, but must now spread all around him that odor of Christ. This means that one must, as much as possible, cooperate in creating a Christian community: at home, in school, during games, in prayer, but especially by active participation in the celebration of the Eucharist.

We also recommend that during the preparation for confirmation attention be given in catechesis to the function of the bishop. It is perhaps one of the few times in their life that the children come so close to the bishop; thus it is a suitable occasion for showing them how we are connected with the bishop. This catechesis is very important in connection with education in Church-consciousness.

The coming of the Holy Spirit on the first Pentecost and its visible effects in the apostles and in the many who accepted baptism helps the children to prepare their minds and hearts for the operation of grace of that same Holy Spirit.

Depending on the amount of time that still remains, we can then deal with several topics in connection with Pentecost and/ or Confirmation:

The Holy Spirit and the spread of the Church;

The Holy Spirit and the martyrs (witnesses);

The Holy Spirit and the hierarchy (successors of the apostles);

The Holy Spirit and the Council;

The Holy Spirit and love of neighbor, prayer, contrition (confession);

The Holy Spirit and holiness (also some modern saints).

7. *Program for the Sixth Grade* (Eleven-year-olds)

Introduction

There are several reasons for the special difficulties attached to the catechesis given to the children of this grade. The differences between the pupils are now more in evidence.

The first difference is that which exists between boys and girls; they are now undergoing different developments. The girls are, generally, in the phase of pre-puberty, while most of the boys are still in the stage of "childhood."

At this time greater differences manifest themselves also because of the milieu from which the children come.

231

Finally there may also be differences arising from the fact that some will eventually go to vocational high schools, others to ordinary high schools or preparatory high schools. Those who are expected to get high grades so as to be accepted in preparatory schools, may on that account, develop a dislike for catechesis. Great stress is sometimes placed on achievements, upon having an excellent scholastic record; thus religious values may be less appreciated. The situation is difficult: on the one hand, we must continue to strive for a sound education and must combat the tendency of overemphasizing achievement; on the other hand, it is also necessary to remain realistic.

All this pleads for great openness with respect to the program of education in general and the catechetical program in particular. That is why, as we advance during the course of this year, we should try to hold conversations with the class for the sake of adjusting ourselves to the particular needs of the children and adapting to their increasing differences. With respect to girls, it is already possible to appeal to their awakening sense of responsibility.

Although we advocate openness regarding the catechetical program, we consider it useful to offer a few fundamental outlines, because most teachers may find it impossible to depend upon their own inventiveness throughout the whole course of this year.

We can say in general that the children of that age, and especially the boys, are more inclined to what is intellectual; we may even say that they sometimes tend to intellectualism. They are more interested in gathering knowledge and making experiments with their potentialities. In spite of that, we must remain faithful to our principles and avoid as much as possible any yielding to one-sided intellectualism. Overloading children with knowledge and frequent repetition, especially in the higher grades, may produce boredom and disgust. Moreover, we profane religious things when we put too much stress on learning and on such means as recitals of lessons, grades and punishments.

What is essential in the primary school is to foster discreetly a Christian attitude and life. In reality it is not easy to indicate concretely what a child of a particular age is able to experience and live by, and what are its potentialities for accepting and living according to the Glad Tidings. Many factors are at work in that. There are always children who find it easy to become involved; others find it difficult to engage themselves. When we work with a group, as is the case in school, we must always bear in mind and take account of the average pupil.

One hears the rather frequent remark that in the higher grades of primary school there is a certain decrease in religiousness. Such critics assume that children of the lower grades are "more religious." But we must ask ourselves whether those conclusions are not drawn principally from the fact that children of the lower grades are more subject to emotions. It is possible that the pupils of higher grades are capable of a more authentic religiousness.

Just now we expressed a warning against intellectualism in our catechesis. It remains true, however, that children of the higher grades must be approached in a different way. Today's teachers stress that the school must offer a pedagogical milieu, but within this milieu there takes place in the successive grades a gradual development toward more instruction.

From the catechetical standpoint, this means that in the lower grades there is little systematic instruction, little subject matter to be "learned"; but there must be a direct integral influencing of the pupils through witness. The religious element must permeate the whole milieu of the child.

This witness continues to occupy the first rank in the higher grades, but its instructional aspect comes more to the fore. This is in harmony with the child's growing need for systematization and its growing ability to survey a greater ensemble.

The older children of the primary school are more attuned to external matters and less capable of admiration and wonder; this is particularly true of boys. Their attention is drawn more strongly to things than to that which is personal. It follows that catechists should avoid giving constantly explicit and emphatic religious witness. Pupils should, of course, be able to experience the catechist's actions and behavior as authentic. It should be his actions themselves that appeal for the pupils' personal commitment rather than his words that ask them to involve themselves. In this way the children are given the opportunity to "stay out of range" if they desire; this is necessary because we must respect their growing freedom.

We should like to make another general remark before proposing a program for the sixth grade. When we outlined the various programs for the primary school, it was not our intention to be complete in every respect. For we believe that the primary school is not the place where we should, for safety's sake, give a completely finished religious formation. Moreover, the children who continue their studies in Catholic schools will receive the additional instruction they need, and so the continuity and continuance of their catechesis is assured. There is a difficulty, however, with respect to the many children who enter public high schools. Methods must be found—and the Confraternity of Christian Doctrine plays a most important role here—to insure that a more complete authentic religious education and instruction be given to those older youngsters. Nevertheless, we must avoid giving in the primary grades what can be given only later, for it is not possible for the children to assimilate what is offered prematurely.

With respect to the program of the sixth grade, because it is, in a certain way, the closing of an important period of life, it is reasonable to give the children a certain frame within which they can now place many things they have heard in the course of the years. This is also why we propose that children should be made somewhat familiar with books of Holy Scripture and with the missal.

Holy Scripture

We already made use of Holy Scripture in the previous years. We now wish to give the children a first acquaintance with Holy Scripture itself. What we have in mind here is especially the Gospels and the Acts of the Apostles; but during the first three months we should like to give some attention also to the Old Testament. We believe we can do this because, in this period, there awakens an awareness of historical connections; the children are becoming interested in the course of history because of their growing consciousness of time. Here are good opportunities for catechesis. For we can clearly show the central place Christ occupies in the history of mankind. There was a time before Christ when people looked forward toward Him; and there is a time after Christ, the time of redemption, the time in which we live at present.

Our primary concern is not the historical sequence itself, but this sequence can shed a Christian light upon our own time; it can help to make God's plan of salvation for men, as it is continued in our present history, a more living reality for the children.

As to the Old Testament, we can content ourselves with giving the children an idea in very broad outline of the history of the People of God. In the New Testament something similar can be offered them regarding the life of Christ and the expansion of the Church. We could make them sufficiently acquainted with the four Gospels and the Acts, then they themselves can find certain texts. We believe, however, that it is better to postpone reading the entire Gospel.

It is useful, in the course of the year, to give some details about the Holy Land, Jerusalem, the Temple and the expansion of the Church, to give the children a measure of familiarity with the world of the Bible. It is not our purpose to give them lessons in the geography and history of Palestine. But those details are important because thus they learn to know better the milieu in which Christ lived during His earthly life, and they thus can better understand His words and His message. Hence those data should not be separated from a personal connection with Christ but they should always function within that connection.

The Missal

A second important aspect of catechesis in the sixth grade can be the introduction of the children to the missal. Like the Bible, the liturgical year as such is not yet a separate topic of our catechesis in the lower grades because, in our opinion, a synthetic understanding of the whole missal is beyond the grasp of those children. Just as the historical vision of salvation, an understanding of the liturgical year requires a somewhat developed notion of time. Of course, we have occasionally made use of various data of the liturgical year. Catechesis was often a preparation for liturgical feasts, and the various principal seasons of this year gave distinct features to the various parts of our catechesis. Now, however, we want to give a more deliberate introduction to the liturgical year, and this we do with the help of the missal.

In the third grade we wanted the catechist to make an appeal to the receptivity of the children for the fundamental symbols of the sacraments and liturgical life in general. With this already done in good time, we can now confront the children more with those signs of the word that appear in the Bible and the missal.

This is a question of introducing the children to two important books that play a capital role in our life of faith. It is not chiefly a matter of giving the children factual knowledge about the books of the Bible and the structure of the missal. It is much more a question of deepening and enriching their life of faith by listening to God's word and participating in the life of the Church.

Regarding the introduction of the children to the missal, we wish to teach them principally how to take part in worship, to make them familiar with the style of prayer used by the Church, and finally to give them an understanding of the fundamental structure of the liturgical year so that they will gradually arrive at participating in it in a conscious manner.

A complete missal does not seem appropriate for children of primary school, but a children's missal can render good service.

It stands to reason that our choice of prayer during this year is dictated principally by biblical and liturgical prayer texts.

Renewal of the Promises of Baptism

Many teachers and priests feel the need of some kind of ceremony marking the end of the phase of education in a religious manner. When First Communion was moved back to an earlier age, this led to the ceremony of the renewal of baptismal promises. But since the Easter Vigil was re-introduced, the renewal of those promises by the children is rightly seen as a "first" renewal, one that must be repeated every year at Easter time. That is why this renewal was placed preferably during Easter Week.

The renewal of baptismal promises has, however, another facet that merits our attention. It was often said formerly that, at this age, the time has come for the child to give a personal

237

witness, a personal promise of fidelity, because the young person must henceforth take his place in society. But we can ask ourselves if the twelve-year-old is capable of doing such a thing. Doesn't this overestimate him as a person and his place in society? Is not a twelve-year-old's attitude determined principally by others, by the group of youngsters of his own age or by the opinion of a respected teacher? In fact, we rarely meet with difficulties in the case of sixth grade children in contrast with youths who raise frequent objections. In their religious conflicts, youths have the feeling that their earlier profession of faith was not authentic or personal. They are convinced that they were then insufficiently aware of what that solemnity meant and implied.

Would it not be better to give the sixth-graders an occasion for solemnly expressing that they are gradually beginning to find their place in the community of adult believers and that, henceforth, they will be permitted to share more and more in the actions and life of this community? Doesn't this signify much better the new phase of life they have reached? In view of this, it seems most suitable to let these children take part *for the first time* in the Easter Vigil. But then they should not be the center of the celebration, but should be participants in it along with the rest of the community.

It follows that, in the program for this grade, we propose for the time before and during Lent a catechesis directed to the children's first celebration of the Easter Vigil. Even if we don't expect that all the children will assist at it, such a catechesis remains meaningful. In that case it would be well to terminate the Lenten catechesis with an Easter celebration. Moreover, there remains the possibility of setting aside some days at the end of the school year to give a relative completeness to the education in a living faith that has taken place in the primary school and to provide an opportunity for jointly thanking God, once more, for all the things they have received during those years.

Until Advent

We recommend that the Bible be introduced in a solemn way by means of some celebration. This, at the same time, raises the Bible above the usual way books are treated in school. It makes the children see the Bible as the Book by which we come in contact with God Himself. We thus try to dispose the children for the word of God from the beginning, a disposition to which we must constantly appeal throughout the further course of catechesis. The cultivation of an attitude of listening attentively to Holy Scripture is one of the most important aspects of the training of these children.

We then pass successively through the great phases of salvation history. We could deal with the following:

Creation as seen by the Israelites and as the first revelation of God's love. Man has a task with respect to creation and principally with respect to his fellow-man.

The fall of man, which is an image of the disrupted world in which we now live. The call of God's love does not receive men's answer.

God calls Abraham and us in him; he is the father of all believers. Ever more clearly God reveals to man who He is and by this man also sees ever more clearly what he himself is and what is his place with respect to God.

God is holy and near us (Moses).

God is our Savior (Exodus).

God is with us (the Covenant of Sinai).

God is our king (entry of David into Palestine).

God lives among us (the Temple of Jerusalem).

Man is unfaithful to the Covenant and puts an obstacle in the way of God's help offered to us (exile).

However, God remains faithful and through the prophets helps His people to arrive at conversion (return from exile).

239

In this way, by the things that take place in the Old Testament, we can throw light upon the various aspects of God's loving concern with us.

Advent

At the beginning of Advent or immediately before it, we introduce the missal. This too can best take place in the form of a celebration. In the course of the year we celebrate in the Eucharist the fact that God is occupied with men and continues to be occupied with them. The beginning of the liturgical year coincides with the beginning of the missal. Here, therefore, is a good time for becoming acquainted with the general liturgical year. The more complete introduction into the missal can be done gradually.

During the weeks of Advent, we try to make the great thoughts of Advent come alive for the children with the help of texts of the missal. We can start from the *parousia* with which Advent begins. We are, like Israel, a people that is on the way (First Sunday). Christ is the Messiah who comes to make all people happy (Second Sunday). He is near, He stands in our midst, He comes to save us (Third Sunday). Christ, the Lord, the Son of the Eternal God, has become man (Christmas).

As to biblical topics, we can speak about the prophets who foretold the Messianic era. Then, for the first time, God would find a man who remained faithful to Him in all things. In this man God would make a new and eternal Covenant. That is why Christ's coming would be a joy for the people. This can be illustrated by the nativity of John the Baptist, the *Benedictus* of Zaccharia, the message of the Angel and the *Magnificat*. Just as under the Old Covenant, a call by God has significance not only for the individual person who receives it but for the whole people.

From January Till the Beginning of Lent

The time of Epiphany provides the children an opportunity to get a deeper realization of the mystery of Christ's Person. This can be obtained through the story of the Magi, of Simeon in the Temple, and especially through what took place at the baptism of Christ in the Jordan. This topic can also be illustrated by various passages from the Bible such as those proposed in the liturgy of those weeks.

We can give some attention during this same time to the structure of the Mass, making use of the missal, to help the children to a deeper meaning of the Eucharistic celebration. Perhaps the catechist can also find time to teach them how to connect the ordinary parts of the Mass with the proper parts.

The Forty Days of Lent

Christ came to restore the intimate relations between God and man: "My Father is also your Father." He came to gather men around Him and lead them to the Father: "No one comes to the Father but by Me." This is God's plan regarding men, His plan of salvation that already began at creation but that was constantly thwarted by man's infidelity (cf. the first three months of this school year). As Christ tries to gather men around Him and lead them to the Father, He constantly encounters sin. It is sin that estranges men from one another and from God.

Christ bridged the distance that separates man from God by a loving donation of Himself to the Father; in submission to the Father He "emptied Himself" and thus overcame sin. The price He paid was His passion and death, but it was at the same time the way to resurrection. He thereby also opened for us the possibility of a return to the Father.

The Risen Savior invites us to fight with Him against evil and overcome sin by prayer and love of neighbor, for the way of

241

salvation is a life of love for God that finds expression especially in love toward men. He who constantly lives this way will meet with suffering as a participation in Christ's passion; but this for the Christian, is precisely the way to resurrection.

This is the fundamental thought of the Lenten liturgy. Hence three principal themes come to the fore during this time:

1. Struggle against evil.

2. This struggle takes place through prayer and love of neighbor.

3. The ultimate consequence of that struggle is suffering, but it leads to the resurrection both for Christ and for us.

At the same time and in connection with these themes, the liturgy of this season also employs the theme of baptism in which we die with Christ in order to rise with Him.

Let us remark that in the Lenten catechesis we must not leave the resurrection out of consideration for any length of time, putting an exclusive emphasis on the suffering and death of the Lord. It is the risen Christ Himself who continues to live in His Church. It is He who invites us during the whole Lenten period to make and renew our choice of Him, so that our whole life is ever more involved in this donation of ourselves to God.

The Lenten Liturgy

In the catechetical program, starting from the pre-lenten season, one could give a series of classes about the liturgy, especially the liturgy of the Sundays, in which he brings to the fore the above-named three topics. If man wishes to attain salvation, he must make greater efforts; yet salvation always remains a free and unmerited gift of God (Septuagesima Sunday). The word of God is sown in abundance but it bears fruit only when we willingly receive it (Sexagesima Sunday). After these weeks, in which the right disposition of generosity and openness have been fostered in us, we now come to the great themes.

Christ announces His death and resurrection. We, too, will have a share in them if we exercise the love of neighbor in all its concreteness (Quinquagesima Sunday). We must not pray and practice love of neighbor in order to receive praise from men (Ash Wednesday). Christ has preceded us in the struggle against temptation; if we cling to Him we shall conquer (First Sunday of Lent). Before Christ entered into His passion, there broke through in His glorification on Mt. Thabor something of the splendor of the resurrection, toward which everything is directed. If we wish to follow God's will to the utmost through love of neighbor, we too must expect suffering in order to attain glorification (Second Sunday).

Being baptized, we must conduct ourselves as children of light. If we again admit the devil into our heart, darkness will have more power over us (Third Sunday). Halfway through Lent, there suddenly emerges something of the joy of Easter in the picture of the superabundance we shall receive, now in this life—especially in the Eucharist—and then in the heavenly Banquet (Fourth Sunday).

At the beginning of Passion Tide we see that there is a growing conflict between Christ and the leaders of the people. Jesus' total commitment to give us life will terminate in the sacrifice of His life; this sacrifice will overshadow all the sacrifices of the Old Testament (First Passion Sunday). On the second Sunday of the Passion (Palm Sunday), we honor Christ who by His Cross became our King. Because He humbled Himself, God exalted Him. We promise to walk the way with Him through death to resurrection.

The hour of victory over sin and death is coming near. Jesus says: "My hour has come; the hour in which the ruler of darkness will be cast out." This is not done by violence, by noisy weapons, but with simple words: "Here I am." Christ goes to the limit in His love for men. He leaves us the Eucharist as His greatest gift. In this way He makes His love-offering always present among us. And by it He makes a permanent appeal to us to love God, as He has loved Him and expressed that love in His love for men. In the Eucharist He gives us the power to do the same (Holy Thursday).

Even at the moment of His greatest suffering, Christ says, "Father, forgive them for they know not what they do." He thus overcomes sin. He thus overcomes death. "We adore Your Cross, O Lord, and we praise and glorify Your Holy Resurrection. For by the wood joy came into the whole world" (Good Friday).

In this way Christ brings about redemption, the new Creation, for His sacrifice is accepted and it leads to His own glorification and to the salvation of all who believe in Him (Easter). The history of man has acquired a new meaning; we are on the way to the final victory when God will be "all in all."

Baptismal Catechesis

Although Christ has saved us, it remains necessary for every man to enter personally and totally into that mystery, to personally join the procession of all those who, with Jesus, are on the way to the Father. Jesus' ascent to the Father must become our own ascent. This event begins in baptism, which is a sign of our dying and rising with Jesus Christ.

As we said above, the theme of baptism plays a role throughout Lent. This presents us with a second topic for a series of classes. This series is most appropriate in the sixth grade as a preparation for the renewal of baptismal vows during the Easter Vigil. Our incorporation into Christ and His people through baptism, however real and important, is not enough. The Christian, in order to continue to participate in the ascent to

244

the Father of Jesus and those who are His own, must again and again renew his mind and heart, so that he may live ever more truly in the spirit of Christ.

Every year during Lent Christians reflect once more upon their fidelity to Christ and to one another. Having acquired in this way the right disposition, they then renew their baptismal promises to express their desire to live a more profound and authentic life of faith. This they do in common, in a public celebration, for they realize that they need and are responsible for one another.

In our catechesis we must first of all make the children clearly understand and appreciate the meaning of the baptismal promises. We should not propose that renewal to them as a purely personal promise of fidelity, but we explain that they have now reached the age when they can join the community of adult believers. This community will have to carry and support them so that they may grow constantly toward and achieve a mature personal commitment to Christ. After this we can give the children a baptismal catechesis in connection with the Easter Vigil ceremonies. They will thus be able to participate more fully in that celebration.

It is evident that we ought to make full use of the biblical ideas forming the background of that celebration. Moreover, it is also meaningful at this time to go together with the children to a baptism.

In the first classes we can speak about the ceremony of light: about the Easter Candle, the procession of the light and the *Exsultet*. We can point out the universal human significance of light. Christ shows Himself as the Light of the world. We participate in this Light and can in turn transmit it to others.

The first two readings of the Easter Vigil, should be given special attention (Gen. 1:1–2; Ex. 14:24–15:1). In connection with the ceremony of the blessing of baptismal water, we can show the meaning of water in Holy Scripture, the symbolism of baptism as a dying and rising with Christ, the principal rites of this sacrament, and we could perhaps speak also of confession as a second baptism. But the point to be stressed is that through baptism we belong to the People of God, we become members of the community of the Church. When explaining the symbolism of water in baptism, we must make it clear that the washing is only secondary.

We can end by dealing with the subjects of the renewal of baptismal promises and the Eucharistic celebration in which the paschal events become a complete reality.

During the course of this baptismal catechesis we should also give attention to the Creed. This must not be approached in·a purely systematic way as giving a synthesis of our doctrine of faith; but we present the Creed as a possibility for authentically professing our faith.

After Easter

Christ's Easter resurrection is the most important feast of the entire history of salvation; it is the high point from which the whole "economy of salvation" gets its power. Christianity stands or falls with the fact that Christ did or did not rise from the dead: "If Christ has not risen, vain is our preaching, vain too is your faith" (1 Cor. 15–14).

To be a Christian means to acknowledge, not only theoretically but practically, that Christ is alive in the sense that the whole life of the Christian must be a witness to his faith in the risen Lord present among us. God continues to be concerned with the world, in Jesus Christ. Jesus is not a distant being who has withdrawn from us and become inaccessible. Man is not abandoned to himself. "Where two or three are gathered together for my sake, there am I in the midst of them" (Mat. 18–20). "I will not leave you orphans; I will come to you. Yet a

246

little while and the world no longer sees me. But you shall see me, for I live and you shall live. In that day you will know that I am in my Father and you in me, and I in you" (Jn. 14:18–20). We speak with the children about some of the stories of the resurrection to enliven their faith that the Lord is near us.

Besides this, we continue the children's initiation in the liturgy. Easter is the high point of the liturgical year. This high point permeates every Sunday; every Sunday is an Easter of the Church. We come together to praise God and give expression to our joy because of the new life. And yet every Sunday and every season of the liturgical year has its particular color.

We now give the pupils a survey of the liturgical year. We look back at its development from Advent to Easter and look forward to Pentecost and the further course of the liturgical year. Here we can also bring out the idea of the *parousia* as it shines forth from the most important celebrations, especially at the end of the year. We show at the same time how the successive years are a constant ascent to a final fulfillment. It stands to reason that we should make constant use of the missal in our explanations in order that the children may find again in them the various subjects we deal with.

Ascension and Pentecost

During the weeks surrounding the Ascension and Pentecost we consider the biblical accounts of those feasts and show in them the significance of those events of salvation for us. We can, besides, give some classes that are built upon materials of the missal.

We celebrate the fact that Christ gave us His Holy Spirit, by which we are able to live according to God's Spirit as He did. Jesus fulfills the will of the Father in the power of the Spirit and continues to fight against sin with a love that forgives everything. It is the same Holy Spirit who brought about the great change that took place in the apostles and that animated the first Christians. This Spirit also continues to fill us through the grace of baptism and especially that of confirmation. He brings us close to one another around our oldest Brother, Jesus Christ, gives us the power to live in love and fulfill our task as true children of the Father.

The End of the School Year

During the remaining time we can talk about the life of the young Church and the problems it met. Many of those questions are still alive in the Church of today. We can speak here about the apostolate, the missions, the adjustment to today's world, unity, ecumenism, etc.

Besides that, it is also possible to bring up some topics that are gradually becoming a problem of importance for those children, for instance, happiness of life, the choice of a profession, vocation, (marriage, the priesthood, the religious state) and other subjects which the children themselves may suggest. When questions come up about man's bodily being, being a man or a woman, we should not evade them. As we already remarked, it is better to deal with those questions in the form of conversations with the children.

APPENDIX
A CONCRETE PROPOSAL FOR COOPERATION BETWEEN THE SCHOOL AND THE FAMILY

When the old-fashioned catechism disappears from the school, parents and teachers might be inclined to imagine that this marks the end of the family's cooperation with the school with respect to religious instruction. There are no more *Questions,* hence children have no longer to learn *Answers.*

On the contrary! Cooperation between the family and the school constitutes the very heart of the new program. Let us briefly show how this cooperation can and should be conceived.

In the Catholic school we no longer give religious "instruction" as more or less separated from authentic "education" in a living faith, but it is precisely this authentic education that must dictate the whole norm and content of religious instruction.

The cooperation between the family and the school thus acquires a totally different content. Until recently, parents were merely asked to make their children learn the answers by heart; after that the teachers listened to the children as they "recited their lessons." This help in the "instruction" of the children is no longer asked of the parents and lest the parents fear worse is to come, there is no other "instruction" that will take the place of the former. For we now realize that the parents have a much more important task with respect to authentic religious education, a task that requires more of them, and is much more fundamental, than cooperating externally with the school.

The parents are the first educators of their children. Their own religious life will ordinarily determine the development of the child's religious life. The task of the school consists in helping the parents; it does not consist in taking the parents' place. But then, because this is so, the school has to realize that it must be most closely attuned to the religious life of the family. Otherwise the school could produce a conflict situation for the child. Here we are not thinking of parents who neglect their children's religious growth. Most parents have an earnest interest in the education of their children in a living faith, though this may not always be equally evident in their words and perhaps even less in their conduct. If we extend a helping hand to them, the parents will often cooperate in the way that is proper to them. Thus we are giving them recognition, and parents will gradually realize that we honestly see them as the first educators of their children. In fact, parents certainly exercise the greatest influence; and it is to this fact that we must attune ourselves.

The Catholic school, of course, has its own specific responsibility. But it cannot bear or fulfill that responsibility in isolation.

249

However difficult it may be in practice, we must seek opportunities to let the parents see that they really have the first responsibility and that, therefore, they must take the lead in the integral religious upbringing of their children.

This situation requires a genuine and growing cooperation between the family and the school, a dialogue between them in which each one listens to the other and makes his own contribution. This cooperation must still be brought about in many parishes; and hence such a cooperation can hardly be expected to be achieved in the first year of the new program. Great changes come about slowly, and it is only gradually that a full development is reached. The parents need to be informed, just as parishioners need instruction about the new liturgy. For this reason special leaflets or folders might be prepared, three for each grade, as is done in Holland. They should reach the parents *by way of the school:* one at the beginning of the school year, one after the Christmas holydays and one after Easter.

In these folders the parents, first of all, are not told what religious *instruction* the children are given in school, but what *education* in living the faith they receive. By means of those leaflets the parents are well posted about the atmosphere of faith and of living the faith which we do our best to foster in the children. We tell them how we try to take account of the particular stage of development of the children and especially—and this is of primary importance—how we want to adapt ourselves to the religious education that the parents themselves give to their children.

The leaflets are set up in the following way. The front has an attractive picture of boys or girls of the particular grade. Then comes a short talk with the parents in which something is said about the phase of life in which the child presently finds itself and, in connection with this phase, something about the child's growing life of faith. Next we tell them what we are doing in each class during that particular part of the year. After that there is a whole page which we call "Our Cooperation with You." Here we show how we attune ourselves to the religious upbringing which the children receive at home and how the parents in turn can attune themselves to what we do: not by taking part in *instruction,* but by accompanying and supporting the child in its *education* at home toward the religious awareness the Catholic school tries to awaken in it.

One or another parent might remark when seeing these folders: "What must we parents *do?* What do they want of us? How can we know exactly what role is assigned to us?" All such remarks proceed from the supposition that the parents somehow are asked to make their children "learn" things by heart. Now this is precisely the thing we do *not* mean at all.

In the plan for the renewal of catechesis the cooperation between the family and the school appears in a totally different form. Together we want to create one and the same attitude and mentality; together we want to *educate* the child in that religious mentality. In other words, it is a question of creating an atmosphere in which the child experiences that the family and the school want to be attuned to each other. And it is precisely for this purpose that those leaflets are given to the parents.

The activities we propose to the parents lie completely within the sphere of the family, for instance, little talks with the child, reading together with, or to, the child from a family Bible.

Those leaflets will achieve their best results when we give them to the parents at the beginning of each three month period. Then, a little later—for instance, on the occasion of a meeting in the evening with the parents of children that belong to a particular class—we can introduce the parents more fully into the spirit of this new project of catechesis. This priests and teachers will find easy to do if they are familiar with this book and its programs. It is the Catholic school that must put that cooperation into motion. That is why all priests and teachers connected with the school are asked to help wholeheartedly for that end. After all, what is our ultimate purpose but to give an authentic religious *education* in the faith to the children God has entrusted to our care?

CHAPTER SEVEN

THE NEW CATECHETICAL PROGRAM FOR STUDENTS IN CATHOLIC JUNIOR AND SENIOR HIGH SCHOOLS

1. *Introduction*

The program presented here is designed for students receiving their education in Catholic junior (seventh to ninth grades) and senior (tenth to twelfth grades) high schools.

The Pastoral Work of the Church

Catechesis forms a part of the pastoral work of the Church. Since this pastoral work constitutes an organic whole, it is only within it that catechesis can be properly understood and can rightly function. When it is isolated from pastoral work we impair its fruitfulness.

In Chapter Two we gave a descriptive definition of pastoral work: It is the endeavor of the whole People of God, as guided by the Holy Spirit, to confront men in their concrete situation with God's offer of salvation in Christ, and thereby to awaken and foster their faith.

The salvation offered us by God is a community-of-love with

Himself and His Son Jesus Christ. This offer does not come to us solely in the sacraments, prayer and the proclamation of the faith; it comes also in and through everything that constitutes our human existence. The whole of reality—hence also the whole of human culture—has a salvific significance. In our dialogue with our fellow-men and the world, we meet God and the invitation He addresses to us.

This offer of salvation becomes a saving reality when man responds to it and commits himself to God by faith. By this believing response, God's invitation becomes actual salvation. It is in this that loving communion with God in Christ is realized.

However, if man wishes to attain faith and grow in it, it is necessary that he come into contact with that divine invitation, that he be confronted with it precisely in his concrete situation.

It is this confrontation that is the task of the Church in her pastoral activity. This activity aims at making man conscious of the reality in which he lives, aware of God's self-giving love, of the effective presence of Christ *in man's whole life*. The Church's pastoral activity, then, wants to help men to discover more and more the salvific meaning of their whole existence, so that they are confronted with Christ coming to them in everything that happens in their lives.

Authentic Education in the Faith

When pastoral work is aimed at children and youths, we call it "education in a living faith." We are then concerned with an educational relationship. Because children and youths are not full-grown, they evidently need the support and guidance of the adults responsible for their education.

That authentic education in the faith functions within the whole of education. It is not something superadded to education, but the whole of education must be orientated by it and permeated with it. Such an education takes place by sustaining and stimulating the pupils to attain an existence that is guided by a correct scale of values and embodied in a Christian attitude of life.

A little child's education in a living faith is still very general. At this time it is a question of a direct and integral influence exercised by their environment, that is, by their parents. Authentic religious education during the first years of primary school remains predominantly general. Insofar as there is here any explicit mention of the faith, it is largely incidental and entirely interwoven with the natural solidarity between children and their educators. But as the children grow older, there occurs a corresponding development in this matter in the pedagogical environment of the primary school. Within the whole of authentic religious education there is an increasingly more explicit dealing with the faith until it becomes a relatively independent function, namely, "catechesis." Educating the child continues to occupy first place, but within it the instructional aspect acquires its own proper character. This is in accord with the need the older child experiences for systematizing its knowledge and with its greater capacity for surveying a larger ensemble.

Catechesis

The school catechesis, as a special function within the whole of education in a living faith, must be seen, like this whole education, as a help to the student in the development of his life of faith. This help consists in illuminating man's existence through God's Revelation. By means of the proclamation of the word, catechesis wishes to give a Christian meaning to human life. This catechesis does by illuminating and showing the whole life of the pupils, as it is lived in the present and directed to the future, as a salvific action of God, as a salvation history. It tries to develop in the students a vision of faith concerning their own life.

This illumination of the pupils' own life is achieved by witnessing to the mystery of Christ by means of the word. For its aim is to present an authentic interpretation of human existence, the interpretation given by God Himself in Christ as it comes to us guaranteed by the living tradition of the Church.

High School. On the high school level it will be necessary to deepen the youngsters' understanding of the faith, to widen their vision and obtain a more critical knowledge of their religion. This is especially true if later they will go on to college and become more or less "intellectuals." But this deepening of their religious understanding should not be divorced from the whole of authentic religious education. Here too it is a question of an understanding in function of living the faith.

One of the reasons for the cleavage between faith and life in the past was undoubtedly the fact that religious knowledge was much too isolated from living one's faith. Faith was reduced to knowing and accepting a certain number of truths which, however, exercised little influence upon practical life. That is why in the renewal of school catechesis there is a shift of emphasis from learning or instruction to education or formation. All the knowledge imparted to the students about Revelation must contribute toward the growth of their vision of faith concerning their own life and must lead them to a meeting with the person of Christ in their whole life and in every situation. Our instruction must continue to function within the framework of authentic religious education; it must form a part of education in a living faith, be attuned to the liturgy and to the reality of the pupil's life in school, at home and everywhere else. Faith is not primarily a matter of knowing a system of truths that are sharply defined and exactly formulated; it is a self-commitment to the living God who is at work in our lives.

This new catechetical approach is a little out of tune with the situation existing in the school. Assigned to a prosaic classroom and sandwiched between English composition and physics, the "religion class" finds a climate of and an interest in transmission of "knowledge," rather than a readiness for a meeting with God. The religious atmosphere is absent as well as the desirable disposition of the pupils. But in spite of this, practice shows that it is possible to use the new approach. Later we shall give a few suggestions for overcoming those obstacles to some extent.

Among educators in general there is a trend of thought that looks for a new approach also with respect to secular subjects, an approach that is more a "formation" of the students than making them "learn things." But even where the new catechesis is ahead of such efforts, it would be wrong to delay its introduction and to retain the old-fashioned system still followed in secular subjects.

The Program

The aim of our proclamation of Christ's mystery is to give meaning to the concrete human existence of these students in this class of this school. It is the saving dimension of their life with all it contains that our catechesis desires to help them discover. It is this life on which our catechesis wants to throw light. That is why our catechesis is essentially a dialogue; a dialogue between the students' life and vision-of-life, on the one hand, and the catechist's own vision of faith on the other.

It is on this basis that a choice is made of a particular program for each class. The program must help the students of a particular class to understand their own life as a salvation history, a dialogue between God and themselves. We must therefore ask ourselves: with what is the pupil's mind occupied at his or her particular age? What are the problems, the questions—sometimes only half-formulated—that arise in the students? What are they wrestling with, what do they seek? How do they see their own lives in that phase of their development? What is the dominant note of that phase?

In the following pages we have tried to give for each grade a program that can function as a religious reply corresponding to the needs of the students of the pertinent age. It goes without saying that such a program cannot be presented here in a fully and concretely worked-out form. Each concrete class has its own peculiarities that distinguish it from other classes. It is possible to draw a general outline and give a summary of the problems that belong to the students of a certain age, but only the catechist who is in actual contact with a group of youngsters is able to discover their particular needs and mental attitudes.

Again, if it be true that the students' own life constitutes the matter that catechesis must enlighten, it stands to reason that the students must as much as possible contribute this material. The catechist can have a general idea of their life, but it is only through a dialogue with them that he can obtain a more precise and detailed picture. Hence the students' own cooperation is an essential part of our catechesis. It is necessary therefore to give our catechesis in such a way that the students—even those of the seventh grade—are constantly involved. A real dialogue is occasionally possible in the ninth grade; in the tenth grade and beyond, it can become a regular feature. By this we do not imply that every class should be a conversation, not even in the highest grade. For the topic we wish to discuss frequently requires that we first give some information to the students. We shall deal with this question in more detail when we propose the various programs.

Another remark we wish to make about the programs concerns its character of completeness. It is our desire to approach the students according to their needs and capacity. Does this mean that certain truths of Revelation will not be considered and hence that we do not want to give everything? Such a question springs from the idea that catechesis is a systematic exposition of a doctrine, of a system of truths or of the course of history over a number of centuries. If such were the case, we could deal with such material in successive classes. The fact is, however, that Revelation constitutes an organic whole which cannot be broken up. If we really wish to shed light on the life of the students and help them see it as a salvation history, the whole of Revelation is always involved, even though all its aspects will not always be fully explicitated.

Finally, with respect to the amount of time to be consecrated to catechesis, in a discussion with many teachers of religion, the consensus appeared to be that two hours a week should be devoted to it. As a matter of fact this rule is followed in many schools.

Is the Proposed Program Too Idealistic? One might wonder whether the proposed program is not too idealistic. Doesn't such an approach demand too much of the teacher and the students?

Formerly people had a different conception of life; their lives were lived in "sectors." One's thinking, willing and feeling were largely separated from one another and each of these sectors led their own more or less individual existences. The separation of religious knowledge from living one's faith was not considered wrong. For each had its own domain and its own framework.

But modern youth approaches life differently. Thought, volition and feeling are experienced as rooted in the unity of the person. It is the whole person who adopts a certain attitude toward what presents itself to him; thus mind, will and feeling cooperate in this as a single unit. As a consequence we can no longer divorce religious knowledge from living one's faith. When a truth of faith is presented to the new generation, they immediately ask what its value is for life. They want an understanding they can live by and a life that is understandable.

It is, therefore, precisely the new generation itself that asks for the new approach. It must be recognized that this approach makes greater demands than a mere transmission and absorption of doctrinal subject matter. But it seems to us that we cannot return to the old ways. Of course, those who are accustomed to the old methods will at first feel awkward when adopting the new program. And in any event there will inevitably be more defects in the realization of the new approach than when catechesis confines itself to imparting information. For the catechist's own personality with all its human weaknesses plays a greater role here.

However, we must not anxiously try to cover up that deficiency for such a camouflage would strip our conduct of authenticity. Nowhere does the teacher stand so much on an equal footing with his pupils as precisely in education in a living faith. He himself stands before the mystery of Christ in an attitude of listening and receiving; he too cannot fully fathom it, but it constantly unfolds before him in accordance with his attempts to respond with a more complete self-commitment. He too is on the way to God; he is certain as only faith can make us certain; but, at the same time, he is gropingly searching for truth and values. Hence, although no one is capable of being completely successful in following the new way, it is valuable to aim high.

Authentic Religious Education in the Whole of the School Milieu

Our catechesis can be fully fruitful only when it functions within the whole of authentic religious education. The school constitutes the milieu within which the catechesis is given and this milieu must also contribute as a whole to education in a living faith.

The description of the Church's pastoral functions, with which we began this introduction, expresses the fact that pastoral work is a task and endeavor of the whole People of God. This holds equally well for authentic education in the faith, which is a pastoral work with children and youths. All adults who have the role of educators of youth are co-responsible for their

260

religious education. This education in a living faith must permeate the whole education and may not be concentrated or segmented exclusively in religious instruction and explicit religious manifestations.

Besides the milieu of the family, the milieu of the school plays a major role in that education. The whole team of teachers, both those who teach profane subjects and the catechists, give education in the faith. They do this, not by means of catechesis, but by the witness given by an authentic life of faith manifesting itself in their entire conduct and actions, both in their relations among themselves and in those they have with their students. The conduct, understanding and mentality of adults is inadvertently and, as it were, spontaneously taken over by the youngsters. Thus it is understandable why their influence is so penetrating. The students constantly identify themselves with their educators.

The students should be able to see a true spirit of collegiality existing among the teachers, a spirit of respect and cooperativeness. The deep influence which parents exercise on their children in the home is paralleled by the great influence of teachers in their relations with their pupils in school.

It must be evident from the teacher's way of dealing with his students that he is orientated to them with sincere respect and interest in their growing personality, that he knows how to stimulate and correct them with patience and gentle understanding. As we have pointed out before, this task does not place an extraordinary burden upon the teachers. It merely specifies a responsibility which every Christian has toward his neighbor, namely, making the Lord present to him. Nevertheless, in the case of young people this responsibility is especially pressing because of their dependence on others and their plasticity.

It should be obvious that we are not asking for a forced piety or an exaggerated exhibition of religious ideas and motives. Sincerity and discretion are necessary conditions for an authentic witness. Everyone must bear witness to Christ according to his own character and possibilities, by a good life that is lived with simplicity and truthfulness.

Finally, we are not advocating a lax permissiveness that does not deserve to be called education. The teacher must remain himself and retain his guiding role. Carrying out this role and, also, taking into consideration the diversity that exists among his students obviously makes great demands of the teacher's educational abilities.

Secular Subject Matter. For authentic education in the faith, not only is the conduct of all the teachers important, but also secular subject matter and the way it is dealt with exercise an influence. All this must be such that it contributes to the formation of a Christian image of man in the mind of the students. It is therefore a question of humanization. Secular subjects must transmit culture in such a way that they aid the students in the unfolding of their humanity. The basis for a life of faith that is fully human can be formed only by an education and instruction in which as many human values as possible are made accessible to the students. Thus an arrogant rationalism that depersonalizes everything and has no eye for man's inmost being or for personal relationships constitutes a danger for authentic religious education.

However, this humanization to be given in the school must be truly Christian. One can humanize only on the basis of a certain view concerning man. All men do not share this same view in every respect. We Christians see man as Christ sees him. If we wish to see the proper value of men and things in all its purity, we must see them also in the light of Revelation. The Gospel has a critical function with respect to our value judgment concerning man and things and, hence, also concerning human culture.

Of course, teachers of secular subjects are bound to a definite program that has a definite subject matter. To what extent changes ought to be made in them is a question that lies outside the scope of our considerations. However, a teacher has, within the existing program of such secular courses, a certain amount of freedom, at least regarding the way he approaches the prescribed topics; that is, the way he deals with that matter and how he integrates it into man's existence.

Hence the contribution made by the secular courses to education in a living faith consists in an unfolding of man's being that is inspired by a Christian spirit and sustained by a Christian vision. While this does not mean we are obliged to give explicit expression to the divine offer of salvation that is included in culture, nevertheless, the kind of secular teaching we have described is a help toward education in a living faith even when no such explicit references are made.

To shed light on culture and show it as having a salvific meaning is precisely the task of catechesis, and we do not try to suggest that instruction in some secular subject should be turned into a lesson in religion. On the other hand, this does not mean when some unexpected opportunity for giving a religious meaning to things presents itself that we must anxiously avoid making any reference to it. He who acts this way does not act authentically if he lives according to a Christian vision of faith. When one makes such incidental references, this can be called occasional catechesis. Here, of course, one must use discretion.

Interaction Between Courses of Religion and Other Courses. There is still another way in which the teachers of secular subjects can contribute to education in a living faith. In their classes they could treat certain topics in a program planned jointly with the teacher of religion. For example, the teacher of geography could cooperate with the catechist concerning the missions and assistance to under-developed countries; the teacher of history could do the same with respect to church history, for

263

instance, regarding the origin and development of the Reformation; there could also be cooperation with the teachers of English on the topic of contemporary literature.

In this field experimentation has only just begun, but it appears to offer favorable perspectives. For the time being, such cooperation will have to be more or less incidental. Much remains to be explored in this matter, so that it would be useful if many teachers contributed their own experiences. As a rule the initiative in this matter must be expected from the teacher of religion.

Communication Between the School and the Family

School education in a living faith becomes less fruitful when it is isolated from what takes place in the other milieus in which youth finds himself, especially his home.

Good communication between the school and the family deserve our utmost attention if we wish to give a solid education in a living faith. Here we could make use of committees of parents. Meetings with the parents, preferably according to the pupils' grades, offer an excellent occasion for speaking with them concerning the authentic religious education and the character formation of their children. These meetings should not be confined to the pupils' scholarly achievements.

We already mentioned several times that the renewal of catechesis manifests a shift of accent from "learning" to "formation." It would be well to begin by explaining this to the parents and showing its importance. This will make them understand, for instance, why we no longer give any grades or marks for religion but record only the degree of interest shown by the children.

Many teachers of religion realize that there threatens to be a cleavage between the old religious knowledge possessed by the parents and the vision of faith with which their children are confronted in school. Such a cleavage can have serious consequences for a true education in a living faith. Most parents greatly appreciate our telling them what is being done in school; they feel through contact with their children that they themselves are in need of supplementary "schooling." We know of a mother who, during Christmas vacation, took her child's book of religion and studied it in the evenings in order to find out what the child was learning at school. This example shows that parents often can be counted upon to cooperate with the school.

In principle, as we explained in Chapter Four, it is the parents who control the religious upbringing of their children. The actual application of that principle is not always simple. Yet the catechist must help find ways in which the religious upbringing that is given in the family and in school can take place without harmful friction.

2. *Program for the Seventh and Eight Grades* (Twelve to Fourteen-year-olds)

GENERAL CONSIDERATIONS

The youth who, after finishing primary school, enters junior high school finds there a relatively new environment. His world becomes different and more complex. He meets with a greater number of teachers and a multiplicity of courses. He is taken up into a community in which there are students who seem to him already grown-up. Here there are other norms and other ways of doing things.

But it is not only his world of life that is different. This school opens for him new fields of reality. He learns about distant countries and times that are long past, about languages and cultures whose very existence he scarcely suspected. A new world unfolds before his eyes.

Moreover, reality is approached here in a different way. He learns to be critical, to reflect and to give reasons. He must meet more scholarly and scientific demands, discipline his thinking, be

265

precise and logical. Reality is no longer simply what spontaneously presents itself but is tested by human reason according to strict methods. The youth learns to place himself thoughtfully at a distance from things and to reflect upon his experiences.

These new educational demands occur at a time when new spontaneous needs proper to his age arise in him; these demands are at least in part attuned to these needs. At this age the youngster is curious and experiences a strong desire for exploration. He wishes to widen his world, to discover new ones; he devours stories about adventures and voyages of discovery and exploration. The outside world is his preferred field of interest and he does not yet worry about real problems of life. While predominantly extroverted and inclined to activity, he is realistic and has a lively interest in facts and actualities. He becomes critical and wants to know if it "really happened." He wants facts and his questions are mostly geared to gathering information. His world expands enormously but has not yet become much more profound.

These youngsters still have much in common with children of the fifth and sixth grades, but they are moving away from that world, for they have broken away from the more or less closed world of childhood. The spontaneous security of their earlier age is disappearing. Liveliness, an urge for exploration and a craving for adventure make them get away from home. These urges are stronger than their fears of the unknown and of the confusion that results from their numerous experiences. The eyes of those youngsters are becoming open to the differences of customs, evaluations and norms of behavior between their home and the outside world. A certain independence is dawning in their thoughts and judgments. They begin to be capable of abstraction, of somewhat freeing their representations and ideas from what is concretely visible and tangible.

During this transition from childhood to adolescence, the students are no longer satisfied with childhood ways, though, on the other hand, they are only just beginning to develop their own personal life. They still wear their childhood ideas and ways of behavior; but these, like an ill-fitting garment, do not coincide with their own convictions and desires, although they are not aware of the fact. They vaguely seek for a life that is fully human, suspecting that there is a secret that must be disclosed to them.

In the field of religion also they are getting away from the habit of uncritical acceptance. They ask questions concerning religious customs and practices, such as certain prayers, confession, Holy Mass and norms of conduct. With respect to Bible stories and miracles, they ask, Is it true? Did that actually happen? How could that be?

In our education in a living faith we shall try as much as possible to adapt ourselves to the attitude of those youngsters and to the new approach to things that prevails in junior high school. The world of men and things expands before their eyes and they explore it in a critical way. Our catechesis, too, must be an exploration of a wider world and, at the same time, must proceed in a more critical fashion.

The new world to which we want to introduce these youths is the Bible itself. We begin with the New Testament in the seventh grade. It is true that in the elementary school the children have already become acquainted with the broad lines of salvation history, but the text itself of the Bible is still largely unknown to them. In any case they have not yet read the Bible in a course. The confrontation of the students with the text itself and the reading of large sections of the Bible gives, at the same time, a more scholarly character to our catechesis.

In some junior high schools, the practice of treating the Old and New Testament in the seventh and eighth grades is already several years old, and their experience shows good results. Educators have weighed the reasons for giving an orientation in New Testament salvation history during the seventh grade and giving another in the Old Testament during the eighth grade. At a catechetical conference held a few years ago, a slight majority of catechists preferred to begin with the New Testament; but to our mind the arguments pro and con are not decisive. The proposal, therefore, to begin with the New Testament should not be approached as if it were a matter of principle.

Whatever choice is made, the catechesis in the seventh grade must, as we have already suggested, assume somewhat the character of an exploration of a new world. As much as possible, teacher and pupils must explore this world together, and this exploration must remain orientated to religious self-commitment.

1. Orientation to Religious Self-Commitment. The catechist will be greatly tempted to limit his classes to the highly interesting presentation of socio-cultural information concerning Sumeria, Egypt, Palestine and the Roman empire. Even though much of our time will be devoted to man's life in antiquity, the intention should not be to make the pupils' memory a museum of ancient Eastern and Greco-Roman culture.

That information must serve to make the pupils understand better the Glad Tidings and to bring the era to life in persons of flesh and blood. Moreover, these Tidings will not be understood if salvation history remains purely a thing of the past. We must find a way to make pupils experience the actuality of that message of salvation.

For students of this age (twelve to fourteen-year-olds) this can perhaps be done best by way of identification, by showing how people reacted to the person of Christ. Nothing serves better to form a personality than example. It is quite possible that the students will find their own situation mirrored in some of the people considered in the Bible.

2. Exploration of a New World. A world that is already known is not a very exciting prospect for exploration. The greatest difficulty in the seventh and eighth grades is to prevent a reaction of "We already had this several times." The new program for the elementary school tries to attune itself more perfectly to the various ages of the pupils. As we said above, those pupils no longer have a course in which they read the Bible. In particular, so little attention is given to the Acts of the Apostles there, that these can now be read *as something new* by the junior high school student. This experience of newness can be strengthened by reading the Acts or one of the synoptic gospels from the standpoint of the reactions Jesus and His message produced in the persons who heard Him. Our aim here is to nourish the faith of the pupils. We wish to explore the Bible in a critical way, but from the viewpoint of faith. This exploration is meant to provide a new way of entering into contact with Christ. The Bible must not become a scholarly but petrified datum from the past but a living reality for us in our day.

This aim we can achieve principally by using the many occasions for identification presented by the persons around Christ and by the Christians of the early Church. It is principally a question here of bringing into relief the attitudes of those persons toward Christ as revealed by their external conduct and deeds. The youngsters of this age are less interested in the interior dispositions of those persons because they are predominantly extroverts and orientated to action.

Here, however, we must make a distinction between boys and girls. We could say, though with some exaggeration, that:

Boys are more sensitive to everything that is exciting and serves to express the manly aspect of their nature. They are more inclined toward strength and control and on that account dramatic, active deeds appeal more to them. They show an inclination to absolutism, a preference for fighting for things that test someone's energy and courage, and for success of an undertaking.

Girls are more attuned to everything that sheds light upon their life in relation to others. The thing that appeals most to them is a person's inwardness and attitude toward some other person; in this way they seek to know themselves better and find support and strength. They undoubtedly have a preference for personalizing womanhood.

3. Common Activity. The students of the seventh grade especially have generally a mentality that is still very similar to that of the fifth and sixth grades and they continue to have a great need for activity. By making them do things together and acting as a team together with them in their lessons, the catechist can make them experience how all of us together are the Church.

Education in Prayer.[1] With respect to educating the students in personal prayer, we can sometimes let them formulate their own prayer in their note-books as suggested by the subject matter of a particular class. We can let them choose from a number of prayers we present to them or let them copy or explain a part of a psalm.

A class prayer is almost totally dependent on the atmosphere in which it is used. The norm here is that it must be authentic. In experiments in many schools, the first class each day begins with a short reading from the Bible. The success of such a practice depends largely on the cooperation of the other teachers. Usually it is not enough to draw up a list of passages to be read, even though these are short. The other teachers are justified in

[1] Cf. above, Ch. V, p. 108.

270

seeking the support and advice of the catechetical director with respect to this practice. Such experiments, we feel, are so important and valuable for many reasons that we beg the schools to consider this matter seriously and not easily give up the search for an appropriate method.

In general we can say that short prayers that are varied according to the situation are most appreciated. Unlike our Protestant brethren, we Catholics are generally still too reluctant to improvise a personal prayer.

In order to make possible an attitude of genuine reverence, it is necessary to carefully avoid overloading the students with prayers. Consequently it might be preferable to have prayers only at the beginning and the ending of the schoolday.

Education in liturgical prayer continues to call for our attention. In schools that have a chapel at their disposal or are located alongside the church, a Mass can be said from time to time for individual classes. Where it is done, this practice is nearly always successful. By greatly distributing functions, both in the preparation for and in the actual liturgical service, we can secure the active participation of many pupils. It is important, however, to respect the pupils' freedom with regard to their taking part in those services.

PROGRAM FOR THE SEVENTH GRADE

Several ways to realize the catechetical purpose we have in mind present themselves. We shall indicate a few. The intention is that one way be chosen, either of those listed here or perhaps even another one, not that we should try to realize them all.

1. A first possibility is reading the Acts of the Apostles. This book, which is probably the best introduction to the New Testament for persons of every age of life, gives an account of the

271

adventures of the young Church which is Christ Himself.[2] The new faith first unfolded within the Jewish nation and then spread throughout the Roman empire. By reliving the great variety of events presented in the Acts, we spontaneously experience wonder about that mighty growth and see that the Spirit of the Lord was with them. He is also with us.

2. A second possibility is reading *one* of the synoptic gospels in our class. The Gospel of St. Mark seems particularly suitable for boys, and St. Luke for girls. Mark, because he is so lively; action never stops, he gives many true to life details and is rich in geographical data. Luke is especially appropriate because he has stories about Jesus' childhood and has very moving passages.

3. A third possibility is retaining the present textbooks, provided they are suitable, and stressing the values of those historical events for the life of the pupils in a simple and unaffected way.

All these possibilities afford an opportunity for touching such questions as:

How is the New Testament put together? The students can learn how to find their way in it, the broad lines of its origin and growth and the historical sequence of the books.

A simple discussion of the question, Is it true? Did it actually happen? Is the New Testament reliable?

A first idea of some literary genres.

Are the miracles "tall stories"?

In order to avoid turning our study of those questions into a dispensing of purely intellectualistic information, we must try to keep this whole catechesis orientated toward a believing and

---

[2] Acts 9:5, where Christ says to Saul "breathing threats of slaughter against the disciples of the Lord": "I am Jesus whom you are persecuting."

living participation in salvation history, a living realization of man's failure and success in that respect.

PROGRAM FOR THE EIGHTH GRADE

Rarely are the students of one class homogeneous. Yet in a class of seventh-graders, the pupils are still "children" and are characterized by playfulness. A change and shift of interest occurs during the eighth grade. There is, with respect to the awareness of the meaning of life, a beginning of interiorization, a tendency to inwardness. Coupled with that, the eighth-graders show a growing need for "actuality" regarding the topics we present to them. When we deal with topics of the Old Testament, we can start—though always avoiding forced comparisons and sensationalism—from a contemporary event, something that belongs to the living Church of today; and we can then shed light on this by pointing to an analogous situation or disposition of the ancient people of God. Or again, the catechist could begin with the Old Testament history and show the pupils how this was fulfilled in the life of Christ and is fulfilled in our own lives.

We already mentioned that boys and girls manifest differences in their attitudes. Sometimes it becomes evident that a particular class of eighth-graders as a whole shows a mentality in the second half of that year which is similar to the mentality of ninth-graders, and we notice that they are ready for the themes of the next grade. We could then give them more opportunity for bringing up their own questions, some of which will be suitable to be dealt with at this time.

In discussing the Old Testament, we try to show how the roving pastoral tribe which later settled down to a permanent home became conscious in its vicissitudes of the active presence of the living God. The primary school child did not yet have a sufficient concept of history to be able to embrace a history of centuries as a coherent, internally structured whole. The eighth-graders are much more developed and can become familiar with the broad lines of that history. For them we should like to illuminate that history by confronting them with the lives of some great personages, how these were called by Yahweh, and the repercussion of this call on their contact with others. For instance:

In connection with Moses we could deal with the vicissitudes of God's people during the Exodus.

After the entrance into the Promised Land, we could con-cretize the broad line of salvation history in one of the Judges, Elias, Samuel, David, Solomon, a weak king, Judith or Esther, in a few Prophets, for example Osee, Isaia, or Jeremia, and finally in the Machabees.

God's call always meant leaving the familiar world for the unknown, a situation that is similar to that of these youngsters. In dealing with those life-stories, we find plenty of occasions for making the pupils understand literary genres; this will make it plain to them in what sense Scripture is true and in what spirit we are expected to read it. When we use and handle the Book, it must always be clear how much we respect it as the Word of God, a respect and love which we would like to foster in those youths.

In speaking about the history of the Jewish people, the open, unprejudiced attitude that we show can be an implicit exposure of the unchristian character of antisemitism.

Boys and girls certainly feel a great need for variety. The teacher of the seventh and the eighth grades should therefore use the opportunities that present themselves to speak about actual questions; this will provide the needed variation in this biblical program.

The experience of cosmic realities, such as water, light, fire, wind, mountain, bread, wine, etc., gives an occasion for lessening the distance that separates ordinary things from the liturgy.

DIDACTIC SUGGESTIONS FOR
THE SEVENTH AND EIGHTH GRADES

1. The Atmosphere.[3] It is to a great extent the teacher who determines the atmosphere of the class, the importance of which it would be difficult to overrate.

a. It is no doubt a great help when the catechesis can be held in a special room that is sober but tasteful. A certain priority should be given to such a room when schools are built or remodeled.

b. Youngsters of this age need order, quiet and peace during the class. They must feel truly "at home" and relaxed; they must be able to speak frankly as though at home and to ask questions.

2. Activities.[4] We can say, in general, that in our catechesis we should give preference to the activities that offer the best opportunity for a religious assimilation of what is given or discovered in that course. For the activities must serve to help the students attain to a more profound faith. Hence, we should not confine ourselves to projects that are principally aimed at giving the youngsters information about facts or making them acquire certain skills. We can let the pupils make their own collection, using loose-leaf folders, in which they can paste or draw pictures, write summaries, transcribe texts and prayers, etc. Sometimes we can let them work together in little groups in such projects. This teamwork can be used also for arranging religious exhibits in the class.

Homework for catechetical classes should be the result of enthusiasm rather than an imposed task.

The use of records, films and the like, as well as reading to the students or letting them read in silence, are well-known

[3] Cf. above, Ch. V, p. 121.
[4] Cf. above, Ch. V, p. 145.

techniques. In summary, we look for a pleasant and useful combination of class and workshop.

3. Marks. Many teachers believe that giving marks is a justified and necessary procedure in the seventh and eighth grades. They argue that the pupils see in those marks and reports a tangible appreciation which stimulates them in their efforts; that they are a support for weak teachers; that pupils will understand the difference between religious knowledge and religious commitment if it is explained to them; and that giving no marks for catechesis makes this course "lose face" in comparison with other subject matters taught in school.

Because we believe that the existing trend will lead to the abolition of marks for religion, we add here the arguments against the old practice. In the future the students will consider it natural that no marks be given for religious knowledge since they have been already abolished in the first six grades. Factual and objective knowledge can be expressed in a mark, but it is, by that very fact, removed from the sphere of faith. The most intelligent pupils usually get the highest marks. Is this our intention? The weak, anxious or ambitious pupils naturally get the impression that it is the achievement which is important.

Many teachers look upon marks as figures expressing the amount of application of a student. Some schools thus try to express the application of the students by using three categories: lack of interest, sufficient interest, great interest.

It goes without saying that the student's fulfillment of a religious project, such as a drawing, recitation or composition must be evaluated. But isn't it possible for the teacher to express this by a few words, by a brief remark?

Concerning the question of memorization, we refer to Chapter Five, p. 139. But, to prevent any misunderstanding regarding this matter of shifting the emphasis, we repeat once more that faith always has a content and, hence, that it is also necessary for us to *know* in Whom we believe.

4. A Note Concerning Guidance for the Pupils' Growth Toward Maturity. The educators of young people have the important task of supporting and guiding them in their development into adult men and women. Educators must help them in the unfolding of their sexuality, that is, the human realization of the sexes by which man and woman can evoke and help each other in true love to achieve the fullness of their human being. The maturing of bodily sexuality constitutes only part of that development. No doubt, in time, the youngsters should receive the necessary information concerning that matter, but this instruction must function within a much broader education toward maturity.

There are still many boys and girls who do not receive such instruction from their parents. This is a matter we should discuss during the meetings we have with the parents of children or when we visit their homes; we can then determine what they would like us to do.

3. *Program for the Ninth and Tenth Grades* (Fourteen to Sixteen-year-olds)

INTRODUCTORY REMARKS

The ninth grade seems, generally speaking, to be the most difficult year. No wonder! people say, for these youths are in the midst of their puberty. And this brings up many questions. Can these young people be classified as a single internally unified group or are external influences perhaps most decisive with respect to their behavior? What kind of parents do they have? In what kind of environment have they grown up? What kind of friends do they seek? What experiences have they gone through? Do they develop in the same way in large cities, small industrial towns and rural villages? Is the development the same now as it was a decade ago? In spite of all these questions and basing ourselves on what is brought to light in teachers conventions, it is possible to present a general image of these youths.

The boy and girl who reach puberty realize that his or her body is undergoing a sexual maturation; this is sometimes experienced as connected with a mystery that is attractive or frightening, and sometimes merely troublesome. Intense emotions arise in them: anxiety, deep affection for another, confusing uncertainty, strong opposition, freedom, guilt and longings.

We may perhaps consider *becoming conscious of one's "ownness"* as the central fact by which the manifold phenomena can be clarified. These youngsters discover that they have their own inner self, that they differ from others. No wonder they often feel lonesome in that phase of development: "No one understands me." "Am I an exception?"

They wish to determine their conduct according to their own understanding of self-discovered values; for instance, in their appreciation of music, which can range from classical music to jazz or Beatle-concerts, in their way of dressing, their interest in sports and hobbies, and their favored "stars" in these matters. Of deeper significance is their discovery of a moral value, such as justice.

In the last analysis it is a question of their growth of freedom, which they manifest by rejecting dependence on others. The only recently discovered autonomy of these youths is still very unsteady. It is easy to understand why at first they believe that they can best protect this autonomy by shutting themselves off from or opposing everyone who seems to be attacking that freedom. In rapidly changing moods, they enter into conflict with parents and with companions of their own age. They refuse all coercion, criticize everything they consider dishonest or valueless, and resist any form of authority whose meaning they do not understand, such as laws, dogmas, precepts and regulations.

Does this represent properly the youth of today who has

reached puberty? Because of greater social mobility and mutual influence through mass communications the youth of today shows greater uniformity. While many youths are soberly realistic and manifest a preference for what is tangible, nevertheless, underneath all of this, the deeper questions remain alive: Who am I? Where do I come from? What do I really live for? What must I do? What is good and evil? What future lies before me? Does God exist and can I reach Him? Can I reach my fellow-man? Where can I find certainty? Is it possible to be permanently happy?

These are questions that arise over and over again in our minds, that occupy our attention throughout our lives. But at the age of these youngsters the questions are asked in a new way, and they can receive a provisional satisfactory answer by the time the youth reaches maturity. We say that they "can" receive such an answer, for this answer is a development which does not take place automatically. The way it takes place also depends on each individual's nature and choice. In this respect it has been pointed out that there are differences between

the naive and the conservative,

the uninterested and those who keep aloof,

those who are still seeking and those who have already made a decision.

Such classification of "types" can be useful for understanding youths provided that in spite of everything, we remain open to what is proper to each of them and firmly believe in their potentialities.

Our catechesis in the ninth and tenth grades aims at keeping open the attitude of search concerning the most profound human questions. This could include

1. Freeing these adolescents from any lingering attitudes that are appropriate only to the world of children.

2. Letting them see the one-sidedness of an approach which deals with men and things exclusively in an attitude that seeks control; we do this by arousing their sense of wonder over the mysterious aspects of the world and especially of the human person.

3. Pointing out the often totally unexpected and sometimes baffling way Christ dealt with men and things.
All this we should like to do by discussing and exploring the realms of human values.

The catechetical purpose could also be formulated in a different way, e.g., to examine together how our conduct, with respect to realms of value that, for instance, are defined in the Ten Commandments, can be seen as a concretization of the one commandment of love and thus contributes to a fully human, that is free, development of man. What such a fully developed humanity implies is made visible in Christ, to a depth that is divine. In other words, we do indeed pick out youths' centers of interest to use them as a starting point; but we want to go beyond them and combine them with a Christian view of man. Hence, we are doing more than merely adapting our catechesis to the students' age; we point toward adulthood.

Finally, in still another description of our catechetical intention, we could say that we try to let the pupils see how God calls us to cooperate with Him in all aspects of our life to help develop a new earth and a new heaven, in which justice dwells.

Because of his theological training, the catechist will spontaneously be inclined to give a logical structure to his program and its development, that is, to follow a scheme that mirrors the structure of the subject matter "in itself." Yet it is more useful with respect to students of this age to seek a "living" structure, one that takes as its guiding principle what the particular topic means for them and tries to take into account their own experience.

As they grow closer to adulthood, however, there will be an increasing need for a more objective structure. This makes it difficult to construct a program for the ninth grade, although Dutch and French teachers of religion show a fairly general agreement about the topics to be chosen. We shall have to learn from experience.

Education in Prayer. These youths often have a growing interest in personal prayer, although they usually are careful not to let others know about it. They are less attracted to fixed prayer formulae. This phenomenon is connected with their growing interiorization; not infrequently—but wrongly—it gives the impression that they are irreligious. They want freedom, spontaneity; they dislike what they call "empty formalism." But they are willing to adore God in their heart, though they do not want this aspiration to be tied down by formulae or laws.

The teacher must be prepared to summarize a topic that has been discussed in a personally spoken prayer when the atmosphere permits it. This is a practice which can be continued in subsequent years.

Experience shows that ninth and tenth-graders still appreciate a celebration of the Eucharist especially arranged for them.

THE NINTH GRADE

Suggested Program

In the summary that follows, groups of connected topics are joined together. We have tried to do it in such a way as to indicate a perspective toward living one's faith, and in this way to avoid a moralism that is entirely divorced from religion.

1. A discussion of the ways men come in contact with one another and the attitude that governs such contact: conversation

—communication—debate—exchange of ideas—listening—quiet —recollectedness—prayer.

2. Growth. How does growth take place? The role played by native abilities, circumstances of life, educators, vicissitudes, one's own decisions.

> the slowness of growth—the need of waiting and commitment—the risks—hopeful expectation—crisis and renewal—the course of life.

3. Dependence and freedom. We present a description of the adults' freedom, in which it is pointed out that their freedom becomes real in giving meaning to their world with restraint. The adults' shortcomings, their greatness and wretchedness, are illustrated by their own testimony.

4. Freedom and authority; the relationship of parents and children.

> make something of your life!—exploring with the class those who really merit our admiration—how did they arrive at that noble way of being man?—the difference between a profession and a vocation.

5. Here we make a reference to Christ's attitude toward earthly goods and consider such topics as: study—work for wages—salary—use of money—respect for property—poverty and hunger.

6. What are you doing with your free time?
Recreational activities:

> sportiveness—comradeship—self-control—choice of reading, movies, television—the role of music—free study and hobbies—vacation—feasts, meals and worship.

Use of free time (this is an important field for the development of their sense of responsibility):
being with others—being alone; time for oneself—time for others; spiritual activity—bodily activity; at home—outside.

7. Certain points can be discussed with respect to study, domestic order, conventions and religious practices:
order—regularity—improvisation—repetition—routine and custom.

8. Friendship—falling in love—love—courtship—marriage —sexuality.

9. Guilt—conscience—law—sin—pardon—confession—fidelity and infidelity with respect to oneself and others.

10. Respect for things (to enjoy them admiringly, to see that they refer us to persons).
Respect for other human beings.
Traffic safety—a good reputation—letting the other be himself.

11. Israel's vision of man and the world (Genesis 1–11):
Man stands in the world together with others, questing for God.
The creation accounts of Genesis 1–3:
How should I read these stories of Creation?—the image of the world in ancient Eastern thought—the biblical image of the world—man before his fall into sin: God's plan—the fall and original sin.
Man in his spoiled world according to Genesis 4–11:
Cain and Abel—the Flood—fathers and sons—the tower of Babel—the just man in creation.
Christ's vision of man and the world.

283

If we realistically deal with those subjects, negative aspects will necessarily present themselves, such as misfortunes, failures, sickness and death. These matters can also become explicit topics of our catechesis if circumstances seem to demand it.

Didactic Suggestions for the Ninth Grade

1. A More Active Role of the Students. In the seventh and eighth grades the teacher talked most of the time, although he tried to stimulate the pupils' active involvement as much as possible. Now that we are dealing with ninth graders we can adopt another attitude. Perhaps we could typify the contrast by saying that, whereas we treated certain topics in those two lower grades, we now wish to take our cue from what is alive among the students.

The teacher will show that now he "takes his students seriously," they now begin to make their own contributions. To "take them seriously" does not mean that we no longer expect naive and unbalanced views, but we show respect for the youths' growing independence. This gives a distinctly different character to the religious instruction of ninth-graders. Generally it will take the form of a conversation with the class in which we try together to list the various aspects of a topic to construct a comprehensive view of it. We can write on the blackboard what the students have contributed. The essential point is that they get the feeling that they are free to present their own views.

2. Questionnaires. This listening to what the pupils have to say does not mean that, class after class, we improvise answers to the questions pupils may bring up. The number of topics in the program listed above most probably is much too great for us to cover in one year. At the beginning of the year we could give each of the students a questionnnaire on which various subjects are briefly mentioned in words he can understand;

and we could ask them to check the subjects they would like to have discussed in class. Collating the various preferences and transferring them to one list, we get an idea of what interests the majority of students in the class. This enables us to draw up our particular program for three or more months. In the plan proposed above, No. 11 is viewed as a summary of the conversations that were held in the course of the whole year. Because of those conversations and discussions in class, the students will get more out of the Biblical texts referred to in No. 11. That is why we consider the topics of No. 11 necessary; they also require much time.

3. Group Discussions. In general, the students of the ninth grade are still considered too young for engaging in frequent religious discussions in small groups or by way of forums. That is why we suggest that such discussions be held only from time to time. Some schools do this in the following way. First the catechist explains the topic to make the students familiar with it; otherwise, the discussion will become mere chatter. Then the class is broken up into groups which are given a few written questions. These are then discussed by the students of the particular groups, each group has one student who reports the results. Finally, there is a joint discussion of the answers, and each student writes the "conclusion" that has been reached in his note-book.

4. Stimulation. Our intention is not to arrive at the final answer of every problem at any price. What we wish to do is to help so that they can throw light on their own situation. In our discussions we should dwell as long as possible on the human motivation of man's conduct. Only when this has been done can the deepest, religious meaning and interpretation of it be sought for together with the students on the basis of Christ's mystery. According to the subject, the capacity of the particular group and the atmosphere of the individual class, this can be done in a short, gripping suggestion or, more fully, by seeking analogous biblical situations. The final summing up of each topic must be a stimulus to further research and thought rather than its conclusion.

5. Discretion. The youth who reaches puberty wants to explore a new world, but he does so with hesitation and uncertainty; on that account he is very vulnerable. That is why, in our conversations, we must not force him to expose himself, but we must give him the chance to remain protected with respect to his own subjectivity. For this reason topics must often be treated in the form of "cases," so that a kind of objective and detached approach is possible. On the other hand, he is eager to have his questions discussed.

Some teachers give the students the opportunity to raise their questions anonymously in writing and to place them in a question box. These questions are not always answered in the same class.

6. Activities. We have already mentioned the most important activity, namely, having the students actively involved in the lesson. When the teacher has chosen the topics together with the class, he can ask one or more students to prepare some of them beforehand.

This can be done by furnishing or letting the students themselves seek literature on the subject; by gathering information concerning the situation of a particular topic in their town; by looking for illustrative material or by documentation. When they are ready, the students report on their research.

It is possible for a class to play host when the teacher invites someone to speak on a subject with which he is familiar because of his profession. This guest can be a fellow teacher or an outsider. His appearance can also assume the form of an interview which the teacher and the pupils together have carefully prepared in the previous class. Because it is not always possible to have a guest come to speak to a class due to the school schedule, a few class representatives could also visit someone who is an expert in a certain field and is willing to be interviewed. This visit too must be carefully prepared in the previous class. What questions should they ask and why?

Sometimes it is possible to make use of the pupils' hobbies, particularly music and photography.

When an opportunity presents itself and homework allows it, we can announce that in the following class we want to discuss a certain film or television program and ask the students to see it.

7. Examinations. We could examine whether it would be useful to give the students the opportunity to express their "religious knowledge" in writing or orally; but this "examination" should not be in the form of testing their familiarity with intellectual information about religion. It should be done in a free form that leaves room for the students to take a personal stand.

This whole catechesis for ninth-graders must be characterized by patience. These youths cannot be manipulated; and we must not force anything. The sacrifice expected of the catechist is that the result of his religious instruction will be such that it cannot be sharply determined and verified. For this reason also, we think that the new approach does not lend itself to being evaluated in marks.

8. Liturgy, Sacraments and Prayer. During the course of the year there will be opportunities for connecting our catechesis with the liturgy and the sacraments. Nos. 6 through 10 of the program listed above are especially open to such possibilities. Prayer is specifically listed; but our aim is to seek prayer possibilities in all topics, so that the students get a broader concept of prayer.

THE TENTH GRADE

Prefatory Remarks

As an introduction to this program, we call attention to the following characteristics:

1. We have said above that becoming conscious of one's "ownness" is a central point at the beginning of puberty. When a certain balance has been regained in his personality, the youth again manifests more clearly his orientation toward others. In this contact with others, he discovers both his fellow-man and himself in a new way. The reality of man acquires a new depth and thus there arise new possibilities for a greater and more profound living of the faith.

2. Because there is now a greater orientation toward community, dialogue acquires a very significant place in the life of the youth. This is why we consider every form of class discussion extremely important for the catechesis in this and the following grades. It is only through conversation and discussion that those boys and girls can be guided to a proper development. This conversation can be:

a) With fellow-students of their own age. Class discussions are a part of it but its center of gravity lies outside the classroom.

b) With adults. The latter should give them an image of man. Obviously this cannot be a one-way affair, an adults' monologue. Youth has always been the privileged locus for a new sense of life to acquire firm footing. The image of man which adults show in their life can mean both an inspiration and a confrontation. But it is something that is offered; not

288

something that is imposed. If we tried to impose it, we would misjudge the new image of man that announces itself in their generation and which they at first find difficult to express in words.

Great faith in their possibilities, a warm interest in their life in all its expressions will enable us to hear, perhaps in a limping formulation, in a halting remark or in a silence, what they really wished to say.

3. Much has been said about the word "witnessing."[5] It may be possible to define the content of that word in terms of the youths' expectations.

For them that term is synonymous with speaking about the faith in a way that is "true to life," that is, "in touch with life." In touch with life is the way God's challenging invitation is mirrored in the life of those whom I encounter; in touch with life is a dogma that can be seen living in someone's external conduct, in touch with life is the truth that means something for a living man, although it is full of conflicts and riddles. The fact that the person who proclaims and announces faith is himself one who seeks security and strives for a solution is appreciated as being true to life. So also is the Christian who honestly, without camouflage, reveals what has really disturbed or consoled him, along with the open questions that still remain unanswered for him.

The fundamental condition for such a witnessing is that one tries to be oneself as a believer. This provides an opportunity for every witness' talent and temperament. Since all witnessing functions between persons, respect and efficacy demand that we adapt our witness to those to whom it is addressed, while fully preserving that fundamental condition. With respect to religious instruction in high schools, this means, among other things, an adjustment to the age, the type of school, the sex of the pupils.

[5] Cf. above, Ch. V, pp. 105–111.

It implies that we shall try to give the students a chance to keep their religious knowledge on the same level as their "profane" knowledge. In our opinion an opposition between catechesis and "scientific" justification of the faith thus becomes something artificial, at least for students of the higher grades who feel a greater need for objectivity.

With respect to the aim of our catechesis, we refer to what has been said for the ninth grade, with this difference: the students who are now continuing to build on self-experience, tend to see themselves in community. On this basis we arrive at the following possibilities for a catechetical program.

PROGRAM FOR THE TENTH GRADE

1. Examination of forms of human community and society such as the family, a fraternity or sorority, the class at school, an association, a movement, our nation, the United Nations. In this matter attention should be given to the relationship between organization and its driving force.

2. The Church as community which, like individual human beings, has her vicissitudes. She is both a gift of God and a scandal in her human aspects. This point can offer an opportunity for a sketch of Church history. In some schools, one of the two weekly hours scheduled for religious instruction in the ninth and tenth grades is devoted to Church history. This course is sometimes given by the teacher of history but it is presented explicitly as the history of man's salvation and ruin.

3. The Church in human society among other Christian churches. A discussion of the ecumenical movement, the churches' search for unity as Christ desired it. This topic will be more explicitly dealt with in the twelfth grade. It stands to reason that the mentality that underlies the ecumenical approach

should permeate our whole religious instruction. Something should be said here about the Reformation.

4. The Church in human society amidst the great world-religions. A first acquaintance with, for instance, Hinduism, Buddhism, Islamism. This introduction will raise such questions as:

Is there a norm by which we can determine which religion is the true religion?

Is it necessary to really know them all in order to make a responsible choice from among them?

How can we claim that Christianity is the true religion?

Are all religions equally good, provided we believe in God?

What does the Church think of the other religions? Consequences of this attitude with respect to the missionary enterprise.

5. War and peace; hunger and the welfare state; racial discrimination.

DIDACTIC SUGGESTIONS FOR THE TENTH GRADE

Practically all the suggestions that were made for the ninth grade can be repeated here. We believe it is essential to have an atmosphere in which the teacher constantly exchanges ideas with the students, as we have explained in No. 1 of the program for the ninth grade. This can take place even if all classroom seats are immobile. If there are movable seats, they can be arranged in one big circle, or when there are more than thirty students, in a double circle, so that everybody can see everyone else.

Beginning with the tenth grade it is possible to have more frequent conversations or discussions between students in small groups into which the class has been divided; these then give an account of the results by means of a reporter; or perhaps some students can constitute a forum. The frequency of such conversations will depend on numerous factors, among which the nature of the topics plays a major role.

Whatever form the discussion assumes, the leader must see to it that the topic is analytically divided into units, and each of these can be introduced by a question. It is always desirable that, at the end of the discussion, the teacher present a brief synthesis in which the whole structure becomes apparent. In this way he will fix the topic more solidly in the students' minds, show how it is related to other topics and opens new perspectives.

4. Program for the Eleventh and Twelfth Grades (Seventeen to Eighteen-year-olds)

Introductory Remarks

The description of the characteristics marking boys and girls in their late teens is borrowed from a well-known textbook in pedagogical psychology.[6] We realized that this phase of life often continues for several years after the students have left school.

"Adolescence is a cultural phenomenon. When it appears, great differences become visible in many respects, both with regard to intensity and duration.

"The peculiar 'being someone' that characterizes puberty has gradually become more and more differentiated. This 'being someone' implies freedom and, as soon as 'being someone' has become natural and unquestioned for the youngster, he experiences freedom. It is by this that *adolescence* announces its arrival. What now captivates him is the fact that 'being someone' contains in a very personal sense a possibility of choice which, as he approaches adulthood, develops into an obligation of choice.

"The adolescent temporarily occupies his mind with the right and the opportunity to have his own preference and, accordingly—at least provisionally—to determine his own life. In the

6 N. Perquin, *Pedagogische Psychologie*, Roermond, 1963.

292

young adolescent this manifests itself principally in the world of ideas. He looks for new views and startling perspectives for their own sake; this is a sort of flirtation with ideas, a cultivation of spiritual sensation. He begins to stretch his wings but does not yet want to bind himself.

"Adolescents, at least nowadays, like to underscore their youthful freedom by the way they dress and behave, individually or toward others.

"Sooner or later, however, in his exploration of freedom the question of *choice* is bound to arise. When this takes place, freedom begins to reveal its deeper meaning to the adolescent. It is no longer experienced as the pleasure of being free from bonds and obligations, but shows itself as the possibility and task of choosing, a choice that has to come from within. The adolescent thus discovers himself as one who has and can bear responsibility.

"This phase of maturation manifests itself also in the way the adolescent determines what his calling in life will be.

"The numerous cases in which adolescents do not or cannot come to a free determination of their calling show how difficult it is to attain adulthood unscathed. The possibilities that lie before them are so numerous and so complex that they cannot come to a decision; thus many may let themselves be guided by secondary considerations rather than by the conviction that their chosen calling signifies *their* way of life.

"Analogous with this situation is that of the *choice of a marriage partner.* When we look at things from the biological and social standpoint, it is reasonable to say that marriages are too long delayed; from the spiritual and affective standpoint, however, the modern marriage demands such a differentiated power to love that it is not surprising that—at least in many cases—youths are only ready for it at a later time. The older adolescent also realizes that he has to make a choice with respect to his view of the world and of life, regardless of whether he has undergone a religious-ethical crisis or not.

"Faith and ethos are becoming a personal attitude which is so deeply rooted in the core of life that its main lines are definitive. For this attitude is one with the person."

Generally speaking, however, the eleventh and twelfth-graders have not yet reached that stage. It seems we are justified in surmising that, for most of them, the existential crisis of faith appears during the years that come after leaving high school.

This brings up the question whether we can, and if so, how we can best prepare them for that time of crisis. This we can do only to a certain degree, for the crisis will arise at least in part from a situation of greater freedom, from a concrete confrontation with other ideas concerning life, or problems that result from higher studies. Now these are not yet fully experienced and realized by the students attending the upper grades of high school.

For this reason, the discussion of their questions—which fortunately are concerned with fundamentals of man's religious existence—is for many of them truly "a flirting with ideas." On the other hand, they are earnest in their desire to occupy themselves with those questions; hence we should help them according to their need for seeing things in larger syntheses and arriving at a provisional, more comprehensive image of man.

This means that we may now organize their questions in an integrally structured whole, according to the internal connection and interrelationship of mysteries, of which they are now also becoming aware.

If in discussing their questions we always think from the standpoint of *one* synthetic theological vision, for example "the encounter with Christ is the Sacrament of the encounter with God," we can help them develop a living Unity from the perhaps disconnected multiplicity of aspects and truths of faith.

During these last two years of high school, we are given a golden opportunity to help the students penetrate to the deepest dimension of what is taking place in our own time, for here are young people who want to find their personal vocation, their proper place in this coming world that should be a world in which every fellow-man can live a life worthy of man.

These youths also make high demands on the authenticity, competence and up-to-date-ness of the catechist. At the same time, they will be grateful to him for giving a justification of the faith which opens the way for the freedom of the children of God.

PROGRAM FOR THE ELEVENTH AND TWELFTH GRADES

Here we suggest a program expressed in questions which are often alive in these students. Because they seek a synthesis, we have grouped the inquiry into an interconnected whole.

We develop the meaning of the proposition that "we believe in the Father, whose 'glory . . . shines on the face of Christ Jesus' (2 Cor. 4:6), whose 'body is the Church' (Col. 1:24) which is animated by the Spirit."

1. We believe

Here we consider such questions as:

Is doubt about one's faith sinful?

What does "to believe" mean for youths from the age of fifteen to twenty-five?

What does "to believe" mean now in our time?

Do we now believe principally because our parents have raised us as Catholics? Did *they* not choose our faith?

What does "to believe" really mean?

What is the certitude of our faith?

Do the natural sciences not give a much greater certitude?

Is it not possible that our technological-scientific age has less need of religion?

Is "to believe" not something that hampers our mind, since faith tells you that you *must* accept this?

Is there even *one* truly clinching proof, one that excludes the possibility of doubt?

II. *In Search of the Living God*

1. The great religions of the world:

Is there a norm by which we can find out which religion is the true one?

Where do we get a foundation for our claim that Christianity is the true religion?

Are all religions equally good, provided you believe in God?

What does the Church think about those other religions?

2. Doesn't every age have its own God, as also every man, every people? (The intention here is to deal with Marxism, with modern areligious humanism, with the problem of religious projection—all this, of course, in terms that these adolescents can understand.)

Is religion not a phenomenon in the development of man, a stage beyond which we now begin to progress?

Is religion not a pipe-dream?

Why must I adhere to a faith?

3. Does an Absolute Being really exist? Here we can deal with certain ways that lead to God starting, for instance, from freedom, love, conscience.

4. How should we read the Bible? How do I know that God speaks through the Bible?

5. The living God:

What is the image of God in the Old Testament?

III. Jesus, the Lord

Why did God create man as a free being? Did He not know that man would misuse his freedom?

Could He not have made man in such a way that he could only say "Yes" to God's offer of His love? The question of predestination.

What can still be the meaning of the word "creation" now that we know that the cosmos is in a state of constant evolution?

How can God be "Love" if He made a world that is without love and without justice?

Is there an answer to the problem of suffering and death?

What is "salvation"? What is it that we must be "saved" from?

How do we know that Jesus is the Son of God?

Is devotion to Mary not out of date?

IV. The People of God

1. Why is there such a thing as a Church? Is it not better for me to have a direct contact with God?

2. Does it still make sense to go to Mass when the Mass means nothing to you?

3. Does it make sense to go to confession when there is no improvement?

Why can't I straighten myself out with God directly?

What exactly is mortal sin? What is a sin?

When am I faithful to my conscience?

What is a vocation? Are we obliged to follow God's call?

How does one know if he has a vocation?

How far must I go in the love of my neighbor?

4. Why can a marriage not be broken?

What is the difference between "being in love" and love?

Why are we not allowed to have intercourse before marriage?
Questions concerning the number of children, contraceptives, and homosexuality.

5. The priesthood: celibacy; is it still reasonable to have contemplative orders in our time?

6. What is the place of the layman in the Church?
When is one a good Catholic? Is it *necessary* to "practice" in order to be a good Catholic?
How must we live our faith in our own time?

7. Is prayer really of any use?

8. What must our attitude be toward Protestants, unbelievers?

V. The Last End
What happens after death?
How must I conceive heaven, hell and purgatory?

Besides explaining such topics and answering the questions, we should find place every year for a series of classes devoted to the exegesis of some Scriptural texts. In this way the students will be confronted with the undiluted wine of God's word and will get some understanding of the methods of exegesis. For instance, we could study together some passages taken from St. John's Gospel and a letter of St. Paul.

Didactic Suggestions[7]

1. Time. The questions mentioned above can serve as an introduction to a particular topic in the class. The time required for a serious examination of the topic will vary according to

[7] Cf. above, pp. 284 f. and 291 f.

circumstances; this will depend also on the interest of the particular group and the time that is at the teacher's disposal.

2. Student Interest. In order to find out what particularly interests the students, we could proceed as follows. At the beginning of the year we could ask the students what subjects they would like to have discussed. Only after they have given their opinion, without being influenced by us, shall we present the list given above, according to the methods we have described in the didactic suggestions for the ninth grade on page 284.

3. Discussion Units. We earnestly recommend that the teacher analytically divide the topic beforehand into discussion units, each of which can lead to further discussion by means of a question. For instance, when we discuss the question, What kind of certainty does faith give us?, we can begin with, What is certainty? and then, How does one attain certainty? There are evidently diverse degrees of certitude, but also various kinds of certitude according to the various methods by which certitude is reached. What kinds of certitude are there? Is the certitude that is obtained by way of experiment and reasoning to be preferred to other types? Is it always possible to make use of the experimental method? What certainties lie at the foundation of our great decisions in life? What certainty has our faith in our fellow-man? What certainty has our faith in Christ? Is this certainty static?

4. Justification of Faith. The earnestness and depth of our discussion will show that critical reflection is possible within the realm of faith. In fact, it is a duty for the well-educated man himself, and also with respect to his fellow-man, to be able to justify his faith in a critical way.

5. Discretion. It is essential here, in our opinion, that the students learn to respect one another's opinion, even though it may completely differ from their own. We are all engaged in a common search for the truth and know that each one must follow his own particular rhythm, that no one has a monopoly on the truth and that we must respect every man's freedom of conscience.

Of course, we may ask the other to justify his point of view. But, as teachers, we must keep in mind that our training in reasoning and formulating things, our knowledge of arguments, can easily give the students the impression that we want to corner them and then stifle their freedom. If our attitude is discreet and is founded on the realization that we, as well as they, stand before the Word in an attitude of openness and readiness to listen and receive, we may then explain the reasons for our personal conviction.

6. Spirituality. Many topics yield an opportunity for steering the discussion into the direction of spirituality. We must learn to "read" our own situation and thus discern the guidance of the Holy Spirit in the course of our daily life, having the courage to commit ourselves to that Spirit.

7. Social Aspects of Faith. We put special emphasis on the social aspects of our faith. If the teacher and the students of a class are capable and the topic lends itself to this, it will be well to place the theme against a historical background. The healthy relativation that will result from this historicity will more clearly reveal the heart of the matter.

8. The Class. It is useful to give the two hours of religious instruction consecutively at the end of the morning or afternoon session. In this way the teacher can really cover a subject well and it also prevents the disadvantage of having a one-hour lesson sandwiched between "secular" courses.

Some teachers use the first five or ten minutes to recapitulate the matter of the previous lesson, allowing the students to make use of their notes. This method serves to recall the general line of thought and shows the place a particular aspect occupies within the whole. After that, the teacher introduces the next topic. Sometimes this introduction must provide the information without which it is impossible to have a useful discussion; but the introduction should always end with a striking representation of the topic, so that the students have a stimulus for getting involved.

9. *Cooperation.* With respect to certain problems, there is a possibility of securing the cooperation of other teachers. There is presently a strong tendency in some quarters toward so-called "project education" which means that a single topic is examined and explained from the standpoints of various sciences; there is then also an opportunity for presenting the religious view on such topics. Some experiments have already been made along those lines.

10. *Charitable Activities.* It may be possible to find or create opportunities to participate in charitable social activities. The student will thus be "one who does the truth" (Jn. 3:21).

EPILOGUE

WE have seriously considered whether it would not be useful to add a chapter to this book in which we would indicate how the fundamental principles and programs described in the preceding pages could be applied to the concrete situation in the United States. This situation differs in several respects from that of Holland. First of all, the American school system is much more uniform than the Dutch system. In Holland the elementary schools consist of only six grades; further education is given in various types of schools preparing for technical functions, office work, and three kinds of schools that aim especially at preparing students for university studies.[1] Secondly, in Holland 97% of the Catholic children go to Catholic elementary schools and 90% of them continue their education under Catholic auspices in the various above-mentioned types of schools. Thus the C.C.D. work for children going to public schools that is so extensive in the United States is practically unknown in Holland. For these reasons the detailed application of the principles to the concrete situation in the U.S.A. would practically demand a new book, and it would have to be based on a thorough

[1] To a certain extent this difference could be taken into account in the translation of this book. However, the reader should keep in mind that the programs suggested for the seventh to the twelfth grades are really meant for the more selective audience of students preparing for college and university studies. (Tr.)

302

knowledge of America. Moreover, one could wonder whether a single program would suffice for the many different situations existing in the United States; e.g., in remote rural areas and in metropolitan parts, in places with large numbers of recent immigrants and in areas with a strongly Spanish-American culture.

Thus it appeared preferable to us to present the proposed renewal as it stands. Even if it cannot be applied at once without adjustment to the local situation, the proposal constitutes an appeal to educators to investigate whether the principles on which it is based prove acceptable to them. If the answer is in the affirmative, they face the task of determining how this can be done.

Accordingly, what this book wants to do above all is to ask questions. Must the child's authentic education in a living faith be conceived in terms of the child himself? We do not mean this merely as a didactic approach by way of which one would arrive at the religious matter as that which one "really" wants. But we ask ourselves whether this should be done as a matter of principle and in a consistent fashion, on the ground that our task goes beyond speaking to the child about the articles of faith, the sacraments and the commandments. This task implies first and foremost the duty to help him find God in his world, that is, in the people and things around him, so that he learns to see the world in its most profound dimension. And in doing that, we would constantly have to ask ourselves what exactly is meant by "the child's world."

Must faith be presented not so much as a system of truths with which the child should become familiar but rather as values addressing a call to us? And in that case what becomes the role of theology in the proclamation of the faith?

What consequences flow from our desire to give an authentic education in a living faith? How should a personalistic catechesis be realized? If such an authentic upbringing in a living faith is accepted as the underlying principle of religious education, what consequences does it have with respect to the time to be devoted to it and the way of "teaching" it? How does knowledge function in this authentic upbringing in a living faith and what practical consequences flow from it?

Is it perhaps necessary to reflect again upon the place of the catechist, the parents and the priest in educating children in an authentic life of faith? And what demands must be made of the catechist's own preparation for his task if we admit that his spiritual attitude is the most important factor?

This book asks questions, it is a challenge. It asks us to seek an answer that can be fruitful for catechesis in the United States.

BIBLIOGRAPHY

Ingo Baldeman, *Biblische Didaktik,* 2nd ed., Fürche-Verlag, Hamburg, 1964.

A. Brien, *Le cheminement de la foi,* Ed. du Seuil, Paris, 1964.

F. Coudreau, *L'enfant devant le problème de la foi,* Ed. Fleurus, Paris, 1961.

F. Derkenne, *La vie et la joi au catéchisme,* 5th ed., Ed. de Gigord, Paris, 1960.

Romano Guardini, *The Life of Faith,* Newman, Westminster, Md., 1961.

J. Mouroux, *Je crois en toi,* Ed. du Cerf, Paris, n.d.

Karl Rahner, *Theology for Renewal,* Sheed and Ward, New York, 1964.

    Nature and Grace, Sheed and Ward, 1963.

    The Christian Commitment, Sheed and Ward, 1963.

    Vom Glauben im Mitten der Welt, Herder, Freiburg i.Br., 1961.

    The Pastoral Mission of the Church, Paulist Press, 1965.

    Gefahren im heutigen Katholizismus, Johannes-Verlag, Einsiedeln, 1950.

H. Renckens, *Israel's Concept of the Beginning. The Theology of Genesis I–III,* Herder and Herder, New York, 1964.

P. Schoonenberg, *God's World in the Making,* Duquesne University Press, 1964, and Gill and Sons, Dublin, 1965.

    Man and Sin, University of Notre Dame Press, 1965.

Günther Weber, *Religionsunterricht als Verkündigung,* Westermann Verlag, Braunschweig, 1961.

H. Wölber, *Religion ohne Entscheidung,* 2nd ed., Göttingen, 1960.

Periodicals:
Lumen Vitae, Brussels.
Catechèse, Paris.
Fiches "Vérité et Vie," Strasbourg.

INDEX OF SUBJECT
MATTER

INDEX OF SUBJECT MATTER

Dialogue with pupils, 112 f.

Development, stages of, 60 ff.; survey of process of, 65 ff.

Didactics, 81 ff., 120 ff., 275 ff., 284 ff., 291 f.

Discretion, 286, 299 f.

Discussion, 285, 299.

Duration of class, 162 f., 300.

Earthly values, salvific meaning of, 114.

Education, renewal of religious, 19; authentic, 56 ff., 154 f., 248 ff., 254 f.; stages of development and, 58 ff.; through identification, 62 ff.; to consciousness of God, Church and sin, 129 ff.; moral, 194 f., 222; project-, 301. See also *Catechesis, Instruction.*

Eucharist, catechesis of, 172, 174 ff.; celebration of, 183 ff. See also *First Communion, Mass.*

Examinations, 287.

Exploration, 145.

Expression, forms of, 145 f.

Faith, as man's response to God, 46 ff., 91 ff.; rendering it more profound, 57 ff.; education in living, 57, 59 ff., 154 ff.; gift of God, 92 f.; as human task, 93 ff.; as union with God, 95 f.; toward living, 98 f.; -consciousness, 107 ff.; justification of, 299; social aspects, 300.

Family, role of, 84 ff., 115 f., 248 ff., 264 f.

Fellowship, 26 f., 28.

First Communion, preparation for, 172 f., 176 f.; time for, 173 f.

Girls, 231, 270.

God, his initiative of love, 31 ff.; entrance into history, 32 f.; union with, 94 f.; -consciousness, 129 f.; 's will, 194 f.

Ground of being, 27.

Guilt, 68.

Holy Spirit, 214 f., 230 f., 247 f.

Humanism, 204 f.

Identification, 62 ff., 268.

Instruction, religious, around 1900, 22 ff.; intellectualistic, 22, 177; moralistic, 22; devotional, 22 f.; closed, 23; ritualistic, 177; versus authentic religious education, 248 f., 250 f.

Intention, 220 f.

Interiorization, 216.

Israel, 32.

Liturgy, 242 ff.

Love, God's initiative of, 31 ff.

Man, former view of, 20 ff.; present view of, 23 ff.; sense of responsibility for world, 25 f.; of human fellowship, 26 f.; social being of, 46, 208.

Marks, 276.

Mass, 175, 184 f. See also *Eucharist.*

Materialism, 204 f.

311